Rural Development and Human Fertility

Rural Development and Human Fertility

Editors
Wayne A. Schutjer
and
C. Shannon Stokes
Pennsylvania State University

Macmillan Publishing Company
A Division of Macmillan, Inc.
NEW YORK

Collier Macmillan Publishers
LONDON

Macmillan Publishing Co.
866 Third Avenue, New York, NY 10022

Collier Macmillan Canada, Inc.

Printed in the United States of America

printing number
1 2 3 4 5 6 7 8 9 10

Library of Congress Cataloging in Publication Data

Main entry under title:

Rural development and human fertility.

Includes index.
1. Fertility, Human—Developing countries—Addresses, essays,
lectures. 2. Developing countries—Population, Rural—Addresses, essays,
lectures. 3. Rural developmenet—Developing countries—Addresses,
essays, lectures. I. Schutjer, Wayne A. II. Stokes, C. Shannon.
HB1108.R87 1984   304.6'32'091734   83-26834
ISBN 0-02-949680-2

Contents

v

Part 3: Policies for Rural Development: Impacts on Fertility

Preface

Poverty and rapid population growth in developing nations are among the world's most urgent problems. The number of people in developing countries who live in abject poverty is estimated at nearly 800 million. The poor are primarily rural and overwhelmingly dependent on agriculture for their livelihood. The population growth problem also has its roots in rural areas of low-income nations where the fertility of rural women is as much as three times higher than that of rural women in the more developed nations.

Within rural areas, the family holds the key to progress in meeting both the poverty and population problems. Rural families make the majority of family-size decisions, as well as decisions about agricultural production and off-farm economic activity by family members. In making these decisions, farm families respond to pressures and opportunities presented by the rural social and economic environment, including government policies and programs. Because of this, public policies directed toward rural poverty and population growth often seek to alter aspects of the rural social and economic environment in order to provide greater economic opportunities for rural families and to reduce the motivation for having large families.

The public policy focus on the rural family and attempts to change economic opportunities and family-size decisions by influencing the rural environment underlies the present volume and the conference that preceded it. Specifically, the issue addressed is: what is known that will provide the conceptual and empirical knowledge base for the coordination and integration of public policy directed at poverty and rapid population growth in rural areas of developing nations? The volume does not provide a set of policy guidelines that will ensure that public policy activities in one problem area do not work at cross-purposes with those in another. Rather, the purpose is to determine what is known that can serve as the basis for the design and implementation of fertility-sensitive, rural economic and social welfare policy.

In April, 1983, the College of Agriculture of The Pennsylvania State University sponsored an international conference on the topic Rural Development and Human Fertility. The present volume is an outgrowth of the conference but is not a conference report. While the conference provided a forum for discussion of preliminary versions of the majority of chapters in the volume, most have been substantially revised and others added.

A number of people contributed to the conference and to the subsequent activities that produced the chapters that appear in the volume. Recognition should go first to the authors who contributed the substance of the conference and who were willing to undertake the revisions necessary for subsequent publication. Samuel Smith, Dean of the College of Agriculture, and Robert McAlexander and J. Dean Jansma of the Office of International Agricultural Programs provided institutional support and were responsible for the majority of the funding obtained for the conference. The Population Issues Research Center contributed both financial support under the terms of its grant from the Hewlett Foundation, and program support by the Director, Gordon DeJong and the research staff, especially, Sarah Harbison and Gretchen Cornwell. The Department of Agricultural Economics and Rural Sociology provided both financial support and the expert clerical assistance of Joyce Kling and Carrie Leitzell.

Wayne A. Schutjer
C. Shannon Stokes

LIST OF CONTRIBUTORS

Ester Boserup is a Danish economist, who has held administrative and research positions with the Danish Government and the United Nations.

Rodolfo A. Bulatao is a consultant to the World Bank and the East-West Population Institute.

E. Kwan Choi is Assistant Professor of Economics, University of Missouri.

Calvin Goldscheider is Chairman, Department of Demography and Sociology, Hebrew University.

W. Whitney Hicks is Professor of Economics, University of Missouri.

Nan E. Johnson is Associate Professor of Sociology, Michigan State University.

James E. Kocher is Director, Center for Development Policy, and Director, Integrated Population and Development Planning Project, Research Triangle Institute.

Shubh K. Kumar is Research Fellow, Food Consumption and Nutrition Program, International Food Policy Research Institute.

Eva Mueller is Professor of Economics, University of Michigan.

Per Pinstrup-Andersen is Director, Food Consumption and Nutrition Program, International Food Policy Research Institute.

Wayne A. Schutjer is Professor of Agricultural Economics and Faculty Associate, Population Issues Research Center, The Pennsylvania State University.

Ozzie G. Simmons is Distinguished Visiting Professor, Department of Sociology and Anthropology, Fordham University.

C. Shannon Stokes is Professor of Rural Sociology and Faculty Associate, Population Issues Research Center, The Pennsylvania State University.

Te-Hsiung Sun is Director, Taiwan Provincial Institute of Family Planning.

Boone A. Turchi is Associate Professor of Economics, University of North Carolina.

Maris A. Vinovskis is Professor of History, University of Michigan.

Robert H. Weller is Professor of Sociology and Research Associate, Center for the Study of Population, Institute for Social Research, Florida State University.

Rural Development and Human Fertility

PART I
Development Processes and Rural Fertility Change

CHAPTER 1
Rural Development and Human Fertility in Developing Nations

Wayne A. Schutjer and C. Shannon Stokes

Rural and poor are terms that characterize the less developed nations of the world. With the use of the World Bank's definition of poverty, 38 percent of the developing nations' population are poor. More than 80 percent of the poor reside in rural areas (World Bank, 1975). The occupation of the rural poor is primarily agriculture and their fertility rates are among the highest in the world. As a result, the world's major poverty problem is inexorably linked with problems of rural development and human reproductive behavior in developing nations.

The agricultural poor include small-scale farmers, tenants, sharecroppers, and landless workers. In 1969, there were more than 80 million small-scale farmers with land holdings to cultivate of less than two hectares. That number is surely greater today. Tenants, sharecroppers, and squatters represented an additional 30 million of the rural poor. Although the number of landless or near landless workers is not known, the available evidence suggests that this group of agricultural families is growing and represents the poorest of rural residents in less developed nations.

The rural poor of the developing nations are not in a separate category in international demographic statistics. It is clear, however, that at an aggregate level both the rurality and poverty of nations are closely related to patterns of human fertility. Specifically, low-income nations have higher fertility, the proportion of the national labor force employed in agriculture is greatest in low-income countries, and high-fertility nations have higher rural fertility rates, both absolutely and as a proportion of urban fertility rates, than do low-fertility nations.

A comparison of the total fertility rates of nations classified by the World Bank as low-, middle-, or high-income countries indicates that fertility rates drop from 5.4 children per woman, to 4.9, and finally to 1.8 as income rises (World Bank, 1980). Similarly, the proportion of the labor force in agriculture declines from 72 percent in the low income group, to 45 percent and 6 percent, respectively, in the middle- and high-income nations. Finally, United Nations data indicate that the rural fertility rate in high fertility nations is three times that of the low fertility nations, and the ratio of rural to urban fertility declines from 1.33 to 1.05 as one moves from the high-fertility to the low-fertility group of nations (United Nations, 1980).

In summary, low-income nations have a large proportion of rural poor who are employed in agriculture and exhibit high fertility rates. The growing rural population creates pressure on governments to accommodate even greater numbers of rural laborers in agricultural production and an increasing flow of rural to urban migrants. At the same time, governments cannot ignore the need for efficiency in agricultural production to accommodate the growing demand for food in both rural and urban areas. Nor can they ignore the recognized need to improve the quality of life in rural areas to meet humanitarian goals and reduce the incentive for rural residents to seek urban residence and employment.

Within this policy context, rural poverty and the resulting employment and migration problems are seen mostly as dependent variables in the population-poverty nexus. It is population growth and migration that are being accommodated in the short-run, so that development and family planning programs can exert a longer-term restraint on rural population growth. This chapter, and the others in this volume, explore theoretically and empirically the inverse of one set of relationships. That is, the extent to which economic and rural development tend to influence the reproductive behavior of rural residents of developing nations. The purpose is not to deny the fact that population pressure influences the rate and structure of rural economic and social development, but to examine the potential for influencing rural fertility rates through variation in the way in which development occurs.

More specifically, the general purpose of this volume is to examine the theoretical and empirical basis for the design of fertility-sensitive rural policy. The task is not to provide a set of rural policy guidelines, but rather, to determine the extent to which a consistent theoretical structure and related research findings are available to serve as the basis for such policies.

The development of rural policy that is sensitive to demographic factors requires that population growth and agricultural production be shown to have a common basis that is subject to change through the use of rural policy. In the sections that follow, the conceptual links between population growth and agricultural output are established and used to demonstrate how interaction between the two forces, operating through the agricultural surplus, determine the course of a nation's early progress. The conceptual discussion provides the background for a review of the components of rural policy and the context for the following chapters in this volume.

AGRICULTURAL PRODUCTION AND HUMAN FERTILITY

The production of agricultural commodities and human reproduction in rural areas both involve biological processes engaged in by families and influenced by a common socioeconomic and cultural environment. Both require an accommodation by the family to the rural environment and are, therefore, both subject to change when the environment is altered. These fundamental commonalities provide an initial theoretical link between the two processes.

The biological basis of each process suggests the importance of technology in determining the level of both agricultural production and family size, and of changes in technology that alter both processes. Gotsch (1972) has demonstrated how the characteristics of agricultural technology interact with the rural social and economic system to determine patterns of output and the distribution of income. It is also likely that changes in agricultural technology have been viewed as a less troublesome way of dealing with difficult rural socioeconomic problems, than changes in institutions to accommodate agricultural development. For example, where crop intensification requires the use of herbicides and pesticides, governments seek to develop pest- and disease-resistant plant varieties, rather than develop educational systems and input delivery systems that would enable small-scale farmers to effectively use agricultural chemicals.

The same situation appears to exist in the case of birth control technology. Investments in the development of birth control pills, injections, and mechanical devices such as the IUD, are all designed to accommodate a wide range of existing social and cultural environments in which families make decisions regarding reproduction. A range of technologies is clearly needed, but its existence does not negate the need for changes in the institutional environment in which family size decisions are made.

Decisions about agricultural production and family size are both made within families, providing a second important link between the two processes. Rural families seek to maximize the short- and long-term welfare of family members within a set of resource constraints. In that process, families can meet current consumption needs through farm and off-farm employment, or borrowing, and provide for future needs through saving and investing. Thus, current consumption can be sacrificed for future goals which may be either monetary or nonmonetary. Family size decisions are an important component in future planning because children represent current and future nonmonetary assets, as well as a potential source of agricultural labor and old age security. The complex set of relationships between children and the economic position of the rural family are explored in detail in the succeeding chapters. At this point, it is important to note that both agricultural production and family size decisions are usually made within the context of individual rural families or households. Other social and economic organizational systems exist, particularly on the production side. However, even within such systems, the family unit appears to maintain economic and social viability.

The common rural environment facing both production and reproduction processes is the third commonality. Most rural policy is directed at changing human behavior through changes in the rural social and economic environment, and this results in the potential for numerous unintended effects, which may or may not be judged desirable, on both processes. The common institutional framework also establishes the possibility of purposeful secondary impacts on demographic processes resulting from agricultural and rural development policy. For example, efforts to increase rural income by the creation of nonagricultural employment opportunities for women may well influence family decisions regarding the number of children desired. At the same time, a labor intensive agricultural technology may influence not only family income, but family size decisions as well. In short, given the need of rural families to adjust both their agricultural production and reproductive behavior to the prevailing rural environment, policies aimed at changing that environment in order to influence one or the other process, will likely have secondary impacts on the other.

RURAL POPULATION GROWTH AND AGRICULTURAL DEVELOPMENT

At the aggregate level, cumulative rural household fertility and production decisions translate into population growth and agricultural production trends. The long-term interaction between agricultural production trends and population growth has been an important topic of concern since Malthus first published his population growth-food production postulates. In the following sections, we review the status of current thinking on the aggregate relationship between the two processes.

The conclusion drawn is that in the short-term agricultural production can increase on the basis of indigenous agricultural technology, but a sustained growth of agricultural production requires a continuing flow of science-based technology that can only be provided through access to inputs produced industrially (Schultz, 1964). The capacity of a nation to produce the science-based industrial inputs is related to the generation and effective use of surplus agricultural output. The potential agricultural surplus is a function of the rural population, consumption standards, and the level of agricultural technology. The realization of the surplus requires a stimulus which may be population growth, urbanization, or pressure from commercial or governmental units with access to the rural sector. In this way population growth and rural-to-urban migration can be a stimulus to growth in agricultural output. Simultaneously, motivations for fertility and migration in rural areas depend upon the nature of the rural agricultural environment. The introduction of agricultural technology, and the institutional changes required to facilitate the adoption and effective utilization of technology, can influence rural demographic processes. Thus, the link between population and agricultural growth is closed, with each being an important element in establishing the level of the other, by influencing the motivations and ability of rural families to alter both family size and the level of agricultural output.

The concept of the agricultural surplus is developed fully in the next section. The surplus concept provides the basis for an examination of alternative growth paths. The notion of an agricultural surplus is clearly not new and, in fact, plays a central role in most models of the growth process. The concept has, however, lost the precision provided by the classical economists' definition of agricultural surplus as the excess of product above the subsistence requirements of the rural population. We find that the term has five possible meanings or interpretations: (1) the classical (Malthusian-Ricardian) surplus; (2) a technological (Boserupian) surplus; (3) an "other goods" (Hymer-Resnick's Z goods) surplus; (4) a "leisure" surplus; and (5) an x-efficiency (Leibenstein) surplus.

The Classical Surplus

The Ricardian-Malthusian Classical Model was powered by two forces: the law of diminishing returns in agriculture, and the tendency for population to grow whenever output exceeds subsistence requirements. The two forces in combination drive the average product of labor to subsistence. Prior to reaching a long-run Malthusian equilibrium, however, there is a period of increasing and then declining average product. During this period, a surplus is available which can be measured by the difference between the agricultural output of a nation, and the subsistence requirements of the rural population.

The Ricardian-Malthusian model provides the classical view of how technical change in agriculture and population interact through the surplus. In its simplest form, technical change increases the surplus, which supports continuing high fertility in rural areas. The development task is to create as large as possible a current surplus and use it to increase future output, while at the same time promoting declining fertility. Under these conditions, the model need not lead to a stagnant equilibrium. If population growth does not occur, or occurs slowly enough, then surplus output can be channeled into investments calculated to shift the aggregate production function upward. Where population stablilizes at less than subsistence average product, a surplus becomes a regular feature of the production process.

The Technological Surplus

The framework advanced by Boserup (1965) argues that there is a potential surplus of output always available in the rural sector in the form of unused technology. She argues that population growth tends to be the stochastic variable in the system, resulting from natural, climatic, and biological forces, as well as variation in economic conditions. In her view, the economic problem for most societies is how best to adapt agricultural output to population, given the supply of land and other factors.   In other words, factor proportions, and per capita income follow from population growth in relation to the resources available, not the reverse.   In this model, shifts from primitive, slash-burn agriculture to short-fallow rotation, and ultimately, to settled, annual cultivation are the responses of society to population pressure. The basic point of view is thus an optimistic one which stresses that most rural societies have an unrealized potential for further techno-logical adaptations if population pressure occurs.

Critical to the analysis of Boserup is a potential surplus of output available to the rural sector in the form of improved or higher-order level technology.   Thus, a technological response to changing man-land ratios, such as movement from long-fallow to short-fallow, suggests a hierarchy of agricultural production functions.   The production functions represent different technologies and do not represent merely discontinu-ities or lumpiness associated with an existing production function. They represent genuine shifts to new production functions (Robinson and Schutjer, in press).

This notion of technology is consistent with the usual economic defi-nition.   Ruttan writes that technological change is: "changes in the coefficients of a function relating inputs to outputs resulting from the practical application of innovations in technology and economic organi-zation" Ruttan, 1959, p. 606).   The Boserupian model posits that increased population leads to a substitution of more labor-intensive techniques for existing techniques at the point at which average labor productivity falls to some critical (or threshold) level.   When this occurs, the next higher technology is adopted and the same inputs pro-duce a larger output, restoring the average product (and income) of labor.   The movement from long-fallow to short-fallow, the introduction of crop rotation, irrigation, and mechanization are all examples of technological changes (1).

The technological-response model argues that some unrealized poten-tial for increased agricultural output with given inputs nearly always exists.   The potential "surplus" is not in underemployed factors, but in the choice of a technology.   The principle of least-effort motivates producers, not the principle of maximizing net surplus.   New technology and increased output are usually thrust on the cultivators by some pressure, with population growth being the most obvious candidate.

Z-Goods Labor Surplus

Lewis (1954) argued that in the rural sector a pool of surplus labor exists that can be withdrawn from the sector with a minimal impact on output.   The view advanced was that tasks are shared by family mem-bers, leisure is too abundant, and long idle spells are characteristic of the annual work cycle.   In classical terms, the point on the production function where the marginal product of rural labor falls below the sub-sistence wage does not represent full employment, and there is a labor surplus which represents the failure to fully mobilize the resources available to the economic system.

The concept of surplus rural labor has enjoyed an enormous vogue. The Fei and Ranis (1964) and Jorgenson (1961) models are elaborations of the Lewis notion that since all workers must be fed, if some are not fully employed at productive activities, then their "idleness" represents a "labor surplus." Hymer and Resnick (1969) focused attention on the role of nonagricultural household productions (which they define as "Z-goods") as one of the ways in which the allegedly unemployed-surplus labor was actually used in rural areas. Housing, clothing, tools, utensils, and decorative and ornamental objects are all integral parts of "subsistence." A peasant economy which produces nothing for the market may actually have little surplus labor. In their view, labor is simultaneously engaged in both agricultural and nonagricultural pursuits, and is thus not surplus to the economic system of the peasant economy (2). From the perspective of agricultural output, however, a surplus exists, as labor employed in "Z"-goods production could be made available for agricultural production.

Leisure Surplus

Chayanov's (1970) theory of the peasant economy provides a second insight into the source of labor surplus to the agricultural production process at current levels of output. He maintains that the rural household is not a net profit (or utility) maximizer in the ordinary microeconomic sense. Instead, the goals of the household are to obtain a satisfactory level of consumption for the household and to provide work for all labor available.

Technology is implicitly static so that, in general, as the needs for consumption and the labor available change, the amount of land cultivated also changes. The theory suggests that there is often an unrealized potential for increased output, because when population pressure does rise, more land is cultivated; if no further land is available, then cultivation can become more intensive on the existing plots. Chayanov implicitly assumes subsistence cultivation with only weak ties to the market and no demand in the rural sector for industrial goods. For his model, the surplus is implied by the deliberate suboptimization of the household. The surplus is created and transferred the moment the agricultural sector acquires a taste for nonhousehold-produced goods, or experiences pressure on food supply, and is willing to sacrifice leisure to obtain more agricultural output.

In any case, the leisure surplus is a deeply-rooted cultural phenomenon and, the existing degree of labor utilization represents a point on some socially optimum production function, consistent with the existing leisure preferences, values and technology. Expropriating the surplus for some nonconsumptive purpose may require improved political and social organization or some exogenous force.

X-Efficiency Surplus

Leibenstein (1978) argues that there may always be a potential for further increases in output per unit of input, depending upon worker motivation, organizational skill, and a host of other qualitative factors. His x-efficiency paradigm is an effort to explain why producing units in all sectors and levels of development frequently can be shown not to be maximizing net profits or to be making the most "efficient" (output maximizing) use of their inputs. Rather than concluding that such firms are irrational, he suggests that they are efficient judged by some more appropriate test. This appropriate but unobserved criterion he calls the x-factor. A firm may thus be foregoing allocative efficiency in order to obtain x-efficiency: market peace with competitors, serving its customers better, or keeping its workers happy. Such "inefficiencies," as judged by the usual criteria, are optional. They can shade off into lethargy and an increase in transactions-costs. But the point for the agricultural surplus is that, under pressure, the unit has the potential for tightening up, increasing output, reducing costs, or otherwise improving its economic position. To the extent that this is possible in the agricultural sector, an unrealized surplus exists.

Realizing the Surplus

Only the classical surplus is an existing surplus, the others are all potential increases in output over and above subsistence needs. Yet all the surpluses require not only a mechanism for stimulating production, but a means for transferring or expropriating it. The creation of any of the latent surpluses depends upon the imposition of pressure on the existing system.

One major candidate to create pressure on traditional systems is population growth. The classical surplus begins to occur due to population growth and economies of scale (in the early stages), but only as the economy becomes monetized, specialized, and trade-oriented. The leisure-labor surplus exists when no central political authority or colonial power exists to require full-employment or change the leisure preference. The local manufacturers' surplus (if it is a surplus at all) exists when tastes are unchanging and no import penetration has occurred. The technological surplus implies a satisfactory present standard of living due to no population pressure, no demand for imports, or other pressures. Much the same can be said of the x-efficiency surplus.

In retrospect, it seems that the great attraction of the labor surplus approach to development policy was that it seemed to promise the creation of an exploitable surplus without the need for any pressure or structural transformation. The framework presented here argues that the latent surplus implied by a strong leisure preference, by poorly integrated domestic economic systems, or by limited material aspirations, may not be easy to change. Thus, countries which argue that they are underpopulated are suggesting that they are still in a range of increasing returns and have an unrealized classical surplus which population growth will create.

Opening an economy with a large potential agricultural surplus to substantial foreign export demand is a second type of pressure which can lead to structural transformation. A country necessarily adopts an export-oriented policy as structural transformation creates larger and larger actual surpluses. But, under colonial conditions, the export-orientation may, in effect, be imposed on a nation by foreign capitalists and plantation administrators. Voluntary or not, the point remains the same. Export demand is an option for creating and capturing potential surplus agricultural output.

A dynamic urban-industrial sector can have the same effect as penetration by an export market and represents a third source of pressure on traditional systems. The demand such a sector generates for agricultural output inevitably leads to growing market penetration into the countryside, changes in tastes, and changes in the allocation of time and other resources. A market-oriented expropriation may or may not be exploitative or noncompetitive. Even in very underdeveloped societies, the urban sector may emerge as the producer of outputs which, when applied to the rural sector, result in increased labor productivity. Included in such outputs are military and police protection, design and control of irrigation schemes, and religious rituals to ensure a favorable harvest.

A potential surplus can be generated and captured in response to at least three forces: population growth, outside market penetration and monetization, and domestic urbanization, coupled with the growth of a central authority eager for the surplus. Once any one or combination of these forces sets the process of surplus creation and transfer in motion, the process becomes cumulative. That is, population growth begins by creating a classical surplus due to economies of scale. Further population growth puts pressure on the system to reduce leisure and shift to a more intensive technology, and finally, forces a more relentless efficiency in production. Similar scenarios can be sketched out for the short- versus long-run effects of market penetration, and of the growth of a coercive central authority. In practice, it is likely that all three interact.

ALTERNATIVE GROWTH PATHS

Central to the analysis of demographic impacts on technical change and rural development is the agricultural surplus and its relationship to population growth. Similarly, the rise of the urban-industrial sector is important for sustained technological change in agriculture. Agricultural surplus was defined to include both actual and potential agricultural output above the subsistence requirement of the sector. Drawing upon the concept of the surplus, we propose a modified, broadened post-Boserupian framework that describes what might be the typical evolution of an agricultural economy.

For example, begin with a traditional, quasi-subsistence rural system as a starting point for the development process. The area is sparsely populated. Cultivation is either shifting, long-fallow, or very extensively farmed though annually planted. A low level of technology and labor utilization exist and there is thus a potential surplus. The actual exploitable surplus is low because the density and settlement pattern militate against trade and specialized crafts and manufacturers. Manufactured goods tend to be home-produced or at least produced for a local market. The urban settlements that exist are small in compari-

son to the total population, and are centered around religious, political, military, and other noneconomic functions. The urban settlements
are, in fact, also essentially rural, and lack real urbanism. This socioeconomic base makes the emergence of any large nation–state, political,
or social entity difficult. The low density implies that, without very
favorable geographical conditions, or without a particularly strong, purposeful political leadership, the creation and transfer from agriculture
of a real surplus will be difficult. Rural households are maximizing
their well-being but are not maximizing output. Little or no actual
surplus is produced or transferred. A considerable amount of population movement may be occurring if cultivation is shifting, less if cultivation is settled (3).

During the traditional agriculture period of development, there is
likely to be a potential agricultural surplus. Increasing population
density, establishment of better communications and transportation,
coupled with the imposition of a strong central political control, or the
attraction of cash markets, will lead to increased specialization in
production, rising total output, the emergence of a transferable surplus,
and the potential for further national economic development. There is,
of course, no reason why these causal factors cannot interact (4).

For our purposes, the question is: what is the logical outcome of
surplus creation and exploitation? The key is the interaction among
three elements: (a) the surplus and the use to which it is put, (b) the
emergence of a domestic urban–industrial sector, and (c) rural population growth.

The Stagnant Involuted Outcome

If the surplus arises in response to rural population growth, we have
the purest Malthusian case. Population consumes the surplus and eventually population growth must cease because of rising death rates or
periodic catastrophies. A surplus exported to world markets leads to
only modest increases in rural income, not to structural transformation.
Moreover, if rural population growth is triggered by the rise in incomes, rural densities may become high enough to eliminate the "transferable" surplus and lead to a Malthusian outcome.

Any sustained rural population growth in the absence of a structural
transformation leads to this outcome. This is true because even the
Boserupian potential surpluses have upper limits. With no inputs from a
science–based, urban–industrial sector, traditional agriculture must
eventually reach an upper level of output such that no further shifts in
technology or rearrangements of factor inputs are possible. This is
"traditional agriculture," rational, maximizing, but in a dead-end. In
practical terms, adding a few more ditches, a new well, or a new draft
animal on the same land, using the same technology, will not increase
agricultural production significantly. For further development to occur,
the agricultural sector must gain access to high-payoff inputs from outside the rural sector. In other words, no further technological change
from inside agriculture is possible (Schultz, 1964).

Under the conditions of a traditional agricultural equilibrium, further surplus development and/or the accommodation of additional population, requires the availability of new technologies embodied in purchased manufactured inputs and a more educated farm manager. If the surplus phase of development fails to create a modern urban-industrial sector which can supply inputs to the rural sector that are capable of supporting further shifts in the agricultural production function, development eventuates in a Malthusian solution in which the combined forces of diminishing returns and continued population growth drive the entire economy to subsistence.   In this case, evolution becomes involution (Geertz, 1968).

The Interacting Rural-Urban Growth Solution

The alternative to the involuted, stagnant, agricultural solution occurs when the agricultural surplus available from the traditional agricultural system provides the basis for interacting rural-urban growth.   As noted previously, handicraft production of nonsubsistence products is virtually always going on in even the most rural economies. However, there are obvious advantages to specialization and efficiency in such production being concentrated in one place in order to internalize within the industry what might otherwise be lost external effects. This occurs in what are already, or what become, urban areas.   Once this begins to occur, trade grows between the rural and urban sectors. The urban sector is transformed from a religious-political center to a manufacturing-service generating sector.   At this stage, the process of change can become self-generating as inputs from the manufacturing sector help continue the transformation in the agricultural sector. Labor requirements fall as labor productivity increases and labor is transferred to the growing urban-industrial sector.   Population growth is still concentrated in rural areas which, coupled with the rapid increases in productivity, and a fall in the amount of labor required, leads to a growing rural-to-urban movement.

This outcome is characterized by dynamic growth in the urban-manufacturing sector such that a demand is generated in the rural-agricultural sector for a growing amount of foodstuff and labor.   Rural-to-urban migration occurs on a large scale as do changes in the structure of the rural sector.   Aspiration levels rise, the level of output rises, and a growing commercialization and consolidation occurs.   The interaction between the sectors leads both to rising levels of output and income.   This scenario can be seen in demographic terms as the early stage of the demographic transition.   The urban sector adopts the small family norm as the micro cost-benefit calculation increasingly turns against large families, and this norm begins to spread outward to the rural areas as well (5).

As the commercialization of agriculture increases, labor is increasingly supplied by hired persons or by selected family members, while others in the household contribute to family income by working outside agriculture.   Farm households become as specialized and dependent on other sectors as other households. The surplus concept is no longer relevant, just as it would be inappropriate to speak of a surplus from a shoe factory, over and above the needs of the workers for shoes. The farmer grows wheat exclusively, but buys bread at the market with everyone else. In this case, migration takes on complex new patterns. Rural-urban differences in income tend to be diminished and population movements more in the nature of a commutation, rather than permanent migration, occur. Both rural and urban populations perceive micro-economic advantages to limit family size, and fertility declines.

The entire economy becomes one marked by a substitution of capital for labor and land; indeed, since output per unit of both land and labor are high, and the demand for food is likely to be relatively inelastic as income rises, the relative need for labor and land in agriculture falls. The rural sector represents a declining share of total national output. In this case, agriculture's success breeds its own relative decline.

Generalizing from the Boserupian model, it can be argued that agriculture does react to "pressures" by creating more output from the potential surplus which was always there. These pressures include rural population growth, but other factors such as exploitation by urban-political authority, colonial exploitation and the penetration of world markets, and growing commercialization, monetization, and tastes for manufactured goods have similar effects. The increased output can come from adopting a new, more intensive technology, but also from reduced leisure, reduced local handicraft production, or an expanded scale of output. If the increase in output is either caused by or accompanied by a growth in the rural population, then the outcome from the entire process will be no growth in real per capita income. Boserupian technological change eventually reaches a point at which any further leap to a new production function requires regular interchanges with, and inputs from, a developing urban-industrial sector that can provide new technologies. The final outcome of the process of change in agriculture depends critically upon the mechanism by which the surplus is achieved, and its interaction with the rate of rural population growth.

The alternative development paths are only abstractions of polar scenarios. The paths do, however, provide an indication of the importance of technological change to sustained agricultural development. In the following section, the process of technical change in agriculture is examined as prelude to an examination of rural development policy and demographic change.

TECHNOLOGY BASED DEVELOPMENT, RURAL DEVELOPMENT POLICY, AND DEMOGRAPHIC CHANGE

The creation of the technological surplus in rural areas requires that farm families adopt and effectively use agricultural technology. The adoption and effective utilization of agricultural technology is closely related to the distribution of productive assets, and the existence and functioning of rural institutions. Both asset distribution and institutions are the subject of rural policy and both have potential implications for rural fertility decisions.

Each rural family has access to assets that can contribute to the agricultural production process, that is, land, labor, or capital. Not all families, however, possess equal amounts of assets. Landless agricultural workers have only their labor to contribute to the production process. Farm owners have land, and if they choose, may also contribute labor. Likewise, capital is not equally available to all rural families. Thus, to the extent that a new technology requires land, labor, and capital in proportions different than that held by a given family, or group of farmers, the technology is less likely to be adopted and/or effectively used.

A similar case can be made regarding the availability of rural institutions such as factor and product markets, the agricultural extension service, rural banks and credit societies, and irrigations associations. Not all rural sectors have a complete range of rural institutions needed for technology adoption and not all farm families within the rural sector have equal access to those institutions that are available.

Technology adoption and use may require access to well-functioning institutions. New varieties of plants may require access to factor markets that can make herbicides and pesticides available. The technology may be very capital intensive, at least from the perspective of the small farmer, and require access to credit for adoption. A technology may be complex to use, e.g., systemic herbicides and pesticides, and require the services of the extension service for effective use.

To the extent that a gap exists between the institutional and asset requirements of the technology, and those available within the rural sector in general, and to specific groups in particular, the adoption and effective use of technology will be limited and selective. Consequently, a great deal of government activity in rural areas is directed at developing functioning rural institutions and changing the distribution of rural assets. To attain that end, policies are directed toward changing the environment within which farm families make production decisions.

The adoption of agricultural technology directly influences the farm family by altering income, assets, and labor demands. It is these direct impacts that combine with the indirect impact of associated institutional change that provide the major link between increased agricultural output and farm family demographic decisions. Not all public policy in rural areas, however, is directed at the introduction and effective utilization of agricultural technology. Other policy concerns such as rural health, education, nutrition, and nonagricultural employment, may in fact dominate rural public policy at times. Thus, a concern for rural development impacts on human fertility must include consideration of the range of public policies in rural areas and their impact on family size decisions.

RURAL DEVELOPMENT POLICY

Rural development policy is directed at increasing agricultural output and improving the quality of life of people who live in rural areas. Within the broad category of rural development policy are three specific sets of activities: rural economic policy, food policy, and rural social welfare policy. Each of the policy domains is represented either explicitly or implicitly in the rural policy of all nations. However, the relative priority given to each and the specific programs and actions vary considerably. The three policy domains are not always separable and may at times work at cross purposes.

A nation that allows free market prices to determine which crops are grown has no less of a policy than one that institutes crop production campaigns with extensive government participation in production decisions. Policies of both nations influence the institutional economic environment facing the farm family—only the strategies are different. The same is true of nations that elect to institute compulsory service in rural areas by recent medical school graduates, and those who allow rural health care to be performed by lay medical personnel in the absence of trained physicians. It is not possible to know in advance which strategies will provide the most output, or the best health care, in either the short- or the longer-term. The bias in the selection of strategies is generally toward activism and short run results, an emphasis that carries over into the analysis of secondary impacts as well. For example, changes in population distribution are much more likely to be perceived as a consequence of rural economic growth policy, than are longer term fertility trends, although both may be markedly influenced by economic policies.

A related issue in establishing rural development policy priorities and implementation strategies is that the policy domains and strategies are often inseparable. For example, a decision to assure an adequate food supply through imports from surplus nations may result in price disincentives for domestic food producers. In this case, the strategy chosen to implement the nation's food policy may have a negative impact on the goal of increased agricultural output and rural income. Complementary relationships between policies are also possible. An investment in a rural health service may have a positive effect on the quality of life in rural areas and simultaneously contribute to increased food output by improving the efficiency of the rural labor force.

The possibility of competing or complementary priorities and implementation strategies is not limited to the rural sector. Often rural development policy is constrained by urban priorities or other national development concerns. An often-cited example is the importation of less expensive food grain as a basis for low urban-industrial wages, which act as a stimulus for national industrialization. The argument advanced is that to provide needed foreign exchange, the nation must either export cheap manufactured goods, or produce industrial products domestically that can substitute for current imports. Low urban food prices help maintain low industrial wages, but often reduce the incentive for local farmers to produce food for domestic urban markets. A similar situation exists when foreign exchange is directed at urban-industrial development through the use of multiple exchange rates biased against the import of fertilizer and other agricultural inputs.

The three major policy domains of rural development are discussed in the next sections. It is important to recognize, however, that the distinctions drawn often fade in the face of the realities of policy formation and implementation.

Rural Economic Growth Policy

Rural economic growth can be defined as an increase in the gross domestic product produced in rural areas. It includes increases in agricultural output and the production of other goods and services in rural areas. This definition is broader than the normal sectoral-based notion of agricultural development, i.e., focusing on improvements in the level and efficiency of agricultural production. However, from the perspective of demographic analysis, the geographical-based definition is more useful. Thus, family size decisions of rural families can be influenced by improvements in income and employment opportunities resulting from either nonagricultural production activities or agricultural development. In fact, an important neglected dimension of the transition from a primarily agriculture base, to a more industrial based economy, is the nonagricultural employment and production activities that occur in small rural communities.

The design of policy to increase agricultural output is relatively straightforward, and the elements are well known. As Mosher (1966) suggested, no farmer will increase output in the absence of markets for his products, supplies and equipment, or production incentives in the form of prices that cover costs of production. Similarly, there must be transportation facilities to assure access to both product and factor markets and, of course, access to technology that is consistent with factor availability and agro-climatic conditions. In addition to these essentials, Mosher notes that farmer education, access to credit, collective or cooperative action related to production and marketing, land improvements such as irrigation or drainage, and coordinated government programs and investments in rural areas can all accelerate the pace of agricultural development.

The vast majority of agricultural development policies and programs are directed at influencing one, or more, or the above essentials or accelerators. The priority placed upon a specific activity reflects past investments and policies, and assessments regarding current constraints on increased output. Similarly, the specific strategy followed to overcome current constraints depends upon both local institutions, and the agro-climatic conditions, and, perhaps most importantly, the political processes involved in the decision.

Policies and programs to increase employment in rural areas of developing nations are not new, but they have taken on increasing priority with rising population pressure and growing rural poverty. Specific activities include direct action to create jobs through public works programs, the introduction or expansion of nonagricultural production activities in rural areas, and a sensitivity to the need for rural jobs in the development and selection of agricultural technology for introduction to farm families.

Public works programs tend to focus on the development of infrastructure needed for economic growth in rural areas. Included in public works activities are the building and improvement of roads, irrigation facilities, land drainage, and market facilities. Reforestation has also been a major focus of employment creation, as have the construction of rural health facilities and rural water supply systems. The latter are directed primarily at improvement in the quality of life in rural areas, but may also contribute to rural economic growth by improving the efficiency of the labor supply.

The creation of employment in nonagricultural production in rural areas has often centered on the development of handicraft industry. These jobs are very intensive of local labor, particularly that of women, but the relatively high labor input reduces output per unit of time, and the economic returns to the rural family are quite low. The advantage of handicraft production from the family perspective is that it generally does not require a structured environment or major equipment, and thus can be performed at home on a time-available basis.

Most nonhandicraft employment creation in rural areas is generally limited to primary industries or the processing of agricultural commodities. Mining, timber, and the initial processing of cocoa, copra, and other tree crops are all important in various developing nations. Manufacturing industry is likely to flourish in urban areas where commercial services exist and access to major domestic and foreign markets is available. Countries such as Taiwan have been able to achieve a less geographically concentrated distribution of manufacturing, but the relatively small area involved, and the well-developed transportation and communication network suggests that this may well be a special case.

Food Policy

Government policies and programs directed toward assuring an adequate and stable supply of nutrients has become increasingly important as the share of population involved directly in agricultural production in the developing nations has declined. Kennedy and Pinstrup-Anderson (1983) suggest that the nutritional status of an individual is a function of five factors: (a) the amount and kinds of food available in the market or on the farm; (b) the ability of the household to obtain the food that is available; (c) the desire of the leading members of the household to obtain the food to which they have access; (d) the use of the food obtained to meet nutritional needs; and (e) the health status of the individual. Food policy is used to influence the factors that underlie each of the five determinants of nutritional status.

Food availability can be influenced by both domestic agricultural production programs and foreign trade and assistance activities. In this case, rural economic growth policy often complements food policy. Policies and programs directed at lowering the cost of food to families or enhancing their purchasing power are the major elements of government activities designed to increase the ability of households to obtain available food. The desire to obtain food is the third principal factor that determines nutritional status. Promotion and advertising are used to influence household food consumption patterns, as are programs and policies that change the intrahousehold distribution of control over income and spending decisions. Finally, both nutrition education and related health care activities are components of an integrated food policy and, as noted below, of national rural social welfare policy.

Rural Social Welfare Policy

The major components of rural social welfare policy with implications for human fertility are governmental efforts to assure rural residents access to adequate education and health services. *Assault on World Poverty* (World Bank, 1975) argues that improved access to education and health are essential to meeting the needs of rural populations in the developing nations. Educational systems in developing nations tend to be heavily biased toward urban populations. The same is true of health systems. For example, the crude death rate for 1960 in rural areas of developing nations was estimated by the United Nations as 21.7 per 1000 as compared with 15.4 for urban areas.

The major constraint rural residents face in gaining access to health and educational services is income. Both low education and poor health reflect the poverty of rural residents in developing nations. Rural economic growth represents one major approach to both the education and health problems of rural areas in developing nations. However, government policies and programs can do much to improve services to rural residents within their economic means.

Current programs and policies consist largely of two major activities. The first is the provision of health and educational facilities such as schools, hospitals, and rural health centers. The second set of activities are the development of nontraditional programs such as functional literacy activities and the distribution of medical services through paramedical personnel. In each case the objective is the same: to improve the overall level of health and education among rural families.

ORGANIZATION OF THE VOLUME

The chapters of this volume are organized into three sections that parallel the previous discussion. The first section examines the major processes in the linkage between urban-industrial development, rural development, and demographic change. The second section examines the determinants of fertility at the rural household level. The final section examines the fertility implications of major rural policy activities.

The issue of population growth and agricultural technology change is central to the rural development-human fertility nexus. Chapter 2 extends previous work in this area by examining the extent to which the relationship between technical change and population pressure is mitigated or enhanced by the prevailing institutional and agricultural production system. Intensification can be viewed as an adjustment to population growth or, conversely, offset the acceptance of a small family norm, depending upon the specific circumstances. The chapter provides a review of alternative outcomes that reflect a range of adjustments under varying agro-climatic and institutional conditions.

Migration from rural to urban areas has long been viewed as a major contributor to declining fertility as migrants adopt the small family norm of urban residents. The process of population redistribution in response to rural modernization, however, has two other major components. First, economic growth does not occur at the same pace throughout rural areas. Moreover, because the agricultural development that occurs in one area often requires a different factor mix than that occurring in another area, a great deal of migration is between rural areas in response to differentials in labor demands. Second, although a great deal has been written on the fertility behavior of rural migrants to urban areas, it is the fertility impact of migration on the people left behind that heavily influences future rural population growth. Both intrasectoral migration and the rural fertility implications of migration are described in Chapter 3.

The linkage between rural development and fertility depends upon the impact of industrial development, migration, and technical change in agriculture on rural family reproductive decisions. Industrial development not only creates nonagricultural employment and raises income, but likely contributes to a breakdown in traditionalism that prevails in rural areas. Chapter 4, on industrial development and rural fertility, draws upon the experience of Taiwan, but the lessons appear to have broader applicability. Urban-industrial development, population redistribution, and technical change in agriculture were also important dimensions of the rural development process in the United States. Chapter 5 reviews the rural fertility decline in the United States and includes all three processes. The conclusion reached is that although the U.S. experience may not be directly applicable to the situations in the developing countries today, it provides the basis for an understanding of the basic processes that influence the decline in fertility that often accompanies rural development.

Section 2 (on microdeterminants) includes a theoretical analysis and reviews of literature regarding the impact of variations in family income, the value of children, and female labor force participation on the fertility decisions of rural families. The theoretical model in Chapter 6 provides a conceptualization of the rural household on which policy and programs ultimately impact, and in which family size decisions are made. The model describes both the biological components of human fertility, as well as variation in the demand for children. The model is sufficiently general to permit consideration of the range of rural policies, and of changes in family decision parameters over time.

Rural development, almost by definition, implies higher incomes among the rural population, or at least greater access to services and opportunities that would usually be associated with higher incomes. Income is thought to influence fertility decisions both directly, and indirectly through intervening variables such as educational and consumption aspirations, infant mortality, female labor supply, and perceptions of old age security. Chapter 7 examines the effect of changing income on human fertility in rural areas, with particular attention given to two intervening variables, educational aspirations and consumption aspirations.

Children present significant demands on time, especially on women's time. Consequently, theoretical expectations suggest that programs and policies that raise the opportunity cost of women's time will, by raising the price of children, be negatively related to family size. The impact is thought to operate both by raising the age at marriage and by reducing marital fertility. The review of the available evidence from rural areas of developing nations finds little consistent evidence to support that theoretical expectation. Chapter 8 concludes that the relationship likely exists, but that the complexity of family decision making under widely different institutional circumstances dictates a more elaborate conception of the relationship.

The value rural families place on children beyond that associated with the joys of parenthood are related to expectations that children will contribute to the agricultural production process and the long-term economic security of parents. Both of these potential contributions are subject to the prevailing rural institutional system and families' positions within the system. Chapter 9 reviews both the economic and socio-cultural value attached to children.

Rural development policy is a multifaceted undertaking, reflecting differences in past activities and prevailing conditions. Within the broad category of rural development policy, a number of policy goals can be identified. The relationship between four major policy goals and human fertility is the subject of the final section: (a) changes in the distribution of rights to land, (b) more equitable income distribution, (c) better nutrition, and (d) the introduction of new technology for agricultural production. The final chapter reviews the impact of community programs on fertility, in recognition of the increasing focus of rural policy at the community level.

The distribution of landholdings and patterns of land tenure are fundamental to the economic and social organization of rural societies throughout the world. Access to land determines to a large extent a rural family's position in the prevailing distribution of power, status, and wealth. As a result, a major focus of rural development policy is alteration of the distribution of land ownership, changes in the conditions of tenure, and the opening up of previously uncultivated areas for settlement by farm families. Chapter 10 examines the relationship between access to land and family reproductive behavior at a theoretical level, and reviews the available empirical evidence within the conceptual framework presented.

An understanding of the relationship between the distribution of income and fertility requires knowledge of the relationship between income and fertility among the various subgroups of a population. The aggregate fertility impact of changes in income distribution is the product of the fertility effects in each subgroup, weighted by the relative proportion of the total population found in each group. Starting from that perspective, Chapter 11 addresses two questions: First, in the course of socioeconomic development and increased per capita income,is fertility affected by changes in national income distribution? Second, if there is a relationship, what is its nature and what are the causal mechanisms?

Food policy may influence fertility through its impact on the nutritional status of women and children, and through changes in other fertility-related factors. The nutrition-food policy link with fertility in rural areas is examined in Chapter 12 within the context of three sets of relationships: (a) the impact of food policy on the nutritional status of women and children; (b) the impact of nutritional status on reproductive behavior in rural areas; and (c) the impact of food policy operating through other mechanisms, such as the value of female time, household income, and intra-household income and budget control.

The impact of agricultural technology on the demand for family labor and other resources provides a major link between agricultural development policy and family reproductive behavior. Chapter 13 provides a theoretical analysis of the impact of changes in the value of family and child labor on the demand for children. Using the model developed, the chapter traces out the effects of a specific set of technologies, i.e., those classified as mechanization. The framework, however, is more general and provides the basis for reviewing other programs or policies designed to influence relative labor prices within the rural sector.

As a pivot between the nation and the household, the small rural community is often the focus for both population and rural development policy. The design of community policy requires more direct contact with the realities affecting the lives of rural people than a focus on national planning efforts. Moreover, a community focus continues to involve a broad social concern that extends beyond the individual level and offers the opportunity for cost effective programs to meet individual needs. Chapter 14 provides a review of community programs designed to influence fertility in rural areas and examines the research available regarding their effectiveness.

Chapter 15 returns to the central issue, does the theoretical and empirical basis for the design of fertility-sensitive rural policy exist? While there is considerable evidence suggesting that the coordination of population and rural development policy is both feasible and desirable, the extant theoretical and empirical basis is deemed inadequate for more than a suggestive or first approximation analysis. Nonetheless, this book identifies areas of fundamental importance to the design of fertility-sensitive rural development policies. Given the long term horizon of many development strategies, the fertility reducing impacts of development programs are not likely to be felt immediately. However, judicious choices among the various policy alternatives may initiate precisely those changes in the institutional structure which are necessary for a sustained fertility decline.

NOTES

1. In a recent empirical study utilizing her basic framework, Boserup (1981) presents an impressive array of aggregate and historical data in support of the technological response-to-population pressure argument. A similar aggregate level analysis of a single intensification strategy, i.e., irrigation, found that investments in irrigation were related to population pressure on rural resources (Simon, 1975). The work of Levi (1976) in Sierra Leone also supports the Boserupian view, as does that of Liu and Lu (1978) in Taiwan.

2. Jones (1969, p. 281) goes further and suggests that the labor surplus found by ". . . Fei and Ranis may be an illusion resulting from their refusal to take seriously when performed by non-Europeans a group of productive activities that account for the largest part of the national income of developed countries."

3. Examples of this situation are perhaps Western Europe in the early period between the breakdown of the classical Mediterranean civilizations and the emergence of new political orders (Slicher Van Bath, 1963); large parts of the Americas and Tropical Africa also fitted this description before European colonization (Wallerstein, 1974).

4. Several historians have pointed out that the densely-settled river valleys of the Near East and Asia are the areas in which irrigation technology, a relatively high degree of urbanization, and also strong, centralized political units first emerged (Krader, 1975; Wittfogel, 1957).

5. Geertz, the scholar who first documented the process of involution in Java, stresses the importance of an integrated rural-urban economy. According to Geertz, Japan had and maintained an integrated economy, but Java had and lost an integrated economy. Population growth in the rural sector in Japan was absorbed by industry, and both output per agricultural worker and yields rose. In Java, output per worker fell while yields rose, because no industrial "escape valve" existed (Geertz, 1968, p. 135).

REFERENCES

Boserup, E. 1965. The Conditions of Agricultural Growth: The Economics of Agrarian Change Under Population Pressure. Chicago: Aldine Publishing Co.

_____ 1981. Population and Technological Change: A Study of Long-Trends. Chicago: University of Chicago Press.

Chayanov, A.V. 1970. Theory of the Peasant Economy. Homewood, Illinois: Richard D. Irwin, Inc.

Fei, J.C.H. and G. Ranis. 1964. Development of the Labor Surplus Economy. Homewood, Illinois: Richard D. Irwin, Inc.

Geertz, C. 1968. Agricultural Involution: The Process of Ecological Change in Indonesia. Berkeley: University of California Press.

Gotsch, C. 1972. Technical change and the distribution of income in rural areas. American Journal of Agricultural Economics 52:326-341.

Hymer, S. and S. Resnick. 1969. A model of agrarian economy with non-agricultural activities. American Economic Review 59:493-506.

Jones, W.O. 1969. The demand for food, leisure and economic surpluses. In: C.R. Wharton, Jr. (ed.) Subsistence Agriculture and Economic Development. Chicago: Aldine Publishing Co.

Jorgenson, D.W. 1961. The development of a dual economy. The Economic Journal 71:309-334.

Kennedy, E.T. and P. Pinstrup-Anderson. 1983. Nutrition Related Policies and Programs: Past Performances and Research Needs. Washington, D.C.: International Food Policy Research Institute.

Krader, L. 1975. The Asiatic Mode of Production: Sources, Development and Critique in the Writings of Karl Marx. The Hague: Assen.

Leibenstein, H. 1978. General X-Efficiency Theory and Economic Development. New York: Oxford University Press.

Levi, J.F.S. 1976. Population pressure and agricultural change in the land-intensive economy. Journal of Development Studies 13:61-78.

Lewis, W.A. 1954. Economic development with unlimited supplies of labour. The Manchester School of Economic and Social Studies 22: 139–191.

Liu, P.K.C. and G.L.T. Lu. 1978. Projections of Agricultural Population in Taiwan, ROC, 1975–1990. Chinese-American Joint Commission on Rural Reconstruction: Taipei, Taiwan.

Mosher, A.T. 1966. Getting Agriculture Moving. New York: Praeger.

Robinson, W. and W. Schutjer. In press. Agricultural Development and Demographic Change: A Generalization of the Boserup Model. Economic Development and Cultural Change.

Ruttan, V.W. 1959. Asher and Schumpeter on invention, innovation and technical change. Quarterly Journal of Economics 73:596–606.

Schultz, T.W. 1964. Transforming Traditional Agriculture. New Haven: Yale University Press.

Simon, J.L. 1975. The positive effect of population growth on agricultural savings in irrigations systems. The Review of Economics and Statistics 57:71–79.

Slicher Van Bath, B.H. 1963. The Agrarian History of Western Europe, A.D. 500–1850. New York: St. Martins Press.

United Nations. 1980. Demographic Year Book 1979. New York.

Wallerstein, I. 1974. The Modern World-System: Capitalist Agriculture and European World-Economy in the Sixteenth Century. New York: Academic Press.

Wittfogel, K. 1957. Oriental Despotism. New Haven: Yale University Press.

World Bank. 1975. The Assault on World Poverty. Baltimore: The Johns Hopkins University Press.

_____ 1980. World Development Report, 1980. Baltimore: The Johns Hopkins University Press.

CHAPTER 2

Technical Change and Human Fertility in Rural Areas of Developing Countries

Ester Boserup

Fertility levels vary from one rural area to another both within and between countries. In countries in which both urban and rural fertility has declined, there has been variation in the timing of declines in both urban and rural fertility. Since the population in rural areas of most developing countries consists primarily of agricultural producers and their family members, it is pertinent to ask: to what extent can the differences in fertility levels, and in the timing of urban and rural fertility declines, be explained by differences in the techniques used in agricultural production? Access to land, tools and methods, annual working hours, and the distribution of family labor are different in various systems of agriculture, and these differences are likely to have an influence on fertility in agricultural families. Therefore, it is necessary to begin with a brief description of the main agricultural production systems prevalent in developing countries.

It is important that these systems be viewed as adaptations to different population densities and environmental conditions (Boserup, 1965). In sparsely populated regions, land may be used for pasturing of herds and flocks, or it may be used for long-fallow agriculture. Since there is more cultivable land than the small local population can cultivate, small plots are cleared and used only until they become infested by weeds, or until crop yields decline for other reasons. When either of these possibilities occur, another plot is cleared and brought under cultivation. The result is a system characterized by long term rotation of productive activity.

In areas of higher population density, the amount of land per inhabitant is insufficient to use in long rotations. The cultivators need to use more of the land for crop production and can leave less as grazing land or fallow for long periods. Thus in regions of medium population density, say 20 to 50 persons per square kilometer, the land is used in rotation in permanent fields in which periods of cultivation alternate with short periods of fallow. During the fallow period, domestic animals may feed on the fallows and other uncultivated land. In regions with still higher population density, there is too little land to permit any of it to lie fallow for years. Here the fields bear a crop each year, and domestic animals have no fallow-land on which to feed. If the animals cannot support themselves in areas unsuitable for cultivation, such as mountains or semideserts, owners of animals must produce fodder crops on a portion of their cultivated area. But some regions are too densely populated even for that system. In very densely settled regions, each cultivating family has only a very small area at their disposal, and a system of multicropping must be used. Under a multicropping system, if at all feasible, two or three successive crops must be sown or planted each year in each field.

If the population in rural communities continues to increase, as is the case in most developing countries, local food production must be steadily expanded, food must be transported between regions, or brought in from other countries. This brief description indicates how continuous expansion of food production is likely to come about. In areas with long-fallow systems, cultivators must increase the number of plots which are cleared for cultivation each year, and they must recultivate plots more frequently than was required when the total population was smaller. The long-fallow system develops into a short-fallow system. If population growth occurs in communities which already have adopted the short-fallow system, the area cultivated each year must expand by eliminating fallow and transforming pastures and forested land into fields, some of which will be used to produce fodder. In communities already using annual cropping, land must be improved so that it can be used for multicropping, or fodder production must be given up, and the number of domestic animals decreased.

THE ORGANIZATION OF PRODUCTION

The organization of agricultural production within each of these systems will determine how this process of intensification is likely to influence fertility. The important elements in the organization are land tenure, the use of child labor, and the existence of possibilities for the use of industrial inputs. Long-fallow systems may be used as a beginning point. In this type of agriculture many operations can be done by small children. In thinly populated areas, consistent with a long-fallow system, the numbers of birds and animals are large, and children perform the time-consuming task of supervising the scattered plots and scaring birds and animals away from ripening crops. Children also gather fruit and other noncultivated food, which provides an important supplement to nutrition in sparsely populated areas. Under the long-fallow system, most, if not all, of the work with vegetable crops is performed by women (Boserup, 1970). Children help their mother carry crops from the widely scattered impermanent plots, often far from the habitations, and with harvesting. Children also help women provide fuel and water for the household, assist with domestic work, and care for younger siblings. Large boys help in felling trees and in preparation of new plots, a task generally reserved for male members of the family.

Child labor is neither the only, nor the most important motivation for desiring a large family in long-fallow agricultural systems. Members of a large family, and of a large local group, provide protection against outsiders, and adult children help parents to survive in old age. The land used for fallow and cultivation may be tribally owned and a family can clear and cultivate the number of plots which they need (Boserup, 1965). If land use is controlled by the local chief, he usually assigns land to a family in proportion to its size, so a man with several wives and a large number of children gains the use of a large area for cultivation (Boserup, 1970). In addition, children contribute to family status since large families are both powerful and respected, and the status of the head of the family is often directly related to its size. In spite of the multiple advantages of large families in many long-fallow communities, family size is relatively small. In these regions, population is small and scattered, and usually far from urbanized areas, therefore, health facilities are poor and morbidity and mortality high. In systems of long-fallow agriculture, most families are unable to rear the number of children they would like to have.

The picture is different in communities employing short-fallow agricultural systems. Some of these communities have recently changed from long-fallow as a result of population pressure, but most communities with short-fallow systems have employed these systems for centuries or millenia. In the latter group of communities, attitudes toward family size may be different from those of long-fallow communities. With greater population density, childrens' work with wild crops and with animal and bird scaring becomes less useful, or disappears. Similarly, while the tools used in long-fallow agriculture are hand tools, in most communities which have utilized short-fallow systems for a long period, ploughs are used for land preparation, and pack animals or animal driven carts are used instead of head transport. The ploughs and carts used in the short-fallow system are nearly always used by men, thus, women in short-fallow systems have less to do and have less need of help from children. Thus, unless the crop rotation includes cotton or other crops particularly well suited for child labor, such labor is not so widely used that it is likely to provide a motive for large family size.

When fallow is shortened, the cultivated land passes into private property, in some cases by legal reforms, but elsewhere by a gradual change of customs. Therefore, the head of a large family cannot obtain additional land for cultivation without cost, but must buy or rent the additional land. Not only is the acquisition of land to accommodate a large family difficult, but a peasant family with many children may be forced to sell land to provide a dowry for daughters.

It may also be necessary either to subdivide the holding or to accept a decline in social status, as some of the sons become wage laborers or tenants for families with fewer children and more land. In peasant communities with private ownership of land, parents in a poor family with more children than they can provide for without losing status are regarded as irresponsible parents. It is the size of the land holding and not the size of the family, which matters for social esteem. In addition to this, land owning peasants can lease out land or engage wage labor in old age, so they are less dependent upon support from adult children.

Many peasant families in different parts of the world have avoided land shortage by means of induced abortion, female infanticide, or other traditional means of fertility control. One example of the adjustment to land scarcity and other economic pressure is Japan. In Japan, female infanticide had disappeared toward the end of the nineteenth century, when economic development made girls useful in silk production and money earners in textile industries. However, after the second world war, when large numbers of settlers returned from former colonies, increasing pressure on land and other employment opportunities induced a sharp increase in illegal abortions and eventually led to the legalization of abortion. The decline of fertility in Japan would probably not have been so rapid, and set in so early after the economic motivation was provided, if a restrictive attitude to family size had not been a traditional custom in Japanese villages.

Concern about land shortage in settled peasant communities with private ownership of land may result not only in deliberate, but also in an unintended reduction in fertility through delayed marriage. If the population is increasing, it becomes more difficult for peasants with many children to arrange favorable marriages for their children, and prolonged, vain, efforts to do so may raise the average marriage age, especially if late-marrying daughters are able to earn money to pay their dowry, as was the case in Japan.

The Japanese example should remind us, the settled peasant communities with very high population density and intensive agriculture, such as prevailed in Japan in the nineteenth century, may have attitudes toward family size which differ from those of less densely populated peasant communities. The smaller land area available per family enhances the motivation for restriction of family size, but with increasing intensification of agriculture, the need for child labor becomes much greater. To understand this, it is necessary to look at the different functions of fallowing. Some of the most important functions of fallowing are to prevent exhaustion of soil fertility, reduce weed growth, and limit the spread of plant disease. These purposes can, however, also be served by use of chemical fertilizer, herbicides, and pesticides. In other words, industrial inputs to agriculture can substitute for fallowing as they do in industrialized countries where fallowing is seldom used. However, chemical inputs are not the only substitutes for fallowing. Soil fertility can be preserved by applying manure and night soil, or vegetable matter gathered in forests and other uncultivated areas, or at the bottom of rivers and lakes. Use of such fertilizing matter is the chief means of preserving soil fertility in densely populated areas in which neither fallowing nor chemical inputs can be used. In such areas, proliferation of weeds must be prevented by repeated hand weeding, and parasites must be removed by hand, or infested plants must be removed. Each of these functions is highly intensive of the type of labor which children can provide.

Use of intensive agricultural systems with frequent cropping not only requires that problems of fertilization, weed control, and pest control be tackled by one of the means mentioned above, it also often necessitates the regulation of the agricultural water supply. Fallowing is sometimes used to preserve moisture in land which is too dry to bear a crop each year. If annual cropping is introduced, the fields must be irrigated. If multicropping is introduced, the second and third crop must be grown outside the most favorable season, requiring irrigation even in areas with a relatively wet climate. Like the operations mentioned above, irrigation can be undertaken either by means of industrial inputs or by labor intensive means. Finally, the control of soil erosion can also be accomplished with a range of techniques. If population density is too high to use the forest-fallow system to prevent erosion created by cultivation of hill sides, erosion can be prevented by means of terracing which can be done either with mechanized equipment or by labor-intensive methods.

In other words, use of intensive agricultural systems requires that problems of soil fertility, weeds, plant disease, water control, and erosion be solved. These problems cannot be overcome by fallowing because of high population density, but a choice remains between industrial inputs and labor-intensive methods. When the latter are used, the demand for labor rises steeply with increased growth of population and increasing cropping frequency. Each additional hectare brought under cultivation, instead of being fallowed, adds to the labor requirement, and the labor input per hectare sown or planted becomes much greater. Women and children gather fertilizing matter, often far from the village, carry it to the fields, and spread it. Women and children are usually the ones who weed, transplant, and try to cope with plant disease. Japanese statistics reveal an extremely high labor input in intensive paddy production as late as the middle of this century, when the use of purchased inputs was already substantial (Ishikawa, 1967).

The need to dig and maintain terraces and irrigation facilities in intensive agricultural systems can also increase the demand for female and child labor because men often compensate for time spent in these activities by making maximum use of female and child labor in the fields. Many densely populated areas with intensive agriculture are often more developed than sparsely populated areas, are closer to urban centers, and have better transport systems. Consequently, they are better able to have labor intensive commercial crops, suited for child labor, in the crop rotation. In short, in intensive agricultural systems, children are likely to contribute more than they cost, not only in families of land owning peasants, but also in landless families, especially if children work for wages in agriculture, separately or together with their parents. Landless workers also depend upon support from children in old age.

TECHNICAL CHANGE AND THE GREEN REVOLUTION

The choice between intensification of agriculture with labor intensive methods, or with chemical and mechanized inputs, is of crucial importance for the use of child labor and thus may provide motivation for, or against, restriction of fertility. It is important therefore, to note, that the Green Revolution techniques, which have spread in many densely populated regions, are a mixture of labor intensive and modern-input methods for the intensification of agriculture. The Green Revolution introduced chemical inputs and certain types of mechanization, but at the same time, land use was shifted to a much more intensive system using irrigation, multicropping, fodder production, labor-intensive commercial crops, and various types of land improvement. Thus the labor input increased, and female and child labor continued to be important. Moreover, there was a sudden, and large, increase in total family income which perhaps made parents feel that they now could afford additional children.

The use of Green Revolution techniques is limited to areas with good infrastructure. Purchased inputs, including chemical fertilizers, must be transported from urban areas, traded, and stocked. In that process, good long-distance transport and local roads to villages and isolated farms are necessary, as are local warehouses. The introduction and use of mechanized equipment requires that fueling and repair services be available locally. An extension network may also be a precondition for the introduction and effective utilization of modern methods, especially if the agricultural structure is one of many small producers. Sometimes large-scale, controlled irrigation must be available, or service facilities and equipment for tube wells and other small-scale irrigation systems. The areas where the Green Revolution has had most success, for instance, Korea, Taiwan, and the Indian state of Punjab, were supplied with basic infrastructure by Japanese and British rulers in the colonial period. These areas now have far better rural infrastructure than is typical for developing countries and, in the case of India, other parts of the nation.

When rural infrastructure is very poor, it may not even be possible to produce commercial crops for export by means of hand labor and animal draughtpower. Because transport of perishable crops may be impossible, and transport of nonperishable products so costly, local prices are so low that production is not profitable. Infrastructural obstacles to agricultural development are likely to be worse in sparsely populated regions than in densely populated regions because it is uneconomic to supply a small and scattered population of agricultural producers with transport facilities and other infrastructure (Simon, 1977; Boserup, 1981). In such a region, the multiplication of population would in the long run improve the possibilities for development by providing an expanded population base for markets and other rural infrastructure. However, for the people living in the region, labor migration by selected family members may be the best, or even the only, way to improve incomes in the short-term. If possibilities for employment or other income-earning opportunities are also poor in other regions of a nation, migrants from labor surplus regions may go to foreign countries that offer better prospects.

The local system of agriculture also influences the sex distribution of migrants which reflects the demand for female and male labor in the local system of agriculture. Similarly, the demand for female and male labor in the areas of destination also affects the sex composition of migrant streams. For example, the migration of women is greater than that of men in regions of Latin America where women's labor input in agriculture is relatively small, and urban demand for female wage labor, especially domestic servants, is large. By contrast, in most of Africa, where women do most of the agricultural work, and where demand for female wage labor in urban areas is small, male migration is much greater than female migration.

Migration may also be large from regions with better agricultural opportunities, especially if there is a possibility for getting stable, urban employment. To have adult children with urban incomes is often regarded as insurance against both fluctuations in harvests and poverty in old age. Therefore, parents are eager to invest in education of their children, and the migration of school leavers to urban areas is large. Where prospects are good that adult children may get urban jobs and send money to the family in the village, migration may contribute to delaying a fertility decline. Sex-selective migration to the United States may have contributed to a delayed fertility decline in rural areas of Mexico.

The large-scale male migration from rural to urban areas in Africa has forced many rural women to provide for their children without male help. However, African women are usually able to obtain a subsistence income for themselves and their children by work in agriculture, small-scale trading, and small informal production and services. These income producing activities are not available to women who belong to cultures which confine women to the household, and to work which can only be done in the home. In rural communities of this type, women are completely dependent upon male family members for their own support, and that of children below working age. All jobs in such communities are male jobs, and there are very few possibilities for divorced, abandoned, and widowed women to earn income. Under these conditions the alternatives available to support such women are often limited to prostitution and begging, unless the women are helped by adult or young children.

In many communities of this type, only men inherit land and other property, while in others, men can freely divorce their wives, and are likely to do so, if they fail to give birth to the desired number of boys. Women have a very strong motive in such situations for bearing many children as quickly as possible (Youssef, 1974). If the age difference between spouses is large and only men inherit, it is important for women to have several sons as soon as possible to assure support should they become widowed or abandoned at an early age. Fertility restriction would likely be more acceptable to such women, if legal reforms gave equal rights to own and inherit land and other property to both men and women, and obliged men to support divorced wives and their children. In order to have a major effect on fertility, however, such reforms need to be accompanied by radical changes in labor market access for women, and the modernization of traditional attitudes. The communities discussed here are the ones in which sex differentials in rural schools are the largest, because only a minority of progressive parents send their daughters to school.   Such sex bias contributes to attitudes conducive to high fertility, as well as limiting access to modern employment by women.

In some rural communities women have considerable liberty to decide their own reproductive behavior, but in most cases, decisions about school attendance, marriage age, use of contraception, and even length of breastfeeding, may be taken by the husband, elder family members, or the village priest.   Under such circumstances, young women have little influence on their own reproductive behavior and dropout rates for acceptors of family planning services are often quite high.   Part of the explanation for the latter phenomenon may be that the person first approached by family planning personnel was not the real decision maker, and this person later sabotaged the effort by not using the services or by putting pressure on the acceptor to discontinue use.

GOVERNMENT POLICY

There is a final category of decision makers relevant to fertility: governments and local government administrations.   Some governments, mainly in densely populated countries, make family planning services available in rural areas, but if the general attitude of the rural population is hostile to fertility restriction they are little used, and an ambivalent attitude by the local staff providing the services contributes to this result.   Other governments, mainly in sparsely populated countries, make more or less successful efforts to prevent the population from restricting fertility.   In addition, and more important, many types of government policy designed for other purposes contribute either to preventing or promoting a fertility decline in rural areas.   Important examples are the alternative strategies of development for urban and rural areas pursued by governments.

Historically, most governments in developing countries focused upon development of industry and the provision of modern services in urban areas, mainly the metropolitan areas, while they did little or nothing to promote rural development.   As a result, before the huge migration to metropolitan areas in developing countries began, these areas nearly always had much better economic and social infrastructure than the rest of the country.   Therefore, when industrialization started or accelerated, nearly all new industries and modern services chose metropolitan locations, and both the increasing demand for labor and the better service facilities attracted high-level, skilled, and unskilled labor to these areas.   The rapid expansion of economic activities, including government administration, and the rapid increase of population in metropolitan areas made it necessary to give priority to expansion and qualitative improvement of urban infrastructure, an effort which continued to be frustrated by further concentration of population in these areas.   In the meantime, few government resources were left for expansion and qualitative improvement of infrastructure in rural areas and smaller towns.   Some of the governments that neglected rural development assumed that because there was no shortage of land resources in the country, market forces would take care of agricultural and rural development. Other governments listened to economic advisors who believed in the now-outmoded theory that agricultural production in developing countries was inelastic, so development could best be pursued by transferring the "rural surplus" of labor to urban areas for employment in industry and modern services.

Because of the neglect of rural infrastructure investment by both central and local governments, the expansion of export crop production and food deliveries to urban areas could only occur in rural areas which already had the necessary infrastructure. The existing infrastructure had been developed to facilitate urban deliveries of food and export crops. But these areas were not sufficient to supply the rapidly increasing urban demand for food. As a result, the increased demand was met to a considerable extent by imports from industrialized countries.

If rapid increases in the share of total population living in urban areas is to be accomplished without increasing food imports, not only must total food production increase, but labor productivity in food production must also increase. Rising labor productivity will not occur if producers can only expand the output of food by means of labor inputs and reduced fallow periods, and are unable to use modern inputs. Such conditions were characteristic of most rural communities in most developing countries in which governments neglected rural development. In Africa, huge, sparsely populated areas had virtually no economic infrastructure, and women who produced the local food supply had no possibilities for using modern inputs, and could at best expand production proportionate to their increase in numbers. In rural African communities which had somewhat better infrastructure, and in which family incomes increased because of increasing production of cash crops or favorable prices for such crops, women would often give up agricultural work, or reduce it, and purchase imported food for family consumption.

Reliance on imported food to supply urban areas had many attractions for governments that were most concerned with financial problems and the welfare of the urban, especially the metropolitan, population. But the reliance on imports made conditions in the already neglected rural areas even worse, because it discouraged food production for the towns, even in areas which hitherto had commercial production for the purpose. Consequently, in many developing countries national production of cereals declined and was replaced by imports. If surplus production of food in the industrialized countries and the need to dispose of the surpluses by means of subsidized exports, or gifts of food, had not made food imports so attractive for many governments in developing countries, many more would have been forced to devote more of their resources to development of their own rural areas. Landowning peasants would have improved their incomes, and landless labor would have had more employment. There would have been less rural to urban migration, and less urban congestion. Moreover, if subsidized exports from the industrialized countries, and their restrictions on food imports, had not discouraged developing countries from developing exports to new markets, some of them, including some of the poorest ones, might have been able to finance rural development by means of food exports.

In rural areas lacking improved infrastructure and modernization of agricultural production, fertility rates have usually remained high, and if urban fertility declined due to industrialization, a gap appeared between urban and rural fertility, or the existing gap became larger. In some of the countries which did not neglect agriculture, but pursued a balanced policy of industrial and agricultural development, fertility rates declined in both rural and urban areas. However, there were also countries that experienced both rural development and continued high fertility. In some cases, this was probably due to cultural obstacles to fertility decline, but it also seems likely that the short term effect of increases in rural incomes may have caused parents to become less inclined to restrict family size.

CONCLUSIONS

It has been suggested that the choice of agricultural policy with radical substitution of mechanized and chemical inputs for traditional labor-intensive techniques could provide motivation for fertility control in peasant families. However, it is not desirable that governments give priority to the likely effects on human fertility in their choice of agricultural policies. Whether fertility rates in rural areas begin to decline rapidly or remain at high levels, rural population increase will continue to be rapid for many decades, because of the increase in the number of young families. To avoid further deterioration of conditions in congested urban areas, a larger share than hitherto of the young families must be able to make a living in rural areas and smaller towns. The creation of economic opportunities in rural areas is more important than a rapid decline in rural fertility. Therefore, the promotion of technological change in rural areas cannot be by means of rapid mechanization of agriculture, even if that might reduce fertility. Rural policy must be designed as a compromise between the labor-intensive pattern and the modern-input pattern, thus ensuring that both employment opportunities and rural per capita incomes increase. In most developing countries, this seems the only way to improve levels of living both in urban and rural areas.

REFERENCES

Boserup, E. 1965. The Conditions of Agricultural Growth. London: Allen and Unwin.
_____ 1970. Woman's Role in Economic Development. New York: St. Martin's Press.
_____ 1981. Population and Technological Change. Chicago: University of Chicago Press.
Ishikawa, S. 1967. Economic Development in Asian Perspective. Tokyo: Knokuniya Bookshop Co.

Simon, J.L. 1977.   The Economics of Population Growth.   Princeton:
    Princeton University Press.
Youssef, N.H. 1974.   Women's status and fertility in Muslim countries of
    the Middle East and Asia.   Paper presented at the Symposium on
    Women's Status and Fertility, American Psychological Association,
    New Orleans.

CHAPTER 3
Migration and Rural Fertility in Less Developed Countries

Calvin Goldscheider

Over the last decade a considerable amount of research has been undertaken to clarify fertility and migration patterns in less developed regions of the world. In addition to national studies and comparative research at the societal level, specific attention has focused on rural-urban fertility differentials, the social and economic correlates of high fertility in rural areas, the fertility patterns of migrants and nonmigrants in urban places, and the determinants and selected consequences of a wide variety of migration patterns. These studies have resulted in theoretical, methodological, and empirical clarification of critical dimensions of population processes in the context of the socioeconomic and political development of the third world.

Yet, the interactions between fertility and migration processes have not been fully investigated. A conspicuous omission in previous research has been the analysis of the relationships between migration and fertility, in general, and between out-migration and rural fertility, in particular. In part, this neglect reflects theoretical biases which have emphasized connections between development and urbanization and have therefore concentrated on urban places and problems. In part, complex methodological problems continue to plague research on migration, specifically the need for a research design which captures the dynamics of migration, tracing selectivity and processes over time, tying out-migration with previous places of origin, and linking it to direction, composition of migrant stream, and permanence of movement.

To be sure, these theoretical biases and methodological problems should be challenges to research rather than obstacles. This is particularly the case since the connections between migration and fertility in rural areas are critical for understanding less developed regions of the world and their societies. Links between out-migration and fertility in rural places of origin operate at both macro and micro levels of analysis, and are located in communities (rather than at national levels) where relationships between population and social change are most salient.

The absence of research materials allowing for a comprehensive assessment of the relationships between out-migration and rural fertility in less developed nations, and the weaknesses and limitations of the individual research studies available, have been noted in the literature (see the reviews, for example, in Dasgupta, 1981; Findley, 1977; Goldstein, 1981; Simmons et al., 1977). The major fertility studies have neglected the migration component or included it in unsatisfactory ways by not specifying type of migration or the characteristics of the migrant at the time of moving; the migration studies have tended to focus on fertility at places of destination for permanent migrants. Few if any studies have focused on the fertility consequences of rural-rural movements.

The objectives of this chapter are to spell out in a preliminary way the basic issues involved in the examination of the migration-fertility nexus in rural areas of less developed countries. Special emphasis will be placed on the types of migration effects on rural fertility, connecting these to broader theoretical and methodological concerns. We start with the identification of the rural context of less developed nations.

THE RURAL CONTEXT OF LESS DEVELOPED COUNTRIES

Urbanization has been a major process in the modernization of societies and rapid urban growth has been a conspicuous feature of less developed nations. As such, it is not surprising that demographic research has focused on the relative socioeconomic adjustment of rural migrants in the cities, including their changing fertility patterns, and has analyzed the demographic components of urban growth in more and less developed societies, including the relative contributions of natural increase and migration. In these contexts, migration has been viewed as a vehicle of change for migrants and as a factor in the redistribution of population from rural to urban areas. As part of urbanization, the study of the relationship between migration and fertility has addressed the extent to which the fertility of migrants approximates the lower levels presumed to characterize the city-born. Issues associated with the fertility of the rural population have often been considered marginal or transitional and, as a result, the study of the impact of migration on rural fertility has been neglected.

The demographic reality of less developed nations suggests that such neglect is unwarranted. The population size and structure of those regions defined as less developed in large part are the consequence of migration and fertility patterns in rural areas. The analysis of the effects of migration on rural fertility is at the core of the demography of less developed countries and of the social, economic, and political correlates of their population processes.   In particular, the proportion rural in less developed countries remains high and most of these nations will remain rural for the next several decades.   Recent United Nations estimates indicate that two-thirds of the population in less developed regions are likely to remain in rural areas until around the first decade of the twenty-first century.   Indeed, more people live in rural areas of less developed countries than the combined total popula- tion of more developed countries and the urban areas of less developed nations.   More than half of the total population of the world will be located in rural areas of less developed countries in 1985 (United Nations, 1982).

These data reveal three additional patterns that provide a context for exploring rural fertility in less developed nations.   First, the size of the rural population is increasing at the same time that the propor- tion in rural areas is decreasing.   In general, this was not the histori- cal (or the contemporary) experience of most industrialized countries (Goldscheider, 1983a; Davis, 1965; Goldstein and Sly, 1977).   Between 1960 and 1980, the proportion rural in less developed countries decreased from 78 percent to 69 percent but the rural population of these same countries increased by 40 percent (from 1632 million to 2285 million).   The United Nations estimates that between 1980 and 2000 the proportion rural in less developed regions of the world will further decrease to 56 percent.   Yet, at the same time, the estimated numerical increase in these areas will be from 2285 million to 2725 million.   Although the projected pace of rural population growth will be slower relative to the previous decades (the proportion increase will be "only" 19 percent), the numerical increase estimated at over 441 million persons is only slightly smaller than the total population size of the United States and the Soviet Union in 1970.

In a very crude way, these data reveal that a substantial amount of population redistribution is occurring in less developed countries. There has been and will continue to be an increase in the level of urbanization, part of which reflects net out-migration from rural to urban areas.   Nevertheless, the amount of rural-urban migration is sub- stantially greater than these net residual movements indicate.   Not all rural-urban migration is permanent; return, repeat, and temporary movements are not reflected in the net redistribution estimates nor are stream-counterstream migrants (i.e., gross migration flows) included.   Of no less importance is the fact that not all rural out-migration is to- ward places defined as urban; some (and often a substantial proportion) is toward other rural areas.   Hence, rural-urban population transfers may represent only a small percent of all rural out-migration.   Taken together, the variety of migration flows from rural areas is greater than the net rural-urban migration inferred from urbanization estimates. Recognizing this, the net rural-urban population redistribution implies high rates of migration and large numbers of rural persons on the move.

A third feature of these data is the heterogeneity of nations included in the less developed regions of the world.   For example, Africa as a whole will remain mostly rural until after the year 2010.   Within Africa the variation in urbanization levels is considerable. Eastern Africa will remain mostly rural (i.e., 50 percent) until sometime after 2025, western Africa until after 2015, central Africa until after 1995, and northern and southern Africa until after 1985. Individual countries within Africa display an even wider range. In contrast, the Latin American region is already mostly urban with only 31 percent estimated to be rural in 1985, but Bolivia will be 64 percent rural in 1985 and will remain rural until the turn of the 21st century.

Similar variations characterize the Asian countries categorized as less developed by the United Nations. It is estimated that less than 30 percent of China will be urban by 1985 and most of the population will remain rural until around 2015. Some east Asian countries (e.g., Korea) are already urban, while Indonesia, Thailand, Vietnam, Bangladesh, and India, with a combined population of 1127 million in 1985 are at least 75 percent rural and will remain so until sometime after the second decade of the 21st century. The increasing size of the rural population, the amount of out-migration, and the enormous variation among countries defined as less developed requires systematic comparative research focusing on fertility and migration. Yet neither the data nor the theoretical frameworks available allow for an assessment of these processes and their interactions.

We have noted that these overall data present but limited hints about the extent of migration. In part this reflects the complex nature of migration and the many types of movement included within the concept migration. There is a wide range of migration types, including local, short distance, temporary, seasonal, and labor mobility, as well as internal and international migrations which are permanent and over long distances. Other criteria for typing migration relate to the composition of the migration stream (e.g., individuals, families, accompanying children, chain, mass) and directionality (e.g., rural-urban, urban-urban, rural-rural, urban-rural). All these distinctions and others as well are based on the implicit assumption that types and intensities of changes (demographic, social, economic, political, and cultural) associated with migration vary by migration type. Before linking migration to other social, economic and demographic processes, there is a need to recognize the diversities of migration and in turn to specify the particular type of migration considered.

In addition, since migration is repeatable and reversible, it is necessary to separate out return and repeat migrants from first-time movers. Combining types of migration and its character involves a complex system of migration flows (Goldscheider, 1971, 1983a,b).

The complexity of migration involving effects on places of origin, destination, and on the migrants and their families, and the wide range of types of movement included in the definition of migration (along dimensions of permanence, distance, boundaries crossed, composition, etc.) imply that migration is not a uniform process. It is not fruitful to search for general relationships between migration and fertility without specifying the type of migration or comparing the variety of migration flows involved in the migration system (Goldscheider, 1983a).

The focus on the links between migration and fertility should note the range of intermediate or proximate variables affecting fertility (Davis and Blake, 1956; Bongaarts, 1976). For some purposes, the analytic issue may be the relationship between migration and fertility change per se, irrespective of whether the change in fertility is a consequence of changes in intercourse, conception, or gestation variables. Nevertheless, we should begin to specify whether a particular migration type affects fertility through changes in marriage patterns, contraceptive usage, abortion, or some combination thereof. Indeed, some effects of rural out-migration are more likely to be related to fertility through the intercourse variables (e.g., changes in rural age structure and sex-ratios generated by selective out-migration) while other effects (e.g., when migration is the mechanism conveying information and modern-urban life styles to rural areas) may operate through increases in the prevalence and use of contraception and abortion.

THE EFFECTS OF OUT-MIGRATION ON RURAL FERTILITY

There are four major types of effects that out-migration may have on rural fertility. These need to be distinguished analytically since the effects do not uniformly operate in the same direction.

Compositional Effects

Migration not only means the movement of a specific number of people from one place to another but the selective movement of persons with particular characteristics. In turn, these characteristics are linked to patterns of reproduction, directly and indirectly.

It is a well-established empirical observation that out-migration from rural areas is selective of younger ages (particularly between the ages of 15 and 29). From a demographic point of view this means an alteration in the age structure of the population remaining in places of origin (in our case the rural areas of less developed regions) as well as the population in places of destination (urban or rural). As a result, studies of rural-urban migration have emphasized that in-migration to cities increases the urban population directly through the transfer of population and indirectly through the influx of higher fertility populations from rural areas. Moreover, the in-migrants tend to be in the prime reproductive ages and hence in the short-run at least there is a structural effect of in-migration on period fertility. These structural effects, combined with the relatively higher fertility of rural in-migrants, the fertility of urban natives, and the direct increase in population size due to in-migration, result in extraordinary high population growth rates in the urban areas of less developed countries.

The pursuit of that line of argument tends to neglect entirely the demographic compositional effects of out-migration in rural areas of origin. These effects depend in part on the extent of rural out-migration (the rate relative to the rural population) and the degree of age selectivity. They also depend on the type of out-migration (in particular its permanence) and the additional selectivity by sex and marital status.

Selectivity by age, sex, and marital status as well as migration type relate to rural fertility not only through compositional changes but through one of the proximate determinants of fertility, marriage. Selective out-migration of males or females who are unmarried may result in a changing rural marriage market; in turn, the timing of marriage may be affected through imbalances in the sex-ratio (by age) of the remaining nonmarried rural population. It is of course difficult to assess this effect among other reasons because migration is dynamic over time. For example, single women may migrate out of rural areas later than single men or men might return to places of origin to marry, returning back to urban areas with their spouses. The permutations are extensive. The important point to note is that the demographic compositional effects of rural out-migration on patterns of rural reproduction occur through the age structural selectivity of migration as well as through sex-ratio imbalances brought about by sex-marital status selectivity. Again, type of migration (its relative permanence and whether primarily of individuals or young families) plays an important role in the extent and direction of these compositional effects.

When type of migration and age, sex, and marital status selectivity are taken into account, another compositional effect emerges. This relates to the extent of temporary or seasonal migration on the separation of spouses and in turn on fertility patterns, particularly its tempo and timing. The absence of husbands from home for a particular season or for some period of time may affect total childbearing, delayed childbearing, and spacing between births.

These demographic compositional issues are important links between selective out-migration and rural fertility. The relative selectivity of migration by age, sex, and marital status do not necessarily imply either modernization or changed fertility attitudes or values in rural areas. Nor can we expect that all rural out-migration will have the same compositional effects on fertility levels, since the extent of selectivity, the rate, and type of migration are critical factors in assessing the impact on rural fertility. Of no less importance is the fact that a change in rural fertility, in particular a decrease in some period measure of fertility, may not necessarily indicate the onset of a continuous decline in fertility. Rather, it may reflect complex compositional consequences of selective out-migration. Fertility changes in rural areas brought about by the effects of selective out-migration on population composition may result in reduced rates of rural population growth (not changed fertility patterns). Reductions in the rate of population growth due to these compositional effects of rural out-migration (over and above changes in size of the rural population due to movement) may have other implications for long-run fertility and migration patterns. We shall return to this point subsequently.

The compositional effects of out-migration on rural fertility relate in complex ways to migratory selectivity along socioeconomic dimensions. Assuming that out-migration from rural areas of less developed countries is selective of the relatively better educated, more ambitious, potentially higher socioeconomic level of the rural poor, we would expect that the remaining rural population would be the least educated, poorest, and least receptive to change. Again, depending on the rate, type, and selectivity of migration, the remaining rural nonmigrants are likely to be characterized by greater resistance to changes in reproductive patterns. This compositional impact may result in relatively higher rural fertility levels than would have otherwise resulted had the out-migration not been selective by socioeconomic status. While the fertility behavior of the rural nonmigrants remains the same, the compositional consequences of selective out-migration by socioeconomic status result in higher overall levels (or sustained high levels) of rural fertility. High fertility at the individual level does not necessarily mean high levels of population growth, which may be affected by compositional changes.

One methodological implication of these compositional effects is that the study of the impact of out-migration on rural fertility needs to relate the socioeconomic and demographic characteristics of migrants to the characteristics of rural places of origin. Another is the need for data over time as the characteristics of rural migrants may change since initial and subsequent selectivity vary. All other effects of out-migration on rural fertility must take these compositional effects as the starting point for analysis.

Diffusion through Migration

A second category of effects of out-migration on rural fertility focuses specifically on the role of migration in bringing new ideas to rural areas, including family and fertility changes. Unlike compositional effects, diffusion of modernity deals directly with real changes in fertility attitudes, motivations, and behavior.

Migration has often been viewed as a vehicle or mechanism of change but almost always in the context of moving "traditional" rural persons into contact with modernity in the city. In this regard, the debates and counterdebates resolve around four core questions: (a) how "traditional" are rural migrants, particularly since rural out-migrants are selective in social-demographic characteristics and are often the least traditional of the rural population; (b) how "modern" are city residents, specifically in their fertility behavior and family patterns; (c) how much contact is there between migrants and the urban-native born population, residentially and occupationally; (d) what are the social, economic, and cultural mechanisms which link migration to fertility changes through exposure to modernity in the city?

These questions have not been resolved for the impact of migration on the fertility of the urban population (migrants and nonmigrants). As long as migration is viewed as one-way from rural to urban areas, the questions of fertility in urban areas are critical. Issues of diffusion relate essentially to when the rural population will become urban-like in its fertility (and related characteristics). However, when types of migration are specified a broader set of questions emerges relating to the direct diffusion of modernity back to rural areas through rural out-migration. Return migrants, temporary and seasonal migrants, as well as visits and other information flows from migrants to places of origin in rural areas bring a variety of types of information and ideas that may influence fertility patterns, directly and indirectly. The range of diffusion types is broad, from specific information about family planning to information about opportunities and alternatives which may influence fertility through changing marriage and family patterns. Diffusion may also occur by way of the transferral of goods and money from out-migrants back to rural areas, thus raising standards of living and consumption aspirations and indirectly affecting fertility.

The extent to which these diffusion processes operate and the specific links to migration need to be examined in the context of the four core questions directed at diffusion in urban settings, noted earlier. Yet conceptualized in broad terms, it is clear that rural out-migration remains a potential mechanism for rural fertility change through diffusion processes. Such diffusion can operate by way of changed attitudes, values conveyed in a variety of ways to the remaining rural population or more indirectly through the diffusion of information about opportunities (hence, changed marriage patterns) or transferral of goods and cash (hence, changed tastes and alternatives to childbearing). These are complex processes that may occur over time, operating at the family, household, and community levels and through kinship-ethnic-occupational networks.

Clearly these diffusion effects do not operate mechanically or automatically and thus are different than the compositional effects of rural out-migration. As before, however, the type of migration is critical in analyzing diffusion as is the context of the broader society, economically and demographically.

Both compositional and diffusion effects of migration on rural fertility have been treated largely in the context of rural-urban migration. We could further specify the type of urban destination, for example, moves to primate (or the largest) cities contrasted with moves to towns and urban places of smaller size. We would expect compositional and diffusion effects to vary with the specific character of the urban destination as well as with the particular type of migration.

Research has repeatedly indicated that rural areas of destination also characterize some rural out-migration. Here the issue is not return migration or counterstream migration from cities to rural places but rural-rural movements. Often, this involves moving from smaller to larger rural areas, to specific rural areas where the relative economic opportunities are greater, or to rural areas as a step closer to more distant urban places. Such rural-rural migration may impact on rural fertility at areas of origin and destination through compositional effects (in more complex ways since the rural effects are located in two populations in addition to the fertility of the migrants themselves) as well as through diffusion, although we would expect that the latter set of effects would be less.

Clearly, we cannot ignore the potential effects that rural-to-rural migration may have on fertility patterns. Since rural-rural moves are not linked directly or simply to modernization processes, links to fertility have been neglected. The relationship between rural-rural moves and the potential for fertility change may best be understood in the two remaining links between out-migration and rural fertility.

Demographic-Behavioral Responses

A third set of migration effects on rural fertility may be derived from the theory of multiphasic responses and its extensions (Davis, 1963; Friedlander, 1969; cf. Mosher, 1980a,b). In broad outline, the general argument is that in the process of transition to low and controlled population growth, populations respond in a variety of ways and with every means to population pressure and relative socioeconomic deprivation. These multiphasic responses include the range of intermediate variables determining control over marital fertility (contraceptive usage and abortion) as well as delayed marriage and internal and external migrations. Multiphasic demographic response theory is a modified Malthusian argument that views migration, in addition to mortality and fertility "checks," as one of the many ways populations respond to the pressures on economic development often brought about by rapid, sustained mortality reduction. Internal and international migrations reduce the pressures of demographic growth by transferring people out of places (or nations) just as fertility reductions reduce growth rates through natural increase.

In rural areas, in particular, the migration response to demographic expansion and the lack of rural economic opportunities is major; the movement out to urban areas provides an outlet for "excess" natural increase. Out-migration fits "the interests and structure of peasant families in the evolving economy" (Davis, 1963, p. 355).

In the original formulation, rural out-migration was viewed as only one of the multiple responses of the rural population in industrializing nations. An extension of the argument emphasized that migration may be a substitute for fertility reduction in rural areas (and vice versa) or a delaying mechanism for alternative responses (see especially Friedlander, 1969). In this view, internal and external migrations are a short-term safety valve relieving population pressures and delaying fertility reduction. Hence, there is an interaction of migration and fertility in the process of demographic transition.

Empirically, in industrializing nations, comparative evidence seems to support the argument that high rates of rural out-migration resulted in longer delays in rural fertility reduction. Those societies that were characterized by low rates of rural-urban movement experienced earlier and more rapid reductions in rural areas (Friedlander, 1969).

On the surface, it appears that the treatment of migration as part of multiple responses to population pressure and economic changes contradicts the position that migration is a substitute for other responses, particularly for fertility reduction. One resolution of this issue conceptualizes the role of migration in the transition to lower fertility as a substitute process in the short-run and as part of multiphasic response in the long-run. Over time (left unspecified), population will respond with every means, including out-migration from rural areas, to the challenge of population growth. However, in the early stages of population transition, and particularly in areas where natural increase is high, migration may be an effective immediate, short-run relief from population pressures. When migration is relatively permanent and rates are high, fertility reductions of the remaining rural population may be slower. Recent research on Puerto Rico and Sweden (Mosher, 1980a,b) demonstrates the utility of this approach as a theoretical guideline for the analyses of demographic transitions. Nevertheless, there has been no clear specification of the socioeconomic and demographic conditions within which migration is a substitute or joint multiphasic response (Goldscheider, 1982).

Social Organizational Changes: Uprooting Effects

One set of effects of migration on fertility beyond connections to the population system links to social organizational changes. In this regard, two key processes of modernization are related to migration: structural differentiation and the expansion of the opportunity structure. The process of moving may involve a break with kinship dominance over economic resources and with family control over status; it may as well relate to changing opportunity structures in rural places of origin or relative opportunities (economic and noneconomic) in places of destination.

The extent of the uprooting effect of migration (particularly the break with family, kin, and community of origin) depends in part on the type of migration, its permanence, distance, and the whole complex of ties retained by migrants with their places of origin. These, of course, take on a variety of forms from visiting and return migration, to remittances and chain migration. Nevertheless, one of the key changes that migration brings about in some degree or another is the removal of total control over resources and status from the family in places of origin. Often it is not clear whether migration is the consequence of the structural differentiation process or its determinant. Yet, over time, moving may facilitate the separation of economic and family structures to be realigned in new ways.

Whatever the specific causal sequence, the relationships between migration and structural differentiation take on particular significance in the context of the migration-rural fertility nexus. Specifically, one of the central axes around which revolve key determinants of fertility change is structural differentiation (Goldscheider, 1982). This involves the separation of family from economic, political, and social roles, and changes in the control exercised by the family and kin groups over economic and political resources. It also includes alterations in the dominance of the broader family-community unit over the status and role of women. Differentiation means the decline in family pressure toward large family size goals as the means to enhance family power and as the major definition of women's contribution to the family, hence status within the community.

The reduced pressure from kin for high fertility is paralleled by growing pressures for smaller families to take advantage of changed opportunity structures and to insure that the next generation will be able to improve living standards. It should be noted further that these changing opportunities exacerbate social class and generation gaps between those who participate earlier in processes of change and the latecomers. Migration of select members of a household further

increases tensions among members even when some resources are returned to the household by the migrant. These emerging inequalities
facilitate the development of new acceptable modes of behavior, including fertility behavior.

The importance of the changing dominance of kin over resources and
shifting control over women's status moves beyond issues of alterations
in the direction of intergenerational wealth flows (Caldwell, 1976). In
addition, fertility changes do not seem to require the shift to western
nuclear family structure in form or function. Rather the key change is
at the level of dominance and control by family-related institutions
over resources and the status and roles of women (Freedman, 1979).

The specific ways in which changes in these control-power mechanisms are set into motion vary. There appears to be no automatic or
universal threshold level or connection to a shift from agriculture to
industry, from extended to nuclear family structure, or redistribution
from rural to urban. Nor is there any specific socioeconomic matrix
linked to the onset of fertility changes (Van de Walle and Knodel,
1967). What emerges is the pluralism in the paths to a common
process of differentiation, changing women's status, and opportunity
structures.

One of the mechanisms linking migration and fertility changes is
therefore the impact of migration on kin control over resources. When
migration results in the decline of kin dominance over economic
resources and over the status of women, then migration would set up
some of the fundamental conditions for fertility reduction. Since not
all migration automatically and inevitably leads to uprooting effects, we
should not expect uniform fertility consequences.

The argument that migration may reflect responses to differential
economic opportunities and may foster the breakdown of kinship dominance does not imply that kinship groups do not facilitate migration or
that all kinship bonds are ruptured in the migration process. To the
contrary: kinship groups often play a key role in the migration of
selected household members and in their integration in places of destination (Hugo, 1981; Goldscheider, 1983b). There is a growing literature identifying the continuous and extensive ties between migrants
and their places of origin (Findley, 1977; Goldscheider, 1983a; Simmons
et al., 1977). Yet, these continuing and new ties do not necessarily
imply kin dominance and control which decline in the process of selected types of movement.

Migration may free the individual migrant, at least in part, from
some of the obligations and constraints of traditional rural societies
and from the ascriptive status of place and family of birth. It may, as
well, weaken the control exercised by the rural extended family over
the lives and opportunities of those who remain in the rural area.
This may also characterize return migrants and other nonpermanent
movements, since migrants do not always fit neatly back into the
social, economic, and political structure of rural areas. Once the
dominance of family-kin groups is challenged by some, it weakens in
other population sectors as well.

While compositional effects of migration are indeterminate in terms of
the predicted direction of change in rural fertility (i.e., it depends on

the selectivity and type of migration), the effects of diffusion following migration would operate over time to reduce fertility levels in rural areas. Similarly, the social organizational effects of migration, particularly the changing dominance of extended families over resources and status, would result in lowered rural fertility levels. In contrast, the demographic-behavioral effects of migration are hypothesized to provide relief from population pressure and are, therefore, alternatives to other responses. It follows that rural fertility would remain high as a result of out-migration.

If demographic theory is correct, then it follows that migration from rural areas will slow down the decline in rural fertility, since an alternative response has occurred. If sociological theory is correct, then it follows that migration from rural areas will facilitate the break between the individual and the family's control over resources and over status; hence, it will indirectly foster a more rapid decline in fertility. Clearly these theories will vary in their predictions depending on the type and rate of out-migration. Both theories may be correct but refer to different societal contexts, economic patterns, and political regimes, or have different time referents.

These hypothesized relations between out-migration and fertility, derived from well-established and theoretical positions, require systematic and detailed empirical testing. As in other social science examples, the contradiction may be more apparent than real, since we need greater specification about short- and long-run effects, and about the societal context within which the out-migration and rural fertility nexus operates. The structure of economic opportunity, the patterns of household-family formation, the political regime, as well as the cultural context, are important specifications.

The different implications of these migration effects for rural fertility are not only of analytic importance. They are of critical significance for questions of policy and programs designed to influence migration and rural development. In general, policies associated with internal migration in less developed countries have ignored the potential uprooting effects of migration. Rural-agricultural or urban-industrial policies, regional decentralized urban programs or centralized urbanization policies (Simmons et al., 1977; Findley, 1977; Goldscheider, 1983a) have not systematically focused on the ways in which selective migration may alter the social organization of rural communities.

The overwhelming concerns (and often with justification) over the enormous growth of urban places and populations in the largest cities of less developed nations have often led to the oversimplified conclusion that policies to stem the tide of rural out-migration would help alleviate the problems of excessive urban expansion. Yet, urban population size will grow even without rural-urban transfers. More importantly, from the point of view of the rural communities, the retention of rural residents in their places of origin compounds the already severe problems of overcrowded agricultural areas. The costs of nonmigration go beyond economic issues of productivity and development, and the allocation of labor accompanying development and even beyond the sheer multiplication of people (Davis, 1975). Nonmigration may delay the separation of economic resources from family-kin domi-

nance and may slow down the differentiation process critical for
modernization, in general, and for fertility reduction, in particular.

CONCLUSION

The relationship between migration and fertility in the rural areas of
less developed nations has been presented as the effects of out-migration on rural fertility. It is clear that the links may work in reverse:
fertility levels in rural areas may influence rates of out-migration.
Indeed, the demographic context of rural population growth has been
hypothesized, as noted earlier, to result in out-migration. Over time,
as rural fertility levels change, less demographic pressure will be
exerted for out-migration, although other pressures (economic and
social) may become more important. Often, because of structural
changes in population due to migration, rural population growth rates
decline and hence generate less subsequent migration. The effects of
fertility on migration operate most directly at the level of households
or extended family units and may be examined at both macro and micro
levels.

The dynamics of the fertility-migration connections imply that often
causal sequences are difficult to disentangle. An interesting example
of this complexity is reflected in a recent study of the relationship
between rural density and fertility change in India which concluded
that increasing density over time dampens fertility (Firebaugh, 1982).
Yet the study also notes that out-migration erodes the social supports
for high fertility in these same rural areas. Does not out-migration
reduce density? Is there no contradiction between high density and
lower fertility, on the one hand, and out-migration and lower fertility,
on the other? While not addressed in that research, it is likely that
both out-migration and reduced fertility are responses to density. More
importantly, out-migration and fertility are linked to each other by way
of the social structure, particularly by way of family structural
supports for high levels of fertility. Nor can these relationships be
viewed statically. The links between out-migration and fertility may
change over time in interaction with each other and within the changing context of the broader social, economic, and political framework
within which they operate.

We noted that the heterogeneity among less developed regions of the
world is substantial in terms of levels of urbanization. Nor are all
rural places within countries similar in terms of their economic and
social structure, ethnic-class composition, and demographic pattern. In
particular, the impact of migration on rural fertility and the effects of
fertility on migration varies with the particular sector of the rural
population. Farmers, workers, owners, landless, service workers, or
agriculturists among other economic and social categories may be affected differently by migration and fertility relationships.

In addition, we must not fall into the theoretical trap of treating
areas and sectors in isolation from the broader societal context of
which they are a part. Often the focus on urban areas has viewed the
rural sector only marginally, as a source of urban population and in
economic relationship to cities. Rural development studies have often

focused only on the rural areas. Emerging from recent theoretical literature is the need to focus on issues of dependencies and sectoral connections within (and between) countries. In interesting ways, the analysis of migration is one of the important mechanisms linking areas and populations.

The outline of issues and specification of relationships should serve as a theoretical map for addressing some neglected patterns of migration and fertility. We need to begin the detailed comparative research in rural areas to build a firmer empirical base for our analytic studies and our policies.

REFERENCES

Bongaarts, J. 1976. Intermediate fertility variables and marital fertility rates. Population Studies 30:227-241.

Caldwell, J. 1976. Toward a restatement of demographic transition theory. Population and Development Review 2:321-366.

Dasgupta, B. 1981. Rural-urban migration and rural development. In: J. Balan (ed.) Why People Move: Comparative Perspectives on the Dynamics of Internal Migration. Paris: UNESCO.

Davis, K. 1963. The theory of change and response in modern demographic history. Population Index 29:345-366.

_____ 1965. The urbanization of the human population. In: Cities. New York: Scientific American.

_____ 1975. Asia's cities: Problems and options. Population and Development Review 1:71-86.

_____ and J. Blake. 1956. Social structure and fertility: An analytic framework. Economic Development and Cultural Change 4:211-235.

Findley, S. 1977. Planning for Internal Migration: A Review of Issues and Policies in Developing Countries. Washington, D.C.: U.S. Bureau of the Census.

Firebaugh, G. 1982. Population density and fertility in 22 Indian villages. Demography 19:481-494.

Freedman, R. 1979. Theories of fertility decline: A reappraisal. Social Forces 58:1-17.

Friedlander, D. 1969. Demographic responses and population change. Demography 6:359-381.

Goldscheider, C. 1971. Population, Modernization, and Social Structure. Boston: Little, Brown and Company.

_____ 1982. Societal change and demographic transitions: Selected theoretical issues and research strategies. In: Department De Demographie (ed.) Population Et Structures Sociales, Chaire Quetelet '81, pp. 83-106. Louvain: Universite Catholique de Louvain.

_____ 1983a. Modernization, migration, and urbanization. In: P. Morrison (ed.) Population Movements: Their Forms and Functions in Urbanization and Development. Liege, Belgium: Ordina Editions.

_____ (ed.). 1983b. Urban Migrants in Developing Countries: Patterns and Problems of Adjustment. Boulder: Westview Press.

Goldstein, S. 1981. Some comments on migration and development. In: J. Balan (ed.) Why People Move: Comparative Perspectives on the Dynamics of Internal Migration. Paris: UNESCO.

_____ and D. Sly (eds.). 1977. Patterns of Urbanization: Comparative Country Studies. Liege, Belgium: Ordina Editions.

Hugo, G. 1981. Village-community ties, village norms and ethnic and social networks: A review of evidence from the Third World. In: G. DeJong and R. Gardner (eds.) Migration Decision-making: Multidisciplinary Approaches to Microlevel Studies in Developed and Developing Countries, pp. 186–224. New York: Pergamon Press.

Mosher, W. 1980a. The theory of change and response: An application to Puerto Rico, 1940–1970. Population Studies 34:45–58.

_____ 1980b. Demographic responses and demographic transitions. Demography 17:395–412.

Simmons, A., S. Diaz-Briquets, and A.A. Laquian. 1977. Societal Change and Internal Migration. Ottawa: International Development Research Centre.

Van De Walle, E. and J. Knodel. 1967. Demographic transition and fertility decline: The European case. IUSSP, Proceedings of the Sidney Conference. Canberra: National University Press.

United Nations. 1982. Estimates and Projections of Urban, Rural and City Populations, 1950–2025: The 1980 Assessment. New York: United Nations.

CHAPTER 4

Urban-Industrial Development as a Force in Rural Fertility Change: The Case of Taiwan, Republic of China

Te-Hsiung Sun

Two of the most significant changes in contemporary societies are urbanization and industrialization. These two changes usually go together. The degree of change, however, varies greatly among societies. For example, the percentage of urban population among countries varies from a high of 100 in Singapore, 95 in Belgium, 90 in Hong Kong, to a low of 5 in Nepal, and 4 in Bhutan and Lesotho (Population Reference Bureau, 1982).

There are at least two types of urban–industrial development. One type is the expansion of existing cities into larger cities or metropolitan areas, accompanied by increases in the industrial population, but leaving large parts of rural areas with little change. This type of development is found in many developing countries. The other type of urban–industrial development includes existing cities, towns, and rural areas. This type of change is characterized by a rapid growth of industrial population in rural areas and tends to be found in the developed and the more advanced developing countries.

As Robinson (1963) pointed out, one of the most important aspects of urbanization is its possible impact on fertility. There have been many studies which demonstrate strong negative correlations between urban-industrial development and fertility (e.g., Friedlander and Silver, 1967; Speare et al., 1973), although some studies indicate a positive or insignificant relation between the two (Gendell, 1967). The important question, however, is how urban–industrial development affects fertility. Spengler (1952, p. 103) speculated on the logic behind a negative relation:

Urbanization . . . concomitant of output-increasing industrialization, has been unfavorable to fertility, presumably because
there has been associated with progress in urbanization an
intensification of more elements (e.g. level and content of
aspirations; relative net cost of rearing children) that are or
can become inimical to childbearing and childrearing than of
elements that are favorable (e.g. better medical care).

There have been many studies at the individual level which have
tried to explain these relationships from economic, psychological, and
sociological points of view. However, there have been few studies at
the aggregate or areal level. Heer (1966) attempted to test the
hypothesis that economic development, while associated directly with
an increase in fertility, at the same time gives rise to a set of
associated circumstances, which prompt a decline in fertility. He
employed the methods of multiple and partial correlation to support his
hypotheses at the cross-country level. He suggested that: (a) while
the direct effect of economic development is increased fertility, the
indirect effect is a reduction in fertility; (b) increased economic
development results in increased literacy and a lower infant mortality
rate; and (c) a high level of education and a low infant mortality rate
result in lower fertility. Massey and Tedrow (1976), however, challenged Heer's methodology and concluded that the methods as implemented by Heer offer no clear support for these basic contentions.
They pointed out a number of errors in statistical reasoning and interpretation in the study. This, however, does not deny that economic
development has an impact on fertility at the aggregate level.

This chapter analyzes the impacts of urbanization and industrialization on rural fertility change in Taiwan at the areal level. It
discusses the data and methods employed, then presents trends in
urbanization, industrialization, and fertility decline in Taiwan. The
third section presents the results, followed by a discussion of the
findings.

DATA AND METHODOLOGY

In the first part of the chapter, time trends for urbanization, industrial development, and fertility are discussed to provide a basis for
further analysis of the impacts of urban-industrial development on
fertility. The trends are presented in the form of urban-rural differentials as much as possible. The decomposition technique is used to
separate the composition/structural effects of education and environ-
mental/period effects on total fertility. Then, multivariate areal
analysis is employed to examine the impact of urban-industrial development on fertility at the aggregate level. The data for 331 townships/
districts of the plain area are used as units of analysis. Path models
have been developed, which view fertility as a function of urban-
industrial development and selected intermediate variables. The
analysis is carried out for all 331 plain townships and for 282 rural
townships, and for both cross-sectional data for 1965, 1973, and 1980,
and changes for 1965 to 1973, and 1973 to 1980.

The data used in this study were obtained primarily from the household registration, supplemented by other registration data, and three knowledge, attitudes, and practice of contraception (KAP) surveys carried out by the Taiwan Provincial Institute of Family Planning and its predecessor. The household registration data are generally good in quality and coverage but, of course, there are some deficiencies. Of the data used in this study, the total fertility rates are regarded as quite accurate, except that the rates before 1974 are based on the date of registration, while subsequent rates are based on the date of occurrence. The proportion of women aged 20 to 24 who are currently married is based on marriage registration and is considered accurate.

The mortality rate for ages under five is based on death registration. The underregistration of infant mortality is estimated to be about 30 to 40 percent, but areal differences are considered to be small (1). The death rates for ages 1 to 4 are quite accurate. There are some minor problems in the data on education. First, data for 1965 are for the population age 12 and above, but those for 1972 and 1980 are for those aged 15 and above. Second, the education registration for ages under 18 is not very accurate because currently enrolled students are not likely to change their education status as long as they continue to receive school education, i.e., the educational level for the population in the younger ages tends to be lower than the actual level. This trend, however, is universal and there is very little areal difference. The data on occupation and industry are not as accurate because: (a) there usually is a delay or even failure to register a change of occupation; (b) since 1968, those who are in the army are registered as "other services"; (c) there is a tendency for retired farmers to retain farmer's status for their own benefit; and (d) the data for 1965 are for the population aged 12 and above, but those for 1973 and 1980 are for those 15 and above. The actual population density of rural townships tends to be lower than recorded, due to underreporting of migration from rural areas to the cities. The data from family planning home visits in the rural areas indicate that around 20 percent of the households with married women under 30 years of age have moved to the cities, but keep their household registration in their place of original residence. This proportion is somewhat higher among remote rural areas. The underreporting of migration also affects fertility data because children born to the couples who moved to the cities without changing their address are registered at the place of origin. The number of contracted doctors for insertion of intrauterine contraceptive devices (IUD) is expressed in terms of person-months obtained from family planning service statistics. Even though the registration data have the deficiencies noted, they are not thought to affect the analysis seriously, except perhaps for occupation.

The KAP data are from the sample surveys conducted by the Taiwan Provincial Institute of Family Planning in 1965, 1973, and 1980, respectively. All surveys were based on probability samples representing women of childbearing age, except for those in the few mountain townships (30 out of 361) where most of Taiwan's small aborigine population lives.

The basic conceptual framework of this study is drawn from the work of Sun (1983), and incorporates key elements of the Easterlin (1975) model.   Stated succinctly, selected aspects of the social structure, environmental conditions, and socioeconomic characteristics of townships are viewed as influencing the demand for children, the supply of children, and the costs of fertility regulation.   The demand and supply of children jointly determine the motivation to control fertility, while motivation and costs of fertility regulation are viewed as directly influencing fertility.   Due to the lack of data, some of the variables (demand for children and motivation to control fertility) are not included in the analysis.   The incompleteness of data to test the analytical scheme may affect the results.

TRENDS IN URBANIZATION, INDUSTRIALIZATION, AND FERTILITY

There are several reasons for using Taiwan as an example to study the impact of urban-industrial development on fertility.   Taiwan has undergone rapid urbanization and industrialization in recent decades. Fertility has been declining quite rapidly until recently.   Finally, Taiwan has comparatively good statistical data for analysis.

As shown in Table 1, the population density of Taiwan has more than doubled in the past three decades from 226 persons per square kilometer in 1952 to 495 in 1980.   The urban population as a percentage of total population increased from 48 to 70.   The proportion of the population served with piped water more than doubled, from 29 percent to 67 percent during the same period.   Urbanization in Taiwan is similar to that in developed countries and the more advanced developing nations.   That is, urbanization has occurred through both the expansion of existing cities and towns, and through changes in characteristics of rural areas.   The number of villages (T'sun and Li) that were classified as urbanized areas increased from 2,877 in 1972 to 3,179 in 1980 (2). Currently, one can find many small factories in towns which attract workers from rural areas, and relatively large factories scattered around rural areas.   The rapid industrialization indicated in Table 1 was accompanied by modernization in many spheres, including a rise in the educational level, a rapid increase in communication media, and improvements in health (Liu, 1976).   It also should be pointed out that, during this period, agricultural production increased 187 percent, largely due to improvements in agricultural technology.   In general, development was faster during 1965 to 1973 than during 1973 to 1980.

The data from three KAP surveys also indicate that there have been significant changes in personal characteristics (Chang et al., 1981). The proportion of married women of childbearing age who had a junior high school or better education increased from about 10 percent in 1965 to almost 30 percent in 1980.   The proportion of husbands engaged in nonagricultural occupations increased from 68 to 87 percent. Respondents (wives) with refrigerators increased greatly from 3 to 95 percent, and those with motorcycles increased from 7 to 74 percent. The proportion of respondents who read newspapers every day increased from 10 to 46 percent.   There were also changes in household types, i.e., an increase in nuclear families.

Table 1. Indicators of Urbanization, Industrialization, and Social Development in Taiwan

INDICATOR	1952	1960	1965	1973	1980
Urbanization indicators					
Population density (persons/km²)	226	300	351	433	495
Urban population as percent of total population[a]	48	50	55	62	70
Population served with piped water (%)	29	30	38	46	67
Industrialization indicators					
Labor force over age 11 in nonagricultural occupations (%)	39	44	46	63[b]	72[b]
Net domestic product from industry (%)	18	25	29	44	45
Total industrial production index[c]	100	243	456	1940	4107
Agricultural production index	100	143	190	243	287
Per capita national income index	100	133	182	350	488
Education indicators					
Population 6 and over who are illiterate (%)	42	27	23	14	10
Primary school graduates enrolled in junior hish schools (%)	34	51	57	84	97
Communication indicators					
Daily newspaper and magazines per 1000 population	–	–	38	76	142
Television sets per 1000 households	–	–	14[d]	738	1020
Health indicators					
Life expectancy, males	56	62	65	68	70
Per capita daily consumption of proteins (grams)	49	57	61	74	78

[a] Urban population = total population – agricultural population.

[b] For labor force over age 14.

[c] Includes manufacturing, mining, electricity, gas, and water.

[d] 1964 data.

Source: Council for Economic Planning and Development, *Taiwan Statistical Data Book*, 1982, and *Social Welfare Indicators*, ROC, 1982.

When the changes are observed separately for cities and urban/rural townships, changes occurred faster in the townships than in the cities. Therefore, the differences between the characteristics of cities and the townships narrowed greatly. This was due largely to rapid urban–industrial development in rural areas which, in combination with agricultural and industrial development in rural areas, greatly increased the productivity of rural areas. The average annual family income increased 169 percent in the cities between 1967 and 1980, but it increased 212 percent in rural townships. Consequently, the income differences between cities and rural areas also narrowed.

In summary, Taiwan has experienced rapid urban–industrial development in the past few decades and development was greater in the rural areas than in the cities. As a result, city-rural differences in socio-economic characteristics and income have been reduced considerably.

These changes in social and economic structure have had a sizable impact on fertility behavior. The total fertility rate was as high as 5,990 in 1959, but decreased to 4,825 in 1965, 3,210 in 1973, and 2,515 in 1980, a decline of 58 percent in 21 years. The trend of decline, however, was different among different periods. The decline accelerated during 1964 to 1975, but slowed up thereafter (Table 2). The decline in total fertility from 1961 to 1978 (Chang et al., 1981), 67 percent, resulted primarily from a decline in fertility for women over 30. When only the effects of marital fertility and the proportion married are considered, 69 percent of the decline in total fertility was attributable to lower marital fertility, and 31 percent to the lower proportion married.

Given the faster development in rural areas, one would have expected that fertility would decline faster in rural areas than in the cities. However, as Table 2 shows, the decline of total fertility occurred almost equally for cities, urban townships, and rural townships. The percentage decline between 1963 and 1981 was 53, 51, and 53 percent for cities, urban townships, and rural townships, respectively. Therefore, the difference in the total fertility rate between cities and rural townships remains almost unchanged. The examination of fertility trends, however, showed that there seemed to be a convergence between urban and rural townships due to a faster decline of fertility in rural townships. When the age-specific fertility rates were examined for areal differentials, the trend was somewhat different. The areal differential increased slightly for the age group 15 to 19 because of a small decline in city fertility, while there was almost no change in rural fertility. Areal differentials remained almost unchanged for ages 20 to 24, but there was convergence in the fertility of urban and rural townships for ages 25 to 29. Areal differences for the age groups 30 to 34, 35 to 39, and 40 to 44 almost disappeared. The analysis indicates that the fertility decline in Taiwan during the past 16 years was faster among women aged 25 and above and faster in the rural areas than in the cities, leading to smaller differences in fertility between cities and rural areas.

Table 2. Total Fertility Rate of Childbearing Age Women by Cities, Chens, and Hsiangs of Taiwan Area, 1963–1981[a]

YEAR	TOTAL FERTILITY RATE			INDEX (Cities = 100)			INDEX (1963 = 100)		
	Cities	Chens	Hsiangs	Cities	Chens	Hsiangs	Cities	Chens	Hsiangs
1963	4,690	5,320	5,880	100	113	125	100	100	100
1964	4,505	5,070	5,565	100	113	124	96	95	95
1965	4,185	4,800	5,355	100	115	128	89	90	91
1966[b]	4,070	4,630	5,150	100	114	127	87	87	88
1967[b]	3,910	4,480	4,980	100	115	127	83	84	85
1968	3,825	4,330	4,810	100	113	126	81	81	82
1969	3,660	4,140	4,595	100	113	126	78	78	78
1970	3,630	3,980	4,405	100	110	121	77	75	75
1971	3,355	3,670	4,085	100	109	122	72	69	69
1972	3,040	3,385	3,740	100	111	123	65	64	64
1973	2,880	3,235	3,610	100	112	125	61	61	61
1974	2,760	3,060	3,390	100	111	123	59	58	58
1975	2,525	2,895	3,210	100	115	127	54	54	55
1976	2,770	3,170	3,445	100	114	124	59	60	59
1977	2,360	2,800	3,090	100	119	131	50	53	53
1978	2,390	2,810	3,055	100	118	128	51	53	52
1979	2,360	2,805	3,015	100	119	128	50	53	51
1980	2,245	2,665	2,845	100	119	127	48	50	48
1981	2,200	2,615	2,765	100	119	126	47	49	47

[a]Cities include national, provincial and prefectual cities; Chens are urban townships, and Hsiangs are rural townships.

[b]Adjusted for biases in registration due to 1966 census.

Source: *Taiwan Demographic Fact Books*, 1973 and 1981. Ministry of the Interior.

DECOMPOSITION OF FERTILITY CHANGE

In the process of urban–industrial development, the level of education also rises. Because of the significant fertility differentials among different levels of education, it has been speculated that the change in educational structure alone will bring down fertility to a very low level. Therefore, it would be interesting to analyze how much of the change in total fertility was due to changes in education structure. As Figure 1 shows, fertility differentials by education continue to exist in Taiwan. A comparison of 1966 and 1980 education–age–specific fertility shows, however, that the difference in fertility between different educational levels for ages 30 and above almost disappeared by 1980 (data not shown). The fertility differential by education remains very significant for younger women. In other words, the urban–rural and education fertility differentials almost disappeared for ages 30 and above but they remain quite significant among younger age groups.

Applying the decomposition technique, it was found that about one–third of the decline in total fertility between 1966 and 1980 (about 46 percent of the 1966 total fertility rate) was due to change in educational structure and about 14 percent due to change in the correlation between age and education. The small decline in total fertility rate between 1975 and 1980 (9 percent), was due largely (91 percent) to a change in educational structure, and the period effect became positive (Table 3). The negative effect of changes in correlation between age and education is also quite large, indicating a large increase in the education of younger age groups, coincident with the extension of compulsory education to the junior high level in 1968. Taking 1966 to 1980 as one period, about two–thirds of the decline in total fertility could not be explained by educational structure change. This change was due to the decline in fertility within each educational level caused by changes in the social and economic environment. It is not clear what factors composed this environmental change, but they may include the family planning promotion program and changes in social norms (Sun, 1978).

When education of respondents and occupation of husbands were taken together to explain changes in ideal number of children and expected number of children (using procedures identical to those used

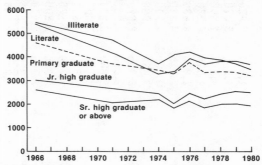

Figure 1. Total fertility rate by level of education, 1966–1980, Taiwan, Republic of China.

Table 3. Decomposition of Total Fertility Rate Change by Education Structure Change and Period Effect in Taiwan

FACTOR	1966-75	1975-80	1966-80
Total fertility rate			
Beginning of period	4676.5	2756.0	4676.5
End of period	2756.0	2514.5	2514.5
Change in TFR due to			
Change in correlation between education and age	-198.0	-97.8	-295.8
Change in education structure	-448.3	-220.3	-745.5
Period effect	-1368.2	+13.2	-1495.2
Interaction	+94.0	+63.4	+374.5
All factors	-1920.5	-241.5	-2162.0
Percent of change due to			
Change in correlation between education and age	-10.3	-40.5	-13.7
Change in education structure	-23.3	-91.2	-34.5
Period effect	-71.3	+5.5	-69.1
Interaction	+4.9	+26.2	+17.3
All factors	-100.0	-100.0	-100.0

in Table 3), a number of important findings emerged. Educational structure change was more important than change in occupational structure in explaining change in ideal and expected number of children. The effect of structural change on the two fertility measures increased over time. A substantial part of the change in these two fertility measures remained unexplained by the structural change of education and occupation, i.e., a period effect. Finally, the contribution of educational and occupational change seemed to be slightly larger for the rural sample than for the total sample. In other words, in the process of urbanization and industrialization, both for cities and rural areas in Taiwan, a part of the fertility decline (about one-third) was due to the change in educational structure, about 5 percent was due to the change in occupational structure, but a substantial part was due to period effects not associated with occupational or educational change. The analysis using areal data and individual data showed the same result.

MULTIVARIATE AREAL ANALYSIS

In order to measure directly the impact of urban-industrial development on fertility at the aggregate level, a path model was developed

(Duncan, 1966). It was postulated that urban-industrial development, represented by population density, proportion in primary industry, and proportion of women with junior high or better education, would exert its influence on fertility, expressed in terms of the total fertility rate, either directly or through proportion of women married (for ages 20 to 24), child mortality (mortality rate for ages 0 to 4), and contraceptive services (number of doctors contracted to do insertion of IUD). The variables considered in the conceptual model are shown in Table 4, and the model is shown in Figure 2. The relationships shown in Figure 2 may be expressed in the following equations in accord with the conventions of path analysis:

$$X_7 = P_{74}X_4 + P_{75}X_5 + P_{76}X_6 + P_{71}X_1 + P_{72}X_2 + P_{73}X_3 + P_{7y}R_y$$
$$X_4 = P_{41}X_1 + P_{42}X_2 + P_{43}X_3 + P_{4u}R_u$$
$$X_5 = P_{51}X_1 + P_{52}X_2 + P_{53}X_3 + P_{5v}R_v$$
$$X_6 = P_{61}X_1 + P_{6w}R_w$$

These relationships take the form of linear-log or log-log expressions (Bollen and Entwisle, 1981).

The analysis was carried out separately for 1965, 1973, and 1980 to permit comparisons of the effects at different stages of development. Because of the delay of socioenvironmental effects on fertility behavior, a lag in the total fertility rate for one and two years was also tried. For example, the effects of the 1965 development variables and intermediate variables on 1966 and 1967 total fertility rates were estimated. A lagged form of regression using 1965 development data, 1973 intermediate variable data, and the 1980 total fertility rate was also used to examine long-term effects.

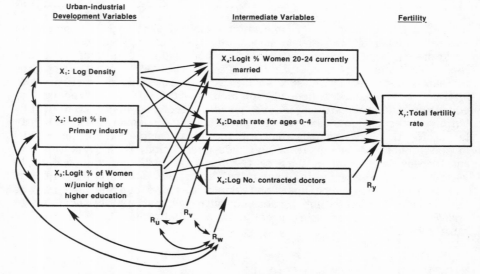

Figure 2. Path diagram of factors affecting total fertility rate.

Table 4. Definitions of Variables in Figure 2[a]

VARIABLE NUMBER	DESCRIPTION
X_1	Log of population density per square kilometer
X_2	Logit of percentage of employed persons in primary industry
X_3	Logit of percentage of women age 12 (for 1965) or 15 (for 1972 and 1980) or above with junior high school or better education
X_4	Logit of percentage of women ages 20 to 24 who are currently married
X_5	Death rate for population of ages 0 to 4
X_6	Log of the person-months of doctors contracted for IUD insertion
X_7	Total fertility rate per 1,000 women, for years t, t+1, or t+2

[a] Logarithmic values (log or logit) for X_1, X_2, X_3, X_4, and X_6 are used to improve the fit between these variables and total fertility, i.e., use of linear-log and log-log specifications.

The units of analysis are 331 townships/districts in the plain area which covers more than 98 percent of the total population of Taiwan. Excluded in the analysis are the 30 mountain townships where most of the aboriginal population live. The analysis was also carried out for 282 urban and rural townships, excluding the districts in the cities to examine the situation in rural areas.

The correlation matrix of the variables used for the development model (Table 5) shows that (a) the correlations are all in the expected direction except for a minor one (r_{56} for 282 townships for 1973); (b) the correlations are generally higher for the combined 331 townships and districts than for the 282 townships; (c) the correlations are generally stronger for 1965 and 1980 than for 1973; and (d) the standard deviations for education, proportion married, child mortality, and total fertility rates decrease over time, indicating increased homogeneity among townships on these variables.

The results of the analysis are presented in Tables 6-8. Table 6 reveals that the six independent variables in 1965 explain more than half of the variance in total fertility and exert a significant influence on total fertility in 1965, 1966, and 1967. The urban-industrial development variables exert their influence on fertility both directly and indirectly through the intermediate variables (X_4, X_5, and X_6). The indirect effects (not shown), although smaller than the direct effects, are significantly large. The relationships hold for both all 331 townships/districts and the 282 urban and rural townships, indicating

Table 5. Correlation Matrix of Variables Used for the Development Model, 1965, 1973, and 1980 for 331 Townships and 282 Townships in Taiwan[a,b]

VARIABLE[c]	X_1	X_2	X_3	X_4	X_5	X_6	X_7 (t)	X_7 (t+1)	X_7 (t+2)	MEAN	STANDARD DEVIATION
1965											
X_1		-0.763	0.606	-0.519	-0.428	0.509	-0.643	-0.579	-0.586	6.588	1.295
X_2	-0.446		-0.786	0.377	0.319	-0.540	0.517	0.504	0.416	0.348	1.377
X_3	0.390	-0.716		-0.516	-0.472	0.582	-0.634	-0.653	-0.582	-2.990	0.929
X_4	-0.517	0.299	-0.483		0.443	-0.334	0.619	0.565	0.573	0.464	0.459
X_5	-0.334	0.178	-0.390	0.391		-0.326	0.578	0.528	0.610	8.933	3.224
X_6	0.373	-0.459	0.489	-0.244	-0.219		-0.504	-0.510	-0.465	1.823	1.541
X_7 (t)	-0.546	0.305	-0.515	0.567	0.516	-0.380		0.899	0.884	5,154	835
X_7 (t+1)	-0.467	0.321	-0.557	0.502	0.464	-0.411	0.874		0.843	5,049	846
X_7 (t+2)	-0.480	0.195	-0.466	0.509	0.554	-0.340	0.861	0.809		4,493	733
Mean	6.207	0.758	-3.188	0.507	9.296	1.595	5,301	5,183	4,601		
Standard deviation	0.811	0.926	0.818	0.456	3.262	1.395	785	810	699		
1973											
X_1		-0.791	0.547	-0.462	-0.393	0.468	-0.461	-0.397	-0.503	6.730	1.362
X_2	-0.555		-0.668	0.423	0.323	-0.503	0.427	0.450	0.582	-0.299	1.428
X_3	0.328	-0.537		-0.480	-0.355	0.496	-0.585	-0.584	-0.690	-1.602	0.772
X_4	-0.375	0.288	-0.393		0.427	-0.325	0.392	0.363	0.370	-0.078	0.373
X_5	-0.309	0.203	-0.269	0.400		-0.177	0.410	0.352	0.332	4.915	2.513
X_6	0.324	-0.450	0.399	-0.238	0.079		-0.372	-0.376	-0.436	2.548	1.523
X_7 (t)	-0.252	0.182	-0.457	0.276	0.345	-0.247		0.812	0.829	3,455	587
X_7 (t+1)	-0.126	0.199	-0.456	0.229	0.274	-0.259	0.765		0.824	3,145	569
X_7 (t+2)	-0.238	0.365	-0.581	0.236	0.237	-0.328	0.793	0.780		3,008	516
Mean	6.331	0.109	-1.752	-0.032	5.179	2.351	3,551	3,238	3,105		
Standard deviation	0.902	1.007	0.708	0.348	2.586	1.426	560	539	467		

VARIABLE[c]	X$_1$	X$_2$	X$_3$	X$_4$	X$_5$	X$_6$	X$_7$ (t)	X$_7$ (t+1)	X$_7$ (t+2)	MEAN	STANDARD DEVIATION
1980											
X$_1$		-0.772	0.584	-0.459	-0.411	0.579	-0.488	-0.482	...	6.778	1.425
X$_2$	-0.583		-0.715	0.547	0.378	-0.544	0.593	0.571	...	-0.671	1.329
X$_3$	0.357	-0.604		-0.661	-0.438	0.603	-0.733	-0.660	...	-0.667	0.463
X$_4$	-0.146	0.306	-0.501		0.286	-0.415	0.527	0.469	...	-0.325	0.303
X$_5$	-0.291	0.244	-0.331	0.139		-0.318	0.341	0.261	...	3.557	1.338
X$_6$	0.434	-0.416	0.484	-0.239	-0.204		-0.421	-0.413	...	2.358	1.765
X$_7$ (t)	-0.164	0.346	-0.616	0.305	0.208	-0.241		0.887	...	2,686	401
X$_7$ (t+1)	-0.129	0.294	-0.491	0.197	0.099	-0.225	0.830		...	2,609	385
Mean	6.379	-0.312	-0.764	-0.265	3.716	2.056	2,775	2,694			
Standard deviation	1.039	1.003	0.398	0.264	1.349	1.626	350	330			

[a]The upper-right half of each panel is for 331 townships and lower-left half is for 282 townships.

[b]t = the year listed.

[c]See Table 4 for definition of variables.

Table 6. Standardized Partial Regression Coefficients (Betas) and Coefficients of Determination (R²) for Specified Combinations of Variables in Taiwan, 1965–1967

DEPENDENT VARIABLES

INDEPENDENT VARIABLES (fixed at 1965)[a]	For 331 townships/districts			For 282 townships		
	1965	1966	1967	1965	1966	1967
Dependent variable: Total fertility rate (X_7)						
X_1 Log population density	−0.339**	−0.253**	−0.393**	−0.283**	−0.204**	−0.265**
X_2 Logit percent in primary industry	−0.183*	−0.207**	−0.374**	−0.184**	−0.211**	−0.325**
X_3 Logit percent with junior high or better education	−0.282**	−0.409**	−0.352**	−0.283**	−0.407**	−0.345**
X_4 Logit percent 20 to 24 married	0.231**	0.179**	0.164**	0.220**	0.155**	0.156**
X_5 0 to 4 death rate	0.217**	0.168**	0.285**	0.232**	0.179**	0.302**
X_6 Log number contracted doctors	−0.118**	−0.140**	−0.114*	−0.116*	−0.155**	−0.118*
R^2	0.63	0.57	0.60	0.53	0.48	0.51
Dependent variable: Proportion married for women ages 20 to 24 (X_4)						
X_1 Log population density	−0.546**			−0.436**		
X_2 Logit percent in primary industry	−0.485**			−0.246**		
X_3 Logit percent with junior high or better education	−0.566**			−0.489**		
R^2	0.39			0.39		

DEPENDENT VARIABLES

INDEPENDENT VARIABLES (fixed at 1965)[a]	For 331 townships/districts			For 282 townships		
	1965	1966	1967	1965	1966	1967
Dependent variable: Mortality rate for ages 0 to 4 (X_5)						
X_1 Log population density	-0.434**			-0.274**		
X_2 Logit percent in primary industry	-0.461**			-0.303**		
X_3 Logit percent with junior high or better education	-0.572**			-0.501**		
R^2	0.31			0.23		
Dependent variable: Number of contracted doctors for IUD insertion (X_6)						
X_1 Log population density	0.509**			0.373**		
R^2	0.26			0.14		

[a] For definition of variables and their means and standard deviations see Tables 4 and 5.

*Statistically significant at the 5 percent level.

**Statistically significant at 1 percent level.

63

that rural development at this stage has significant effects on fertility. It should be noted, however, that the direction of influence of industrialization on fertility was positive, even though zero-order correlations between the two variables were negative. Fertility was positively related to the proportion of population in primary industry, i.e., negatively correlated with the proportion in secondary and tertiary industries. This suggests that while urbanization and the rise in educational levels worked to reduce fertility, industrialization, which increased income, operated to raise fertility when the influence of other factors was controlled. The negative zero-order correlations between industrialization and fertility were artifacts of the correlation with other factors. Because of its high correlation with population density and education, when industrialization was excluded from the model, the proportion of explained variance in total fertility was reduced only slightly (about 1 to 2 percent). As noted earlier, this finding could only be attributed partially to problems in the data and, therefore, deserves further investigation.

The relationships between urban-industrial development and fertility were much weaker in 1973 than in 1965 (Table 7). However, the effect of education on fertility, especially the direct effect, was particularly strong. Population density had a significant effect only on the 1973 total fertility of the 331 townships/districts. Industrialization still had a positive effect on fertility in 1973, but this changed to a negative effect by 1975 for the 331 townships/districts. The influence of child mortality on fertility was stronger in rural areas than in the cities. The number of doctors contracted to do IUD insertion still had a significant negative effect on 1974 and 1975 total fertility in rural areas, but no longer in the cities. Finally, industrialization had no significant effect on the proportion married or child mortality in 1973, while urbanization and education still had strong effects on these two intermediate variables.

The picture changed greatly by 1980 to 1981. The only factor which had a strong effect on total fertility was education, and its effect was much stronger than in previous years. The effect of industrialization on total fertility was negative, but significant only for 1981. Other factors in the model no longer had significant effects on total fertility. At the same time, the indirect effects became almost negligible. The situation was quite similar for the 331 townships/districts and for the 282 rural and urban townships.

In summary, urban-industrial development had a strong effect on fertility in the early stages of fertility decline, but its influence became weaker toward the later stages of the fertility transition. While the effects of urbanization and the increase in education on fertility was negative, the short-term effects of industrialization on fertility was positive. However, it appears that the long-term effect of industrialization on fertility was also negative. For example, the 1973 industrial level had a positive effect on 1973 total fertility, a weak negative effect on fertility in 1974, but a significant negative effect on 1975 fertility (Table 7). An increasingly strong negative effect was also found in the 1980 data (Table 8).

Table 7. Standardized Partial Regression Coefficients (Betas) and Coefficients of Determination (R²) for Specified Combinations of Variables in Taiwan, 1973 to 1975

DEPENDENT VARIABLES

INDEPENDENT VARIABLES (fixed at 1973)[a]	For 331 townships/districts			For 282 townships		
	1973	1974	1975	1973	1974	1975
Dependent variable: Total fertility rate (X7)						
X1 Log population density	-0.208**	0.003	0.051	-0.121	0.066	0.000
X2 Logit percent in primary industry	-0.157*	0.045	0.146*	-0.211**	0.091	0.033
X3 Logit percent with junior high or better education	-0.448**	-0.432**	-0.506**	-0.420**	-0.419**	-0.507**
X4 Logit percent 20 to 24 married	0.040	0.040	-0.017	0.008	0.008	-0.040
X5 0 to 4 death rate	0.187**	0.148**	0.079	0.225**	0.186**	0.101
X6 Log number contracted doctors	0.085	0.098	0.079	0.115	0.138*	0.113*
R²	0.42	0.38	0.51	0.29	0.25	0.36
Dependent variable: Proportion married for women ages 20 to 24 (X4)						
X1 Log population density	-0.323**			-0.297**		
X2 Logit percent in primary industry	-0.064			-0.050		
X3 Logit percent with junior high or better education	-0.346**			-0.323**		
R²	0.29			0.22		

65

Table 7. Cont.

	DEPENDENT VARIABLES					
INDEPENDENT VARIABLES (fixed at 1973)[a]	For 331 townships/districts			For 282 townships		
	1973	1974	1975	1973	1974	1975
Dependent variable: Mortality rate for ages 0 to 4 (X_5)						
X_1 Log population density	-0.356**			-0.274**		
X_2 Logit percent in primary industry	-0.119			-0.064		
X_3 Logit percent with junior high or better education	-0.240**			-0.214**		
R^2	0.19			0.13		
Dependent variable: Number of contracted doctors for IUD insertion (X_6)						
X_1 Log population density	0.468**			0.324**		
R^2	0.22			0.11		

[a]For definition of variables and their means and standard deviations see Tables 4 and 5.

*Statistically significant at the 5 percent level.

**Statistically significant at 1 percent level.

Table 8. Standardized Partial Regression Coefficients (Betas) and Coefficients of Determination (R^2) for Specified Combinations of Variables in Taiwan, 1980 to 1981

INDEPENDENT VARIABLES (fixed at 1980)[a]	DEPENDENT VARIABLES			
	For 331 townships/districts		For 282 townships	
	1980	1981	1980	1981
Dependent variable: Total fertility rate (X_7)				
X_1 Log population density	-0.047	-0.086	0.050	0.057
X_2 Logit percent in primary industry	0.112	0.151*	-0.002	0.033
X_3 Logit percent with junior high or better education	-0.627**	-0.528**	-0.659**	-0.547**
X_4 Logit percent 20 to 24 married	0.057	0.027	-0.006	-0.070
X_5 0 to 4 death rate	0.011	-0.061	0.018	-0.064
X_6 Log number contracted doctors	0.073	0.029	0.057	-0.000
R^2	0.55	0.46	0.39	0.25
Dependent variable: Proportion married for women ages 20 to 24 (X_4)				
X_1 Log population density	-0.047		0.053	
X_2 Logit percent in primary industry	0.118		0.036	
X_3 Logit percent with junior high or better education	-0.549**		-0.498**	
R^2	0.45		0.25	

Table 8. Cont.

DEPENDENT VARIABLES

INDEPENDENT VARIABLES (fixed at 1980)[a]	For 331 townships/districts		For 282 townships	
	1980	1981	1980	1981
Dependent variable: Mortality rate for ages 0 to 4 (X_5)				
X_1 Log population density	−0.270**		−0.224**	
X_2 Logit percent in primary industry	−0.064		−0.059	
X_3 Logit percent with junior high or better education	−0.326**		−0.287**	
R^2	0.23		0.15	
Dependent variable: Number of contracted doctors for IUD insertion (X_6)				
X_1 Log population density	0.579**		0.434**	
R^2	0.33		0.19	

[a]For definition of variables and their means and standard deviations see Tables 4 and 5.

*Statistically significant at the 5 percent level.

**Statistically significant at 1 percent level.

In order to test the long-term effects of urban-industrial development on fertility, a lagged path analysis was undertaken in which 1980 total fertility was taken as a function of 1973 intermediate variables and 1965 urban-industrial development variables. The model was tested on data for both the 331 townships/districts and also for the 282 urban and rural townships. The results are shown in Figures 3 and 4. It appears that all three urban-industrial development variables had significant effects on the 1973 intermediate variables. These development variables also had strong direct effects on 1980 total fertility. The effects of the 1973 intermediate variables on 1980 total fertility were not statistically significant; therefore, the indirect effects of the development variables on 1980 fertility were also weak. The effect of industrialization on 1980 fertility was negative and was the strongest path observed, even stronger than that for education. This statement applies to both the 331 townships/districts and to the 282 townships, even though the relationships were somewhat weaker in the rural townships. The direct influence of population density on fertility was positive, indicating that fertility change was greater in the rural (low-density) areas. This finding was also supported by a subsequent first-difference analysis.

In order to remove area-specific time-invariant effects which can bias the results obtained in single cross-sections, a first-difference model was employed. In this model both the dependent variable (total fertility) and independent variables (X_2, X_3, X_4, X_5, and X_6) were

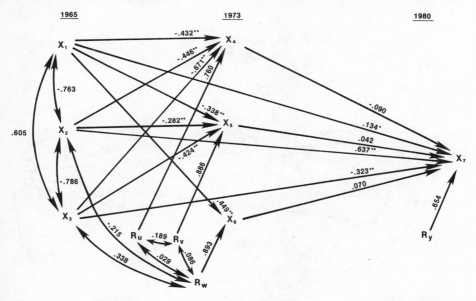

Figure 3. Lagged form of path diagram for the impacts of urban-industrial development on total fertility, Taiwan, Republic of China. N = 331 township/districts.   *Statistically significant at the 5% level. **Statistically significant at the 1% level.

measured in terms of changes between 1965 and 1973, 1973 and 1980, and 1965 and 1980. The original X_1 (population density) was replaced by a classification of townships in 1965 (coded "0" for cities and "1" for urban and rural townships). The results, shown in Table 9, may be summarized as follows: (a) Changes in the urban-industrial and inter-mediate variables explained about one-fifth of the variance in total fertility change for the periods 1965 to 1973, and 1973 to 1980, but explained about one-third of the variance in the period 1965 to 1980. (b) All six independent variables except X_5 (change in child mortality) had significant direct effects on change in total fertility for the period 1965 to 1973, but only three independent variables (X_3, X_4, and X_5) had significant direct effects in the period 1973 to 1980. (c) The effect of 1965 township class on total fertility change was negative, indicating a faster fertility decline in rural townships. (d) The change in industrialization had a significant positive effect on change in total fertility for the period 1965 to 1973, but became negative (not signifi-cant) in the period 1973 to 1980. (e) The change in educational level had a strong negative effect on total fertility change. (f) The change in child mortality had positive effects on total fertility change, and became very important in the later period (1973 to 1980). (g) The negative effect of the increase in the number of contracted doctors for IUD insertion became insignificant in the later period. In summary, the changes in urban-industrial development did have strong effects on the change in total fertility in the early stages of the fertility transi-

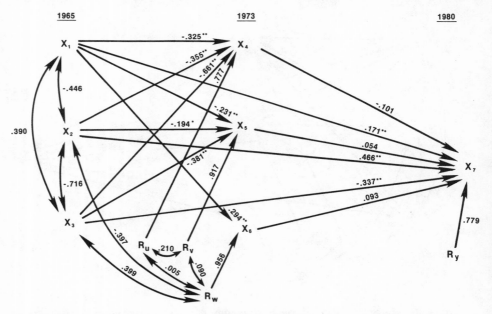

Figure 4. Lagged form of path diagram for the impacts of urban-indus-trial development on total fertility, Taiwan, Republic of China. N = 282 townships. *Statistically significant at the 5% level. **Statistical-ly significant at the 1% level.

tion, although the direction of influence for industrialization was contrary to expectations. In the later stages of the fertility transition, however, changes in the proportion married and child mortality seem to have more impact on total fertility change than urban-industrial development. It was also found that fertility change was greater among rural townships than among the cities.

Table 9. Standardized Partial Regression Coefficients (Betas) and Coefficients of Determination (R^2) for Specified Combinations of Variable Changes in Taiwan

INDEPENDENT VARIABLES[a]	331 TOWNSHIPS/DISTRICTS		
	1965–73	1973–80	1965–80
Dependent variable: Total fertility change (X_7)			
X_1 Class of townships fixed at 1965	−0.176**	−0.007	−0.117*
X_2 Change in logit percent in primary industry	−0.219**	0.083	−0.013
X_3 Change in logit percent with junior high or better education	−0.153**	−0.106*	−0.232**
X_4 Change in percent 20 to 20 married	0.215**	0.290**	0.400**
X_5 Change in 0 to 4 death rate	0.046	0.223**	0.160**
X_6 Change in log number contracted doctors	−0.103*	−0.053	−0.049
R^2	0.19	0.19	0.36
Dependent variable: Change in proportion of women 20 to 24 married (X_4)			
X_1 Class of townships fixed at 1965	0.033	0.170**	0.212**
X_2 Change in logit percent in primary industry	−0.105	− 0.050	−0.085
X_3 Change in logit percent with junior high or better education	−0.044	−0.077	−0.294**
R^2	0.01	0.03	0.08
Dependent variable: Change in 0 to 4 death rate (X_5)			
X_1 Class of townships fixed at 1965	−0.065	−0.100	−0.043
X_2 Change in logit percent in primary industry	0.024	−0.068	0.060
X_3 Change in logit percent with junior high or better education	−0.055	−0.120*	−0.265**
R^2	0.01	0.03	0.09

Table 9.   Cont.

	331 TOWNSHIPS/DISTRICTS		
INDEPENDENT VARIABLES[a]	1965–73	1973–80	1965–80

Dependent variable: Change in number of contracted doctors
for IUD insertion (X_7)

X_1 Class of townships fixed at 1965	0.059	0.198**	0.121*
R^2	0.00	0.04	0.01

[a] X_1 has been replaced by the class of townships in 1965, which is coded "0" for cities and "1" for other townships. The changes are expressed in terms of the values in the later date minus the values in the earlier date. For definition of variables and their means and standard deviations, see Tables 4 and 5.

*Statistically significant at the 5 percent level.

**Statistically significant at the 1 percent level.

SUMMARY

Urban–industrial development and fertility decline have been quite rapid in Taiwan during the past two decades.   Population density increased 65 percent; the percentage of urban population to total population increased from 50 to 70; and the total fertility rate decreased 58 percent, from 5990 to 2515.   The speed of fertility decline and urban–industrial development, however, was much faster during the earlier stage (1965 to 1973) than in the later stage (1973 to 1980), and also faster in the urban/rural townships than in the larger cities.   A result was a faster rise in income in rural areas than cities, narrowing the gap between the two types of areas.   Urban–industrial development in Taiwan was characterized by both the expansion of existing cities and towns, and by changes in the characteristics of rural areas.

This chapter analyzed the impacts of urban–industrial development on fertility in Taiwan at the aggregate level, especially in rural areas using township data, supplemented by KAP survey data.   The decomposition of the total fertility rate, ideal, and expected family sizes indicated that change in educational structure had significant effects on fertility, but a large portion of variance in fertility change remained unexplained by education and occupation, especially in the early stage of fertility decline.   These unexplained "period effects" need further study.

The multivariate areal analyses show that urban–industrial development had strong effects on fertility in the early stages of the fertility transition.   Most of this effect was direct, but part was indirect, operating through intermediate variables such as the proportion married and child mortality. While the effects of urbanization and the rise in education on fertility were negative, the short-run effect of industriali-zation on fertility was positive, but its effect changed to negative in the long-run. It was also found that, in the later stages of the fertil-ity transition, changes in the proportion married and child mortality seemed to have more impact on total fertility change, i.e., the indirect effects of urban-industrial change became stronger than the direct effects.   Fertility change during the study period was greater among the rural townships than among the cities.

Even though there were deficiencies in the data used, the results confirm that urban-industrial development in Taiwan had significant impacts on fertility change, especially in the early period and in rural areas. However, the study also found that urban-industrial development could not explain all of the variation or change in fertility. The models presented here likely are not adequate in measuring fully the "period," "environmental," or "cohort" effects which are outside of the structural or compositional effects. It is generally recognized that two persons of similar background, but of two different generations or co-horts, behave differently. This may have been caused by their expo-sure to different social and economic environments. Better measure-ment of the "cohort" effect, including controls for the time period of exposure to certain levels of modernization at different ages is called for. This, however, is difficult with aggregate level analyses. There is a need for a methodology which can deal with both aggregate and indi-vidual data simultaneously.

This study did not consider changes in population and family planning policy and their implementation, which are considered to have had con-siderable impact on fertility decline in Taiwan. Hermalin (1973, 1979) has pointed out that the family planning program had an effect on fertility decline independent of modernization. However, it is not clear as to how modernization and the family planning program interacted to facilitate fertility decline.

Industrial development in rural areas in Taiwan provided an increased number of off-farm opportunities. Although this situation is reflected in the decrease in the proportion of the work force in primary industries, the mechanism of interaction between industrial development and fertil-ity change in rural areas requires special attention. This was not attempted here due to limitations of data.

There are a number of additional ways in which urban-industrial development probably influenced fertility change in Taiwan and which deserve consideration (Freedman et al., 1980). Chief among these are:

a)   Technical change in agriculture by increasing the income of farmers and providing them with opportunities to acquire new ideas and living styles may have influenced fertility by exposing rural families to nontraditional attitudes and modern fertility behavior (Lee and Sun, 1972).

b)   The high population density and mechanization of agriculture created a surplus of labor in rural areas, leading to increased migration to the cities and to increased employment in off-farm activities. Both migration and off-farm employment led to increases in income, adoption of new ideas and, hence, likely contributed to lower fertility.

c)   Migration from rural areas to the cities not only reduced population pressure in rural areas, but also improved the living standard of rural areas by the transfer of money and modern durable goods back to the place of origin. The intensive communication ties with the place of origin and the return of migrants operated to modernize rural areas, and may have led to lower fertility.

d)   The improvement of living conditions in rural areas reduced urban-rural differentials, and the concomitant equalization of incomes may have worked to lower fertility (Kocher, 1973).

e)   Improvement in food and nutrition in rural areas contributed to earlier puberty and lower maternal mortality which, combined with decreases in breastfeeding, would increase fertility. However, lower infant and child mortality probably operated to reduce fertility.

f)   The land reform which changed land ownership greatly seems to have had positive effects on fertility in the short-run, but negative effects in the long-run.

g)   The great emphasis the family planning program put on rural areas helped to minimize urban-rural fertility differentials (Liu and Sun, 1979).

Although these points appear reasonable, they require more empirical work to establish the relationships and also to measure the relative importance of these developments in changing the fertility of Taiwanese couples.

NOTES

1.   Based on the vital registration follow-up survey of the Taiwan Population Studies Center from 1966 to 1968.

2.   The Li and T'sun are the basic administrative units under township/ district. The Li or T'sun that have any of the following charac-teristics are classified as urbanized areas (based on household registration data):

a)   More than 60 percent of the employed males are in nonagricul-tural occupations.

b)   With three or more urban type facilities, such as schools of different levels, hospitals or clinics, post office, theater, recreation center, and park.

c)   Population density exceeds 2,000 per square kilometer.

d)   The site of township/district office.

e)   T'suns or Lis which are surrounded by the T'suns or Lis with above characteristics.

ACKNOWLEDGMENTS

The author wishes to thank Yin-Hsin Liu for his assistance in the data processing, including computer programming, and also Jack M. C. Chang and H. S. Lin for their valuable comments.

REFERENCES

Bollen, K.A. and B. Entwisle. 1981. Economic Development and Fertility: A Curvilinear Specification. Research Report No. 81-7, Population Studies Center, University of Michigan.
Chang, M.C., R. Freedman, and T.H. Sun. 1981. Trends in fertility, family size preferences, and family planning practice: Taiwan, 1961-80. Studies in Family Planning 12:211-228.
Council for Economic Planning and Development. 1982. Taiwan Statistical Data Book. Executive Yuan, ROC.
Duncan, O.D. 1966. Path analysis: Sociological examples. American Journal of Sociology 72:1-16.
Easterlin, R.A. 1975. An economic framework for fertility analysis. Studies in Family Planning 6:54-63.
Freedman, R., A. Hermalin, T.H. Sun, and K.C. Liu. 1980. Factors Related to Taiwan's Fertility Decline: A Review of the Evidence. Taiwan Population Studies Working Paper No. 44. Population Studies Center, University of Michigan.
Friedlander, S. and M. Silver. 1967. A quantitative study of the determinants of fertility behavior. Demography 4:30-61.
Gendell, M. 1967. Fertility and development in Brazil. Demography 4: 143-157.
Heer, D.M. 1966. Economic development and fertility. Demography 3: 423-444.
Hermalin, A.I. 1973. Taiwan: Appraising the effect of a family planning program through an areal analysis. In: Population Papers, Institute of Economics, pp. 73-111. Taipei: Academia Sinica, ROC.
_____ 1979. Multivariate areal analysis. In: The Methodology of Measuring the Impact of Family Planning Programmes on Fertility, pp. 97-111. Population Studies 66(Manual IX), United Nations.
Kocher, J. 1973. Rural Development, Income Distribution and Fertility Decline. New York: Population Council.
Lee, T.H. and T.H. Sun. 1972. Agricultural Development and Population Trends in Taiwan. Seminar on Effects of Agricultural Innovations in Asia on Population Trends. Manila: Ramon Magsaysay Award Foundation.
Liu, P.K.C. 1976. The Relationship Between Urbanization and Socioeconomic Development in Taiwan. In: Institute of Economics, Conference on Population and Economic Development in Taiwan, pp. 617-646. Taipei: Academia Sinica.
Liu, K.C. and T.H. Sun. 1979. The Determinants of Fertility Transition and Their Implications in Taiwan, ROC. Industry of Free China 52(2 and 3).

Massey, D.S. and L.M. Tedrow. 1976.   Economic development and fertil-
   ity: A methodological re-evaluation.   Population Studies 30:429–437.
Merrick, T.W. 1974.   Interregional differences in fertility in Brazil,
   1950–1970.   Demography 11:423–440.
Ministry of the Interior. 1973 and 1981.   Taiwan Demographic Fact
   Books. Taipei, Taiwan.
Population Reference Bureau. 1982.   World Population Data Sheet.
   Washington, D.C.
Robinson, W.C. 1963.   Urbanization and fertility: The non-Western
   experience. The Milbank Memorial Fund Quarterly 41:291–308.
Speare, A. Jr., M.C. Speare, and H.S. Lin. 1973.   Urbanization, non-
   familial work, education, and fertility in Taiwan.   Population Studies
   27:323–334.
Spengler, J.J. 1952. Population theory.   In: B.F. Haley (ed.) A Survey
   of Contemporary Economics, Vol. II, pp. 83–128.   Homewood, Illinois:
   Richard D. Irwin, Inc.
Sun, T.H. 1978.   Demographic Evaluation of Taiwan's Family Planning
   Program. Industry of Free China 49(4 and 5).
_____ 1983.   Future Research Directions on Factors Related to Fertility Decline in Taiwan, ROC.   International Conference on Population
   and Family Planning (Jan. 6–8) Taipei, Taiwan.

CHAPTER 5

Historical Perspectives on Rural Development and Human Fertility in Nineteenth-Century America

Maris A. Vinovskis

Scholars seeking to understand the relationship between rural development and human fertility frequently look to the demographic experiences of North America and Western Europe for guidance and data since these areas experienced considerable social and economic development as well as a sustained decline in fertility during the nineteenth and twentieth centuries. Although studies of the decline in rural fertility in the West may not be directly applicable to the situations in the developing countries today since conditions in those different areas and eras are by no means identical, they may nonetheless provide the basis for developing a broader and more comprehensive framework for analyzing rural development and demographic change.

While historical demographers have analyzed the causes of the general decline in fertility in the West (Knodel, 1974; Lesthaeghe, 1977; Wrigley and Schofield, 1981), most of them have not specifically addressed the issue of rural development and fertility. Fortunately, a few scholars, especially economic historians, have indirectly dealt with this question in trying to explain the decline in rural fertility in nineteenth-century America. Using their work as the point of departure, this chapter will evaluate their methodology, review their findings, and try to arrive at some tentative statements about the relationship between rural development and human fertility in the past.

DECLINE IN FERTILITY IN NINETEENTH-CENTURY AMERICA

Fertility levels in nineteenth-century America were considerably higher than in other Western European countries, in large part due to the earlier ages at marriage and the higher proportion marrying in the New World. Whereas the crude birth rates per 1000 in 1800 in Denmark, France, Norway, and Sweden, for example, were approximately 30, the white crude birth rate in the United States was 55 (Mitchell, 1975; Coale and Zelnik, 1963; McClelland and Zeckhauser, 1982). Yet by 1800 fertility had already begun a steady decline in America (Vinovskis, 1981a; Wells, 1982), while most European countries did not witness a sustained decline in fertility for another 50 or 60 years (Wrigley, 1969; Coale, 1969).

One of the recurring explanations advanced to account for fertility differentials and trends in nineteenth-century America is the urban and industrial development of the country. Potter (1965, p. 678) argued, for instance, that urbanization and industrialization played a key role in the decline in fertility in the United States:

> The findings have to remain inconclusive. But the evidence still seems to support the view that industrialization and urbanization with the accompaniment of higher living standards and greater social expectations (but possibly also higher infant mortality), were the main reasons for the declining rate of population growth either through the postponement of marriage or the restriction of family size.

The urban-industrial explanation of the decline in fertility is attractive because it is commonly assumed that it is more expensive to raise a large family in an urban area than in a rural setting because of the higher costs of food and lodging and the lower utility of young children's labor off the farm. Urban populations are also usually better educated than their rural counterparts and more likely to be employed in white-collar occupations. As a result of these and other similar factors, scholars have frequently turned to an urban-industrial explanation to account for declines in fertility (Jaffe, 1942; Robinson, 1963). The plausibility of this interpretation for the United States is enhanced by the fact that there were definite rural-urban differences in birth rates during the nineteenth century (Bash, 1955; Easterlin, 1971, 1976; Forster and Tucker, 1972; Hareven and Vinovskis, 1978; Leet, 1975, 1976; Potter, 1965; Vinovskis, 1976b,c, 1978b, 1981a,b; Yasuba, 1962).

Despite the initial attraction of an urban-industrial explanation of the decline in fertility, most historians, however, are now skeptical since only a small proportion of the population lived in urban or industrial areas. Even if one defines urban as towns of 2500 or more persons, only 5.1 percent of the population were in urban communities in 1790 and 19.8 percent in 1860. Even if one focuses on the percentage of the labor force in nonagricultural occupations rather than on those living in rural areas, the results are very similar. Although there was a sizable increase in nonagricultural workers (from 28.1 percent in 1820 to 41.0 percent in 1860), most Americans in the antebellum period were still engaged in agriculture (Vinovskis, 1981a). Thus, it is impossible to account for the overall decline in fertility in America by any urban-industrial explanation. In fact, Forster and Tucker (1972) have estimated that in the period 1810 to 1840, 78 percent of the overall decline in white fertility was due to a drop in rural birth rates, 11 percent to a decline in urban birth rates, and another 11 percent to a population shift from rural to urban areas. A similar calculation for the period 1840 to 1860 produced nearly identical results although the rural-to-urban population shift now increases to 16 percent of the total absolute decline in white fertility.

The failure of the urban-industrial explanation to account for most of the decrease in nineteenth-century fertility has led most American scholars to focus almost exclusively on the determinants of rural fertility. Interestingly, while American social historians during the past twenty years have almost abandoned the study of rural populations in order to investigate urban life, demographic historians have pursued just the opposite strategy. One unfortunate consequence of this divergence in the research agenda of social and demographic historians is that we have relatively little information about the nature of nineteenth-century rural life except for patterns of childbearing. As a. result, it is difficult to tie changes in rural social and economic development at the household level to families' demographic experiences since analyses of the former are limited or nonexistent.

AVAILABILITY OF EASILY ACCESSIBLE FARMLAND

Most of the studies of the decline in rural fertility in nineteenth-century America have been undertaken by economic historians (Yasuba, 1962; Forster and Tucker, 1972; Easterlin, 1971, 1976, 1977; Easterlin et al., 1978; Leet, 1975, 1976; Schapiro, 1982). They noted that fertility was higher in newly settled areas than in older agricultural regions and that it declined as these areas became more economically developed.

The most frequent explanation for the decrease in rural fertility is the declining availability of easily accessible farmland in an area as it became more settled and developed (Yasuba, 1962; Forster and Tucker, 1972; Easterlin et al., 1978; Leet, 1975, 1976; Schapiro, 1982; Laidig et al., 1981). Since the United States was predominantly an agricultural society, access to land constituted a major source of economic opportunity. Any decreases in the availability of farmland might lead to lower fertility as couples postponed their marriages in order to acquire enough resources to set up an independent household. In addition, marital fertility might also decline as the need for children's labor on the farm decreased as farms became smaller and had a higher proportion of improved acreage. Particularly important to this theory is the assumption that parents wanted to establish each of their children on a nearby farm but could no longer expect to do so as unimproved land became scarce. Rather than further fragmenting their own farms or not providing their children with an adequate bequest, farm families curtailed fertility. Thus, as both the ages at first marriage and marital fertility changed due to the decreasing availability of nearby farmland, overall rural fertility diminished in nineteenth-century America.

Much of the current debate on the decline in rural fertility revolves around the definition of land availability. Modell (1971) used population density as a measure of agricultural opportunity, but this does not take into account either the quality of the land or the extent of settlement in that area. Furthermore, population density not only measures agricultural opportunity in rural areas, but also the number of people living in villages and towns. Yasuba (1962) tried to avoid these problems by defining agricultural opportunity as the number of persons per 1000 arable acres. The population estimates were obtained from the nineteenth-century federal censuses while the data on arable acres came from 1949 figures on cropland. Yasuba used the latter data because he wanted some measure of the potentially arable land rather than the amount of land actually being cultivated in the antebellum period. Because twentieth-century farming technology and practices are considerably different than those of the nineteenth century, other analysts believe that the cropland figures from 1949 are not likely to reflect actual or even relative levels of potential farming areas in the nineteenth century (Forster and Tucker, 1972; Leet, 1975, 1976; Vinovskis, 1976b,c, 1978b, 1981a).

In order to avoid some of these problems, Forster and Tucker (1972) used the number of white adults per farm based upon the white adult population in the census year under investigation and the number of farms in 1850, 1860, or 1880. Their index has the advantage of reflecting nineteenth-century farming conditions and practices more accurately than either Modell's or Yasuba's indices. Even Forster and Tucker's index of land availability, however, leaves much to be desired. At the state level, an index of white adults per farm is highly correlated with the percentage of the population engaged in nonagricultural occupations and the percentage of the population in urban areas. Therefore, we cannot be sure whether the high correlation between the white adult-farm ratio and the white refined fertility ratio is due to the availability of farms, to the percentage of the population in nonagricultural occupations, or to the percentage of the population living in urban areas.

Land availability has also been calculated at the township level in 1790 and 1840 from the Massachusetts state tax valuations which provide information on the number of tilled acres, unimproved acres, and unimprovable acres. By using the number of unimproved but improvable acres of land per white adult male for the index of farmland availability in a given township, one can compare the agricultural opportunities in the different communities of the Commonwealth, especially if those townships that are already largely urban or engaged in other activities such as fishing or commerce are eliminated from the analysis (Vinovskis, 1981a). The advantage of this index is that it provides a measure of potential agricultural development as perceived by individuals living at the time rather than based upon the eventual settlement or economic development of that area at some future date. Like the other measures mentioned earlier, however, this one still fails to reflect either the cost or the quality of the acres still available for cultivation.

Another approach to measuring land availability was first developed by Leet (1975, 1976) who measured agricultural "stress" among antebellum Ohio counties by computing the available potential farmsites as well as the number of young adult males who might be competing for them. Laidig and his colleagues (1981) employed similar methodology in studying fertility in Pennsylvania counties in 1850 and 1860, as well as adding information on the quality of the land and the required labor inputs. This approach represents an improvement upon the estimates by Yasuba (1962) or Forster and Tucker (1972) by taking into consideration new farmsites created by the death of farm operators as well as employing a more refined estimate of the young adult males presumably in the market for one of these farms, but it still has conceptual and empirical limitations. As in all of the previous indices of land availability, there is no attempt to ascertain the cost of the farmland, although at least the Pennsylvania study attempts to measure variations in the quality of the labor and land. Furthermore, calculating the increased farmsites due to the mortality of its current owners is useful conceptually, but the absence of detailed mortality data at the county-level forced both studies to employ a constant multiplier which may or may not reflect actual mortality rates among the different counties and time periods. Since we know that there were considerable fluctuations in American mortality patterns, especially between 1850 and 1860, the application of any constant rate may be misleading (Vinovskis, 1972, 1978c).

One of the more puzzling aspects about the efforts to measure the availability of farmland has been the lack of attention to farm costs, especially surprising since most of the calculations have been done by economic historians who usually are otherwise quite concerned about costs. Simply estimating the number of available farmsites does not tell us much about the relative difficulty of someone acquiring them. Indeed, the preoccupation with farmsites rather than farm costs presupposes that the cost of establishing a new farm does not vary greatly among the states, counties, or townships under investigation, an assumption which has not been established empirically.

When one is discussing the availability of farms, we are in effect considering the relative costs of establishing a farm. Ideally, we would like to have information on the overall cost of establishing new farm households. Unfortunately, that information currently is not available for the nineteenth century. We do have data, however, on a very crude approximation of this: the average value of a farm. Using this index, it becomes evident that there was a wide geographic variation in the costs of farms in antebellum America. To take an extreme example, in 1860 the average value of a farm in Kansas was $1179, whereas the average value of a farm in Louisiana was $11,818 (Vinovskis, 1976c). Or, in more typical situations, Easterlin et al. (1978) found the value of the average Northern farm in 1860 was $1388 in newly settled areas while it was $3545 in the oldest sections.

The almost exclusive focus on the availability of undeveloped farmland or potential farmsites without taking into consideration the actual cost of that land or farm has also had another unfortunate consequence: it has diverted the attention of scholars from studying the relationship between farm income and fertility. As the availability of farmland or farms decreased in an area, the value of existing ones rose. Thus while the decreasing availability of land may reduce fertility by postponing marriages or curtailing the family size of farmers who worried about bequests for their children, the overall rise in farm values and farm incomes should have allowed, all other things being equal, farm families to have more children.

The rise in farm values as an area became more settled also might have made it even easier for parents to assist their children in acquiring their own farms. Even if parents chose not to sell any of their own property to finance a new farm for their offspring, they still would have been in a much better position to underwrite their children's credit, an important factor for anyone aspiring to farm ownership in the nineteenth century (Bentley, 1893). Combined with the increasing availability of farmland in the Midwest and West during the antebellum period, the rise in farm values in the settled areas should have made it easier for the children of farmers to establish themselves, especially once the federal government provided free or low-cost land for homesteaders.

The proponents of the land availability theory acknowledge that in many regions in the United States more farmland was becoming available as new lands were opened for settlement, especially in the decades prior to the Civil War (Forster and Tucker, 1972; Leet, 1975, 1976; Easterlin et al., 1978; Schapiro, 1982). But they point out that parents wanted to settle their children nearby so that the availability of less expensive farmland elsewhere was not a real alternative. Indeed, the assumption that parents and children placed such a high premium on living close to each other that they were willing to ignore the large cost differentials in farm prices is fundamental to the land availability thesis since most studies only measure the difficulty of acquiring nearby farm land or farmsites.

Yet the evidence that parents and children assigned such a high priority on living near each other is based almost entirely upon conjecture. Certainly nineteenth-century parents preferred, whenever possible, to have their children living in the same neighborhood or township. But the nature of farmlife during those years made this a hard goal to achieve in the first place and even more difficult to maintain thereafter. Most farmers simply did not remain very long in any particular community, thus significantly reducing the benefits of trying to settle their children nearby. Only 46 percent of the farm owners present in Wapello County, Iowa in 1850 remained there in 1860 (Throne, 1959). Similarly, in the decade following 1860 the persistence rate for families in Kansas counties was usually under 30 percent and never higher than 42 percent (Malin, 1935). Thus, with less than half of the farmers in the Midwest remaining in the same county from one decade to another, the assumption that parents considered only the availability of nearby farmland or farms in planning for their children's prospects twenty years hence seems overstated.

Indeed, one of the major proponents of the land availability approach (Easterlin, 1976, p. 65) seems to have significantly altered the assumptions behind this model by acknowledging that "the provision of one's children does not necessarily take the form of land whether at home, nearby, or far away. What is sought is equal treatment of offspring in terms of money values. . . . It is then, the prospective 'increase of capital,' an ever present concern of farmers, that chiefly governs the changing size of farm families."

Easterlin's statement that the prospective increase of capital is the major factor that governs the changing fertility of farm families is a major departure from earlier formulations of the land availability model and raises questions about the appropriate focus of attention on further research. If parents are more concerned about providing a set and equal amount of capital for each child rather than establishing them on a nearby farm, then we should be spending more effort in studying trends in farm income and wealth rather than the availability of easily accessible farmland or farmsites. Studies of farm income and wealth, for example, should concentrate more on farm costs and agricultural production, changes in transportation and markets for farm products, and rates of return on farm investments. Although some of these factors may be related to the availability of nearby farmland and farmsites as Easterlin (1976) suggests, they are by no means identical. In fact, if one accepts Easterlin's suggestion of the importance of the prospective increase of capital in determining family size, existing studies of human fertility among farm families are very weak conceptually and empirically in trying to measure this factor.

In addition to questions about the assumptions underlying the land availability model of household behavior, there is also a need to reconsider the nature of rural society. One of the major reasons for abandoning the urban-industrial explanation of the decline in nineteenth-century fertility and turning to land availability is that most Americans lived in the countryside and most of the absolute decrease in fertility rates occurred in rural rather than urban areas (Forster and Tucker, 1972). But the proponents of the land availability theory of fertility decline need to take into consideration, for example, what proportion of the rural population was engaged in agriculture and what percentage of those in agriculture were farm owners.

In making decisions about when to marry or how many children to have, persons directly engaged in agriculture were probably more likely to be influenced by the expected availability of farmland than those in nonagricultural pursuits. The federal censuses of 1820, 1840, 1850, and 1860 provide information on the proportion of the antebellum labor force engaged in agriculture (Vinovskis, 1981a). In 1850 the percentage of white males over fifteen engaged in agriculture was 44.7 percent, ranging from 32.7 percent in the Middle Atlantic states to 61.2 percent in the South Central states. While the land availability theory may reflect the needs and aspirations of farm families, it is less likely to represent those who are no longer directly engaged in agriculture. Furthermore, the fact that increasing numbers of white adult males could and did enter nonagricultural occupations meant that many farm families may not have expected or even wanted all of their children to become farm owners.

Not all of those engaged in agriculture were farm owners or could realistically expect to become farm owners or operators. In 1850 only about 60 percent of white males ages fifteen and above in agriculture had farms (Vinovskis, 1981a). While some of those without farms might anticipate obtaining one in the future, others may have resigned themselves to continuing to be farm laborers or tenants (Schnob, 1975; Cogswell, 1975). Therefore, analyses of the relationship between fertility and land availability should take in to consideration the proportion of those in agriculture who owned their farms, rented them, or worked as agricultural laborers.

The land availability hypothesis assumes that the age at first marriage is lower in areas where farmland is more plentiful because it is easier to establish new households. There has been no effort, however, to consider the possible differences in the age at first marriage for farm owners, renters, and laborers or how the age at first marriage might have shifted for each group as farmland became more scarce. Although there are no studies on the age at first marriage in rural areas by occupational class for the nineteenth century, there are a few analyses for the early twentieth century. The results of these studies suggest that the age at marriage for wives of farm laborers was lower than that of wives of farm renters or farm owners. In addition, the age at marriage for wives of farm renters was usually lower than that of wives of farm owners (Notestein, 1931).

The inverse relationship between the age at marriage for women and the occupational class of their husbands in rural areas suggests the need for refining the hypothesis that the age at marriage increased as farmland became more scarce. As an area became more developed, there was an increase in the proportion of those in agriculture who were renters or laborers. Therefore, although the increasing scarcity of land might discourage early marriage among prospective farm owners, the increase in the percentage of farm renters or laborers might operate in the opposite direction since they tended to marry younger than farm owners.

Another unresolved problem with the hypothesis that a diminishing supply of land causes an increase in the age at marriage is that no empirical evidence has been gathered to test directly that relationship. Prospective farm owners probably did marry later than farm laborers, but this might be simply a reflection of differences in their relative social status and backgrounds rather than of the difficulty of obtaining their own farms. Since many farm owners did not purchase farms until they were in their 30s, the fact that their average age at marriage was probably in the mid-20s suggests that many of them married before acquiring their own farms. If this were the case, the increasing scarcity of land in an area might be less a factor in postponing marriages as the norms for prospective farm owners would be to marry even before they could afford to purchase their own farms.

We have already seen that there is often an inverse relationship between the age at marriage and occupational class among farmers in the early twentieth century. Studies of rural fertility also indicate an inverse relationship between fertility and social class, in part due to earlier marriages among farm laborers and renters than among farm owners. But even after controlling for the age at marriage, there is usually a higher fertility rate for wives of farm laborers and renters than for wives of farm owners (Bash, 1955; Kiser, 1933). Therefore, as in the earlier discussion of marriage, as an area becomes more settled and developed, the lower rate of fertility among farm owners concerned about their children's inheritance would be offset to some degree by the increasing presence of farm renters and laborers who had more children than farm owners.

The land availability model postulates that parents expected to establish their children on nearby farms but curtailed their fertility as it became apparent that it would be difficult to achieve this goal. It presupposes that indeed most parents wanted or tried to help finance their children's farm ownership at the time they left home, yet the evidence for this important assumption is scanty. It is not clear, for example, how many of the sons of farmers received their inheritance upon reaching adulthood. Perhaps some parents did not transmit significant amounts of capital to their offspring when these children reached their majority, either because they could not afford to do so or because they had already assisted them through other forms of investment such as their education. The pattern and timing of bequests are essential to the land availability argument, but very little attention has been paid to the relationship between inheritance and the age at marriage or marital fertility (Bogue, 1976). As a result, it has not yet been demonstrated that most parents consciously reduced their family size because of the expectation that they would have to make a significant bequest to each of their offspring when they reached adulthood or that children frequently benefited from such a practice when they were about to set up an independent household.

This review of the problems of defining and measuring land availability as well as of the implicit assumptions behind such an approach suggests that this model needs further conceptual clarification and refinement before we can even properly interpret any results. In addition, some of the existing land availability studies (Forster and Tucker, 1972) are plagued by statistical shortcomings ranging from the inclusion of territories with unusual sex ratios to the presence of multicollinearity in the regression equations. Since the statistical weaknesses of these efforts have been detailed elsewhere (Vinovskis, 1976b,c, 1981a), they will not be repeated here.

A further methodological problem with the empirical studies of the relationship between land availability and fertility is that almost all of them are based upon cross-sectional analyses of aggregate data at the state (Yasuba, 1962; Forster and Tucker, 1972; Vinovskis, 1976c), county (Leet, 1975, 1976; Vinovskis, 1976b; Laidig et al., 1981), or township levels (Vinovskis, 1978b, 1981a). The results of these studies are mixed. While most of them claim to find strong support for the land availability theory (Yasuba, 1962; Forester and Tucker, 1972; Leet, 1975, 1976; Laidig et al., 1981; Schapiro, 1982), others which have either reanalyzed the earlier works (Vinovskis, 1976c) or done additional work (Vinovskis, 1978b, 1981a) have found problems with this interpretation.

One of the problems inherent in all of these aggregate-level studies is that they can only inform us about the relationship between fertility and land availability among different ecological units such as states, counties, or townships. Because of the problems associated with the "ecological fallacy" we cannot infer that the relationships at the aggregate level necessarily reflect those at the individual level. While there are theoretical ways of minimizing these difficulties, investigators using ecological regressions in these studies seem to be unaware of the problem and frequently implicitly assume that the results from their areal analyses are representative of the experiences of individuals, a particularly hazardous procedure in studies such as these which usually cannot fully specify their models and where both individual and contextual variables influence the behavior of the individuals being investigated (Langbein and Lichtman, 1978; Vinovskis, 1980). Particularly question- able is the reliance on the standardized measures in ecological regres- sions to infer the strength of relationships at the individual level. Therefore, even if these aggregate-level studies find a strong or weak correlation between the measures of land availability and the index of fertility, we cannot be certain that a similar relationship would exist at the individual household level as the theory predicts.

One can avoid the "ecological fallacy" by investigating the relation- ship between fertility and land availability at the individual or house- hold level.   This is an important methodological improvement as it permits the investigator to analyze the experiences of farm families without confounding them by the inclusion of other groups or indivi- duals.   Ideally, one would code the characteristics of the individual and the household as well as adding contextual information about the community.   In practice, information is usually assembled and analyzed on the individual or household, but not on the environment since often only a single community is being investigated.   The difficulty in con- ducting individual or household level analysis is that it requires much more effort and expense to code that information from the manuscript federal population and agricultural censuses than if one is doing areal analysis.

The use of federal manuscript censuses to study nineteenth-century rural populations was developed by Curti (1959) and his associates. Since then almost all of the efforts using this source have been devoted to urban rather than rural populations (Vinovskis, 1977).   Sur- prisingly, very little effort has been made by scholars to use these sources for the analysis of the land availability model.

The few studies of land availability and fertility that have used the individual-level data from the federal manuscript censuses have pro- duced mixed results.   Easterlin and his colleagues (1978) found support for the land availability thesis in their analysis of northern farm families, but their findings so far are limited only to demonstrating that fertility levels are higher in the newly settled areas (except for the frontier area) than in the more developed regions.   They have not yet published any findings based upon a household-level analysis which demonstrates that farm families with larger amounts of unimproved, but improvable land were likely to have a higher fertility rate.   On the other hand, an analysis of fertility differentials at the household level in Weston, Massachusetts from 1800 to 1820 found no statistically significant relationship between the amount of land and the level of fertility, even though several different measures of land availability were used (Notzon, 1973).   Similarly, a study of residents in Washtenaw County, Michigan, in 1850 did not find a consistent relationship between the amount and type of property a farmer owned and the level of the wife's fertility (Trierweiler, 1976).   Thus, while the land availability model is a very useful first step in the analysis of the determinants of rural fertility, it will undoubtedly need further testing and refinement at the household level before we can accept its validity and importance.

MARRIAGE PATTERNS, VALUE OF CHILDREN, AND MORTALITY CHANGES

So far we have concentrated on the land availability explanation for the decline in rural fertility in nineteenth-century America. Now we will turn to three other factors which may be associated with reduced fertility: a rise in the age at first marriage and a decrease in the proportion married, changes in the value of children, and decreases in mortality. Although all three factors have been incorporated (especially the first two) in the land availability model, we will consider each of them in more detail.

Changes in the ages at first marriage and the proportion marrying, especially in societies where marital fertility remains high, can greatly affect birth rates. The relatively high birth rates in early America compared to Western Europe are often explained by the earlier ages at marriage in this country.

Since very little direct information is available on ages at marriage, many scholars have relied upon indirect indices such as the sex ratio of the population which presumably reflects the availability of marriage partners in a given area. T'ien (1959), for example, asserted that the sex ratio of the population at the state level was very important in explaining fertility differentials and trends in the antebellum period. Yasuba (1962, p. 126) dismissed this argument:

> In conclusion we might say that, although it is reasonable to assume that the sex ratio affected fertility through marriage customs, it is doubtful that it was an important factor in causing interstate differentials in fertility and in reducing fertility over time. Significant positive correlations between the sex ratio and fertility are likely to have been chiefly the result of correlations between these two variables, on the one hand, and one or more other variables, say interstate migration, the degree of urbanization, or the availability of land, on the other.

Yasuba was correct that changes in the sex ratio in antebellum America cannot account for the decline in fertility because there was little overall change in that sex ratio. He was incorrect, however, in concluding that the sex ratio was unimportant in predicting fertility differentials once other variables were taken into consideration (Vinovskis, 1976b,c, 1981a; Laidig et al., 1981). Furthermore, a detailed analysis between the sex ratio and the percentage of the population that is married found that the two items are highly correlated (Vinovskis, 1978a).

Unfortunately, we have few studies of the changes in the ages at marriage in nineteenth-century America. Easterlin and his associates (1978) used an indirect measure of the age at marriage and found that early marriages and a higher proportion of the population married were characteristics of northern farm families in the newly settled areas rather than in the older regions, thereby lending support to their interpretation that the decreasing availability of nearby farmland forced couples to postpone their marriages. Similarly a study (Osterud and

Fulton, 1976) of a small community in Massachusetts found that the increases in the age at first marriage from 1730 to 1850 accounted for nearly one-half of the decrease in fertility in that village. Other analyses (Vinovskis, 1981a), however, have found a significant increase in the age at first marriage for Massachusetts women in the eighteenth century, but no major changes in the first half of the nineteenth century. It is too early at this time to speculate exactly on the changes in the ages at marriage or the proportion married in antebellum America, especially once we leave New England, but it is unlikely that a rise in these two factors can explain most of the decline in rural fertility, although they may have been contributing factors as suggested by the land availability models.

Children are often considered an economic asset to their families because they provide labor on the farm, contribute to the family income after leaving home, or support their parents in old age. Therefore, in some circumstances it is economically advantageous for the individual family to have more children, especially when the costs of raising them are not very high (Easterlin, 1976; Caldwell, 1982).

While there is no consensus on the net worth to parents of farm children, the most detailed and careful assessment (Lindert, 1978, p. 121) concludes that "the farm child's work contribution was not great enough to match the total time-plus-commodity costs of his rearing." Since few American children, particularly the males, felt obligated to send money to their parents when they left home, the economic value of the child was not enhanced. Similarly, though children sometimes did assist aged parents in the nineteenth century, most of them do not appear to have made large economic contributions as most elderly still sustained themselves by working and living alone (Achenbaum, 1978; Graebner, 1980). Thus, while greater economic opportunities in the New World made it possible for parents to support the larger families which their society valued, the large family probably was more of an economic liability than an asset, at least while the children were still growing up at home.

Whether the relative value of children increased or decreased as an area became developed is not clear. On the one hand, farm labor was scarcer in newly settled areas and wages were higher, thus suggesting the willingness of parents to have larger families (Easterlin, 1976). On the other hand, the type of work that young children could do was more suited to farms in the more developed areas where dairy products and garden vegetables were grown for urban markets (Easterlin et al., 1978), thereby mitigating some of the apparent benefits of the larger family in the newly settled areas.

Although we cannot be sure whether the relative value of children's labor on the farm increased or decreased during the nineteenth century, it does appear that the costs of raising a child may have increased substantially as children could not enter schools as early as before and yet were likely to be enrolled longer overall. Whereas it was not uncommon for three- or four-year-olds to be enrolled in public or private schools in the early nineteenth century, thus relieving their mother of the burden of caring for them, it was no longer deemed desirable to send such youngsters into the schools by the mid-nineteenth century (May and Vinovskis, 1977). Furthermore, as rural schools were extended in length and as the rates of overall enrollment as well as daily attendance rose, the total amount of time farm boys spent in school increased (Kaestle and Vinovskis, 1980).

In addition to the increased time spent in school at older ages, the type of care that was expected of the parents, particularly of the mother, greatly increased in the nineteenth century (Cott, 1977; Degler, 1980; Kuhn, 1947). The greater emphasis on the mother's role in childrearing in the late eighteenth and early nineteenth centuries meant that women were expected to spend more time with their children, especially as their offspring were now more likely to stay in the home longer before entering school. Therefore, even if the potential benefits from the labor of children did not change much during the nineteenth century, the costs of raising them probably increased substantially.

One of the fundamental tenets of the demographic transition model was that mortality declined prior to the reduction in fertility. As the death rates decreased, parents no longer had to have as many children to insure that a certain number of them would survive into adulthood. While most scholars have abandoned the traditional demographic transition model as being too simplistic, many individuals still connect the decline in fertility with a preceding or simultaneous reduction in mortality.

At first glance it appears that the case of the United States supports the notion that the decline in fertility in the nineteenth century was accompanied by a substantial reduction in mortality. The standard interpretation of mortality trends in the United States set forth by Thompson and Whelpton (1933) and recently reaffirmed by Easterlin (1977) is that there was a steady increase in life expectancy in the United States during the first half of the nineteenth century. But Easterlin's (1977) argument rests heavily on the use of the Wigglesworth life table of 1789 and the Jacobson life table of 1850, and both of these have been discredited (Vinovskis, 1971, 1972, 1978d).

While we simply do not have enough mortality information, particularly outside of New England, to be certain of mortality trends in the nineteenth century, the available evidence points to little change in death rates in rural areas (Vinovskis, 1978d). Only in the South is there likely to have been a major change in mortality levels and much of this probably occurred in the seventeenth and eighteenth centuries. Therefore, it is unlikely that the sharp decline in fertility in rural America in the nineteenth century was brought about by a large decline in death rates. However, there is a possibility that even though death rates did not decline substantially in antebellum America, people might have thought they had, since they had greatly overestimated the extent of mortality, particularly adult mortality, in the seventeenth, eighteenth, and early nineteenth centuries (Vinovskis, 1976a). If people's perception of mortality came closer in line with their actual experiences in the mid- and late-nineteenth century, then perhaps it may have still played some role in persuading rural parents to have fewer children.

MODERNIZATION

Several scholars (Smith, 1978; Vinovskis, 1976b,c; 1981a,b; Wells, 1975, 1982) have questioned whether socioeconomic factors by themselves will suffice to explain the decline in fertility in the nineteenth century. Rather than seeking separate explanations for the changes in urban and rural fertility, they observe that the declines in birth rates in these two areas were nearly parallel throughout this period, thereby suggesting perhaps that some more basic changes, often labelled as modernization, were affecting fertility in both settings. Contemporary studies (Miller and Inkeles, 1974) have found an inverse relationship between fertility and modernization and several American historians (Brown, 1972, 1976) are now arguing that the United States was undergoing a period of modernization in the eighteenth and early nineteenth centuries.

The concept of modernization is not without its critics. In fact, the use of the term in the other social sciences has been severely criticized (Bendix, 1967a,b; Smelser, 1968). The chief complaint has been the lack of a precise definition. Modernization as a term has been used so loosely as to become meaningless from an analytical point of view. Furthermore, modernization is frequently equated with urbanization and industrialization so that other scholars find it difficult to apply such a concept to a preindustrial era. Finally, modernization is often a very value-laden term which implies the notion of progress even though in practice it creates hardship and turmoil in the lives of many people.

Considerations of space necessarily limit our discussion of the role of modernization during the nineteenth century. But we can conclude that in terms of many of the attitudinal and structural characteristics often associated with modern societies, the United States in the first half of the nineteenth century probably was becoming a more modern society. There were major changes in the extent and quality of education available to both men and women in the antebellum period (Kaestle and Vinovskis, 1980). During these years there was also large increases in the amount and type of information available to Americans through magazines and newspapers (Pred, 1973). American society also became more commercially-oriented in both its agricultural and industrial sectors (Henretta, 1973). As workers were brought into the market economy, they acquired a broader outlook and increased their desires for material goods. There was also a fundamental change in American attitudes as people became convinced that they could improve not only their own lives, but the lives of others as well (Barnett, 1973; Howe, 1979; Thomas, 1965). The reform spirit swept through the United States and encouraged people to join together to undertake reforms to eliminate many of the social problems they found present in that society. Finally, and perhaps most important of all, there was a major change in the role of women in nineteenth-century society as they began to play a larger role within their homes (Cott, 1977; Degler, 1980). These developments merely illustrate a few of the changes that were occurring and that might be considered as part of the modernization of American society.

Though demographers and economists have been very reluctant to look beyond socioeconomic explanations of the fertility decline in nineteenth-century America, it is important that we also consider some of the broader attitudinal and cultural shifts that were occurring in society. The fact that the concept of modernization had been badly misused by some scholars in the past should not deter us from analyzing the possibility that American society in the late-eighteenth and early-nineteenth centuries experienced major changes that might be appropriately summarized under the heading of modernization. Statements by economists (Schapiro, 1982, p. 582) that "there is little evidence of changes in attitudes" during the period 1760 to 1870 are simply incorrect given the large amount of recent work on this issue by social historians. Although it is impossible to prove or even to demonstrate convincingly at this time, it is very likely that broad attitudinal and cultural shifts in American society played a key role in the decline in fertility in both rural and urban areas.

CONCLUSION

The major declines in fertility in nineteenth-century America occurred in the countryside. Therefore, it is only fitting that scholars have turned to an analysis of the relationship between rural development and human fertility.

The major thrust of the work up to now has been to study the relationship between easily accessible farmland and fertility. While this has been a fruitful avenue for analysis of farm fertility, it still needs considerable conceptual and statistical improvement, especially since even its most able proponents cannot seem to state clearly exactly what the model says or implies. Better measures of land availability will have to be devised which take into account both the quality and cost of the land as well as of the other investments needed to start a new farm. In addition, many of the crucial assumptions encompassed within the land availability approach need reformulation and testing, especially those concerned with the transmission of capital from parents to children as the latter reach adulthood. The land availability theory also needs to take into consideration the effects of the increases in per capita farm income during most of the nineteenth century (Fogel and Rutner, 1972). Indeed, what is interesting is that farm fertility declined as sharply as it did during the nineteenth century even though the rise in farm income made it easier to maintain large families if all other factors had remained constant. Finally, much of the earlier work on land availability is limited not only by its statistical procedures, but also by its almost exclusive reliance on aggregate rather than individual- or household-level analysis. But despite these shortcomings, the land availability approach continues to be an important and exciting area for research by social and demographic historians.

One of the fundamental limitations of the work on land availability, however, is that it often confuses declines in the fertility of farm families with those of the rural population in general. As we have noted, large numbers of individuals living in rural America were engaged in nonagricultural tasks and increasing proportions of those who were in agriculture had little realistic expectation of ever becoming a farm owner rather than a tenant or laborer. Furthermore, as an area became more settled, the tendency for individuals to live and work in small villages becomes an important factor—especially since fertility among villagers seems to have been lower than that among farmers (Modell, 1971). In other words, those interested in the relationship between rural development and human fertility should develop a broader research agenda than the present almost exclusive focus on the role of land availability on the demographic experiences of farm families.

In addition to examining the role of land availability and rural development, we also need to look at other factors such as the changes in the ages at marriage and the proportion married, the costs and benefits of raising children, and shifts in mortality patterns. Of these three factors, the first two are likely to provide some additional explanatory power as the ages at first marriage may have been rising in the nineteenth-century rural America (particularly in the second half) and the costs of raising children rose as the amount of formal education they received increased. At this time, it appears doubtful that there were significant enough reductions in rural mortality to account for the decline in fertility, but this entire issue, including individuals' perceptions of the death rates, awaits further research.

One avenue of analysis that most economic and demographic historians have not taken very seriously is whether or not there may have been large changes in the attitudes and values of nineteenth-century Americans which might had led them to reduce their family size. Recent work by social historians, for example, suggests that there may have been such changes during this period. Whether one loosely classifies them under the heading of modernization or not is not as important as whether one takes seriously the possibility that such changes were occurring and that they may have affected fertility. One of the tentative conclusions from studying trends in rural fertility in the West is that changes in attitudes and values of a society may play a much larger role in explaining the decline in fertility than most scholars have acknowledged.

REFERENCES

Achenbaum, W.A. 1978. Old Age in the New Land. Baltimore: Johns Hopkins Press.

Barnett, R. 1973. From Philanthropy to Reform: Poverty, Drunkedness, and the Social Order in Massachusetts, 1780-1825. Ph.D. dissertation, Harvard University.

Bash, W.H. 1955. Differential fertility in Madison County, New York, 1865. Milbank Memorial Fund Quarterly 33:161-186.

Bendix, R. 1967a. The comparative analysis of historical change. In: T. Burns and S.B. Saul (eds.) Social Theory and Economic Change, pp.125-146. London: Macmillan.

——— 1967b. Tradition and modernity reconsidered. Comparative Studies in Society and History 9:292-346.

Bentley, A.F. 1893.   The Condition of the Western Farmers Illustrated by the Economic History of a Nebraska Township.   Baltimore: Johns Hopkins Press.

Bogue, A.G. 1976.   Comments on paper by Easterlin.   Journal of Economic History 36:76-81.

Brown, R.D. 1972.   Modernization and the modern personality in early America, 1600-1865: A sketch of a synthesis.   Journal of Interdisciplinary History 2:201-228.

_____ 1976.   Modernization: The Transformation of American Life, 1600-1865.   New York: Norton.

Caldwell, J.C. 1982.   Theory of Fertility Decline.   New York: Academic Press.

Coale, A.J. 1969.   The decline of fertility in Europe from the French revolution to World War II.   In: S.J. Behrman, L. Corsa, and R. Freedman (eds.) Fertility and Family Planning: A World View, pp. 3-24.   Ann Arbor: University of Michigan Press.

_____ and M. Zelnik. 1963.   New Estimates of Fertility and Population in the United States: A Study of Annual White Births from 1865 to 1960 and of the Completeness of Enumeration in the Census from 1880 to 1960.   Princeton: Princeton University Press.

Cogswell, S., Jr. 1975.   Tenure, Nativity and Age as Factors in Iowa Agriculture, 1850-1880.   Ames: Iowa State University Press.

Cott, N.F. 1977.   The Bonds of Womanhood: "Women's Sphere" in New England, 1780-1835.   New Haven: Yale University Press.

Curti, M. 1959.   Making of an American Community.   Stanford, California: Stanford University Press.

Degler, C.N. 1980.   At Odds: Women and the Family in America from the Revolution to the Present.   New York: Oxford University Press.

Easterlin, R.A. 1971.   Does Human Fertility Adjust to the Environment? American Economic Association, Papers and Proceedings 61:399-407.

_____ 1976.   Population change and farm settlement in the northern United States.   Journal of Economic History 36:45-75.

_____ 1977.   Population issues in American economic history: A survey and critique.   In: P.J. Uselding (ed.) Research in Economic History, Vol. I, pp. 133-158.   Greenwich, Connecticut: JAI Press.

_____, G. Alter, and G.A. Condran. 1978.   Farm families in old and new areas: The northern states in 1860.   In: T.K. Hareven and M.A. Vinovskis (eds.) Family and Population in Nineteenth Century America, pp. 22-84.   Princeton: Princeton University Press.

Fogel, R.W. and J.L. Rutner. 1972.   Efficiency effects of federal land policy, 1850-1900: A report of some provisional findings.   In: W.O. Aydelotte, A.G. Bogue, and R.W. Fogel (eds.) The Dimensions of Quantitative Research in History, pp. 390-418.   Princeton: Princeton University Press.

Forster, C. and G.S.L. Tucker. 1972.   Economic Opportunity and White American Fertility Ratios, 1800-1860.   New Haven: Yale University Press.

Graebner, W. 1980.   A History of Retirement: The Meaning and Function of An American Institution, 1885-1978.   New Haven: Yale University Press.

Hareven, T.K. and M.A. Vinovskis. 1978.   Patterns of childbearing in late nineteenth-century America: The determinants of marital fertility in five Massachusetts towns in 1880. In: T.K. Hareven and M.A. Vinovskis (eds.) pp. 85–125. Princeton: Princeton University Press.

Henretta, J.A. 1973. The Evolution of American Society, 1700–1815: An Interdisciplinary Analysis. Lexington, Massachusetts: D.C. Heath and Company.

Howe, D.W. 1979. The Political Culture of the American Whigs. Chicago: University of Chicago Press.

Jaffe, A.J. 1942. Urbanization and fertility. American Journal of Sociology 48:48–60.

Kaestle, C.F. and M.A. Vinovskis. 1980. Education and Social Change in Nineteenth Century Massachusetts. Cambridge: Cambridge University Press.

Kiser, C.V. 1933. Trends in fertility of social classes from 1900 to 1910. Human Biology 5:256–273.

Knodel, J.E. 1974. The Decline of Fertility in Germany, 1871–1939. Princeton: Princeton University Press.

Kuhn, A.L. 1947. The Mother's Role in Childhood Education. New Haven: Yale University Press.

Laidig, G.L., W.A. Schutjer, and C.S. Stokes. 1981. Agricultural variation and human fertility in antebellum Pennsylvania. Journal of Family History 6:195–204.

Langbein, L.I. and A.J. Lichtman. 1978. Ecological Inference. Quantitative Applications in the Social Sciences, No. 10. Beverly Hills, California: Sage Publications.

Leet, D.R. 1975. Human fertility and agricultural opportunities in Ohio counties: From frontier to maturity, 1810–60. In: D.C. Klingaman and R.K. Vedder (eds.) Essays in Nineteenth Century Economic History: The Old Northwest, pp. 138–158. Athens: Ohio University Press.

_____ 1976. The determinants of the fertility transition in antebellum Ohio. Journal of Economic History 36:359–378.

Lesthaeghe, R.J. 1977. The Decline of Belgian Fertility, 1800–1970. Princeton: Princeton University Press.

Lindert, P.H. 1978. Fertility and Scarcity in America. Princeton: Princeton University Press.

McClelland, P.D. and R.J. Zeckhauser. 1982. Demographic Dimensions of the New Republic: American Interregional Migration, Vital Statistics, and Manumissions, 1800–1860. Cambridge: Cambridge University Press.

Malin, J.C. 1935. The turnover of farm population in Kansas. Kansas Historical Quarterly 4:339–372.

May, D. and M.A. Vinovskis. 1977. A ray of millenial light: Early education and social reform in the infant school movement in Massachusetts, 1826–1840. In: T.K. Hareven (ed.) Family and Kin in American Urban Communities, 1700–1930, pp. 62–99. New York: New Viewpoints.

Miller, K.A. and A. Inkeles. 1974. Modernity and acceptance of family limitation in four developing countries. Journal of Social Issues 30:167–188.

Mitchell, B.R. 1975. European Historical Statistics, 1750–1970. New York: Columbia University Press.

Modell, J. 1971. Family and fertility on the Indiana frontier, 1820. American Quarterly 23:615-634.

Notestein, F.W. 1931. Differential age at marriage according to social class. American Journal of Sociology 37:22-48.

Notzon, F. 1973. Fertility and Farmland in Weston, Massachusetts: 1800-1820. Master's thesis, University of Wisconsin.

Osterud, N. and J. Fulton. 1976. Family limitation and age at marriage: Fertility decline in Sturbridge, Massachusetts, 1730-1850. Population Studies 30:481-494.

Potter, J. 1965. The growth of population in America, 1700-1860. In: D.V. Glass and D.E.C. Eversley (eds.) Population in History: Essays in Historical Demography, pp. 631-688. Chicago: Aldine Publishing Co.

Pred, A.R. 1973. Urban Growth and the Circulation of Information: The United States System of Cities, 1790-1840. Cambridge, Massachusetts: Harvard University Press.

Robinson, W.C. 1963. Urbanization and fertility: The non-Western experience. Milbank Memorial Fund Quarterly 41:291-308.

Schapiro, M.O. 1982. A land availability model of fertility change in the rural northern United States, 1760-1870. Journal of Economic History 42:577-600.

Schob, D.E. 1975. Hired Hands and Plowboys: Farm Labor in the Midwest, 1815-60. Urbana: University of Illinois Press.

Smelser, N.J. 1968. Essays in Sociological Explanation. Englewood Cliffs, New Jersey: Prentice-Hall.

Smith, D.S. 1978. The context of marital fertility change in Hingham, Massachusetts. Paper presented at the American Historical Association Meeting, San Francisco.

Thomas, J.L. 1965. Romantic reform in America, 1815-1865. American Quarterly 17:656-681.

Thompson, W.S. and P.K. Whelpton. 1933. Population Trends in the United States. New York: McGraw Hill.

Throne, M. 1959. Population study of an Iowa county in 1850. Iowa Journal of History 5:305-330.

T'ien, H.Y. 1959. A demographic aspect of interstate variation in American fertility, 1800-1860. Milbank Memorial Fund Quarterly 37: 49-59.

Trierweiler, W.C. 1976. The Differential Child-Woman Ratios in Washtenaw County, Michigan, 1850: An Investigation into the Patterns of Fertility Decline in Ante-Bellum America. Honors thesis, University of Michigan.

Vinovskis, M.A. 1971. The 1789 life table of Edward Wigglesworth. Journal of Economic History 32:570-590.

_____ 1972. Mortality rates and trends in Massachusetts before 1860. Journal of Economic History 32:184-213.

_____ 1976a. Angels' heads and weeping willows: Death in early America. Proceedings of the American Antiquarian Society 86:273-302.

_____ 1976b. Demographic History and the World Population Crisis. Worcester, Massachusetts: Clark University Press.

_____ 1976c.   Socio-economic determinants of interstate fertility differentials in the United States in 1850 and 1860.   Journal of Interdisciplinary History 6:375-396.

_____ 1977.   From household size to the life course: Some observations on recent trends in family history.   American Behavioral Scientist 21:263-287.

_____ 1978a.   Marriage patterns in mid-nineteenth-century New York State: A multivariate analysis.   Journal of Family History 3:51-61.

_____ 1978b.   A multiple regression analysis of fertility differentials among Massachusetts regions and towns in 1860.   In: Charles Tilly (ed.) Historical Studies of Changing Fertility, pp. 225-256.   Princeton: Princeton University Press.

_____ 1978c.   Recent trends in American historical demography: Some methodological and conceptual considerations.   Annual Review of Sociology 4:603-627.

_____ 1978d.   The Jacobson Life Table of 1850: A critical re-examination from a Massachusetts perspective.   Journal of Interdisciplinary History 4:703-724.

_____ 1980.   Problems and opportunities in the use of individual and aggregate level census data.   In: J.M. Clubb and E.K. Scheuch (eds.) Historical Social Research: The Use of Historical and Process-Produced Data, pp. 53-70.   Stuttgart, Germany: Klett-Cotta.

_____ 1981a.   Fertility in Massachusetts from the Revolution to the Civil War.   New York: Academic Press.

_____ 1981b.   The fertility decline in the West as a model for developing countries today: The case of nineteenth-century America.   In: Nick Eberstadt (ed.) Fertility Decline in the Less Developed Countries, pp. 228-253.   New York: Praeger.

Wells, R.V. 1975.   Family history and demographic transitions.   Journal of Social History 9:1-20.

_____ 1982.   Revolution in Americans' Lives: A Demographic Perspective on the History of Americans, Their Families, and Their Society.   Westport, Connecticut: Greenwood Press.

Wrigley, E.A. 1969.   Population and History.   New York: McGraw Hill.

_____ and R.S. Schofield. 1981.   The Population History of England, 1541-1871.   Cambridge, Massachusetts: Harvard University Press.

Yasuba, Y. 1962.   Birth Rates of the White Population in the United States, 1800-1860: An Economic Study.   Baltimore: Johns Hopkins Press.

PART II
Rural Fertility Determinants: Household Perspectives

CHAPTER 6
Rural Development Policy and Fertility: A Framework for Analysis at the Household Level

Boone A. Turchi

Rural areas in the third world have over the past two decades been subjected to an impressive array of public programs designed to accelerate their rate of economic and social development. A more modest set of programs has been directed toward the reduction of human fertility in these areas, primarily through the supply of birth control products and services. That rural development policy and fertility reduction policy should be closely coordinated follows from the widely accepted view that rapid population growth impedes the development of low income regions.

However, there is very little evidence that rural development and fertility reduction policies are in fact coordinated in the majority of developing nations. Typically, the responsibility for development and administration of the two policies has resided in separate ministries and the result has often been a lack of coordination or even familiarity with respective programs. The scientific literature relating to these two fields are equally unconnected; the rural development literature very rarely considers the fertility impact of rural development programs even though it is widely believed by social scientists that economic and social transformation is a major factor in the fertility transition.

Research on fertility reduction policy is, on the other hand, primarily directed toward the supply side of family planning programs. Policy studies in this area tend to focus on the issues surrounding development of institutions appropriate for the dissemination of family planning knowledge, commodities, and services. To the extent that the demand for these services is studied, it is studied in a very general social science framework that is far removed from the immediate and practical concerns of program planners and administrators. These concerns have been succinctly described by Ilchman (1965, p. 16):

> To be useful to policymakers, the knowledge of the correlates of fertility should instruct those who must make choices, with or without such guidance, about their policy interventions: who might be the objects of intervention, what degree of change might be achieved by how much and what kind of resources, what methods of intervening make what difference to the outcome, how long the intervention should last until the behavior is self-sustaining in enough people, what are the costs of intervention from the point of view of those who provide the means of intervening, whether enough resources are available publicly to achieve the purpose, and whether too many or not enough resources are available to the objects of the intervention so that the desired behavior might not be forthcoming.

By these criteria it is clear that much of the cumulative social research on third world fertility does not aspire to policy relevance (1).

Although there is little evidence available, it is likely that the lack of coordination between fertility policy and rural development policy has significant ramifications for each. Rural development policy is designed to affect the social and economic environment within which reproductive behavior takes place; however, measures of the productivity of this policy rarely ever include its fertility impact. If fertility levels do indeed affect the pace of rural development to the extent commonly believed, failure to account for fertility effects will lead to potentially significant errors of measurement of the impact of rural development policy. Likewise, the effectiveness of population policies in rural areas depends upon the degree to which social and economic conditions encourage or impede their successful implementation. Rural development projects may, therefore, have important positive or negative consequences for population programs that may, in the absence of coordination, result in significant misallocations of public resources.

What is needed is a framework for fertility research that is more consciously oriented toward policy questions. This framework should facilitate the study of mechanisms by which rural development policy is linked to the reproductive behavior; it should help development planners and administrators to produce programs that complement fertility reduction policy and it should provide a conceptual basis for the interpretation and synthesis of two literatures that today remain largely separate. Finally, it should provide a basis for the collection of new data that are more appropriate to the analysis of policy issues.

This chapter proposes and describes such a framework for household-level research. The discussion is motivated by a conviction that successful analyses of the rural development/fertility relationship must be guided by a theoretical framework that emphasizes possible linkages, offers a basis on which to interpret and integrate existing literature in relevant fields, and guides the collection of new data. The emphasis of this theoretical framework is on the collection of data that will allow policy relevant rural development/fertility research of the sort just described.

The following section presents a household-level theory of fertility and attempts to make explicit the connections that reproductive behavior has with the social and economic environment. A third section describes the kinds of variables that are appropriately collected in any attempt to estimate versions of the model, while a subsequent section relates the theoretical structure to data collection procedures for policy relevant research. A final section concludes with further discussion of rural development policy and fertility research.

A SOCIOECONOMIC MODEL OF REPRODUCTIVE BEHAVIOR

Rationale for an Economic Model

Beginning with the pathbreaking work of Leibenstein (1957) and Becker (1960), the use of models based on the economic theory of the consumer for fertility analysis has become quite common. Becker argued that, since couples in industrial societies exercise a considerable degree of control over family size, it is proper to treat reproductive behavior as a form of decision making under resource constraint. The decisions of parents to limit family size below the maximum that is biologically attainable are properly viewed as resource allocation decisions, since child rearing requires sizable amounts of parental time and financial resources (Espenshade, 1977; Turchi, 1975).

Becker argued that these allocative reproductive decisions are in essence no different than the kinds of decisions that individuals make in allocating scarce resources over a set of consumption possibilities. Consequently, it may be useful to conceive of parents as utility maximizers who choose a family size that is consistent with their other consumption aspirations and that leads to the highest level of psychic welfare (utility) attainable. This process of utility maximization leads formally to a demand equation for children

$$K = D \ (PK, I)$$

where, K, the number of children demanded in a completed family depends upon preferences (the functional operator, D), the opportunity cost (price) of a child (PK), and a measure of economic resources available over the family's life cycle (I). Becker's formulation has been extended and modified by a number of authors, particularly in the context of fertility analysis in industrial countries (Willis, 1973; Turchi, 1975).

There are, however, a number of objections that have been raised to the use of the microeconomic model of fertility, both in industrial and in third world countries.

The assumption of "rationality" is untenable with respect to fertility. Critics of the microeconomic model of fertility point to numerous instances in the industrial as well as third world nations where reproductive behavior appears to be anything but rational and they argue that the basic behavioral axioms of the model are so often violated as to make its use inappropriate.   There are two immediate objections to this sort of criticism.   First, in the industrial countries at least, conscious control over fertility is virtually universal.   Some set of criteria must be motivating this control and the rational-consistent assumption of economic theory provides an attractive motivational basis for this behavior (Turchi, 1975, pp. 27-29).   Clearly, there are other motivational bases that might be guiding the purposive behavior of couples, but they are not particularly well spelled out.   The burden of proof would appear to be on critics of the microeconomic theory to present viable alternatives and to provide evidence of their superiority.

Another problem with common criticisms of the rationality assumption is that they often confuse "process rationality" with "outcome rationality."   If the process by which a certain family size is achieved does not appear to be "rational" then the critics argue that the outcome of the decision process also cannot be a "rational" outcome.   This sort of criticism of the microeconomic model often paints a derisory picture of couples making use of "bedside calculators" to compute the costs and benefits of another birth before retiring in the evening.   However, economists have never argued that a decision process must itself appear to be rational in order for the outcomes of that process to be consistent with the decisionmaker's achievement of a maximum of psychic welfare given the social, biological and economic constraints that he or she faces.   In traditional third world settings this point is particularly important: reproductive behavior that appears to be anything but rational to western observers may in fact be entirely consistent with the sociocultural and economic constraints that limit the choices available.   Caldwell (1977) has made this point forcefully with respect to West African and other societies.   An advantage of the microeconomic model, as elaborated below, is that it offers the opportunity to delineate fairly precisely how the changing social and economic conditions that characterize socioeconomic development serve to widen the options available to traditional couples in the third world so that the choice set comes to include low-fertility options as well as the high-fertility options that characterize traditional society.

The economic model does not allow for the impact of institutional factors on reproductive behavior.   Sociologists (Blake, 1968; Goldberg, 1975) and others have argued that the economic model of fertility cannot take adequate account of the numerous social and cultural factors that influence reproductive behavior outside of the narrow set of income and price variables usually associated with that model.   The fertility literature does indeed contain a number of examples in which the economic model is applied without much attention to the normative environment within which reproductive behavior is occurring; however, lack of attention to the sociocultural environment is in no way an essential feature of the economic models. Economists (Easterlin, 1978; Easterlin et al., 1980; Leibenstein, 1975) have incorporated a wider noneconomic viewpoint into their analyses of fertility in developing countries, and Easterlin (1969) and Turchi (1975) have explicitly included noneconomic factors in their studies of American fertility. Indeed, it will be argued below that the economic model of fertility offers a particularly attractive framework for the systematic inclusion of environmental and contextual factors in analyses of fertility by providing a causal theory as to how these factors operate directly and indirectly upon reproductive behavior. Because this causal structure exists, the impact of hypothesized changes in the economy and society can be traced through and predictions can be offered on the basis of a more systematic analysis of that structure. Support for this assertion will be provided later in this section.

The economic model erroneously assumes that individuals can precisely control their fertility in the same manner that they can purchase a consumer durable. Critics have argued that, at best, the economic model applies to affluent groups in the industrial countries, since it is those groups that can effectively control their fertility. However, there is nothing inherent in the economic theory of the consumer that posits a situation in which perfect satisfaction of consumption plans is costlessly achieved. The sequential model of fertility to be outlined below demonstrates how the costs inherent in fertility regulation can result in failure to achieve fertility intentions. Moreover, the model demonstrates the linkage between family planning programs that are designed to reduce the costs of effective fertility regulation and other programs that might serve to raise the demand for those family planning programs.

Even if the economic model is conceded to apply to the industrial nations, it is poorly suited for application to the traditional regions where none of the conditions for rational, independent, purposive decision making exist. Again, criticisms of this sort confuse process with outcome. Behavior that appears to be irrational from one viewpoint may indeed be seen to be eminently rational once the relevant constraints to behavior and the alternatives available are known. The economic model has the advantage of forcing the researcher to define explicitly the constraints that he believes to be operative and the alternatives that are open to the decision maker. Theories of fertility that are not based on a decision-theoretic framework of this sort allow the analyst to avoid a rigorous specification of the factors that immediately affect decision making. As a result, interpretation of findings is often problematic and ad hoc.

The range of alternatives available to the individual need not be wide for a decision theoretic framework to be appropriate. Indeed, consumer theory requires that the decision maker have only two choices in order to be relevant to the analysis of that decision. Moreover, the model is flexible enough to account for those social settings in which the psychosocial rewards to parenthood are so high and the opportunity cost of children are so low that uniformly high fertility is the norm. Even in this extreme case of sociological determinism the economic model can identify the factors that produce uniformity of behavior and that will be likely to change with socioeconomic development.

A Static Model of Completed Fertility

In this section a prototype microeconomic model of completed family size is developed in order to illustrate the uses and advantages of the decision-theoretic approach to fertility analysis. Our subject is a

"representative third world woman" who is currently participating in a
sexual union.   The factors that are hypothesized to influence her current demand for a completed family of a certain size are illustrated in
Figure 1.   This figure illustrates those variable sets (2) or "factors"
that the microeconomic theory identifies as being central to the determination of the woman's demand for children (3).

Although the model presented is designed to be as comprehensive as
possible, it is difficult to present a model that can be immediately
applied to any particular third world setting.   The economic model,
like any other, must be adapted to the culture and institutions being
studied and this may require substantial changes in terminology and
viewpoint.   We will, for example, refer to "marriage," "husband," and
"wife" throughout this discussion even though for a number of cultures
this terminology and viewpoint will be inaccurate.   The purpose of this
discussion, however, is to illustrate the features of the socioeconomic
model and to demonstrate how it may be modified to encompass the
special conditions present in different settings.

Because a woman acquires her children over time, her intentions regarding the size of the completed family are subject to change, both as
a result of changes in factors that determine her demand for children
and as a consequence of her experience with children of early parity.
Therefore, life cycle models that characterize a woman as choosing a
completed family size early in the reproductive life cycle and then
maintaining that intention over a fifteen to twenty year period are
probably doing considerable violence to the facts of reproductive

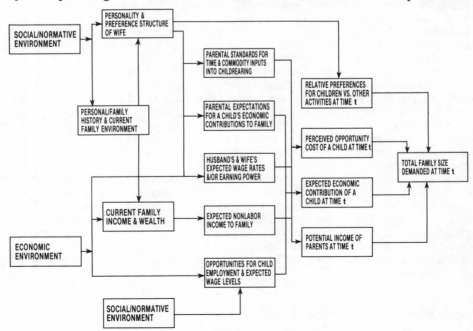

Figure 1.   A woman's demand for children at time t.

decision making. The static theory of consumer behavior requires that consumption decisions be based on the set of decision factors that are operative at the time of the decision; if those factors change, then consumer behavior can be expected to change. Consequently, the decision model in Figure 1 characterizes a woman's situation at a point in time, recognizing that as time passes the factors that affect her choices may change, causing her to revise her intentions.

THE UTILITY MAXIMIZATION MODEL. The microeconomic theory of fertility characterizes an individual woman as choosing a completed family size that, together with a set of activities not related to child rearing, leads to her greatest perceived happiness. Because children require time and market goods and services, this choice is constrained by the resources available to the decision unit.

The theory of constrained maximization identifies four variable groups, or factors, that directly influence the demand for children: relative preferences for child rearing versus other activities, the opportunity cost or price of a child as perceived by the parent, the expected economic contribution of a child, and the potential income available to the family. If the demand for children changes, at least one of these four factors must also have changed, and these immediate decision factors serve as the paths through which all external factors must affect family size choices.

In standard models of consumer behavior, and in some microeconomic theories of fertility, attention to determinants of demand stops with a consideration of prices and income. Relative preferences are often assumed to be homogeneous or randomly distributed in the population, and therefore cápable of being ignored in statistical analyses. However, a number of economists (Easterlin, 1969; Leibenstein, 1975; Turchi, 1975) and sociologists (Blake, 1968; Ryder, 1976; Goldberg, 1975) have forcefully made the case that to limit analysis to the study of prices and incomes and their effect on fertility would be a major error for several reasons.

First, since reproductive behavior occurs in a particular sociocultural setting, a primary goal of fertility researchers is to understand the relationship between that setting and reproductive behavior. Not only is this relationship often the primary focus of scholarly interest, it is also the channel through which public policy may have an effect on fertility. Rural development policy, for example, often affects directly the social and economic context that only indirectly alters the demand for children. Therefore, in order to understand the fertility impact of development policy, it is necessary to understand the connections between the socioeconomic environment, the immediate decision factors, and the demand for children.

In addition, there is a practical reason for understanding the linkages between the social, cultural, and economic context and the immediate decision factors. These factors are often unmeasured or poorly measured in the available data, and attribute variables such as education, occupation, or race, and community level variables such as wage levels, distribution of wealth and income, occupational structure, or health conditions are often by necessity employed as proxies for them. Without a theory that attempts to explain the various paths through which these proxies may operate, interpretation of statistical analyses of fertility data is liable to be unsystematic, ad hoc, and incomplete.

ENVIRONMENTAL LINKS WITH THE CONSUMER MODEL. The basic economic model of fertility consists of four immediate decision factors: (a) relative preferences for children versus other activities, (b) perceived opportunity costs of children, (c) expected economic contributions of children, and (d) potential income of the parents at the time(s) decisions are made. These four factors are defined to be the only paths through which the demand for total family size can be altered. All other determinants operating out of the social and economic environment in which a person resides must act through them. The connections between the socioeconomic environment and these immediate decision factors ought to be subjected to intense study, and we now sketch some important theoretical relationships that should be examined.

Relative Preferences for Children. A woman's relative preferences for children are determined by her own personality and preference structure, which is, in turn, determined to some degree by her current family environment and family history (Figure 1). In turn, the social/normative environment affects family preferences and the woman's preferences directly. Consequently, the economic model is open to systematic influence by noneconomic factors operating through relative preferences. Economists and others who ignore noneconomic factors are making the (acknowledged or unacknowledged) assumption that the impact of these factors on relative preferences is either uniform or random. This assumption may be a reasonable starting point in the study of demand for small consumer durables or nondurables, but, given the strong social and psychological role of children in most societies, it seems to be especially problematic with respect to the study of fertility determinants. The decision-theoretic model of Figure 1 explicitly displays the hypothesized linkages by which social/normative factors ultimately may affect the demand for children (4).

Perceived Opportunity Cost of a Child. The economic theory of fertility postulates that a woman approaches child rearing with a set of expectations and standards regarding the opportunity cost, in terms of parental time and financial resources, of a child. In particular, she is hypothesized to possess a set of standards regarding the quantity and quality of time necessary for child rearing; the types, quality, and quantity of market goods and services necessary for child rearing; and a sense of the extent to which the various inputs into the child rearing process may be traded off. This set of standards (Figure 1) is formally analogous to the economist's notion of a production function for children, where instead of technology the production function consists of the social norms and biological requirements that limit the range of options open to parents in child rearing.

To the extent that these standards vary across social, geographic, ethnic, or religious groups, it is necessary to consider the social and economic environment that produces a particular perception of the opportunity cost of a child. Figure 1 presents a schematic view suggesting that the social/normative environment, operating through an individual's preference structure and through the family, determines the production function ("parental standards" box) for children, while the economic environment determines the prices of time and market commodities required in the production of children. Clearly, systematic differences in these prices between locations may lead to systematic differentials in the opportunity cost of a child and, ultimately, in fertility. As many authors have perceived, but infrequently documented, rural/urban differentials in fertility in the third world may be due in large part to differences in the opportunity cost of children.

Expected Economic Contribution of a Child. Likewise, environmental factors play a major role in determining the scope of a child's economic contribution to the family. Recently, a number of authors have begun to describe the economic contributions that children make to their families in different third world settings (Nag, 1976; Cain, 1977; Caldwell, 1977; Nag et al., 1978; Evenson et al., 1980; Tilakaratne, 1978; Khuda, 1980; Mueller, 1976), and have thereby alerted students of fertility to another difference in reproductive motivation between the third world and industrial societies. The model of Figure 1 suggests that social norms operating directly and through the family determine parental expectations regarding the economic return of their children.
The economic environment also plays a major role in determining the value of children's economic contributions. The labor market determines the extent of availability of jobs for children and the wage rates that they might receive. The kind of agriculture practiced, the level of technology, the capital stock in place, etc., all determine the value of contributions to home production that children can make. Again, geographical differentials in fertility may be linked significantly to differentials in the potential economic contribution of children. The potential importance of rural development policy in affecting the economic value of children should also be obvious.

Potential Income of Parents. The size of the family that can be supported by a couple is ultimately constrained by the economic resources available to it for consumption purposes. The "potential income" block of Figure 1 represents that collection of variables that determines the maximum value of resources available over the couple's life cycle, and it is this value that constrains the family size that can be supported (5).
Clearly the social/normative and economic environments play an important role in determining the potential income of the parental household. The labor market determines the wage rates available to husband and wife, the availability of jobs, and the constraints placed on women in the labor force. The land tenure system, size of the capital stock, fertility of the land and market prices for agricultural products determine the productivity, hence the implicit wages, of men

and women in agriculture. In addition, family structure and the social
relationships between families of orientation and families of procreation
determine the extent of economic assistance that the latter will receive from the former.

It is important to note, however, that the impact of income or
wealth upon fertility depends fundamentally upon the price of children.
Income serves as a constraint upon family size only to the extent that
children are costly to rear. Much of the research upon determinants of
fertility, both in the third world and in the industrial countries has
focussed upon income with little or no reference to the price of a
child. The results are, understandably, inconclusive, because the role
of income in determining fertility levels and differentials cannot be
adequately assessed in the absence of specific attention to the role of
the price of a child in determining fertility levels.

A Sequential Model of Reproductive Behavior

The static consumer model of economic theory assumes that the
desired level of consumption can be attained in any given time period.
When applied to reproductive behavior this assumption is no longer
tenable since children are acquired sequentially. Hence, even though a
woman may, at any point in time, have an idea of her optimum completed family size, she may be able to undertake behavior that achieves
only part of her goal. Consequently, the goal of the fertility researcher is often to describe or predict behavior over a time period that is
too short to allow achievement of an optimum family size. The sequential model of Figure 2 shows the manner in which the static model
can be modified to account for reproductive behavior over time.

The model of Figure 2 suggests that eventual family size goals at a
point in time are potentially important determinants of the demand for
children in the immediate future. Other factors, however, also play a
role in determining short-run reproductive behavior, the most important
being the set of variables labelled "reproductive history." These
factors, including such variables as length of open birth interval,
experience with fetal, neonatal, postneonatal, or child deaths, fecundity, previous complications in pregnancy, and breastfeeding status will
be important determinants of the timing of a subsequent birth.

Other factors can influence the short-run demand for a birth, in
particular the competing demands for a woman's time. For example, a
woman may strongly desire another pregnancy in the immediate future,
but, because she is a recent migrant to a city, be forced to postpone
pregnancy while working in the labor market in order to assist in the
acquisition of housing for the family. Issues such as this suggest that
in any particular time period, the demand for an additional birth
affects the demand for competing activities and vice versa. Note also
that the model suggests that the short-run demand for an additional
birth may be significantly affected by the demands of spouse and
extended family members or other important acquaintances. Thus pressure regarding family size may influence not only the demand for a
completed family, but for the timing of births as well.

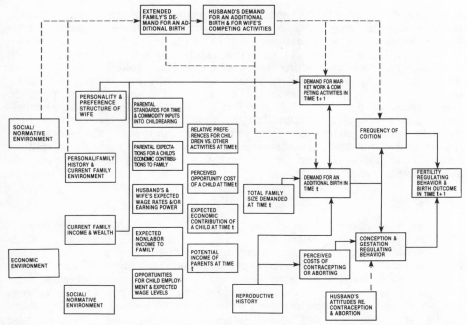

Figure 2. A sequential model of fertility and reproductive behavior: time t to t+1.

At any point, therefore, a woman's demand for an additional birth may range the continuum from a strong desire for the birth, through indifference, to a strong aversion. The strength of the demand for an additional birth will determine in large part a woman's conception and gestation regulating behavior, and possibly, the frequency of sexual intercourse with her husband. Ultimately, therefore, whether or not a birth occurs in the immediate future depends upon a woman's fecundity, the frequency with which she engages in sexual intercourse, and the measures she takes to prevent conception or gestation (6).

As was discussed previously, the vast bulk of resources spent on fertility programs in the third world has been in the area of conception and gestation control. Publicly and privately funded efforts alike have concentrated upon the tasks of improving the distribution of contraceptives, developing new methods that are safer, more effective, and less esthetically disruptive, and toward extending the availability of improved methods of abortion and sterilization. The goal, in terms of Figure 2, has been to reduce the perceived costs of contraception or abortion so that women will be better able to act to achieve their family size intentions. For the most part, the focus of these programs has been supply-side oriented. Even at this relatively late date very little is known about the precise factors that influence the demand for children and, by extension, the demand for contraception. It should be clear from Figures 1 and 2 that the demand for children is expressed out of a complex cultural milieu, and that even if the psychosocial and economic costs of fertility control were reduced to practically nothing, there would in many parts of the third world continue to exist a pervasive demand for large families.

Finally, Figure 2 attempts to make explicit the context within which reproductive decision making takes place. The broken lines show the influence that spouse, members of extended family and friends may have on the intentions and behavior of a woman at any particular point in time (Ben Porath, 1980). Clearly the cooperation (or at least acquiescence) of the spouse is fundamental in determining the success with which a woman undertakes family planning, and the influence of the spouse and other members of the family or social network are of potentially major importance in determining the nature of birth outcomes in a particular period of time.

Summary

The socioeconomic model outlined in this section offers a comprehensive and flexible framework for viewing reproductive behavior. It is based upon the postulate that, even in very traditional societies, reproductive behavior is an allocative process that is influenced directly by a set of well defined decision factors that are, in turn, affected by a host of social/normative and economic factors external to the actors. The socioeconomic model provides a set of hypothesized paths by which the social/normative and economic environments may influence the demand for children and short-run reproductive behavior.

The model is flexible because it is capable of incorporating a wide range of analytical frameworks in a consistent and coherent manner. It is able to provide a theoretical structure for "demographic transition theory" by offering an explanation about how secular changes in society and economy work to alter the fertility of individuals. It provides a link for the normative theories of sociologists (Freedman, 1974; Ryder, 1976) by postulating a set of immediate decision factors that are influenced by normative variables and that in turn directly affect fertility. The biosocial models of Davis and Blake (1956) and Bongaarts (1978) are also compatible with the extended sequential model of Figure 2. Ultimately, a model such as this is useful because it provides a unified framework within which the contributions of researchers working out of quite different research paradigms can be synthesized.

Moreover, the socioeconomic model offers a guide to data collection, because it specifies precise areas in which data needs arise and it emphasizes the sorts of connections that researchers ought to be attempting to make in their analysis of fertility data. In the following section an attempt is made to specify more precisely the sorts of variables that a researcher studying rural fertility determinants might wish to collect.

VARIABLES IMPLIED BY THE SOCIOECONOMIC MODEL

In a general exposition such as this it would not seem to be particularly wise to attempt to list all of the variables that one should collect in order to study fertility. Not only would this leave the author vulnerable to the reader's dissatisfaction that a "particularly important set of variables" has been omitted, but it pays no regard to the fact that research questions must be precisely formulated before a list of variables to be collected can be developed.

Moreover, the list of potential variables that might be included is essentially infinite, even in the most narrowly restrictive economic model. For example, a model of demand for a commodity should, according to the economic theory of the consumer, contain income, relative prices, and, possibly, relative preferences, as explanatory variables. However, theory offers no guidance at all as to how large the list of relative prices or the set of relative preferences should be. Moreover, when the economic model of fertility is extended as in Figure 1 to include community-level and family-level variables, the problem of where to stop collecting data becomes paramount.

However, the attractions of the economic model lie not so much in its ability to specify precisely the variables to be collected, but in its categorization of the types of variables that should be collected and its emphasis on the linkages between the sets of variables. Clearly researchers operating in geographically and culturally diverse places might develop lists of variables that superficially bear little common resemblance; however, if those various data sets have been collected using the socioeconomic model as a framework, researchers should be able to relate their data to that framework in a way that allows a rigorous comparison of research findings in a way not often currently possible.

Table 1 is offered, therefore, not so much as a definitive list of variables that every fertility researcher ought to try to collect, but as a list suggestive of the kinds of variables that characterize each box in Figures 1 and 2 and as a basis for a brief discussion of the sorts of interconnections pictured there that a researcher should seek to explain.

Table 1 is organized into four main divisions that correspond to groups of boxes in Figures 1 and 2: (a) community level factors affecting demand for completed family size; (b) family level factors; (c) individual decision factors; (d) factors affecting reproductive behavior and birth outcomes in a subsequent time period. Each division contains sections corresponding to the boxes in Figures 1 and 2, and each section contains variables that are candidates for collection and analysis because they measure to some degree the theoretical concepts represented by the boxes.

Again, it is important to emphasize that the primary purpose of fertility research is often to illuminate the causal chain that connects events or conditions in the society or economy with reproductive behavior. The socioeconomic model of fertility presented in Figures 1 and 2 represents a theoretical view of how differentials arise and how rates change over time. The corresponding variables in Table 1 are suggested by the model and should be collected in a form that will facilitate the analysis of the interrelationships specified in the diagrams.

Table 1. Variable List for Comprehensive Fertility Model

COMMUNITY LEVEL FACTORS AFFECTING THE DEMAND FOR
COMPLETED FAMILY SIZE

Social/Normative Environment
    Family structure (nuclear, extended, etc.)
    Social role of children and parents
    Educational opportunities for males and females at given ages
    Important reference groups: castes, tribes, racial groups, religious
       groups, occupational groups
    Evidence of recent rapid social change? Social mobility?
    Determinants of prestige
    Women's role in family and society
    Locus of political power. Children's contribution to political power

    Demographic context
       Sex ratio
       Marriage market conditions, local, regional
       Population density
       Prevailing age of entry into sexual unions
       Types of sexual unions
       Stability of sexual unions

    Health environment
       Mortality conditions
       Morbidity conditions
       Nutrition levels

Economic Environment
    Labor market conditions
       Options for women of relevant age/wage rates
       Options for men of relevant age/wage rates
       Aggregate unemployment levels and trends: local, regional, national
       Market vs. traditional employment options
       Geographic labor mobility patterns
       Child labor restrictions and opportunities/wage rates
       Seasonality of labor demand

    Geographical and production environment
       Types of agriculture practiced and labor required (especially child
         labor)
       Growth potential for agriculture
       Types of nonagricultural production activities

    Macroeconomic framework
       Income and wealth levels: local, regional, national
       Distribution of income and wealth
       Land tenure system
       Economic growth rates and prospects: local, regional, national

Table 1. Cont.

Housing supply: size, price, quantity
Organization of enterprises (family vs. other)
Consumption alternatives available

FAMILY LEVEL FACTORS

Personal/Family History and Current Family Environment
Family of orientation
Racial/ethnic identification
Number of children
Social prestige
Religion/degree of religiosity
Occupation of head
Region of origin/migration history
Wealth

Current family situation/background of subject
Education
Occupational qualifications
Age
Living with own or spouse's family of orientation?
Personal migration history
Locus of decision making power in household

Current family income and wealth
Assets: financial, land, other
Access to assets of extended family
Current income by source and person:
Income from self employment: agriculture, other
Wage income
Asset income

INDIVIDUAL DECISION FACTORS DETERMINING DEMAND FOR
CHILDREN

Relative Preferences for Children vs. Other Activities
List of available alternative activities:
Consumption activities and labor market opportunities
Relative preference measures: child rearing vs. alternatives

Perceived Opportunity Cost of a Child
Required parental time inputs into child rearing
Required commodity inputs into child rearing: e.g., housing, food,
clothing, education, etc.
Prices of goods and services required in child rearing
Opportunity value of time required in child rearing

Table 1. Cont.

_____

Expected Economic Contribution of a Child
  Jobs that a child can/will perform: in home, market
  Age at which economic contribution begins
  Probability that contribution will actually be forthcoming
  Quantitative estimates of present value of contribution

Potential Income of Parents
  Present value of income from assets
  Present value of maximum parental income from wage labor
  Present value of income from gifts, transfers, etc.

Total Family Size Demanded at a Particular Stage in Reproductive Life
  Cycle

FACTORS AFFECTING REPRODUCTIVE BEHAVIOR AND BIRTH
OUTCOME

Frequency of Coition

Conception and Gestation Regulating Behavior
  Use/nonuse of contraceptives, by type
  Sterilized?
  Attitude toward and use of abortion

Costs of Contraception or Abortion
  Information costs: level of knowledge of available methods and their
    effectiveness
  Perceived health effects of relevant methods
  Perceived psychic costs of relevant methods
  Access costs: costs of acquiring methods (time, money, psychosocial)

Demand for an Additional Birth/Strength of Desire to Avoid Pregnancy

Reproductive History
  Parity (and number of sons)
  Family planning use history
  History of fetal, infant, child deaths
  Age of entry into sexual union
  Fecundity

Demand for Market Work and Competing Activities

Spouse and Family Influences on Reproductive Behavior
  Husband's attitudes regarding contraception and abortion
  Husband's demand for an additional birth
  Husband's demand for wife's participation in competing activities
  Extended family's demands for additional birth(s)

_____

GUIDES FOR DATA COLLECTION AND ANALYSIS

Implications of Misspecification

Many social scientists who use quantitative methods appear to understand only partially that estimation of incomplete models leads to inferences that are biased and unreliable. For example, it is not uncommon to find studies in the fertility literature that attempt to determine the impact of "income" on family size (7). Some of those studies, in effect, regress a measure of fertility on family income and label the resulting slope coefficient the "effect" of income on fertility. However, the socioeconomic model specifies that other variables such as relative preferences, opportunity cost and expected economic contributions of children all have a role to play in determining fertility levels. If the opportunity cost (price) of a child is omitted from a regression analysis in which income is included, the resulting regression coefficient on income may well be biased. Bias can be expected to occur because the price of a child and family income are likely to be related to each other and to fertility. If price is omitted while income is retained, the net effect is to produce an income coefficient that is biased toward zero (8).

Thus, even ostensibly simple models do not escape the problems that arise with misspecification, and a complete theoretical model is useful even if one cannot collect all the data that the model requires. It allows the analyst to assess the expected direction of bias that will occur when theoretically important variables are omitted (Turchi, in press).

Decision Criteria for Data Collection

Although the main purpose of development of a comprehensive theory of fertility is to identify all those theoretical variables that are potentially important, it is also useful in helping the researcher reduce the size of the data collection effort. Budget limitations usually make it impossible to collect all the variables required by a comprehensive theory of fertility. Each variable that is collected, therefore, becomes a precious commodity that has been selected over competing items. If the data collection instrument has not been designed with an explicit theoretical model in mind, it is likely that resources will be wasted in collecting data that overlap extensively, are poor measures of theoretical variables of interest, and that contain crucial gaps in coverage.

The socioeconomic model assists in the data collection process by forcing researchers to consider explicitly every theoretical factor. When decisions must be made regarding the paring of the set of variables to be collected, the model offers guidelines for excluding potentially relevant data. First, the variables proposed for measurement of each factor (9) can be examined for duplication in order to reduce the number collected for each. Second, the analyst can search the set of factors for those factors that, in a particular research context, will exhibit no variation and will, therefore, contribute little or nothing to explanation. For example, if in a study of rural fertility the home production responsibilities of all children in the population are virtually identical, factors dealing with the expected economic contribution of children may be safely omitted from the data set collected for that study.   Consequently, the informed elimination of theoretical factors and the careful "thinning" of the variable sets remaining is made easier and more precise if a comprehensive model serves as the basis for these activities.

Research Design

Careful attention to theory will also salvage research from the effects of faulty research design. One of the reasons that there are so few examples of rural development/fertility research available at the household level is that the appropriate data are rarely present.   In assessing the impact of rural development programs on reproductive behavior, the analyst ideally should have experimental data.   These data should provide a set of baseline measures before the policy is implemented and should supply a set of post-policy measures at appro-priate intervals after the policy has had a chance to be effective. Moreover, these measures are required both for the population being subjected to the policy and for control populations.   In laboratory experiments, assignment to treatment and control groups can be ran-domized, and the resulting statistical analyses often are quite simple as a consequence.

Rural development and fertility data rarely even approximate the laboratory standard.   Most often the data available have not been collected with policy analysis in mind; even when they have, they fall far short of the ideal experimental situation because: (a) no baseline data are available; (b) data have been collected only in the area affected by the policy so that there are no control groups; or (c) if there are control groups, assignment to them is not randomized and systematic differences remain.   In each of these cases a well-articu-lated and comprehensive theory offers virtually the only means by which to interpret the data. The weaker the experimental design, the more important it is that theory guide the data analysis, because only then can some idea be had of the possible direction of the biases present therein.

Even when the analyst has the funds and the time to collect data, careful attention to theory will pay dividends, not only with respect to variable selection but with respect to choice of policy sites and con-trol areas. The better the theoretical preparation, the more likely it will be that the sites surveyed will be comparable and that remaining differences will be adequately controlled through multivariate analysis (10).

RURAL DEVELOPMENT POLICY AND FERTILITY

Figures 1 and 2 suggest numerous opportunities for household-level research designed to relate rural development programs to reproductive behavior. However, human fertility and rural development policy are rarely connected in research at the household level. Research at an aggregate level, reviewed more fully elsewhere in this volume, is somewhat more plentiful and it provides useful perspectives from which to develop micro-level studies. Mueller and Anderson (1982), for example, undertake a retrospective study of the fertility effects of the Comilla Project in East Pakistan (now Bangladesh). Using aggregate data from a variety of sources, they employ a theoretical framework in order to sort out the conflicting demographic effects of development policy. Herrin (1979) employs a simple socioeconomic framework to interpret the effects of rural electrification programs in Mindanao. He must also employ data from a variety of sources and the theoretical framework serves as a means to supply missing links that the available data do not provide.

Because of the lack of examples of household-level research available in the literature, we will limit our discussion to some "as if" theorizing of the sort undertaken by Jain (1982) with respect to education sector policies and fertility in India. We will now consider a hypothetical nation with two regions that have high fertility rates (11).

Water Reclamation Project

Suppose that a water reclamation project in a district leads to a major increase in the availability of water for irrigation. What are the predicted impacts upon fertility? First, it is to be expected that the additional availability of water will have an important impact on the economy. If it is an agricultural area, the water project may lead to changes in the crops planted and/or in the kinds of agricultural cultivation practiced. To the extent that labor requirements are changed (assume that the demand for field labor increases), the role and economic value of a child in a household will also change. The expected contribution of a child to household production might increase and the value of the child's contribution might also increase. Consequently, the expected economic contribution of a child may rise and, ceteris paribus, a family's demand for children might also rise. The socioeconomic model suggests the causal reasoning just presented and it suggests the sorts of variables that might be collected to pursue that reasoning.

Mandatory Schooling

Suppose that the fertility effects of a new policy mandating school attendance to age fifteen in another region of the country are the subject of study. How might the socioeconomic model be used to address the issue? The analyst might reason as follows: provision of mandatory schooling is a significant change in the social/normative environment that might lead to revised expectations about the social role of children and delayed entry into marriage, among others. In addition, a child's economic contribution to the family might be reduced in the near term because of school time required (12). Likewise, the attendance of children at school might imply additional money expenditures on clothing, school supplies, etc., that would lead to a rise in the opportunity cost of a child. The net hypothesized effect might well be a decline in the demand for children in the district and, over time, the decline in demand might well be reflected in lower fertility rates.

Introduction of a New Family Planning Program

In the two regions described above, the Ministry of Health plans to make a major improvement in the delivery of family planning services by opening new clinics and introducing new methods, with the intended result that the economic and psychic costs of fertility regulation will be reduced. How successful will the programs be in reducing fertility rates? Clearly the answers might be considerably different, depending upon the region in question. In the region containing the water reclamation project, fertility rates might not decline at all because of a general rise in the demand for children. On the other hand, the new family planning program may have a major impact in the second region because the demand for children is declining, and the reduction of the cost of fertility limitation is complementary to that trend in demand. As the socioeconomic model makes explicit, the fertility effects of family planning programs depend both upon the nature of the programs and upon the strength of demand for improved means of fertility reduction.

The variables listed in Table 1 represent the sorts of variables that an individual researcher might select for analysis on the basis of the socioeconomic model. Each researcher must, of course, determine the variables to be collected and analyzed based on an extensive consideration of the research questions that are to be proposed. Figures 1 and 2 emphasize the factors that, in general, should be considered in the analysis of fertility and it is the researcher's responsibility to collect the appropriate empirical variables in a way that facilitates the analysis of the causal interconnections between them.

CONCLUSIONS

Vast sums of public funds are spent annually in the third world on projects designed to increase the rate of economic development. A significant proportion of these funds are targeted either to rural development programs or to fertility reduction programs without any real understanding of the mutual impacts that these programs have on each other. This chapter has attempted to examine this issue and to suggest ways to approach policy relevant research on rural fertility. It makes the fundamental point that this research requires a theoretical framework capable of delineating the paths by which rural development policy can affect an individual household's reproductive behavior.

Prevailing social demographic and economic theories of fertility are in many ways inadequate, the former because they do not deal directy with variables affected by rural development policy and the latter because they often ignore the social and economic environment within which reproductive decision making takes place. The theoretical framework presented here attempts to correct both these deficiencies. It explicitly recognizes that, even in traditional cultures, reproductive behavior can profitably be characterized as a resource allocation process; on the other hand, it delineates the paths through which a society, economy, and government can alter the outcomes of that process. Finally, it unifies population policy research by integrating the analysis of the demand for children with the analysis of supply-side factors that determine the nature and cost of the reproductive control methods supplied by public agencies.

A comprehensive theoretical framework also allows the effective collection of relevant data. Because it defines the hierarchy of causal factors, it forces the researcher to collect appropriate data in a coherent and organized manner. Table 1 illustrates the sorts of variables that ought to be collected in order to analyze the effects of public policy on fertility. This list is, of course, only suggestive; however, the purpose of a comprehensive model is to provide a framework from which specific applications can be tailored. The list itself is impossibly large for any particular study, but it provides the basis by which smaller studies can be performed without introduction of bias and a resulting loss of causal interpretability.

Many analysts will not, of course, have access to specially collected data sets and it is in this case that a well articulated theoretical model becomes even more essential. Use of secondary data for fertility policy analysis requires a rigorous assessment of the quality and suitability of such data. This assessment can be undertaken only in the context of a theoretical model that provides a standard against which judgments can be made. Then the problems inherent in nonexperimental data analysis can be minimized, and a better understanding of the relationship between rural development and fertility can be achieved.

NOTES

1. Bulatao and Lee (1983) provide a comprehensive review of the determinants of fertility in developing countries.
2. Each box in Figure 1 represents a collection of empirical variables that together measure the influence of a particular theoretical variable. Each collection of variables in a box will be termed a "decision factor" in the discussion that follows, partly for purposes of expositional clarity and partly to acknowledge that the empirical researcher is often obligated to create indexes representing theoretical magnitudes out of collections of variables. The variables that might be contained in each box will be described more fully in the following section.
3. An analogous model can be developed for the woman's spouse.
4. Specific attention is given to the contents of the boxes discussed here later on in this chapter.
5. We are implicitly assuming here that children represent a net economic drain on their parents. Although there is accumulating evidence that children in many third world settings do provide an

economic return that somewhat offsets their demands on the family budget, we find Mueller's (1976) conclusion that children still represent a net drain to be convincing.

6. The reader will recognize that the variables just mentioned constitute the bulk of the well known intermediate variables (Davis and Blake, 1956). Missing in this discussion are the variables concerning formation and maintenance of sexual unions that also form a part of the Davis-Blake framework.

7. We ignore here the serious problems accompanying the proper measurement of income in fertility analysis (Mueller and Cohn, 1977).

8. See for example Turchi, 1975, pp. 57-58.

9. A factor, remember, is represented by each box in Figures 1 and 2.

10. See Turchi (in press) for a discussion of statistical problems associated with policy relevant fertility research.

11. These examples are extremely abbreviated and lacking in institutional realism. They are meant to illustrate the kind of reasoning that might motivate a researcher's analysis of rural development programs and reproductive behavior.

12. Of course, the long-term expected contribution of the child may rise also. Ideally, the researcher would attempt to acquire information on both the near and longer terms.

REFERENCES

Becker, G.S. 1960. An economic analysis of fertility. In: Demographic and Economic Change in Developed Countries (Universities-National Bureau of Economic Research), pp. 209-231. Princeton: Princeton University Press.

Ben Porath, Y. 1980. The F-Connection: Families, friends, and firms and the organization of exchange. Population and Development Review 6:1-30.

Blake, J. 1968. Are babies consumer durables? Population Studies 22: 5-25.

Bongaarts, J. 1978. A framework for analyzing the proximate determinants of fertility. Population and Development Review 4:105-132.

Bulatao, R.A. and R.D. Lee (eds.). 1983. Determinants of Fertility in Developing Countries: A Survey of Knowledge, 1983 (two volumes). New York: Academic Press.

Cain, M.T. 1977. The economic activities of children in rural Bangladesh. Population and Development Review 3:201-227.

Caldwell, J.C. 1977. The economic rationality of high fertility: An investigation illustrated with Nigerian survey data. Population Studies 31:785-830.

Davis, K. and J. Blake. 1956. Social structure and fertility: An analytical framework. Economic Development and Cultural Change 4: 211-235.

Easterlin, R.A. 1969. Towards a socioeconomic theory of fertility. In: S.J. Behrman, L. Corsa, Jr., and R. Freedman (eds.) Fertility and

Family Planning, pp. 127-156. Ann Arbor: University of Michigan Press.

_____ 1978. The economics and sociology of fertility: A synthesis. In: C. Tilly (ed.) Historical Studies of Changing Fertility, pp. 127-156. Princeton: Princeton University Press.

_____, R.A. Pollack, and M.L. Wachter. 1980. Toward a more general economic model of fertility determination: Endogenous preferences and natural fertility. In: R.A. Easterlin (ed.) Population and Economic Change in Developing Countries, pp. 81-149. Chicago: University of Chicago Press.

Espenshade, T.J. 1977. The value and cost of children. Population Bulletin 32:1-47.

Evenson, R.E., B.M. Popkin, and E.K. Quizon. 1980. Nutrition, work, and demographic behavior in rural Philippine households: A synopsis of several Laguna household studies. In: H.P. Binswanger, R. Evenson, C. Florencio, and B. White (eds.) Rural Household Studies in Asia. Singapore: Singapore University Press.

Freedman, R. 1974. The Sociology of Human Fertility: An Annotated Bibliography. New York: Seminar Press.

Goldberg, D. 1975. Socioeconomic theory and differential fertility: The case of LDC's. Social Forces 54:84-106.

Herrin, A. 1979. Rural electrification and fertility change in the southern Philippines. Population and Development Review 5:61-86.

Ilchman, W.F. 1975. Population knowledge and fertility policies. In: W.F. Ilchman, H.D. Lasswell, J.D. Montgomery, and M. Weiner (eds.) Policy Sciences and Population. Lexington, Massachusetts: Heath-Lexington Books.

Jain, A.K. 1982. Education sector policies, educational attainment and fertility: A case study for India. In: R. Barlow (ed.) Case Studies in the Demographic Impact of Asian Development Projects. Ann Arbor: Center for Research on Economic Development, University of Michigan.

Khuda, B. 1980. Time Allocation Among People in Rural Bangladesh. Development Research and Action Programme Publications No. 101. Bergen, Norway: The Chr. Michelsen Institute.

Leibenstein, H. 1957. Economic Backwardness and Economic Growth. New York: John Wiley and Sons.

_____ 1975. The economic theory of fertility decline. Quarterly Journal of Economics 89:1-31.

Mueller, E. 1976. The economic value of children in peasant agriculture. In: R. Ridker (ed.) Population and Development: The Search for Selective Interventions, pp. 98-153. Baltimore: Johns Hopkins University Press.

_____ and R. Cohn. 1977. The relation of income to fertility decisions in Taiwan. Economic Development and Cultural Change 25: 325-347.

_____ and J. Anderson. 1982. The economic and demographic impact of the Comilla Project in Bangladesh: A case study. In: R. Barlow (ed.) Case Studies in the Demographic Impact of Asian Development Projects. Ann Arbor: Center for Research on Economic Development, University of Michigan.

Nag, M. 1976.   Economic value of children in agricultural societies: A review and proposal.   In: J.F. Marshall and S.F. Polgar (eds.) Culture, Natality and Family Planning, pp. 3-23.   Chapel Hill: Carolina Population Center.

_____, B.N.F. White, and R.C. Peet. 1978.   An Anthropological Approach to the Study of Economic Value of Children in Java and Nepal.   New York: Population Council Working Paper No. 11.

Ryder, N.B. 1976.   Some Sociological Suggestions Concerning the Reduction of Fertility in the Developing Countries.   Paper No. 37 of the East-West Population Institute.   Honolulu: East-West Population Institute.

Tilakaratne, M.W. 1978.   Economic change, social differentiation, and fertility: Aluthgana.   In: G. Hawthorn (ed.) Population and Development, pp. 186-197.   London: Frank Cass.

Turchi, B.A. 1975.   The Demand for Children: The Economics of Fertility in the United States.   Cambridge: Ballinger Publishing Co.

_____ In press.   The specification and estimation of models of fertility.   In: G.M. Farooq and G.B. Simmons (eds.) Fertility in Developing Countries: An Economic Perspective on Research and Policy Issues. Geneva: International Labour Office.

Willis, R.J. 1973.   A new approach to the economic theory of fertility behavior.   Journal of Political Economy 81(2, Part II), March/April: S14-S64.

CHAPTER 7

Income, Aspirations, and Fertility in Rural Areas of Less Developed Countries

Eva Mueller

Rural development, almost by definition, implies higher incomes among the rural population. The purpose of this chapter is to examine the effect of changing income on fertility in rural areas, giving particular attention to two variables which intervene between income and fertility: educational aspirations and consumption aspirations. Aspirations are not the only things that change when income rises. For example, infant mortality, female labor supply, and people's sense of security may be affected and may in turn alter reproductive behavior. These other intervening variables are largely disregarded here in order to limit the focus of the chapter and to allow the aspirations link to be examined in greater depth.

Accordingly, the first part of this chapter is devoted to the income/fertility relation in rural areas of less developed countries (LDC). It appears that in rural areas at the micro level the effect of income on fertility is nonlinear: positive at low levels of income and negative at relatively high levels. The second part of this chapter deals with educational aspirations and the so-called quantity/quality trade-off. It will be shown that the conventional wisdom, which holds that rising educational aspirations lead parents to opt for smaller families, may not always be applicable to poor rural populations. This may be one reason why a demographic transition is slow to appear in such populations. The third part of the chapter examines the hypothesis that a negative income/fertility relation is more likely once a transformation of consumption aspirations has occurred. Aspirations to invest in physical

121

capital, a parallel concept in consumer-producer households, receive only passing attention because they have been almost completely neglected in research and in the literature. Within each section of the chapter some theoretical and methodological issues are discussed, and then followed by a review of the research literature.

A great many empirical studies have examined the effect of income change on fertility in LDCs. Quite diverse results from these studies suggest that this relation may vary from one stage of economic development to the next and from one social and economic context to another. Furthermore, as will become evident, the income/fertility relation is quite complex, and the data sets available for analyzing it are seldom ideally suitable. One is likely to have reservations about much of the empirical work. The task then is to search for whatever regularities may exist in studies using quite different approaches methodologically and conducted in quite different socioeconomic settings. For this reason a broad overview of research results is needed.

The consequences of income change for children's education for consumption, and for fertility are most appropriately observed at the household level where income change affects the consumer choice process. On the other hand, our interest in the income/aspirations/fertility sequence reflects concern with a dynamic process which is believed to reduce the demand for children over time. Cross-sectional data are not ideally suited for a study of dynamic change. Relevant time series are not available. We shall therefore consider some macro-level evidence along with micro-level studies.

INCOME AND FERTILITY

Theoretical and Methodological Considerations

In order to alert the reader to the complexity of the income/fertility relation, a model of this relation is outlined in Figure 1 (1). The model depicts some of the ramifications of this relation without trying to be complete. Most importantly, the model depicts only influences on the demand for children. Supply-side factors such as health, nutrition, age at marriage, and access to contraceptives may be influenced by income, just as the demand side variables are, but are not included in Figure 1.

On the demand side, income acts as a constraint on the family's ability to obtain goods and services that yield utility. Thus when agricultural development provides a family with more income, the family can expand the quantity, quality, and assortment of utilities it acquires, including the utilities derived from children. The pure income effect is here defined as the change in the demand for children which is attributable directly to a change in income (the heavy line on Figure 1). In addition, income change may affect the demand for children indirectly via other variables which are causes of consequences of income change. Important among these indirect effects are those which operate through changes in the value of time, costs of children, aspirations, perceived benefits from children, female and child labor force participation, and

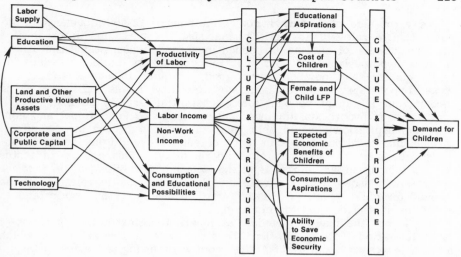

Figure 1. Income and the demand for children. This diagram is illustrative only: more variables and more arrows could have been added.

the family's sense of optimism and security regarding its financial future. The total income effect encompasses both the pure and indirect effects.

A pure income effect can only be observed after the income/demand for children relation has been purged of the impact of price, taste, attitude, and other changes that are causally related to income. Empirical studies cannot completely expurgate the indirect effects, if only because such variables as the value of time invested in children, tastes, and benefits from children are difficult to measure. Thus the pure income effect cannot be readily observed, and our belief that it must be positive rests largely on theoretical grounds, i.e., the implausibility of viewing children as "inferior goods."

The left side of Figure 1 reminds us that, in the larger context of rural development, income itself is an endogenous variable and that the effects of income change may depend on how income is changed and whose income is changed. For example, if rural development raises the value of time, especially women's time, fertility may be reduced while income is enhanced. In view of the focus of this chapter on aspirations, it is important to recognize that technological advances and capital accumulation, in the very process of generating more income, transform the economy. A variety of new and better and/or cheaper consumer goods will be manufactured at home, or their import will be facilitated by the expansion of export industries. Also, the process of economic development creates a need for a more literate and skilled labor force, leading to investments in educational facilities. One hypothesis of this chapter is that, to the extent that these new opportunities emerge in rural areas, they enhance (in conjunction with income increases) consumption and educational aspirations. Such changes in tastes may eventually reduce the demand for children.

The right side of Figure 1 depicts a number of consequences of income change relevant to fertility analysis. Of particular interest here are the effects of income on educational and consumption aspirations. A weak hypothesis would hold that the demand for children's education (child quality) and new consumer goods is quite income-elastic. This weak hypothesis could explain why fertility levels off with rising income, but it cannot account for a substantial fertility decline.

A stronger hypothesis, linking income change to educational and consumption aspirations, would hold that, in addition to the income effect, income change alters tastes in favor of educated children and new consumer goods at the expense of child quantity. This change in tastes implies (among other things) that the demand for child quality becomes progressively more income-elastic and less price-elastic relative to the demand for child quantity. In that case income increases could lead to a decline in the demand for children.

This is not the place to review at length theories of the dynamics of taste formation (Pollak, 1978). The issue here is the extent to which income serves as a catalyst in the process of changing tastes or aspirations. At the macro-level, rising income is associated with the appearance of new consumption opportunities and a more easily accessible and affordable infrastructure including schools, transportation, and communication. Given these stimuli, the initial demand for new goods and services by households may stem from higher incomes, along with relatively attractive prices or, in the case of education, high rates of return. Beyond this, income increases facilitate the diffusion of new consumption and educational standards, since rising income promotes contacts with a larger world and raises people's sights. Rising incomes enable rural people to take trips into town, visit friends or relatives outside the village, buy radios, newspapers, and magazines which acquaint them with new consumption and educational opportunities, small family norms, and fertility control. Or, to put it differently, income increases make new ideas and new opportunities more widely known. In economic terms, they lower information costs. Assuming that consumer preferences are interdependent among families, the acquisition of watches, bicycles, or higher child quality by higher income and urban families creates a demonstration effect. A felt need for these goods and services is then induced among lower- and middle-income families who become acquainted with them. Demand therefore should rise more than the reduction in financial constraints or price changes alone would warrant, i.e., preference functions should be modified at the expense of children and other traditional goods (2). Once higher consumption and educational aspirations are acquired, they may be passed on to the next generation, regardless of the economic fortunes of that generation, as Easterlin (1973) postulates. Thus income advances together with the inter-family and intra-family interdependence of tastes may bring about a secular decline in the demand for children.

The strength of the causal process outlined above, leading from income change via changes in aspirations to changes in fertility, depends (a) on the responsiveness of consumption and educational aspirations to rising income and (b) on the responsiveness of the demand for children to changes in these aspirations. Figure 1 suggests that both kinds of responses are conditioned by cultural factors and the structure of the economy. Coale (1973) and his associates found that in Europe "culture" was an important determinant of the speed of the demographic transition. Likewise it appears that in LDCs structural characteristics of the economy and society may affect rates of fertility decline.

Alternative Income Measures

Before we turn to empirical studies of the income/fertility relation, it is necessary to consider some alternative income measures; for the way income is defined may have important effects on the observed impact of income on fertility.

The first issue concerns the use of current income data, while it is likely that the demand for children is influenced by long-term or "permanent" income. Even if fertility decisions are made sequentially, a commitment to the support of another child is likely to be based on long term income, past and expected. In a cross-section of households, recipients of large current incomes may include a disproportionate number of units with temporarily high incomes and the reverse for recipients of small current incomes. In rural areas land is a proxy for permanent income. The land/fertility relation may therefore yield valuable insights.

A second issue concerns adjustments in income for differences in the size of the receiving unit. If income is to be a measure of welfare or financial latitude, it has to be adjusted for the number of people it supports. A common solution is to measure income on a per capita basis. However, income per capita is affected by the number of children in the household and the labor force participation of wives and children. Unless children are fully self-supporting, dividing income by family size biases the income/demand for children relation in a negative direction. Further, high fertility is likely to reduce the wife's contribution to income, thereby reinforcing the negative bias. The per capita income measure may also introduce a nonlinearity into the income/ fertility relation (Boulier, 1982). In strict logic, household income per capita is an endogenous variable determined simultaneously with the demand for children (Conger and Campbell, 1978).

In an attempt to reduce the negative bias, a few investigators have regressed fertility measures on income per adult or income per member of the labor force rather than on income per capita. Others have used husband's income as a proxy for permanent income, assuming that husband's income is independent of fertility (3). Only a small number of studies relating to LDCs have investigated the income/fertility relation by means of simultaneous equation models.

Empirical Investigations of the Income Effect

The foregoing review of theoretical and methodological issues makes it clear that it is difficult to measure the income/fertility relation statistically in a satisfactory manner. And indeed, empirical studies do

not show a consistently positive or negative effect of income on fertility, and often the measured relation is not statistically significant.   I
believe it would be erroneous to infer that income has no effect on the
demand for children.   For one thing, the inconsistent results may be
due to different methodologies.   Secondly, positive and negative
indirect effects of income on fertility may vary in strength in different
economic and cultural settings.   Consequently, the total impact of
income growth may be positive or negative, depending on the balance
of indirect effects.

The empirical relation between income and fertility may be studied
at the country- or at the household-level.   A recent review of macro-
level studies for LDCs (Mueller and Short, 1983) found that more often
than not the income/fertility relation was not significant.   Among 15
macro-level regressions reviewed where income was significant, its
relation to fertility was positive in 3 cases, negative in 12.

Macro-level studies involve a number of problems which may account
for their inconsistent results.   For one thing, they are handicapped by
the difficulty of obtaining comparable data for a sufficiently large group
of countries which are reasonably homogeneous.   A further problem
arises from the sensitivity of results to the controls used, given the
collinearity between income and various other concomitants of development.   Variables which are exogenous at the household-level but endogenous at the country-level are usually held constant in order to
approximate household-level relationships.   Thus there tend to be
controls for the various determinants of income shown in Figure 1.
Still, there are few studies which treat income as an endogenous
variable and present reduced form as well as structural coefficients.
Likewise, the likelihood that fertility affects per capita income, or is
determined simultaneously with income, is seldom taken into account.
Several of the simultaneous-equation models exhibit a positive, though
not significant, income/fertility relation in contrast to the negative
relation typical of single-equation models.   DaVanzo (1972) and Rosen-
zweig/Evenson (1977) make a distinction between male, female, and
children's wages in their simultaneous equation models (wages acting as
a proxy for income) and find fertility positively related to the male
wage and negatively to the female wage, as the Columbia-Chicago
school postulates.

Two strategies are available for dealing with the consequences of
income change.   One strategy would control for as many consequences
(i.e., indirect effects) as possible in order to approximate a pure
income effect.   An alternative strategy would control only variables
exogenous to household decisions with the aim of measuring the total
income effect, pure and indirect.   Many studies adopt a hybrid approach.   We find controls for some, but not all, of the following: female
labor force participation, child school attendance, newspaper circulation, and child mortality; less frequently we find controls for consumption aspirations, educational aspirations, or age at marriage, although
all these are part of the complex of choices which confronts the household when it earns more income.   Consequently, the income effect
which these studies capture is neither the total nor the pure income

effect. Rather it is a conglomerate of the pure income effect and the indirect income effects via the omitted variables. The likelihood that the omitted variables are sensitive to income change and that on balance they tend to reduce fertility, may be a major reason for the predominance of negative income coefficients at the macro-level.

The distinction between demand for children and fertility tends to be blurred in these models since most of them ignore supply-side influences. Another problem is the specification of the functional relationship between income and fertility. Most studies assume a linear relationship without justifying that choice (4).

Table 1 summarizes some investigations based on household level data, largely for rural areas in developing countries. Most of these studies seem to be intended to measure the total income effect. Common controls are age of wife and/or duration of marriage, education of one or both parents, occupation, and infant or child mortality, variables that are presumably exogenous to the household. Even though these studies tend to focus on the total income effect, most of the significant income coefficients are positive ones (10 out of 15); however, we again see many nonsignificant coefficients.

Among the micro-level results a fairly consistent pattern does however seem to emerge: the relation between income and fertility (usually measured by children every born) is positive in poor rural populations with low life expectancy, but levels off or even becomes negative in rural populations with higher incomes (Table 1). Further, the income/fertility relation tends to be negative in urban populations. There are, however, some exceptions to this generalization, and the results sometimes lack statistical significance. Encarnacion (1974), in a study of Philippine households, was one of the first to show that the income/fertility relation may be positive in rural households, while it is negative in urban households. Encarnacion's negative relation for urban areas is consistent with Ben-Porath's (1973) findings for urban wage earners in Israel, Anker and Knowles' (1982) findings for urban Kenya, Khan and Sirageldin's (1979) results for urban Pakistan (in the TSLS model only), and Schultz's (1981) results for husband's wages in urban Colombia. However, Kelley (1980) obtains a positive relation for urban Kenya and Farooq (1979) for urban Nigeria. Encarnacion's positive relation for rural areas is consistent with Anker's (1977) results for 11 Indian villages, Makhija's (1978) results for a cross-section of households in rural India, Anker and Knowles' (1982) results for rural Kenya, Schultz's for men's wages in rural Colombia, Khan and Sirageldin's for rural Pakistan, Chernichovsky's (1976) for agricultural income and income from unskilled occupations in India, and Chernichovsky's (1981a) findings for rural Botswana.

One may conjecture that in traditional rural areas the rich and the poor are less differentiated in terms of tastes and attitudes than is the case in urban areas. Hence the unmeasured negative indirect effects would be weaker in rural areas.

The evidence regarding a positive income fertility relation in rural areas that have not experienced much development is strengthened by studies of the land size/fertility relation. Measures of land quantity

Table 1. Studies of the Income/Fertility Relation in LDCs, Micro Level

AUTHOR, DATE	SAMPLE	METHOD	FERTILITY	INCOME	SIGN	OTHER VARIABLES INCLUDED
Anker, 1977	India, 11 rural villages, 454 households	MCA	Ideal family size	Income per adult	+[c]	Parent's education, % economic benefit of children, felt economic burden, caste, development level of village, urban contact, ownership of consumer durables, perception of economic change, no. rooms per adult, husband occupation, use of abstinence
			Completed family size		+[c]	
Anker & Knowles, 1982	Kenya, 1888 married women	OLS	CEB	Annual household income per adult	−	Age,* age squared,* parents education,[a] urban residence,[a] parents siblings,[a] wife work experience,[a] average child child school enrollment,[a] educational aspirations,[a] migrant,[a] child survival rate,[a] family planning participation, polygamous,[a] husband's residence,[a] health, breastfeeding experience[a], land,[a] livestock,[a]
	Subgroups Rural n = 1605	OLS	CEB	Annual household income per adult	+	
	Urban n = 283	OLS	CEB	Annual household income per adult	−*	

AUTHOR, DATE	SAMPLE	METHOD	FERTILITY	INCOME	SIGN	OTHER VARIABLES INCLUDED
Boulier,[b] 1982	Philippines (3425 observations)	OLS	CEB	Husband's annual income	+*	Age of wife,* cumulative natural fertility,* % births surviving, husband employed in agriculture,* education of wife,[a] education of wife squared*
			No. living children		+*	
Canlas, 1978	Philippines nationwide (subsample, 2342 observations)	OLS	CEB	Annual family income below subsistence	All +* Rural + Urban +	Age cohort*, age at marriage*, labor force participation[a], education[a]
				Annual family income above subsistence	All + Rural - Urban +	
Chalamwong et al.,[b] 1979	Thailand, 21 villages, 840 farm households	OLS	CEB	Agricultural income	-	Farm size,* ownership status,* land quality, age at marriage,* female education,* child labor participation*
				Nonagricultural income	+	
Chernichovsky, 1976	India, 212 households	OLS	CEB	Total income (subsample n = 128)	+*	In mother's age,* mother's age at marriage,* mother literate, father's schooling,[a] no. children died[a]
				Income from agriculture	+*	

Table 1. Cont.

AUTHOR, DATE	SAMPLE	METHOD	FERTILITY	INCOME	SIGN	OTHER VARIABLES INCLUDED
				Income from unskilled occupation	+*	
				Income from skilled occupation	-	
Encarnacion, 1974	Philippines nationwide, 7237 households	OLS	No. live births	Annual family income, various subsamples in which Y- = below approximate median income; Y+ = above approximate median income	All - Urban - Rural + Y- +* Y+ - Urban Y- +* Urban Y+ - Rural Y- +* Rural Y+ -	Wife's age at marriage,[a] duration of marriage,* duration of marriage squared,* wife's education
Khan & Strageldin, 1979	Pakistan, 1024 married women	SE	No. live births	Current monthly income: Total sample Urban Rural	 - -* +*	Child mortality,[a] husband education,[a] wife's age,* age at marriage,[a] husband's age, travel time to medical place, binary variables for wife liter-

AUTHOR, DATE	SAMPLE	METHOD	FERTILITY	INCOME	SIGN	OTHER VARIABLES INCLUDED
Mueller & Cohn, 1977	Taiwan, island-wide, 2100 couples	MCA	No. living children, ideal no. children	Income per adult	+[c] +[c]	ate,[a] land owned,* house owned,[a] nuclear family,[a] child in school,[a] wife in labor force,[a] wife aware of family planning,[a] income adequate,* urban,[a] child <5 yrs present
Repetto,[b] 1979	Puerto Rico, 6300 households	OLS	CEB No. own children under 2 years old	Income per person	–* –* '	Wife's age, marriage duration, family structure, husband's education, wife's education Age of wife,* age of wife squared,* income per capita squared,* number of children in excess of two,* neighborhood level education,* legal* or consensual[a] marriage, women employed,* no. children enrolled,* variance of income in husband's occupation,[a] years school completed by women,* neighborhood level fertility*

Table 1. Cont.

AUTHOR, DATE	SAMPLE	METHOD	FERTILITY	INCOME	SIGN	OTHER VARIABLES INCLUDED
	Korea, 4570 currently married women	OLS	CEB	Income per person	-*	Age at marriage,* preferred family size,* number of sons,* contraception use, no. years at current residence,* nonfamily paid employment, current age,* education-al aspirations,* expected old age support,* respondent's education, husband's occupation
Rosenzweig, 1976	Philippines, countrywide, 8434 households	OLS	Expected additional children	Husband's expected wage	–	Wife's age at marriage, wife's age,* no. living children,* wife's education, wife's education x age,* husbands education, husband's age, child mortality rate, wife's knowledge of contraception,* husband in farm work, wife's work experience, work experience x age*

AUTHOR, DATE	SAMPLE	METHOD	FERTILITY	INCOME	SIGN	OTHER VARIABLES INCLUDED
Rosenzweig, 1978	Philippines, countrywide, 7237 households	OLS	CEB	Husband's expected wage	–	Child's wage rate,* wife's schooling,* age,* husband's schooling, husband's age,* farm residence, infant mortality rate,* religion, knowledge of contraception

*Statistically significant.

ªSignificant in some specifications.

ᵇAppears in other tables also.

ᶜNo tests of statistical significance available.

show a quite consistent positive association with fertility, in most cases statistically significant.   These studies are discussed in the chapter by Stokes and Schutjer and need not detain us here.   Admittedly, the positive effect of land quantity on fertility may not be due to income alone.   Other factors may be at work as well, such as inheritance or dowry targets, the complementarity between land and children's labor, and in some places lower female labor force participation among families with larger land holdings.   The point remains that in rural areas landholdings are a reasonable proxy for permanent income.   Indeed, amount of land owned tends to be more accurately measured than long-term income prospects.

Encarnacion refined his analysis by testing the hypothesis that the income/fertility relation is nonlinear.   He divided his rural Philippine sample into subgroups falling above or below median income, and found a significantly positive income/fertility relation for the group below median income.   This result was retested by Canlas (1978) with a later data set for the rural Philippines, confirming the positive income/fertility relation below median income.   A study by Ron and Schutjer (1982) in rural Thailand shows a similar nonlinearity, but the turning point occurs well above median income.

The constraints on fertility in poor rural households may be in part on the supply side.   That is, they may be physiological in nature, reflecting poor nutrition and poor health of the mother.   Studies of the effect of malnutrition on fertility, conducted in Bangladesh and Guatemala, suggest that moderate chronic malnutrition depresses fecundity only to a small extent (Bongaarts, 1980).   However, since it is difficult to measure nutritional status accurately for a large sample of women, the negative impact of malnutrition on fertility may be somewhat underestimated in these studies.   With regard to health, both Anker (1978) and Winegarden (1980) find in macro-level studies that at low levels of life expectancy, women's morbidity and mortality have substantial negative effects on fertility.

In addition, there seem to be behavioral constraints on the demand for children in very poor households.   If the enjoyment of children is a "normal" commodity, the demand for children should be depressed by low income and rise as the economic status of couples improves.   However, when some income threshold is reached, taste changes may begin to occur which over time will lower the demand for children.   In urban areas especially, changes in consumption and educational aspirations are to be expected, with the result that the rich and the poor, i.e., those living in the modern and traditional sectors, have quite different tastes.   The taste differentials may then outweigh the positive pure income effect.   In rural areas, as long as modernizing influences remain weak, rich and poor households tend to be homogeneous in their aspirations and attitudes.   Better-off rural households may be slower than urban ones to develop new educational and consumption aspirations.   Therefore some of the negative indirect income effects may be weak in rural areas, leading us to observe a positive relation between income and fertility.

EDUCATIONAL ASPIRATIONS AND FERTILITY

Theoretical Considerations

It is widely believed that rising educational aspirations lower the demand for children. This notion was formalized in the economic literature by Becker and Lewis (1974) and plays a major role in the "economic theory of fertility" propagated by the Columbia-Chicago school. Generally, economic theory would lead us to expect that a growing taste for new consumer goods and services would be counterbalanced by small declines in the demand for a large array of more traditional goods and services, including children (5). A quite different situation is postulated by Becker and Lewis as regards educational aspirations. As the expression "quantity/quality trade-off" implies, they see education as having a unique and sizable negative relation to fertility. Becker and Lewis state clearly that they do not see child quality and quantity as close substitutes. Rather, in their view, the "special relation" between the quantity and quality of children rests on the assumption that quantity and quality interact in such a way that child quantity raises the cost of quality and child quality raises the cost of quantity. Because of this interaction, a rise in educational aspirations may reduce the demand for quantity by more than an ordinary price effect would; indeed, the measured income elasticity of demand for child quantity may become negative when the income elasticity for quality is high (6).

The crucial assumption underlying Becker's theory is that parents want all children (at least those of the same sex) to be of the same quality. By contrast, if parents merely desired one educated son, the cost of a second or third son or of daughters would be unaffected by educational aspirations, although the income available to raise other children would be reduced. We shall later examine the validity for LDC settings of the assumption that parents feel obligated to treat all children alike.

Becker and Lewis' theory of the trade-off between quantity and quality of children was formulated with industrial societies in view. I shall argue that on theoretical grounds in less developed rural areas the relation between children's education and fertility may be only weakly negative; there may be no relation, or the relation may even be positive. I shall further hypothesize that a quantity/quality trade-off, i.e., a strong negative relation, is more likely to occur in urban than in rural areas and at later rather than earlier stages of development. In other words, in traditional rural areas educational aspirations may not only be slow to rise, but they need not necessarily be incompatible with high fertility, when they first emerge. Cochrane (1979) has shown that the relation between adult education and fertility may be non-linear. The same may be true of the relation between child quality and quantity.

The demand for educated children may be viewed as a function of income, price (educational costs), tastes, and the structure of the

economy and society.   Becker takes preferences as given and makes
the assumption that quality is more income elastic and more price
inelastic than quantity.   This assumption is valid only when education
has a high degree of priority in people's preference function.   In
developing societies, particularly in rural areas, educational aspirations
are bound to gain strength only gradually.

Looking at the bundle of satisfactions that people derive from children in traditional rural societies helps to clarify this point (7).   It is
difficult to know whether psychic satisfactions from children are
enhanced more by quantity or quality.   Presumably, as long as the risk
of child mortality is high and education is not valued as a consumer
good or for status reasons, quantity may be more satisfying psychologi-
cally than quality.   Perceived economic benefits from children likewise
may be tied more closely to quantity than to quality at early stages of
development.   As long as children are desired in part for the unskilled
labor they can perform, quantity could be more desirable than quality.
Also at that stage, larger income transfers and more substantial old
age support from children may be associated with larger numbers.
Education will have a greater expected payoff than numbers only when
villagers become aware of the rising demand for skilled and educated
labor in the country.   At that stage parents should also have altruistic
motives for educating their children.   In brief, the conditions which
prevail in rural areas with little developmental activity are not
conducive to a genuine commitment to education.   Hence, even when
parents take some interest in the education of their children, quality
may be slow to become more income elastic and more price inelastic
than quantity.   Moreover, outlays on quality may reduce traditional
expenditures other than those for quantity such as costly weddings and
other ceremonies.

Further differences between MDCs and LDCs are evident when one
considers educational costs, i.e., Becker's negative price effect.   Starting with direct costs, when Becker and Lewis wrote about the quanti-
ty/quality trade-off, they probably were thinking about the cost of a
U.S. college education, which is high indeed.   In rural areas of LDCs,
rising educational aspirations refer to the desire to send children to
school for 3 to 4 years rather than allowing them to remain illiterate;
and at a somewhat more advanced stage of development educational
aspirations may refer to the demand for 6 rather than 3 years of
primary education.   The direct cost of primary schooling in rural areas
may be quite low.   There often are no school fees at that level, although parents incur some other costs.

Foregoing children's labor, the indirect costs of schooling may be
more significant.   In some peasant societies, educational aspirations are
likely to be so low, or held by such a small proportion of people, that
they do not have an appreciable effect on behavior.   Child quantity
may be determined by natural fertility, possibly modified by some other
factors such as child mortality, but not educational aspirations.   People
who happen to have more living children can more easily spare some of
them from farm work.   Thus, the larger the number of children, the
more education they may receive, with education being a second priority time use.   In such a setting we would observe a positive association

of quantity and quality, quantity being a determinant of quality, but not vice versa.

Recognition that the indirect cost of education may be influenced by the number of siblings who can substitute in farm work raises the possibility that at somewhat more advanced stages of development, when educational aspirations become important or compulsory education is extended, people may have more children in order to facilitate school attendance and get the necessary work done.   In that case quantity and quality could continue to be positively related (8).   To be sure, other outcomes are possible as well.   When school attendance interferes with child labor, parents may send their children to school irregularly or not at all, or they may indeed reduce quantity, depending on the price elasticity of the demand for education.   If school hours are short (which often is the case) and vacations coincide with the busy season, schooling may not interfere appreciably with child labor.   In that case educational costs could remain low and need not impinge greatly on quantity.

Next we must consider that parents may view education of children as an investment from which they themselves may profit.   In MDCs parents no longer expect an economic benefit from educating their children (or at best a small benefit).   Therefore costs of education are not offset by returns from education, although there may be psychic rewards.   In rural areas of LDCs, parents may reap substantial net financial gains by educating their children, if education gives children access to well-paying, nonagricultural jobs and if educated children remit some of their earnings to parents.   It may then pay parents to have and educate many children.   In the East-West Population Institute's "Value of Children" studies, husbands were asked about the help they expected from children.   Expectations of receiving part of sons' salaries were expressed frequently in all participating countries: by over 60 percent of respondents in the Philippines, Turkey, Korea, and Taiwan, slightly over 50 percent in Thailand and Indonesia, but only 29 percent in Singapore.   Expectations of receiving part of daughters' salaries were only slightly less frequent.   That is, in rural areas where earnings in agriculture are low relative to urban earnings, the expected payoff from raising children may be highly education elastic with the result that there is no quantity/quality trade-off.

The obvious difficulty with this argument is that, timewise, investments in children precede returns from these investments.   How can low-income families educate numerous children when their ability to borrow is severely restricted?   In some cultures there are social mechanisms which take care of this problem.   Relatives who are better off or have few children of their own may help to defray educational costs.   A more frequent mechanism seems to be the so-called "chain arrangement" which, according to the literature, is quite common in Asia and Africa.   Under this arrangement the oldest child is educated at the parent's expense and is then obliged to contribute to the education of a younger child, who in turn pays for a still younger child.   The "Value of Children" study throws some light on this practice.   In the Philippines, Turkey, Indonesia, and Thailand over 80 percent of fathers said they expected "support for siblings' schooling" from their sons; for Taiwan the figure was 79 percent, Korea 60 percent, and Singapore 35 percent. The expectations for educational assistance from daughters were almost as high.

To summarize, quantity and quality of children may be positively related (a) under a regime of natural fertility, (b) if the opportunity cost of school attendance is seen as being lower in large than in small families, (c) if net rates of return to parents from educating their children are perceived as being positive, and (d) if siblings and relatives share in the cost of children's education. Even when the quantity/quality relation is negative, it is likely to be weak as long as rural families do not attach high priority to education. Whether one or more of these conditions prevail and are of importance clearly depends on cultural and economic conditions. Therefore we may expect to find a positive relation between quantity and quality of children in some settings and a negative relation in others. Overall, it would appear that the more rural and the less developed a society is, the higher is the value of unskilled child labor (and therefore the incompatibility between small family size and school attendance), the more universal is the expectation that educated children will turn over some of their earnings to parents, and the stronger are kinship ties and obligations. Thus there may be no quantity/quality trade-off in some rural societies, although such a trade-off should occur and become stronger at more advanced stages of development.

Empirical Findings Regarding the Quantity/Quality Trade-Off

Data on educational aspirations or actual schooling of children are seldom collected in connection with demographic investigations in LDCs; and very few studies have been specifically designed to test for a quantity/quality trade-off. Most studies which address this relationship do so peripherally as part of a broader exploration of fertility determinants. The complicated causal relationships reviewed above are seldom sorted out satisfactorily. Still, it is interesting that the available evidence points to a positive relation between quantity and quality in some countries, a negative one in others, and in some cases no relation at all.

To start with, there is little data which would allow us to test the validity for LDCs of Becker and Lewis' key assumption, that parents want all their children (of the same sex) to have the same education. There are historical writings on China which speak of a tradition of educating one son; there also are anthropological writings for various LDCs which report that parents invest differentially in their sons. On the other hand, statistical data collected in Asia in recent years are in accord with the Becker and Lewis assumption. For example, data for Taiwan show great similarity in educational attainment among children of the same sex within a family (Wei, 1981). A study of the determinants of school enrollment and continuation rates in the Bicol region of the Philippines by King and Lillard (1983) finds that, after taking account of various socioeconomic determinants of school enrollment and continuation, the intrafamily residual correlation among children is 0.49 and is unaffected by sex.   Caldwell et al. (1982, p. 717) write with reference to South Indian villages:

> No one doubts that there is economic strain imposed on a family by keeping their children at school. . . . We repeatedly asked whether the solution was to send some children to school, but not others, but were consistently told that families just cannot do this. . . .

One interpretation of the quantity/quality trade–off is that quantity and quality are jointly determined.   That is, variables which raise the demand for quality may reduce the demand for quantity, without any direct causal connection between quantity and quality.   Rosenzweig and Evenson (1977) have shown that in rural India the child wage is positively related to fertility and negatively to education.   Another joint determinant is mother's education to matriculation.   Such high educational attainment lowers fertility in rural India and raises school attendance.   However, father's education and lower levels of mothers' education show no significant effect.   A somewhat similar study by Rosenzweig (1978) in the Philippines again reveals a negative relation of mother's education to fertility and a positive relation to children's schooling.   The child wage has a positive impact on fertility and a negative (but not significant) impact on schooling.   Becker and Lewis clearly had more than joint determination in mind.   By reasoning that quantity raises the cost of quality, and quality raises the cost of quantity, they postulated a simultaneous and direct relation between the two.

I am aware of three studies conducted in Africa relevant to the direct quantity/quality trade–off.   Using data collected in 1968 and 1969 in a mostly urban area of Sierra Leone, Snyder (1974) observes a positive association between children's education and number of children born, controlling for an appropriate array of other variables.   The positive relation is most significant for women under 35 and becomes weaker at older ages.

The Rural Income Distribution Survey conducted in Botswana in 1974 and 1975 also points to a positive relation.   An analysis of time use by Mueller (1981) reveals that as numbers of children in the household increase, economic work per child is reduced, while average school hours per child rise.   In other words, a family with more children finds it easier to send some children to school and still obtain the needed child labor for cattle and farm operations (9).   Chernichovsky (1981b), using school enrollment and number of grades completed as dependent variables, shows that in rural Botswana the number of children aged 7 to 14 in the household is positively related to schooling.   This result is obtained after controlling for head's education.   Not unexpectedly, head's education is positively associated with children's schooling and negatively with fertility.   Only in that limited sense is there a negative quantity/quality relation.   The findings for Botswana are of particular interest because a large percentage of uneducated young men migrate to South Africa to work in the mines for some period.   Thus parents can obtain appreciable remittances from uneducated children.

This suggests that the opportunity cost of school attendance may play an important role in the quantity/quality decision.

Anker and Knowles (1982) analyze the quantity/quality trade-off separately for urban and rural areas of Kenya. They observe that in rural areas "higher levels of school attainment seem to have a stimulative effect on fertility. It appears that parents view education for their children as a 'good investment'. . . ." That is, in rural areas education variables are significantly related to fertility in a positive direction. In urban areas, by contrast, neither the actual school enrollment rate in the location of residence nor the wife's expectations regarding her children's education is significantly related to fertility. Anker and Knowles attribute this contrast to the greater strength of family ties in rural areas.

Looking next at other parts of the third world, a study of work participation and conditional hours worked by children in Malaysia by De Tray (1982) yields results similar in some respects to the Botswana time use analysis. The Malaysia data indicate that the larger the number of children of working age (over 10) in the family, the less each child works, especially each child in the 5 to 14 age group. This is true for housework as well as economic work. De Tray does not explore the implications of shorter working hours for school attendance, but time use studies generally show school attendance and working hours to be inversely related. However, De Tray also shows that the more children under 10 a household has, the more work each child 5 to 14 does, presumably substituting for the mother who is busy with young children.

Other time use studies in rural areas differ from the Botswana and Malaysia results in that they disclose a positive relation between number of children and hours worked per child. This presumably implies a negative relation between number and school attendance. Nag et al. (1978) found that in Java and Nepal work activity per child increases with number of siblings. Similarly, Clark's (1979) data for rural Guatemala indicate that school attendance is reduced and work time increased when there are one or more siblings of the same sex aged 15-18 in the household. Nag et al. (1978) attribute this phenomenon to the supervisory function of older siblings which, he believes, enhances the labor productivity of younger children. Clark offers an explanation more congenial to economists. She points out that large numbers of children reduce per capita income and that the depressing effect of lower income on school attendance may outweigh the stimulative effect of large family size via the lower opportunity cost of children's time.

The most ambitious analysis of the quantity/quality trade-off in rural LDCs has been undertaken by Ron and Schutjer (1982). It relates to rice farming families in the Central Plain of Thailand. Because of the exceptional care and detail involved in that study, it is of great interest that it shows a negative quantity/quality relation. Ron and Schutjer estimate a simultaneous equation model (indeed 5 simultaneous equations) where children ever born affect expected years of schooling, and expected years of schooling affect children ever born. That is, quantity enters the schooling equation as a proxy for the cost of quality, and quality enters the fertility equation as a proxy for the cost of quantity. Both cost proxies have the expected negative sign and are highly significant statistically in accordance with the Becker and Lewis theory. The measured income elasticity of expected children's education is greater than the income elasticity of children ever born, also in accord with Becker and Lewis' hypothesis. The very size and complexity of the Ron and Schutjer model makes it vulnerable to criticism. Especially, one may question whether all 5 equations are properly identified, a perpetual concern regarding simultaneous equation models.

Caldwell et al. (1982), using in-depth anthropological interviewing techniques in rural South India, arrive at the conclusion that a quantity/quality trade-off is now operating there. They observe that, in view of the fragmentation of landholdings, parents strongly desire urban jobs for their sons and well-educated husbands for their daughters. They also report (p. 700) that sons with urban jobs or local off-farm employment usually provide some kinds of assistance to the family.

> Strategies of this type necessitate schooling and inevitably lead in the Indian situation to choices between an unlimited number of children with a lower level of schooling and a limited number with a higher level.

Caldwell et al. (1982, p. 724) add the following footnote:

> The situation is different in tropical Africa, where sibling chains of assistance can be established so that each educated child makes it more likely that the next will be educated.

My own study in Taiwan in 1969 and the East-West Center studies of the "Value of Children" yield some additional evidence of a negative quantity/quality relation. These studies asked questions about the perceived cost of children and of children's education (Mueller, 1972; Arnold et al., 1975; Bulatao, 1979). Perceived costs were then related to income and to desired fertility or contraceptive use. Bulatao and Arnold (1977, p. 155) report:

> One disvalue that was broadly important in all countries . . . in the first phase of the VOC study was the financial costs of children. With social and demographic variables controlled, this disvalue still affected fertility preferences and behavioral intentions negatively, though less in some cases than in others.

However, in a number of VOC countries perceived cost of children does not seem to rise with income, nor does perceived cost rise with income across countries. One reason may be that ability to pay and what parents expect to spend on their children approximately keep pace. In addition, the proportion of educational costs which parents themselves bear, while rising with income in a cross-section, may not rise with development; indeed it may fall. Most important, however, perceived educational costs seem to be influenced by expected number of children, which often declines with income (Bulatao, 1979). If one accepts this interpretation, the data are broadly consistent with a quantity/ quality trade-off: as educational aspirations rise with income, parents stabilize the perceived burden of education by balancing off quantity against quality.

In brief, there is empirical evidence in the literature that there is a quantity/quality trade-off in some developing countries. However, there is theoretical as well as empirical support for the idea that rising educational aspirations may not lead to a decline in the demand for children, indeed may make for an increase. The trade-off seems to be contingent on institutional and economic circumstances which vary from country to country. Whether the positive relation is peculiar to Africa or whether it is more generally associated with early phases of rural development is not clear. There are not enough studies available to establish with confidence the hypothesis which I put forward, that a negative relation is more likely at later than at earlier stages of rural development.

CONSUMPTION ASPIRATIONS AND FERTILITY

Aspirations to acquire modern consumer goods are another potentially important negative indirect effect of income on fertility. Studies of consumption patterns in LDCs generally show a high income elasticity of demand for consumer durable goods, along with education, transportation, modern recreation and other modern services. In the course of development, the relative cost of modern consumer goods is likely to decline, reinforcing the growing demand for new goods. Data are not available to demonstrate a decline in relative price statistically, but it appears probable in view of economies of scale, increasing experience with indigenous production, and increasing competition among producers. I argued earlier that quite apart from income and price, development should also shift tastes in favor of modern consumer goods.

It is plausible that aspirations for modern forms of consumption would be slow to emerge in rural areas when income rises from very low levels. People at first have unmet needs for necessities, especially higher quality food. Moreover, consumption aspirations are related to other modernizing influences and depend on the availability of modern goods and services in local or nearby markets. There is very little research on changing consumption patterns in rural areas. Musgrove (1978, p. 164) reports for Latin American cities:

> It appears that such [durables] expenditures may increase
> only slightly relative to total spending at very low incomes,
> then rise sharply in an intermediate range, and thereafter
> level off or at least increase more slowly.

Freedman (1972) shows that in Taiwan couples who are in touch with modern influences, via education, the mass media, and modern employment are more interested in modern consumption than others. She further reports that high aspirations for modern forms of consumption do not have an adverse effect on either educational aspirations or saving. It follows that there is a shift in demand away from traditional goods. The question is whether children are among the "traditional goods" which seem less attractive as new goods become available.

Freedman (1970, 1976) and Mueller (1972) found that in Taiwan in the early 1970s there was indeed a negative relation between consumption aspirations and fertility after controlling for income, education, age, and some other variables. Actual consumption of durable goods and modern services as well as desired consumption were shown to be significantly related to ideal family size and to contraceptive use. The relationships were not very large, but consistently significant. The finding that this negative relation is modest is consistent with the expectation that child services are only one of several traditional modes of consumption which may be reduced when new consumer goods and services become popular. That is, consumer goods are not substitutes for children, nor do they raise the cost of children, as education may do.

Since the early 1970s the "aspirations hypothesis" has often been referred to in the literature but relatively little data collection has occurred which would allow tests at later points of time and in places other than Taiwan. We shall now review some of the scanty new evidence which has become available. The VOC study for Taiwan (Wu, 1977) collected data on the number of durable goods actually owned. It was found that ownership of durable goods was negatively related to desired family size, thus substantiating the results of an earlier Taiwan study. The VOC study for Korea (Lee and Kim, 1979) likewise collected data on number of durable goods owned, but made relatively little use of this information in the analysis. We merely learn that ownership of modern durables is one of a series of socioeconomic status variables, each of which has a strong positive relation to knowledge and use of contraception and a negative relation to desired family size.

For another Asian country, Indonesia, there is reasonably convincing evidence that consumption aspirations contributed to a recent fertility decline. According to McNicoll and Singaribrum (1982):

> Consumerist values seem to be blossoming, and not just within an economic elite. . . . Improvements in transport and greater media penetration seem to be eroding rural-urban differences in values and consumption patterns.

They further explain:

> The spread of consumer values is another change affecting individual aspirations, this one not principally a cohort phenomenon. Widely remarked upon (and frequently deplored) within Indonesia, this is seen as a byproduct on the one hand, of the economic recovery and, for many, the relative prosperity created by the oil revenues and agricultural gains, and, on the other hand, of the government's encouragement of private economic activity and discouragement of political activity. The contrast with the economic austerity of Sukar-

noist Indonesia . . . is striking. The earlier discussion noted
the likelihood of income and substitution effects bearing on
fertility, from the new array of consumption opportunities.

A link between consumption aspirations and fertility in Indonesia is
demonstrated statistically by Chernichovsky and Meesook (1981). In a
multivariate analysis (controlling among other variables, for parents'
education and income) they found that ownership of modern durables is
positively and significantly associated with knowledge and use of contraception and negatively with children ever born.

A quite different piece of evidence for a relation between aspirations
and fertility comes from a study of rural electrification in the Philippines (Herrin, 1979).   Herrin reports that a marked fertility decline
occurred in Misamis Oriental Province, a rural area in Southern Philippines, during a period when a large-scale rural electrification project
was being implemented.   Apparently birth rates declined more in the
area receiving electrification than in adjacent areas which benefited
equally from other governmental development efforts and had comparable family planning programs.   Referring to the same area, Yotopoulos
(1982) shows that conscious fertility control was appreciably greater in
the electrified portions of the province than elsewhere.   The specific
reasons for the fertility decline cannot be identified unambiguously from
the available data.   According to Herrin, income increases were much
larger in the electrified area than in surrounding areas because the
availability of electricity attracted new business firms, facilitated the
expansion of irrigation, enhanced employment opportunities, and allowed
households to work at night.   More women entered the labor force, and
their working hours rose, one possible reason for the fertility decline.
While electrified households did spend money on electricity installation
and electric consumer durable goods, they differed most sharply from
households in the surrounding areas in regard to their investment
pattern.   In the electrified area farmers invested, individually and
cooperatively, in pump sets, equipment, irrigation systems, greater use
of fertilizer, pesticides and herbicides, electrification of community
facilities, and nonagricultural businesses.   King and Lillard (1983) show
that in the Bicol area of the Philippines electrification is positively
related to school attendance when other socioeconomic characteristics
are controlled.   Herrin (1979) concludes:

> The increased household incomes and the social and economic
> opportunities that rural electrification and other development
> inputs helped bring about generated changes in the consump-
> tion and investment patterns and aspirations of rural house-
> holds.   The felt need to save and to invest in electricity
> installation, in farm and business enterprises and in human
> capital . . . tended to raise the opportunity cost of addition-
> al children, thereby creating pressures for limiting further
> childbearing through contraception.

On the basis of the available evidence for the Philippines, one may at
least conjecture that rising investment aspirations were more important

than consumption aspirations in lowering the desired number of children.

In all, there are few studies on the indirect effect of income on fertility via consumption aspirations. Those studies which have been made consistently show a negative indirect effect. There simply is not enough empirical evidence to assess in how many countries consumption aspirations play a similar role as in Indonesia and how often they have a substantial, as opposed to marginal, negative impact on fertility.

CONCLUSION

A review of the empirical evidence regarding the income/fertility relation in LDCs indicates that the relation is negative in urban areas and in rural areas where development is relatively advanced. It seems, however, to be positive in rural areas at earlier stages of development. In other words, the pure positive income effect may be reinforced by indirect positive effects in poor rural populations. In such populations, income increases may lead to better health, nutrition, and higher survival rates among women of childbearing age. Rising income may also lead to more optimistic expectations regarding permanent income; and in some countries, rural women may withdraw from the labor force or reduce work inputs when the farm earns more money. At later stages of rural development, negative indirect effects of increasing income on fertility may outweigh the positive ones. Rising educational and consumption aspirations are among these potential negative indirect effects; but there are of course others, especially the anticipation of declining economic benefits from children.

The observed income/fertility pattern suggests first that aspirations respond more strongly to income advances in urban than in rural settings and during later than during earlier phases of rural development. Secondly, it suggests that the sensitivity of fertility to rising aspirations may be quite low in traditional rural societies. This second proposition derives support from an analysis of the quantity/quality trade-off. While there is evidence for a number of societies that a growing interest in education may constitute an effective inducement to limit family size, this does not seem to be a universal reaction. Especially in the African setting, and perhaps more generally at early stages of rural development, quantity and quality of children may be positively associated or unrelated. In some societies what appears to be a negative influence of educational aspirations on fertility is in fact a case of joint determination; higher parents' education and a diminishing need for work contributions by children both seem to raise school attendance and lower desired family size.

Rising consumption aspirations (or consumerism) often are viewed with mixed feelings by development planners. While the depressing effect of consumption aspirations on fertility seems to be modest, it does appear that a policy of austerity with regard to new consumer goods may make it more difficult to lower birth rates.

Investment aspirations have been neglected in the literature. A policy of creating conditions conducive to investment in nonhuman capital for a broad spectrum of rural households is desirable in its own right.   If high investment aspirations also lowered birth rates, they would represent a doubly valuable policy goal.   It seems plausible that, once advances in rural technology have raised the marginal productivity of farm investments, the rising demand for investment funds would raise the opportunity cost of children.   Mueller (1975) presented some evidence for this hypothesis relating to Taiwan.   Herrin's (1979) study of rural electrification in the Philippines provides some additional support. Still, the question under what conditions children's labor facilitates investments and under what conditions the presence of more mouths to feed is perceived by parents as an obstacle to investment requires more attention from researchers.

NOTES

1.   The term "income" refers to current household income as defined in national income accounts.
2.   An example may be the growing taste in some countries for educated children, even in the face of falling rates of return to education.
3.   In a self-employed household husband's income cannot be readily separated from the earnings of wife and children.
4.   Bollen and Entwisle (1981) show that a logarithmic form provides a better fit than a linear one, and a quadratic exponential form a still closer fit.   They also argue that a quadratic exponential specification reflects most adequately the historic or ideal shape of the demographic transition.
5.   Easterlin, however, seems to believe that relative economic status affects the demand for child quantity much more than the demand for most other goods.   No explanation for this assumption is given.
6.   For formal proof of these propositions, see Becker and Lewis (1974) and Becker (1981).
7.   See also Ben-Porath (1973).
8.   The notion that the value of children's labor diminishes with an increase in the number of children in the household assumes that children are employed only on family farms or in family businesses. If children have earnings opportunities independent of their family's situation, the value of child labor is equal to the child market wage and is unaffected by the number of children in the household. It appears that only the poorest households hire out their children and that in most countries the wage labor market for children is very limited.
9.   The data cannot tell us whether children take turns going to school or whether some are educated and others are not.   Knowledgeable informants say that they often do take turns.

REFERENCES

Anker, R. 1977.   The effect of group level variables on fertility in a rural Indian sample.   Journal of Development Studies 14:63-78.

_____ 1978.   An analysis of fertility differentials in developing countries. Review of Economics and Statistics 60:58–69.

_____ and J.C. Knowles. 1982. Fertility Determinants in Developing Countries: A Case Study of Kenya, International Labour Office. Liege: Ordina Editions.

Arnold, F., R.A. Bulatao, C. Buripakdi, B.J. Chung, J.T. Fawcett, T. Iritani, S.J. Lee, and T.S. Wu. 1975.   The Value of Children: A Cross-National Study, Vol. 1, Introduction and Comparative Analysis. Honolulu: The East-West Center.

Becker, G. 1981. A Treatise on the Family. Pp. 103–112. Cambridge, Massachusetts: Harvard University Press.

_____ and H.G. Lewis. 1974.   Interaction between quantity and quality of children.   In: T.W. Schultz (ed.) Economics of the Family, pp. 81–90. Chicago: University of Chicago Press.

Ben-Porath, Y. 1973. Economic analysis of fertility in Israel: Point and counterpoint. Journal of Political Economy 81:S202–S233.

Bollen, K.A. and B. Entwisle. 1981.   Economic Development and Fertility: A Lesson in Functional Form Misspecification. Ann Arbor: Population Studies Center, University of Michigan, Working Paper 81-#7.

Bongaarts, J. 1980.   Does malnutrition affect fecundity?   A summary of evidence. Science 20:564–569.

Boulier, B.L. 1982.   Income redistribution and fertility decline: A skeptical view. Population and Development Review Supplement 8: 159–173.

Bulatao, R.A. 1979. On the Nature of the Transition in the Value of Children.   Current Studies of the East-West Population Institute. No. 60–A. Honolulu: East-West Center.

_____ and F. Arnold. 1977. Relationship Between the Value and Cost of Children and Fertility: Cross-Cultural Evidence.   International Population Conference, Mexico 1:141–155.

Caldwell, J.C., P.H. Reddy, and P. Caldwell. 1982.   Demographic change in rural South India. Population and Development Review 8:680–727.

Canlas, D.B. 1978.   A qualitative study of fertility and wife's employment in the Philippines: 1973.   The Philippine Economic Journal 36 XVII (1 and 2):88–121.

Chalamwong, Y., M. Nelson, and W. Schutjer. 1979.   Variation in land availability and human fertility among Thai rice farmers. Paper presented at the annual meeting of the Population Association of America, Philadelphia, Pennsylvania.

Chernichovsky, D. 1976. Fertility behavior in developing economies: An investment approach. Paper presented at IUSSP Seminar on Household Models of Economic-Demographic Decision-Making, Mexico City, November 4–6.

_____ 1981a.   Socio-Economic Correlates of Fertility Behavior in Rural Botswana. Population and Human Resources Division, Discussion Paper 81-48. Washington, D.C.: World Bank.

_____ 1981b.   Socio-Economic and Demographic Aspects of School Enrollment and Atendance in Rural Botswana. Population and Human Resources Discussion Paper 81-47. Washington, D.C.: World Bank.

_____ and O. Meesook. 1981.   Regional Aspects of Family Planning and Fertility Behavior in Indonesia.   Staff Working Paper No. 462. Washington, D.C.: World Bank.

Clark, C.A.M. 1979.   Relation of Economic and Demographic Factors to Household Decisions Regarding Education of Children in Guatemala. Unpublished Ph.D. Thesis.   Ann Arbor: University of Michigan.

Coale, A.J. 1973.   Demographic transition reconsidered.   International Population Conference, Liege, Vol. 1, pp. 53-72.

Cochrane, S.H. 1979.   Fertility and Education: What Do We Really Know?   Baltimore: Johns Hopkins University Press.

Conger, D.J. and J.M. Campbell, Jr. 1978.   Simultaneity in the birth rate equation: The effects of education, labor force participation, income and health.   Econometrica 46:631-661.

DaVanzo, J. 1972.   The Determinants of Family Formation in Chile, 1960: An Econometric Study of Female Labor Force Participation, Marriage, and Fertility Decisions.   R-830-AID, August.   Santa Monica California: Rand Corporation.

De Tray, D. 1982.   Children's Economic Contributions in Peninsular Malaysia.   WD-1471-AID.   Santa Monica, California: Rand Corporation.

Easterlin, R.A. 1973.   Relative economic status and the American fertility swing.   In: E.B. Sheldon (ed.) Family Economic Behavior, pp. 170-223.   Philadelphia: J.B. Lippincott.

Encarnacion, J. 1974.   Fertility and labor force participation: Philippines 1968.   The Philippine Review of Business and Economics XI:113.

Farooq, G.M. 1979.   Household Fertility Decision-Making in Nigeria. Revised Version of the Population and Employment Working Paper No. 75 (July).   Geneva: International Labour Office.

Freedman, D.S. 1970.   The role of consumption of modern durables in economic development.   Economic Development and Cultural Change 19:25-48.

_____ 1972.   Consumption aspirations as economic incentives in a developing country—Taiwan.   In: B. Strumpel (ed.) Human Behavior in Economic Affairs: Essays in Honor of George Katona.   Amsterdam: Elsevier.

_____ 1976.   Mass media and modern consumer goods: Their suitability for policy interventions to decrease fertility.   In: R.G. Ridker (ed.) Population and Development: The Search for Selective Interventions, pp. 356-425.   Baltimore: Johns Hopkins University Press.

Herrin, A.N. 1979.   Rural electrification and fertility change in the southern Philippines.   Population and Development Review 5:61-86.

Kelley, A.C. 1980.   Interactions of economic and demographic household behavior.   In: R.A. Easterlin (ed.) Population and Economic Change in Developing Countries, pp. 403-470.   Chicago: University of Chicago Press.

Khan, M.A. and I. Sirageldin. 1979.   Education, income, and fertility in Pakistan.   Economic Development and Cultural Change 27:519-547.

King, E.M. and L.A. Lillard. 1983.   Determinants of Schooling Attainment and Enrollment Rates in the Philippines.   N-1962-AID.   Santa Monica, California: Rand Corporation.

Lee, S.J. and J.O. Kim. 1979.   The Value of Children: Korea.   Honolulu, Hawaii: East-West Population Institute.

Makhija, I. 1978. The Work Done by Children in Poor Rural Areas: Effects on Fertility and Schooling. Chicago: University of Chicago Press (mimeo).

McNicoll, G. and M. Singaribrum. 1982. Fertility Decline in Indonesia: II. Analysis and Interpretation. Population Council, Center for Policy Studies, Working Papers 92 and 93.

Mueller, E. 1972. Economic motives for family limitation. Population Studies 26:383-403.

_____ 1975. The impact of agricultural change on demographic development in the third world. In: L. Tabah (ed.) Population Growth and Economic Development in the Third World. Leige: International Union for the Scientific Study of Population.

_____ 1976. The economic value of children in peasant agriculture. In: R.G. Ridker (ed.) Population and Development: The Search for Selective Interventions, pp. 98-153. Baltimore: Johns Hopkins University Press.

_____ 1981. The Value and Allocation of Time in Rural Botswana. Population and Human Resources Division. Discussion Paper No. 81-44. Washington, D.C.: World Bank. (Forthcoming in Journal of Development Economics.)

_____ and R. Cohn. 1977. The relation of income to fertility decisions in Taiwan. Economic Development and Cultural Change 25:325-347.

_____ and K. Short. 1983. Effects of income and wealth on the demand for children. In: Panel on Fertility Determinants, pp. 474-517. Washington, D.C.: National Academy of Sciences.

Musgrove, P. 1978. Consumer Behavior in Latin America. Washington, D.C.: The Brookings Institute.

Nag, M., B.N.F. White, and R.C. Peet. 1978. An anthropological approach to the study of economic value of children in Java and Nepal. Current Anthropology 2:293-306.

Pollak, R.A. 1978. Endogenous tastes in demand and welfare analysis. American Economic Review 68:374-379.

Repetto, R. 1979. Economic Equality and Fertility in Developing Countries. Baltimore: Johns Hopkins University Press.

Ron, Z. and W. Schutjer. 1982. An Econometric Analysis of Fertility, Schooling, and Time Allocation among Thai Agricultural Households. Bulletin 840. University Park, Pennsylvania: Pennsylvania State University College of Agriculture.

Rosenzweig, M.R. 1976. Female work experience, employment status, and birth expectations: Sequential decision-making in the Philippines. Demography 13:339-356.

_____ 1978. The value of children's time, family size, and non-household child activities in a developing country. In: J. Simon (ed.) Research in Population Economics 1, pp. 331-347. Greenwich, Connecticut: JAI Press.

_____ and R. Evenson. 1977. Fertility, schooling, and the economic contribution of children in rural India: An econometric analysis. Econometrica 45:1065-1080.

Schultz, T.P. 1981. Economics of Population. Reading, Massachusetts: Addison-Wesley Publishing Co.

Snyder, D.W. 1974.   Economic determinants of family size in West Afri-
    ca. Demography 11:613-628.
Wei, S.P. 1981.   The Effect of Family Structure on Siblings' Status
    Achievement: The Case of Taiwan. Ph.D. Dissertation.   Ann Arbor:
    University of Michigan.
Winegarden, C.R. 1980.   Socioeconomic equity and fertility in develop-
    ing countries. De Economist 4:530-557.
Wu, T.S. 1977.   The Value of Children: Taiwan.   Honolulu: East-West
    Population Institute.
Yotopoulos, P.A. 1982.   Equilibrium of the Household: An Application
    with Demographic Decision-Making. Working Paper No. 8202.   Stan-
    ford, California: Food Research Institute.

CHAPTER 8

The Gainful Employment of Females and Fertility—With Special Reference to Rural Areas of Developing Countries

Robert H. Weller

The relationship between female labor force participation and fertility is a variable whose sign and causal nature vary from woman to woman and from context to context. In some instances, women who are in the labor force have lower fertility than those who are not; in others the two groups of women have the same fertility; and in other instances those women in the labor force have higher fertility than those not in the labor force. The causal nature of the relationship is also variable. For some women, fertility apparently affects their labor force activity; for others evidence suggests that labor force participation affects fertility. In yet other cases, the relationship seems to be reciprocal.

One central theme of this chapter is that female labor force participation and fertility are each multidimensional variables. It is also asserted that the categories "in the labor force" and "not in the labor force" contain a significant amount of heterogeneity with respect to several important factors and that the composition of each category with respect to these factors is an important predictor of the existence and causal nature of the relationship between female employment and fertility.

In turn, the internal composition of each category is affected by the institutional structure of the society, including the nature of the economic opportunity structure, the conditions surrounding employment, the normative structure surrounding womanhood and employment of females, and family structure. Those who ignore such factors in making blanket

151

recommendations that increased employment opportunities for women will, by itself, be sufficient to induce declines in fertility in less developed countries do so at the risk of greatly oversimplifying reality and ignore a great deal of literature to the contrary.   As Hull (1977, p. 43) suggests after reviewing a number of studies on the employment status of females and fertility, it is all too common for "results" to be accepted and used without sufficient background knowledge:

> It is understandable that policy makers may want to embrace such conclusions given their recent exposure to speeches, conferences, and various statements proclaiming that female employment and education are the keys to fertility decline. When data are produced showing the desired relationship, the tendency is to accept the result as evidence of the hoped-for pattern, rather than to further investigate the probable causes and mechanisms that produced the finding.

This chapter is organized around a brief, selective geographic review of the recent literature examining relationships between female employment status and fertility, paying particular attention to research on the rural areas of developing countries.   This is followed by a discussion of the heterogeneity existing with respect to several key factors within categories of employment status.

GEOGRAPHIC COVERAGE

Weller (1977) reviewed the already voluminous literature on female employment and fertility and reached several conclusions about the probability of observing a negative relationship between the two variables.   This probability was described as being higher in the more modernized countries than in the developing ones.   In the latter, the probability of observing a negative relationship between female employment status and fertility was greater in urban areas than in rural areas, if the wife were employed away from home rather than at home, and if she were in a white collar occupation rather than some other occupation, particularly that of agricultural laborer.   At the same time, Safilios-Rothschild (1977) also summarized the literature and concluded (p. 361):

> In summary, within societies (mostly the developing), social classes (mostly the working class), and contexts (the rural more often than the urban), in which the mother role is viewed as compatible with the work role and women's most important identity and fulfillment is considered to be mother-hood, women's work may either be unrelated to fertility or positively related to it.

Anker et al. (1982), Youssef (1982), and Mueller (1982) have subsequently reviewed the by now even more voluminous body of literature and report that the negative relationship between work and fertility is found almost exclusively in urban industrialized settings. However, as Standing (in press) points out, even establishing a causal nature between more urban, modern types of employment and fertility levels is problematical. This will be discussed in greater detail later.

Although Gille (1981) has cited Egypt as a case study demonstrating that employment opportunities for women would contribute to fertility declines in rural areas, Loza-Soliman (1981) and Loza (1982) conducted an analysis of Egyptian data and conclude that the fact that women work outside the home may not necessarily affect their fertility. Vallin (1978) reports that Algerian employed women have less children than other women at all ages. Arowolo (1976) and Lewis (1979) find no relationship between the two variables in urban Nigeria (also see Fapohunda, 1981, p. 236). DeLancey (1982) reports a similar lack of association in her study of the Southwestern Province of Cameroon.

Timur (1978, p. 68) reports a strong negative association in Turkey between employment and fertility and children ever born and concludes:

> Our data suggest that female employment depresses fertility. However, it is also clear that, in Turkey, the relationship between women's working status and fertility is weaker than the relation of other socioeconomic variables with fertility.

And Indonesian data show that working women desire fewer additional children than nonworking women, leading the authors to conclude that as women become more economically active fertility rates will decrease (Lembaga Demografi, 1974, p. 20). Mason and Palan (1980, p. 21) report that among rural Chinese and Indian women there is a nonnegative employment-fertility relationship and that among rural Malay women the negative relationship is very weak. Fapohunda (1981, p. 241) reports that the fertility of uneducated economically active Sinhalese women was found to be higher than that of economically nonactive Sinhalese women of all ages.

Gurak and Kritz (1982) studied urban women in the Dominican Republic and observed no relationship between employment status and fertility. Hollerbach (1983) notes that although female employment produces considerable time constraints, as shown by various Cuban time budget surveys, the exact association between fertility and female employment cannot be ascertained from the available Cuban data. Fapohunda (1981) reports marked differences between active and nonactive women in El Salvador but notes a lack of control for differentials in proportion married.

In an areal analysis, Jones (1977) shows a positive correlation between the number of children under 2 years of age and the percent of females 15 to 44 economically active in political subunits of Barbados. The U.S. Bureau of the Census (1983) has conducted a cross-national study in which the percent of females in the labor force and percent of females in the labor force who are in white collar occupations are compared to the total fertility rate. Although differences emerge between major regional groups (e.g., African and Asian Muslim countries vs. developed countries), little consistent relationship is noted within these regions at the aggregate level of analysis.

In addition to these studies relating current employment status to fertility, numerous studies have examined whether previous employment of females is related to fertility.   Chaudhury (1978) reports the absence of any relationship between duration of work since marriage and cumulative fertility in a metropolitan city of Bangladesh.   Data from rural portions of Bangladesh, however, show that women who have ever worked have lower fertility in all age groups than do those who have never worked (Sohail, 1981).   In rural Turkey, Moslem women who had never worked had 4.2 births vis-a-vis 3.9 for those who had been employed in agriculture (Shaw, 1980).   Lebanese women not working since marriage averaged 4.5 children ever born, compared to 3.4 among those who had worked since marriage (Chamie, 1983).   A similar negative association is reported between wife's work before marriage and number of children ever born.   However, a multivariate analysis reveals only minimal net differences.   Ogawa and Rele (1981) report that in Sri Lanka work status before marriage negatively affects cumulative fertility directly, as well as indirectly through age at marriage.   Kim and Choi (1981) conclude that, after controlling for prior variables, the contribution of work experience before marriage to a lowered desire for more children remained statistically significant while work experience after marriage did not.   Data from rural Egypt also show a negative association between the woman's employment before marriage and her cumulative fertility (Department of Statistics, PFPD, 1982).   In Thailand, data suggest that, in both rural and urban areas, women who had worked for wages before marriage had fewer children than women who had not (Standing, 1978, p. 179).   Jamaican data show that the work experience of young women appears to have a negative effect on the women's actual and desired fertility (Standing, 1981).

A Methodological Note on Definitions

Many persons seem to think of the economic activity of females as though it were easy to measure and as though it usually takes place in the "modern" (i.e., Westernized) sector of the economy, perhaps picturing Rosie the Riveter going off to her 8 to 5 job in an auto assembly plant or Susie the Stenographer going off to take dictation from her male supervisor.   However, it is not always like that in the developing countries, especially in the rural areas.   In contrast to the Western experience, female workers in developing areas are more likely to be self-employed than wage earners, to work seasonally rather than year-round, to be underemployed rather than formally employed, and to engage in a fluid or sporadic pattern of diverse and shifting activities (Dixon, 1982, p. 541).   Moreover, the boundary between domestic production for the household's own consumption and economic activity for sale or exchange is less clearly drawn in developing countries, especially among women in rural areas (Boserup, 1975; Dixon, 1982).
    As Safilios-Rothschild (1977, p. 362) points out,

> most data tend to classify women as working or nonworking
> according to conventional, male-oriented and wages-oriented

Western models and are often . . . quite crude in that many
working women in developing nations, especially in the rural
and nonmodern urban sector, are not counted as such.

Many women participate directly in economic activities but are not
paid for doing so and may not consider themselves as "working."
Housework may be considered to be "nonwork" or peripheral to the
economic well-being of the family, yet women engaged in housework
may engage in such essential activities as producing and storing foods,
caring for domestic animals, making clothes, and collecting fuel for
heat (Ahdab-Yehia, 1977; Chamie, 1983).

Other women may report themselves to be nonworking even though
they are paid wages. This may be the case if they are engaged in
illegal activities such as brewing alcohol, black market trading, or
prostitution. In one of the few studies of its kind, Harter and
Bertrand (1979) report that prostitutes in Cali, Colombia have about
national average fertility. In this particular case, apparently the
fertility preceded the trade (cf. Harter and Bertrand, 1975).

Also some women may not define themselves as working due to their
desire to maintain the image in the eyes of their husbands, kin, or
society in general that they are not working. Whether women who
work define themselves as working may have important consequences
for their fertility by indicating the relative importance placed upon the
occupational vis-a-vis the parental and domestic roles (Oppong, 1980).
One could reasonably hypothesize that gainfully employed (i.e., paid)
women who report themselves as "nonworking" have higher fertility
than gainfully employed women who report themselves as "working."

Bulatao and Fawcett (1981, p. 437) discuss the link between occupational career involvement and fertility delay, stating that those women
with higher occupational career aspirations or higher expectations are
more likely to postpone childbearing in order to get ahead in their
occupational careers. They explain this delay as a desire to accumu-
late work experience, to become more secure in one's job, or even to
save additional money before leaving the labor market. Although the
evidence they cite is gathered in North America, it supports the notion
that women who emphasize the occupational role vis-a-vis that of
parent have lower fertility than other women. Tickamyer (1979) also
supports the idea that different processes are involved in the fertility-
work relationship depending upon tastes and that there is a significant
interaction between sex role orientation and the existence, sign, and
strength of the relationship between female labor force participation
and fertility.

Women may also be reported by other persons as not working, either
because of the seasonal nature of the employment or because of normative strictures to do so. Thus, Youssef (1977) reports that under-
enumeration of women in agriculture in Muslim countries is due largely
to the reluctance of male farmers to report that their wives and
daughters work outside the home. Also, census or survey interviews
may choose to ignore women's work, especially for some age groups or
marital statuses (cf., Blacker, 1978, 1980; Standing, 1977, for examples).
Dixon (1982) contains an excellent discussion of the entire problem of

measurement regarding women in agricultural activity in developing countries.

To the extent that gainfully employed women report themselves (or are reported by others) to be nonworking and to the extent that these women have fertility levels higher than those of women who report themselves to be working, there is systematic measurement error that would bias toward the outcome of "working" women having lower fertility than "nonworking" women. Such measurement error also has implications for aggregate level analyses relating rates of female labor force participation to fertility levels. Hull (1977) has demonstrated how a change in the definition of work, by asking rural Southeast Asian women whether they had taken part in the preceding agricultural season, resulted in a percentage of women almost twice as great as that obtained when a more conventional question was asked (53 and 23 percent, respectively). Chamie (1983) reports similar results using Lebanese data.

HETEROGENEITY OF WOMEN

Heterogeneity of Nonworkers

In addition to the difficulties involved in classifying women as workers or nonworkers because of definitional and measurement problems, one must deal with the considerable heterogeneity of women within the category of nonworker. For one thing, many of them may have prior work experience. These women have varying work histories before and after marriage as well as before and after a particular parity level. Also there are women with varying degrees of satisfaction about the idea of remaining in the nonworkers category. Some are unemployed and would like to work if it were available. Others are content to remain as nonworkers temporarily but not permanently. This might be the case with a woman who has just married or given birth and is willing to forego employment in order to be a "homemaker," in the short run. Other women may be quite satisfied to remain in that category (Safilios-Rothschild, 1977, pp. 364-366).

Heterogeneity of Workers

The circumstances surrounding the gainful employment of women need to be taken into account, as does the need to control for differences in educational attainment (cf. Cochrane, 1979). One important source of variation is the occupational composition of the female labor force.

Occupation

Occupation may affect the female employment-fertility relationship in several ways. For one thing, occupation may be associated with the relative ease (or difficulty) with which the roles of mother and worker

may be combined. Other things equal, the more difficult it is to combine the two roles, the more the woman is forced to choose between
them and to substitute one for the other. Which choice is actually
made will depend upon a number of factors which need to be specified
in future research. However, the greater the necessity to choose
between the two roles, the stronger should be the differences between
the fertility of workers and nonworkers.

It should be pointed out in this context that the choice is not
always between employment and fertility. Women engage in a variety
of activities, and Mueller (1982) points out that women in developing
countries often find time to care for babies and small children by
cutting down on leisure and housework. Time is not a very scarce
resource in these countries. Thus women's market work and earnings
may be reduced only to a small extent by the arrival of another child.
Mueller bases this observation on time-use studies of rural women
whose work time is much more divisible than the work time of women
who are employed in the modern sector. (Also see Kossoudji and
Mueller, 1979 and Ho, 1979, for time-use investigations in rural low-
income areas which show that young children primarily reduce women's
leisure rather than their work time.) Boulier (1977) suggests that both
work and leisure time are reduced by the presence of young children.
As Standing (in press) and Freedman (1975) suggest, if the primary
effect is on leisure time, this may help to explain why educated
women, who have a greater financial ability to enjoy leisure, want
fewer children. Also, as we explore later, it is possible to substitute
the labor of other persons in the care of young children.

Occupation is also an important consideration because it normally is
associated with the locus of the market activity itself, the human
capital (in terms of education in particular) the person possesses, a
particular level of wages and set of fringe benefits, the level of
satisfaction and prestige to be gained from engaging in market activity,
and the ease with which child care may be arranged. In turn, each of
these factors is affected by the institutional structure of the society
and of the area in which the woman lives.

The locus of employment is important because working away from
home may make it more difficult to combine employment and motherhood. It is generally accepted that wage employment away from home
is much more incompatible with fertility than nonwage activity,
whether on farms, in trading, in unpaid family work, or in small-scale,
family based forms of production (Standing, in press). McCabe and
Rosenzweig (1976) report that women in Africa frequently carry children on their backs while they are engaged in retail or agricultural
activities and that, in this case, children may not be very intensive of
the wife's time. Hermalin et al. (1979) states that in Taiwan women
working away from home have lower subsequent fertility than women
working at home or not working at all. Finally, a study of married
women in twelve rural zones of Thailand shows a significant relationship between fertility and nonfamilial work, although most of the
explained variance was due to life-cycle variables and to "modernity"
(Cook and Leoprapai, 1977). Data collected in Thailand as part of the
World Fertility Survey show the expected pattern, with women in

professional and clerical occupations having much lower fertility than manual workers and sales and service workers.   Interestingly, women not working had lower fertility than women in farming occupations, even when differences in duration of marriage were controlled (Institute of Population Studies, 1977, p. 50).

Omran and Standley (1976, p. 133) report that in the rural portions of the Manila area, women in clerical or professional occupations have less children ever born than agricultural or industrial workers, who in turn have less children ever born than women in other occupations or housewives.   In the urban area, no clear relationship between parity and occupation is reported, a finding similar to that of Gurak and Kritz (1982) for urban women in the Dominican Republic.

Cahill (1977) reports that one reason there is not a negative relationship between employment and fertility in India is mainly because the occupations available to Indian women are those in types of industries (agriculture and cottage) in which it is readily possible to combine the roles of mother and worker.   Omran and Standley (1976, p. 105) report no distinct pattern between occupation of females and children ever born in Gandhigram, India.

In the Egyptian rural fertility survey, women in professional, clerical, crafts, or sales occupations reported 2.5 children ever born, compared to 3.4 for those with household productive activities and 4.4 for those working in agriculture (Department of Statistics, 1982, p. 40).   Data from the Sudan show a similar pattern (Government of Sudan, 1981).

Lebanese data show that among both Shiia and Maronites housewives experience higher parity than those engaged in professional and clerical jobs (Omran and Stanley, 1976, p. 120).   Sohail (1981) reports that women in rural Bangladesh working in the traditional sector do not have higher fertility than women working in the modern sector.   However, ESCAP (1982) states that self-employment is often associated with high fertility because it presents less conflict with child rearing and because it is the form of employment most readily available to women with minimal education.   Professional employment is reported as generally associated with lower fertility.

Hermalin et al. (1979) and Coombs and Freedman (1979) report a weak but statistically significant relationship between female employment and fertility in Taiwan but report that women working at home or for relatives have the same fertility as those not working at all. The fertility differences present were primarily those between women in the impersonal market sector and all other women.   Dixon (1976, p. 298) echoes a similar theme when she states:

> only when agricultural wage labor takes women away from the home for very long hours on a more-or-less permanent basis--thus approximating the conditions of nonagricultural employment--or when handicraft production is organized around a central work setting where women are placed in active contact with each other does the expected negative relationship between female employment and fertility in rural areas begin to appear.

However, establishing a causal relationship between employment in the modern sector and fertility levels is less certain than one might believe. For one thing, the amount of role incompatibility associated with a particular type of economic activity may vary from one institutional setting to another. Thus, contrary to the situation in the other contexts, DaVanzo and Lee (1978) report that Malaysian agricultural activities appear to be less compatible with child care than sales or production activities. Nearly 50 percent of the women in sales or production with children under 10 years of age take some of these children with them to work, compared to 24 percent of those in agricultural activity and 22 percent in service. By contrast, very few women engaged in other market occupations take their children along. Thus, Mueller (1982, p. 82) is correct when she states that children are indeed time-consuming yet child rearing need not interfere with market work. DeLancey's (1982) study in Cameroon provides another interesting illustration of this. She reports that half of the women at the Tole Tea Estate worked and that there was a day care center (creche) available there, free of charge, for children under school age. Yet only 7 percent of the wage-employed women at Tole (with young children) used the creche. Some 62 percent of the women had their young children cared for by siblings, co-wives in polygamous families, or other members of the extended family. Indeed, many families bring along a young relative from their ethnic homeland specifically to help around the house and to care for the children, thus supporting Ware's (1977, p. 13) assertion that, as long as relatives are willing to come and assist with household tasks, female employment may actually delay fertility reduction in Africa by slowing the trend toward the nuclear family system.

More modern, urban jobs may actually facilitate and subsidize childbearing, providing high incomes that enable women to afford children, and providing maternity leave and pay (Standing, in press). Thus, Ware (1977, p. 18) reports that, in a study of young women in Ibadan, housewives had the lowest fertility and that, in Lagos, white collar women workers, despite their relatively late age at marriage, still had more children on the average than those with no occupation. Also, any inverse relationship between fertility and modern, urban employment may be due more to job commitment effects or to differences in amount of schooling rather than to the amount of role incompatibility involved. It may also reflect a tendency for selection of nontraditional jobs by women having attitudes and attributes restricting their fertility (Standing, in press). This may account for the results of Cook and Leoprapai (1977) cited earlier as well as those of Stokes and Hsieh (1983), who use a national probability sample and report that female labor force participation is only weakly related to fertility behavior in Taiwan. Various dimensions of female employment, including occupation, are related to fertility preferences, length of first birth interval, and actual fertility, but Stokes and Hsieh report that most zero-order differences by employment characteristics are attributable to compositional differences in duration of marriage, education of wife and husband, residence, and husband's employment locus. They conclude that even with increased participation of women in the modern market sector, female employment by itself apparently has little impact on fertility preferences or behavior.

Income

Based upon research in the United States and other developed countries, one would expect that higher levels of income would be associated with lower fertility (Bulatao and Fawcett, 1981; Ermisch, 1981; Kyriazis, 1979; Razin, 1980; Snyder, 1978; but see Kyriazis and Henripin, 1982).   However, one point of this chapter is that one cannot generalize from a Western-based model for developed countries to the experience of less developed countries.   Ridker (1976, p. 20) points out that an increase in wife's market wage will have two economic effects: (a) to increase household income, making it possible to afford a larger family (the income effect) and (b) to increase the opportunity costs of the wife's time spent in nonmarket activities, thus inducing her to reallocate her time in favor of market activities (the substitute or price effect).   Studies in developed countries indicate that the substitute or price effect tends to outweigh the income effect but studies in less developed countries have frequently indicated that the income effect is greater.   Ridker explains this in terms of: (a) the income effect as being much stronger at the lower levels of income than at the higher levels; (b) the ready availability of family members to assist in child care; and (c) the less degree of incompatibility between the roles of mother and worker in less developed countries than in the more developed ones.   McCabe and Rosenzweig (1976, p. 535) also note a positive relationship of female wages with fertility if mothers can find maternal surrogates or engage in occupations that are more compatible with raising children when the value of their time increases.
Schultz (1981, p. 177) has analyzed Colombian census data in which an imputed wage is assigned to all women.   He reports that fertility is negatively associated with wife's wage in urban areas but in the rural areas the association is negative only for the younger wives, among whom childbearing may only be delayed.   DaVanzo and Lee (1978) report that an increase in wives' or husbands' wage rate leads to a transfer of child care to other persons (servants or relatives) and a decrease in child care by mothers, fathers, and siblings.

Child-Care Arrangements

In addition to containing women engaged in a variety of occupations and working at a variety of pay levels, the work force is heterogeneous in several other ways that have important implications for the work-fertility relationship.   Some women find it easier than other women to arrange child care for their young children, either by taking the children with them while they work or by having older children, a relative, or a servant care for them.   Such an arrangement is more likely when there is a closely knit extended family or when the cost of the domestic labor needed to provide substitute childcare is low. Also, as Standing (in press) points out, the constraints imposed by fertility on women's work are reduced when the desired schooling of children is low or where the desired input of parental time is small. Thus a low educational norm, likely to be present in the rural areas of developing countries, reduces the degree of role incompatibility. DeLancey's (1982) study in Cameroon, cited earlier, provides a case study of the role an extended family can play in providing surrogate child-care while the mother works. Under such circumstances, the opportunity costs of childbearing are reduced because the mother need not forego earning income in order to have children.

Reasons for Employment and Labor Force Commitment

Another major source of heterogeneity within the female work force lies in the reasons the women work and in their degree of commitment to labor force participation. Not all women work for the same reason, nor do all women have equally strong tastes for market activity. Bulatao and Fawcett (1981) report that those women with higher occupational aspirations or expectations, generally, also the more educated, are more likely to postpone early childbearing in order to get ahead in their careers. The extent to which such an attitude is present is at least partially a product of broader societal forces. Salaff and Wong (1977, p. 136) conclude that evidence from the three Chinese societies of Hong Kong, Singapore, and the People's Republic of China points toward social group pressures rather than individually generated attitudes that commit women to remain in the labor force. Attitudes toward work may indeed originate at the individual level, but wider social structures must also support the woman's labor force participation in order for the attitudes to be manifest in work commitment. Some of these wider social structures are more conducive to high degrees of work commitment than others. Safilios-Rothschild (1972) contains an excellent discussion of the effect of work commitment on fertility.

Moreover, not all women work because they are committed to having a career. Women may be in the work force because they are infertile or because their large number of children forces them to seek additional income for the family (ESCAP, 1982; Hull, 1977; Peek, 1975). Others work because they are poor and need the income. When work is done because of economic need and if fertility norms are high, then additional children will induce women to work more to meet increased consumption requirements (Standing, in press). Thus, low income women may have both high rates of market activity and high fertility, and under such circumstances work cannot be held to influence fertility decisions. Hull (1977, p. 45) points out another way in which the reasons a woman works can affect the relationship between her employment status and her fertility, citing findings from a rural village in Java:

The lower fertility among working women in this area of
Java, which has caused some to suggest the value of female
employment in reducing fertility, was found to be not so
much a result of women's working per se as their poverty.
The poor, who have little choice of whether to work or not,
have fewer births and fewer surviving children for a number
of reasons, many of them involuntary.

Thus, Loza-Soliman (1981) writes that most women work outside the
home out of subsistence necessity rather than self-actualization. Youssef (1982) also reports that poverty forces women into the labor market
and that these women work because they have to, not necessarily because they want to, and that therefore their working may not affect
their fertility decisions.   Other women may work because of marital
dissolution or the temporary absence of the husband from the home,
e.g., migrant workers (Sohail, 1981; Wainerman, 1980).   Finally, Ware
(1977, p. 21) reports that the major constraints on fertility discovered
in the Value of Children Study conducted in Southwest Nigeria were
problems of finance, especially the costs of education, health problems,
and marital dissolution.   She adds: "Some African women, and especially
those in polygamous marriages, work in order to be able to have a
large number of children who, in turn, will support their mother in her
old age."

Causality

Scholars have been aware for some time that even the existence of a
negative association between female employment status and fertility
does not necessarily mean that the employment status causes the lower
fertility.   This is even the case in the United States, the model from
which so much extrapolation to less developed countries has so often
improperly been made.   Cain and Dooley (1976), Butz and Ward (1977),
and Waite and Stolzenberg (1976) conclude there is a large effect of
female employment on fertility but only a negligible effect of fertility
on employment.   Siegers and Zandanel (1981) reach a similar conclusion
using Dutch data.   However, Cain (1979), Cramer (1979), Hout (1978),
and Smith-Lovin and Tickamyer (1978) reach opposite conclusions.   Bagozzi and Loo (1978) assert that female employment and fertility affect
each other; and Cramer (1980) attempts to shed light on the contradictions inherent in earlier work on the U.S. experience by stating (p.
167) that: "the dominant effects are from fertility to employment in the
short run and from employment to fertility in the long run."   Dixon
(1978) concludes that recent studies have leaned heavily toward the
interpretation that fertility influences labor force participation more
than the latter affects fertility.   Azzam (1979) notes a negative and
significant relationship between fertility and female labor force
participation in the Arab world and gives fertility the prime causality.

Intermediate Variables

There has been a considerable amount of research relating female
labor force participation to several of the intermediate variables which

can affect fertility. Gaisie (1981) reports that the shortening of postpartum abstinence among the Yorubas is positively associated with employment by either spouse in a white collar occupation. This would tend to increase the fertility of working women, but numerous studies have tested the hypothesis that gainful employment is related to factors which could lead to lower fertility: (a) a higher age at marriage and (b) an increased use of contraception.

Dixon (1978) points out that because of a working daughter's economic contribution to the home, parents may find it advantageous to postpone her marriage and may even decide to have fewer children as they become less dependent upon sons for economic survival. Fawcett and Khoo (1980) report that labor force participation is usually correlated with education and also tends to delay marriage, and Chen–tung (1979) finds that married Singaporean women who are economically active tend to have a higher ideal age at marriage than other women and that females in different occupational groups also differ in their opinion of the ideal age at marriage. Both Omran and Standley (1976) and Ogawa and Rele (1981) report differences in age at first marriage by occupation, with women in the clerical or professional occupations having the highest age at marriage.

The evidence is more ambiguous with respect to contraceptive use. Dow and Werner (1983) report that approval and knowledge of family planning is greater among rural Kenyan wage earning women than among women not earning wages but these differentials are not translated into differentials in use. Data from Bogata and Sao Paulo show no relationship between employment status and contraceptive use (Bertrand et al., 1982). Regmi (1981, p. 216) reports that whether the woman worked before or after marriage is at best weakly related to contraceptive knowledge. Peng and Abduraham (1981) find that the wife's work pattern (in relation to marriage) does not provide differentials in contraceptive use among women in peninsular Malaysia. And Fawcett and Khoo (1980) report that working women in Singapore began practicing contraception earlier in their marriage than did nonworking women but that differences between the two groups are minimal with respect to their attitudes toward family planning or the level of current use.

In Bangladesh users have a slightly higher percentage of women who have worked than do the nonusers (Rahim, 1981, p. 168; also cf. Chaudhury, 1978). Timur (1978) also reports differentials in contraceptive use by employment status, and World Fertility Survey data for Java-Bali show that 30 percent of the exposed women who have never worked are currently using efficient methods compared to 35 percent for those working in the traditional sector and 39 percent for those working in the nontraditional sector. Data from rural Egypt show no differences in use among housewives and workers in agriculture but sharply higher use among professional workers (Department of Statistics, 1982).

CONCLUSIONS

The categories of working and nonworking women are not homogeneous units. Each contains women in a variety of circumstances and with a variety of characteristics which have implications for fertility behavior.   Whether female employment and fertility are related will depend in part upon the composition of each category.   It must be emphasized that the relationship between female labor force partici- pation and fertility is a variable between two multidimensional concepts and that the nature of this variable is affected by the social and economic milieu in which it is observed.

All working women do not have lower fertility than all nonworking women.   Whether working women in the aggregate have lower fertility than nonworking women in the aggregate will depend upon the internal composition of each category with respect to the factors described earlier.   In turn, the composition of each category is affected by the institutional framework of the society: the normative structure sur- rounding motherhood and the importance placed upon it as a means of justifying one's existence; the normative structure surrounding female labor force participation and the extent to which work vis-a-vis motherhood can be a means to achievement; the structure of husband- wife and familial relationships; the economic opportunity structure, particularly the extent to which underemployment and unemployment are present, the extent to which this structure is closed to women, and the extent to which continuous gainful employment is rewarded and discontinuities in employment are not; and the occupational structure and conditions surrounding employment.

A great deal more research is needed on the effects of the nature of the economic opportunity structure on the relationship between female employment and fertility, but Ross (1974) and Standing (in press) point out that, in the United States, "interruption costs" have encouraged both fewer children and a closer spacing of children to concentrate the period of labor force withdrawal.   High levels of unemployment may be important if women leaving a job to care for a child are unable to get work again when they want to, thus increasing the costs of discontinu- ities in employment.   On the other hand, high levels of underemploy- ment are typical in situations where supply of labor exceeds demand. This reduces wages and increments in wages with experience.   A field hand who earns $20 per week, perceives she will receive no increase in weekly salary even if she accumulates seniority, and perceives she will have little difficulty in acquiring similar work in the future (at a similar wage) has less incentive to forego childbearing during a given year than a woman who expects to increase her wages through a con- tinuity effect.   The effects of openness of the economic opportunity structure to females on the relationship between female labor force participation and fertility likewise needs further clarification.   Standing (in press) points out several ways that discrimination against women can alter the opportunity costs of fertility: (a) by excluding women from industrial and high-income forms of employment; (b) by reducing the extent to which self-esteem and status can be realized through employment; (c) by affecting the intrafamily division of labor and the comparative advantages of time allocations within families; (d) by assigning women to less "progressive" and increasingly "static" jobs; and (e) by reducing women's income and ability to contribute to family production, thus reducing their relative autonomy in decisionmaking.

Given these considerations, it is clear that increased employment, even paid employment, of females will not automatically mean lowered fertility and that, in the words of Kupinsky (1977, p. 380), "work for women is not a panacea for the world's population explosion."

This does not mean, however, that policy-makers should be discouraged from trying to lower fertility by attempting to increase the gainful employment of females. Under some circumstances the gainful employment of females is associated with increased age at marriage and contraceptive use. These may be associated with decreases in family size or with delayed childbearing. Such effects might be heightened if there were family planning facilities near the women's work places or if some sort of "family life" education were done on site (cf. Dixon, 1976 for some suggestions; also cf. Loza, 1979). In addition, the possibility of an intergenerational effect exists, whereby the current gainful employment of women legitimizes the idea of such employment in the future for their offspring and provides the notion that motherhood is not the only element in the definition of womanhood (cf. Presser, 1971). Thornton et al. (1983) also report that mother's sex-role attitudes and experiences play an important role in shaping the attitudes of their offspring (also see Macke and Mott, 1980).

However, one's enthusiasm for this measure as a means of reducing fertility must be tempered with the stark realization that, at the current time, the available evidence does not always show a negative association between the gainful employment of females and fertility, especially in the rural areas of developing countries, and that even when present such a negative relationship is seldom strong and may have an ambiguous causal nature. Thus, any effects of employment on fertility are likely to be long-term rather than short-term. Rather than viewing increased female labor force participation as a meritorious means of reducing fertility and also reaching a variety of economic and social goals, perhaps we should view it as one element in the complete restructuring of society which is necessary to reduce fertility in these areas, a process that is likely to be lengthy and filled with apparent contradictions as well as with setbacks.

REFERENCES

Ahdab-Yehia. 1977. Women, employment, and fertility trends in the Arab Middle East and North Africa. In: S. Kupinsky (ed.) The Fertility of Working Women, pp. 172–187. New York: Praeger.

Anker, R., M. Buvinic, and N.H. Youssef. 1982. Introduction. In: R. Anker, M. Buvinic, and N. Youssef (eds.) Women's Roles and Population Trends in the Third World, pp. 11–28. London: Croom Helm.

Arowolo, O.O. 1976. Female labour force participation and fertility: The case of Ibadan City in the Western State of Nigeria. Paper presented to the 15th International Seminar on Family Research, Lome, Togo.

Azzam, H.T. 1979. The Participation of Arab Women in the Labour Force: Development Factors and Policies. Working Paper No. 80, World Employment Programme Research. Geneva: ILO.

Bagozzi, R.P. and F. Van Loo. 1978.   Fertility as consumption: Theories from the behavioral sciences.   Journal of Consumer Research 4:199–228.

Bertrand, J.T., R. Santiso G., R.J. Cisneros, F. Mascarin, and L. Morris. 1982.   Family planning communications and contraceptive use in Guatemala, El Salvador, and Panama.   Studies in Family Planning 13: 190–199.

Blacker, J.G.C. 1978.   A critique of international definitions of economic activity.   Population Bulletin of ECWA 14:47–54.

_____ 1980.   Further thoughts on the definitions of economic activity and employment status.   Population Bulletin of ECWA 19:69–80.

Boserup, E. 1975.   Employment of women in developing countries.   In: L. Tabah (ed.) Population Growth and Economic Development in the Third World, Vol. 1, pp. 79–107.   Dolhain, Belgium: Ordina.

Boulier, B.L. 1977.   The influence of children on household economic activity in Laguna, Philippines.   Journal of Philippine Development 4: 195–222.

Bulatao, R. and J.T. Fawcett. 1981.   Dynamic perspectives in the study of fertility decision–making: Successive decisions within a fertility career.   In: International Union for the Scientific Study of Population, pp. 433–449.   International Population Conference, Manila, 1981, Vol. 1.   Liege: Imprimerie Derouaux.

Butz, W.P. and M.P. Ward. 1977.   The Emergence of Countercyclical U.S. Fertility.   R-1606-NIH.   Santa Monica, California: Rand Corporation.

Cain, G. and M.D. Dooley. 1976.   Estimation of a model of labor supply, fertility, and wages of married women.   Journal of Political Economy 84:S179–S199.

Cain, P.S. 1979.   The determinants of marital labor supply, fertility and sex role attitudes.   Paper presented at annual meetings of the Population Association of America, Philadelphia, Pennsylvania.

Cahill, R. 1977.   The status of women, work, and fertility in India. In: S. Kupinsky (ed.) The Fertility of Working Women, pp. 146–171. New York: Praeger.

Chamie, M. 1983.   Employment, underemployment, unemployment, and unacknowledged employment: A case study of Lebanese women.   In: Institute for Women's Studies in the Arab World (ed.) Arab Women in Population, Employment and Economic Development.   Hague: Mouton Publishers.

Chaudhury, R.H. 1978.   Female status and fertility behavior in a metropolitan urban area of Bangladesh.   Population Studies 32:261–273.

Chen–tung, C. 1979.   Fertility, employment, and fertility behavior.   In: P.S.J. Chen and J.T. Fawcett (eds.) Public Policy and Population Change in Singapore, pp. 167–186.   New York: The Population Council.

Cochrane, S. 1979.   Fertility and Education: What Do We Really Know? Baltimore: Johns Hopkins University Press.

Cook, M.J. and B. Leoprapai. 1977.   Labor Force Participation, Village Characteristics and Modernism and Their Influence on Fertility Among Rural Thai Women.   Bangkok: Mahidol University, Institute for Population and Social Research.

Coombs, L.C. and R. Freedman. 1979. Some roots of preference: Roles, activities and familial values. Demography 16:359-376.
Cramer, J.C. 1979. Employment trends of young mothers and the opportunity cost of babies in the United States. Demography 16:177-197.
_____ 1980. Fertility and female employment: Problems of causal direction. American Sociological Review 45:167-190.
DaVanzo, J. and D. Lee. 1978. The incompatibility of child care with labor force participation and non-market activities: Preliminary evidence from Malaysian time budget data. Paper presented at International Center for Research on Women Conference, Women in Poverty: What Do We Know? Belmont, Maryland.
DeLancey, V. 1982. The relationship between female wage employment and fertility in Africa: An example from Cameroon. Paper presented at the annual meetings of the Southern Economic Association, Atlanta, Georgia.
Department of Statistics, PFPB. 1982. Marriage, fertility and family planning: Summary of the major findings of the Egyptian rural fertility survey 1979. Population Studies: Quarterly Review 60:37-49.
Dixon, R.B. 1976. The roles of rural women: Female seclusion, economic production, and reproductive choice. In: R.G. Ridker (ed.) Population and Development, pp. 290-321. Baltimore: Johns Hopkins University Press.
_____ 1978. Rural Women at Work: Strategies for Development in South Asia. Baltimore: Johns Hopkins University Press.
_____ 1982. Women in agriculture: Counting the labor force in developing countries. Population and Development Review 18:539-566.
Dow, T.E. and L.H. Werner. 1983. Perceptions of family planning among rural Kenyan women. Studies in Family Planning 14:35-42.
ESCAP. 1982. Regional Seminar on Strategies for Meeting Basic Socio-Economic Needs and For Increasing Women's Participation in Development to Achieve Population Goals. New York: United Nations.
Fapohunda, O. 1981. Research for population policy design: Main findings of five case studies. In: International Union for the Scientific Study of Population, International Population Conference, Manila, 1981, Vol. 1, pp. 223-246. Liege: Imprimerie Derouaux.
Fawcett, J.T. and S. Khoo. 1980. Singapore: Rapid fertility transition in a compact society. Population and Development Review 6:548-579.
Freedman, D.S. 1975. Consumption of modern goods and services and its relation to fertility: A study in Taiwan. Journal of Development Studies 12:95-117.
Gaisie, S. 1981. Mediating mechanisms of fertility change in Africa: The role of post-partum variables in the process of change. In: International Population Conference, Manila, 1981, pp. 95-114. Liege: Imprimerie Derouaux.
Gille, H. 1981. Use of certain case studies for population policy design. In: International Union for the Scientific Study of Population, International Population Conference, Manila, 1981, Vol. 1, pp. 247-258. Liege: Imprimerie Derouaux.
Government of the Democratic Republic of the Sudan, Ministry of Health and World Health Organization. 1981. Infant and Early Childhood Mortality in Relation to Fertility Patterns. Khartoum.

Gurak, D.T. and M.M. Kritz. 1982. Female employment and fertility in the Dominican Republic: A dynamic perspective. American Sociological Review 47:810-818.

Harter, C.L. and W.E. Bertrand. 1975. Live-in maids and prostitutes in Cali, Colombia: Social demographic similarities and dissimilarities. Human Mosaic 9:15-31.

_____ 1979. An exploratory study of the fertility of live-in maids and prostitutes in a Colombian city: Suggestions for further research. Canadian Studies in Population 6:143-151.

Hermalin, A.I., R. Freedman, T.H. Sun, and M.C. Chang. 1979. Do intentions predict fertility?   The experience in Taiwan, 1967-74. Studies in Family Planning 10:75-95.

Ho, T.J. 1979.   Time costs of child rearing in the rural Philippines. Population and Development Review 5:643-662.

Hollerbach, P.E. 1983.   Determinants of fertility decline in post-revolutionary Cuba.   In: W.P. Mauldin (ed.) Fertility Decline in Developing Countries: Case Studies.   In press.

Hout, M. 1978.   The determinants of marital fertility in the United States, 1968-1970: Inferences from a dynamic model. Demography 15: 139-160.

Hull, V.J. 1977.   Fertility, women's work, and economic class: A case study from Southeast Asia.   In: S. Kupinsky (ed.) The Fertility of Working Women, pp. 35-80.   New York: Praeger.

Institute of Population Studies, Chulalongkorn University and National Statistical Office. 1977.   The Survey of Fertility in Thailand: Country Report, Volume I, No. 1.   Bangkok, Thailand.

Jones, H.R. 1977.   Fertility decline in Barbados: Some spatial considerations.   Studies in Family Planning 8:157-163.

Kim, N.I. and B.M. Choi. 1981.   Preferences for number and sex of children and contraceptive use in the Republic of Korea.   In: Multivariate Analysis of World Fertility Survey Data for Selected ESCAP Countries.   Asian Population Studies Series, No. 49, pp. 30-60. Bangkok: ESCAP.

Kossoudji, S. and E. Mueller. 1979.   The Economic Status of Female-Headed Households in Rural Botswana.   Mimeo.   Ann Arbor: University of Michigan.

Kupinsky, S. 1977.   Overview and policy implications.   In: S. Kupinsky (ed.) The Fertility of Working Women, pp. 369-380.   New York: Praeger.

Kyriazis, N. 1979.   Sequential fertility decision making: Catholics and Protestants in Canada.   Canadian Review of Sociology and Anthropology 16:275-286.

_____ and J. Henripin. 1982.   Women's employment and fertility in Quebec. Population Studies 36:431-440.

Lembaga Demografi. 1974.   Premliminary Report: Indonesian Fertility-Mortality Survey 1973.   Report 1: West Java.   Jakarta: Lembaga Demografi (Demographic Institute), Fakultas Economia, University of Indonesia.

Lewis, B. 1979.   Fertility and employment: An assessment of role incompatibility among African urban women.   Paper presented at the Conference on Women and Work in Africa, University of Illinois, Urbana-Champaign.

Loza, S.F. 1979. Employment of women action programme: Ready-made clothes factory, South Tahrir. Population Studies 6:1-19.

———— 1982. Social Science Research for Population Policy Design: Case Study of Egypt. IUSSP Papers No. 22. Liege: IUSSP.

Loza-Soliman, S. 1981. Roles of women and their impact on fertility: An Egyptian case study. In: International Population Conference, Manila, 1981, Vol. III, pp. 571-585. Liege: Imprimerie Derouaux.

Macke, A.S. and F.L. Mott. 1980. The impact of maternal characteristics and significant life events in the work orientation of adolescent women. Research in Labor Economics 3:129-146.

Mason, K.O. and V.T. Palan. 1980. Female employment and fertility in Peninsular Malaysia: The maternal role incompatibility hypothesis reconsidered. Population Studies Center, Research Reports No. 81. Ann Arbor: University of Michigan.

McCabe, J.L. and M.R. Rosenzweig. 1976. Female employment creation and family size. In: R.G. Ridker (ed.) Population and Development, pp. 322-355. Baltimore: Johns Hopkins University Press.

Mueller, E. 1982. The allocation of women's time and its relation to fertility. In: R. Anker, M. Buvinic, and N. Youssef (eds.) Women's Roles and Population in the Third World, pp. 55-86. London: Croom Helm.

Ogawa, N. and J.R. Rele. 1981. Age at marriage and cumulative fertility in Sri Lanka. In: Multivariate Analysis of World Fertility Survey Data for Selected ESCAP Countries. Asian Population Studies Series, No. 49, pp. 117-168. Bangkok: ESCAP.

Omran, A.R. and C.C. Standley (eds.). 1976. Family Formation Patterns and Health. Geneva: World Health Organization.

Oppong, C. 1980. A Synopsis of Seven Roles and Statuses of Women: An Outline of a Conceptual and Methodological Approach. World Employment Programmes Research, Working Paper No. 94. Geneva: ILO.

Peek, P. 1975. Female employment and fertility: A study based on Chilean data. International Labor Review 112:207-216.

Peng, T.N. and I. Abduraham. 1981. Factors affecting contraceptive use in Peninsular Malaysia. In: Multivariate Analysis of World Fertility Survey Data for Selected ESCAP Countries. Asian Population Studies Series, No. 49, pp. 94-130. Bangkok: ESCAP.

Presser, H.B. 1971. Like mother, like daughter? The demographic push for alternative roles. Paper presented at annual meeting of the Population Association of America, Washington, D.C.

Rahim, M.A. 1981. Determinants of contraceptives use in Bangladesh. In: Multivariate Analysis of World Fertility Survey Data for Selected ESCAP Countries. Asian Population Studies Series, No. 49, pp. 163-190. Bangkok: ESCAP.

Razin, A. 1980. Number, spacing and quality of children: A microeconomic viewpoint. In: J.L. Simon and J. DaVanzo (eds.) Research in Population Economics, Vol. 2. Greenwich, Connecticut: JAI Press.

Regmi, G. 1981. Differentials in contraceptive knowledge in Nepal. In: Multivariate Analysis of World Fertility Survey Data for Selected ESCAP Countries. Asian Population Studies Series, No. 49, pp. 204-226. Bangkok: ESCAP.

Ridker, R.G. 1976. Perspectives on population policy and research. In: R.G. Ridker (ed.) Population and Development, pp. 1-35. Baltimore: Johns Hopkins University Press.

Safilios-Rothschild, C. 1972. The relationship between work commitment and fertility. International Journal of Sociology of the Family 2:64-71.

_____ 1977. The relationship between women's work and fertility: Some methodological and theoretical issues. In: S. Kupinsky (ed.) The Fertility of Working Women, pp. 355-368. New York: Praeger.

Salaff, J.W. and A.K. Wong. 1977. Chinese women at work: Work commitment and fertility in the Asian setting. In: S. Kupinsky (ed.) The Fertility of Working Women, pp. 81-145. New York: Praeger.

Schultz, T.P. 1981. Economics of Population. Reading, Massachusetts: Addison-Wesley.

Shaw, R.P. 1980. Population policy and education in the Arab world. Unpublished manuscript.

Siegers, J.J. and R. Zandanel. 1981. A simultaneous analysis of labor force participation of married women in the presence of young children in the family. De Economist 129:382.

Smith-Lovin, L. and A.R. Tickamyer. 1978. Nonrecursive models of labor force participation, fertility behavior and sex role attitude. American Sociological Review 43:541-557.

Snyder, D. 1974. Economic determinants of family size in West Africa. Demography 11:613-627.

_____ 1978. Economic variables and the decision to have additional children: Evidence from the survey of economic opportunity. American Economist 22:12-16.

Sohail, M. 1981. Differentials in cumulative fertility in rural Bangladesh. In: Multivariate Analysis of World Fertility Survey Data for Selected ESCAP Countries. Asian Population Studies Series, No. 49, pp. 181-203. Bangkok: ESCAP.

Standing, G. 1977. Studies of Labour Force Participation in Low-Income Areas: Methodological Issues and Data Requirements. Geneva: International Labor Organization.

_____ 1978. Labor Force Participation and Development. Geneva: International Labor Organization.

_____ 1981. Unemployment and Female Labour Supply in Kingston, Jamaica. London: Macmillan for the International Labor Organization.

_____ In press. Women's work activity and fertility. In: R.A. Bulatao and R.D. Lee (eds.) Determinants of Fertility in Developing Countries. New York: Academic Press.

Stokes, C.S. and Yeu-sheng Hsieh. 1983. Female employment and reproductive behavior in Taiwan, 1980. Demography 20:313-331.

Thornton, A., D.F. Alwin, and D. Camburn. 1983. Causes and consequences of sex-role attitudes and attitude change. American Sociological Review 48:211-227.

Tickamyer, A.R. 1979. Women's roles and fertility intentions. Pacific Sociological Review 22:167-184.

Timur, S. 1978. Socioeconomic determinants of differential fertility in Turkey. In: J. Allman (ed.) Women's Status and Fertility in the Muslim World, pp. 54-76. New York: Praeger.

U.S. Bureau of the Census. 1983. International fertility indicators. Current Population Reports, Series P-23, No. 123 (February).

Wainerman, C.H. 1980. The impact of education on the female labor force in Argentina and Paraguay. Comparative Education Review 24:2, Part 2:180-195.

Waite, L.J. and R.M. Stolzenberg. 1976. Intended childbearing and labor force participation of young women: Insight from non-recursive models. American Sociological Review 41:235-251.

Ware, H. 1977. Women's work and fertility in Africa. In: S. Kupinsky (ed.) The Fertility of Working Women, pp. 1-34. New York: Praeger.

_____ 1981. Women, Demography and Development. Canberra: Australian National University.

Weller, R.H. 1977. Demographic correlates of woman's participation in economic activities. In: International Population Conference, Mexico, 1977, pp. 447-516. Liege: IUSSP.

Youssef, N. 1977. Women and agricultural production in Muslim societies. Studies in Comparative International Development 12:41-58.

_____ 1982. The interrelationship between the division of labour in the household, women's roles and their impact on fertility. In: R. Anker, M. Buvinic, and N. Youssef (eds.) Women's Roles and Population Trends in the Third World, pp. 173-201. London: Croom Helm.

CHAPTER 9

Rural Development and the Value of Children: Implications for Human Fertility

Nan E. Johnson

Demographers have long sought a theory to account for the inverse relationship between human fertility and economic development. Classical demographic transition theory explained the nineteenth-century European fertility decline as due to the rising levels of urbanization and industrialization (Notestein, 1945, 1953). These residential and economic changes were thought to shift dependence from relatively self-contained local institutions (e.g., the family farm) to institutions of the larger society (e.g., the factory) (Freedman, 1963). As one's system of interaction expanded outside the family, children were hypothesized to become less critical to economic survival. At the same time, children supposedly became more costly because parents wanted to invest more in themselves or their children and because children made it harder to take advantage of new nonfamilial opportunities (Freedman, 1979). As such, demographic transition theory put the locus of fertility innovation in an urban industrialism which reduced the economic benefits and raised the cost of children. For a long time, the urban bias implicit in demographic transition theory discouraged international development efforts in the rural sector, since some feared that these efforts would only stimulate high human fertility and overwhelm any potential rise in agricultural productivity (see Lieberman, 1980, p. 305).

Recently, economic historians and demographers have noted some new findings which urge a revision of classical transition theory. For example, fertility decline began in France before the Napoleonic Revolution, a time when the population was largely illiterate farm owners.

French fertility may even have been lower in rural than in urban areas (Goldscheider, 1971, p. 159). It is, hence, illogical to attribute the fertility decline in France in the late eighteenth century to urban industrial growth, since the source of fertility decline was apparently indigenous to rural areas, since industrial expansion was minimal at that time, and since rural-to-urban migration was insignificant (Goldscheider, 1971, p. 156).

Similarly, a fertility decline had begun in the U.S. by 1810, seven decades before the decline in the more industrialized England. Ironically, the majority of the U.S. population was rural; and the rural population was growing at a rate exceeding two percent annually (Johnson and Beegle, 1982). Petersen (1961, p. 218) calculated that 56 percent of the U.S. national fertility decline between 1810 and 1940 was due to a reduction in childbearing in rural areas, 24 percent due to a reduction in urban childbearing, and 20 percent due to rural-to-urban migration. These nineteenth-century fertility trends in the U.S., together with those of eighteenth-century France, beg a revision of demographic transition theory to consider the rural farm economy as a locus of human fertility decline.

THE WEALTH-FLOWS THEORY OF FERTILITY

A reformulation of demographic transition theory was offered by Caldwell (1976, 1977a,b, 1978, 1980, 1982, 1983). Caldwell argued that there are only two kinds of society: one in which it is economically rational to have an unlimited number of children; and one in which it is economically rational to be childless. Since no surviving society has reproduced at the biologically maximal level, a ceiling on human fertility has been imposed by social and personal constraints. However, that ceiling has been higher in the first kind of society.

The Pre-Transitional Society

The cultural superstructure of the first (pre-transitional) society is a family morality (Caldwell, 1978). Decision-making authority in both production and reproduction is based on the high status accorded to males. Consequently, patriarchs contribute to farm production not so much by physical labor as by the decisions on what to do and when to do it (White, 1975, p. 136). Male elders govern reproduction by controlling the nuptials of their children. The marriages of sons are often arranged late so as to lengthen their contribution to the family farm economy and to preserve intrafamilial heirarchies by age and sex. For example, Middle-Eastern males are typically wed at about age 25 to women five to ten years younger. This mature age at male marriage supports greater lengths between male generations, and the age difference between spouses encourages emotional distance between them (Caldwell, 1978, p. 564). Thus, females begin to marry and children begin to work when both are young and docile; and for the rest of their lives, their labor benefits husbands and fathers. The family morality commands wives/children to work hard, obey their husbands/ fathers, and demand little in return.   Indeed, sharp distinctions are often not perceived between the social roles of wives and children (Caldwell, 1982, p. 336) (2).   Put simply, wives and children are economically valuable and cost little in the long run.   In such a society, the greater material advantage accrues to adult males from polygamy and high fertility.

From an early age, children are miniature workers in a pre-transitional society.   They perform the less preferred chores which their elders cannot or will not do: carrying messages, fetching water or fuel, sweeping, and caring for farm animals or younger siblings.   While such tasks may not directly produce income or food, they are necessary for household maintenance.   The performance of these "children's jobs" releases older family members to do more directly productive work and hence are of indirect economic value (Caldwell, 1976, p. 344).

Java would appear to be a society based on a family morality.   In Javanese households with insufficient capital to purchase farm animals, children care for the animals of another farm household in exchange for a daily wage and half of any litter born during the tenure (White, 1975).   While the daily wage is quite small, this method of acquiring newborn farm animals is an important economic contribution since a large cow in Java is worth about half of a poor family's annual income (Nag et al., 1978, p. 295).   A time-use study of the village of Kali Loro near Yogyakarta showed that children spent more time than adults in animal care (White, 1975).   Similar relationships were observed in a relatively inaccessible Nepalese village, where boys and girls aged six to eight years spent an average of about two hours each day tending animals (Nag et al., 1978) (3).   Likewise, Javanese and Nepalese girls aged six to eight spent nearly two hours daily watching younger siblings and releasing mothers for other work.

As Javanese children grow larger, they are able to begin the heavier tasks of rice cultivation.   The chores are segregated by sex with males doing the ground preparation, females the planting, males the weeding, and females the reaping.   White (1975) found that by age 13 to 15, boys could earn as much as men for hoeing and weeding rice, while girls aged 13 to 15 could earn as much as women for planting and harvesting rice.   Mueller (1976, p. 122) alleged that the proximity of White's village to Yogyakarta (21 miles) heightened the demand for farm products and handicrafts and thereby exaggerated the economic value of Javanese children.   Yet a more geographically scattered survey of 1000 households in Central Java showed that a large majority of wives and husbands cited economic benefits as a first response to an open-ended question on the advantages of having children (Darroch et al., 1981, p. 26).

Unlike in Java, the practice of female seclusion (purdah) keeps Bangladeshi females within or near the house.   Thus, Bangladeshi households depend primarily on young sons to forage for cooking fuel, potable water, and animal feed (Cain, 1977).   This search is quite time-consuming, as the increasing intensity of cropping has led to severe deforestation and loss of pasture (Cain, 1977, p. 204; Briscoe, 1979).   By ages eight to nine, boys begin weeding, hoeing, transplanting, and harvesting rice.   In contrast to their brothers, Bangladeshi girls begin sweeping floors, washing dishes, and tending chickens at about age six.   By the time they are nine, the girls are strong enough to begin husking rice with a heavy wooden plank which is attached to the fulcrum and operated seesaw fashion (see Cain, 1977).   Although husking rice is labor-intensive, it is practically always for home consumption; and, consequently, rice processing is socially defined as maintenance rather than as productive labor.

When Bangladeshi females do engage in market labor, purdah restricts the geographic and social distance they may travel; for example, they may work only for employers with whom a prior social relationship has been established (e.g., through kinship) (Cain et al., 1979).   Females are less likely to find employment and must work for lower wages than males (Cain et al., 1979, p. 430).   Hence, while girls aged 13 to 15 work as many hours as do similarly aged boys, the socially constructed value of female labor is less than what they consume (Cain, 1977). Yet boys can earn enough to be net producers by age 12, to compensate for their cumulative consumption by age 15, and to repay their own and one sister's cumulative consumption by age 22 (Cain, 1977, 1978).   The inaccessibility of wage labor to females in Bangladeshi agriculture may explain why a sample of Bangladeshi men expressed a strong preference to have sons instead of daughters (Williamson, 1978, p. 8).

Pre-transitional societies are characterized by an environment of risk. One type of risk is crop-destroying vagaries of nature such as floods, droughts, or insects.   Cain (1981, p. 461) wrote that children, regardless of age, are unlikely to be of much help to their parents in times of natural disaster, since younger and older generations are apt to suffer equally.   However, women disproportionately suffer the social risks attending divorce, widowhood, or permanent celibacy.   Thus, in patriarchal societies like Bangladesh, where women are systematically denied access to wage labor, husbands and adult sons are forms of risk insurance against economic deprivation (Cain, 1978).   Because a Bangladeshi wife is, on average, about eight years younger than her husband (Durch, 1980, p. 11), the probability of widowhood is great; and her future welfare is uncertain in the absence of sons (4).   Indeed, a Bangladeshi widow must have borne children by the deceased husband in order to claim his bequest (Cain et al., 1979, p. 408).

Unlike in Bangladesh, daughters are a form of risk insurance in Java, even after they marry.   Most married daughters live nearby and can regularly assist parents with food, labor, or care.   As mentioned previously, planting and harvesting rice are exclusively female tasks in Java; and the labor of nonhousehold female relatives is preferred to that of neighbors or strangers (Hull and Hull, 1977a).   The pay of such preferred workers is a larger share of unhulled rice (White, 1975). Women who participate in planting the paddies of others expect also to assist in harvesting and, in turn must reciprocate that invitation if they cultivate paddies of their own.   Hence, larger networks of female relatives are able to retain more of the rice harvest within the extended family, to the greater benefit of their spouses, children, and parents (Hull and Hull, 1977a).   In addition, elderly Javanese in the village of Kali Loro were almost equally likely to reside with daughters as with sons (Nag et al., 1978, p. 299). As such, there is no preference for having sons rather than daughters in the village of Kali Loro [a finding also reported in a larger study of Central Java (see Darroch et al., 1981)]. The stronger economic status of women in Indonesia than in Bangladesh may create weaker pronatalist pressures in the former country and may contribute to its somewhat lower fertility (5).

Another kind of risk in pre-transitional societies is that posed by depredation (Cain, 1981). In environments where legal or political institutions are weak or corrupt, there is strength in numbers. In Nigeria and Ghana, where economic and political institutions are capricious, parents can insure themselves against loss by investing in the education of one or two children. Education is the only route to a job in the modern political or economic bureaucracy; but once in place, the educated child can pressure the local authorities in behalf of his family (Caldwell, 1976, p. 349). The risk environment is, however, pronatalist, since some children must be spared for farm labor to support their sibling in school (6). Similarly, since men have absolute control over the police force and the courts of Bangladesh, women have little legal protection there unless "closely identified with and supported by a man" (Cain et al., 1979, p. 407). The vulnerability of women against property crimes doubtless creates strong motivations to have sons in Bangladesh. However, social and political ties are gained not only through childbirth but also through marriage. Arranged marriage, common in the pre-transitional countries of Africa and Asia, insure that the interests of the patriarch are served by the union.

Aside from being insurers against the risks of pre-transitional societies, children can be interest-bearing investments. Ware (1978) mentions the practice of child-pawning in Nigeria and Ghana, where parents borrow money and hand over a child as collateral. The service the child renders to the creditor is deemed interest on the loan. Later, children may become a source of old-age support, particularly in countries where institutional alternatives do not exist. Thus, the Value of Children Study in five Asia nations (Japan, Taiwan, Thailand, South Korea, and the Philippines) found that over 70 percent of the rural respondents expected old-age/financial support from their children (Arnold et al., 1975). Since this study covered more economically developed Asian countries, the percentage would likely be higher elsewhere on the continent.

But children convey a security beyond the economic. For example, the Javanese derive contentment from attention and entertainment provided by others. This atmosphere is best achieved in a household bristling with activity, and small children are major contributors to this mood. More than material goods, elderly Javanese want solicitude from their children; and these expressions are vital psychological supports in times of illness or crisis (Hull and Hull, 1977a). In other words, children insure parents not only agains economic risk but also against alienation and in this way provide comfort in both the material and personal sense.

There are few alternatives to the functions children hold in a pre-transitional society. While elderly Javanese might receive gifts from other relatives, children are clearly the preferred source. Gifts are valued as symbols of the child's eternal debt for the ultimate gift of life itself. As such, the material gifts of support from the younger to the older generation are offerings which reaffirm the parent-child bond. Hoffman and Hoffman (1973, p. 69) wrote that if children satisfy a value for which there are few alternatives, then people will brook heavy costs before they will reduce their fertility. Thus, Caldwell (1976, 1977b, 1980, 1982, 1983) concluded that fertility will be high in societies where a family morality requires a net wealth flow from child to patriarch.

A criticism of the wealth-flows theory holds that children and wives do not generate more than they consume in pre-transitional societies. An aggregate-level study of peasant agriculture in 27 lesser developed countries concluded that at ages 15 to 19, boys' work contribution is only 75 percent of that of men aged 20 to 54 (Mueller, 1976, p. 118). Making some assumptions about annual hours worked and productivity per hour, the same study argued that females at any age had much lower labor contributions than did males of the same age. However, Mueller's study defined "work" as any activity which contributed to the gross national product: agricultural labor, house construction, and preparation of food for sale. By excluding maintenance housework and child care, this definition was biased against recognizing the work contributions of children and women. Secondly, for a given time unit of "work," Mueller used agricultural wage rates as indicators of the relative productivity by age and sex. The problem with this approach is that wage rates are not an objective indicator of productivity because they reflect the social valuation of the laborer. Recall that the sex-segregated market activities in Bangladesh create fewer wage-earning opportunities for females and pay them lower wages (Cain et al., 1979). For these reasons, Mueller's conclusion that third-world children's and women's farm labor is "seriously underutilized" cannot be drawn from her data.

In a vein similar to Mueller's, Cain (1982) renounced his original contention that the productivity of Bangladeshi boys was great enough to compensate for their lifetime consumption by age 15, an average of nine years before their marriage (Durch, 1980, p. 11). Rather, Cain later argued that when the net productivity of boys is discounted by a positive interest rate on what they consume, it is no longer certain they can repay their lifetime consumption before their nuptials. Yet Caldwell (1982, p. 334) cautioned that estimations of the net economic value of children should not start with birth and end in marriage; instead they should start when the individual first begins fertility decision making and conclude only at death. Indeed, parents can and do tap the income streams of married sons in Bangladesh.

Cain (1982) asserted that what children consume represents a larger proportion of the family budget in a pre-transitional than in a transitional society, where average family incomes have risen above the subsistence level. In other words, he concluded that children cost relatively more in pre-transitional societies; but he ignored the issue of who pays the cost. A family production unit may encounter stages of the life cycle when children are a potential drain on paternal resources (as after the birth of children but before any are old enough to do productive or maintenance work). However, the food deficit will fall disproportionately on children and women (Caldwell, 1982). As an example, lower food–consumption levels by children and women than by men in Bangladesh is suggested by higher rates of infant and female mortality and by anthropometry (Chen et al., 1981).

Contrary to what the wealth-flows theory suggests, Cain (1982) reasoned that extended-family networks providing mutual economic support might bring about lower fertility. He noted that in three Indian study villages (Shirapur, Kanzara, and Aurepalle), extended family residence was twice as high and joint cultivation of farms by brothers was far more common than in the comparison village of Char Gopalpur, Bangladesh. He concluded that fertility was much lower in the Indian villages perhaps because lateral kinship bonds were strong enough that children were not the only kin-based insurance against risk (p. 173). However, the Indian and the Bangladeshi villages differed by the presence of medical facilities, schools, and credit cooperatives in the former. These institutions supplied contraceptive services, information from the outside world, and nonfamilial sources of financial aid, all of which facilitated lower fertility or reduced the rewards of higher fertility in the Indian villages. Therefore, the lower fertility in the Indian villages as compared to Char Gopalpur can be accounted for without reference to the relative strengths of lateral and filial bonds.

In addition, the wealth flow from patriarch to child in the Gonja tribe of Ghana is weak enough that bequests are often made within rather than between generations. Yet this same tribe has high fertility and high rates of fosterage. Fosterage is an adult-centered mechanism for acquiring the services of children; it is practiced instead of adoption because children are not valued as heirs (Goody, 1973). The Gonja tribe does not support Cain's thesis that strong lateral bonds are an antinatalist alternative to the economic contributions of children.

Another criticism of the wealth-flows theory is that English fertility did not begin to decline in the 1830s and 1840s, when the Factory Acts severely restricted child labor and, hence, the economic value of children. Rather, the English fertility decline began between 1871 and 1881, when only 17 percent of the population was still in primary production (Caldwell, 1980, p. 246). Likewise, by 1850, urban children in Australia were probably no longer a productive asset; but Australian marital fertility did not begin falling until three decades later. A way of understanding these anomalies is to consider them representative of a threshold era, when wealth is no longer directed upward to the patriarch but is not yet directed downward by him (Caldwell, 1980, p. 232, 248; 1982, p. 346). One might say that at the threshold of fertility decline, the chief monetary value of children to the patriarch is that they are relatively costless.

The Transitional Society

The second (transitional) society envisioned by Caldwell is one based on a community morality. Community morality emotionally nucleates individuals from the natal family and creates felt obligations to the community or state. Community morality teaches the subordination of family authority to employer authority, makes citizens out of sons and daughters, and equips them to be loyal and efficient producers in the state economy. By investing in compulsory school education, the state economy introduces technical knowledge as a source of decision-making authority. In so doing, community morality legitimates a net wealth flow from parents to school children, since parents must protect the state's investment in its future decision makers.

Subordination in a two-tiered global system forces contemporary developing economies to import not only some of the technical knowledge which is their grist but also the means by which it is created: to wit, organizational models, syllabi, teachers, and textbooks from Western schools. A content analysis of primers in Ghana, Nigeria, and Kenya showed no support for such African traditions as polygamy, witchcraft, condemnation of sterile women, or stronger loyalty to the family at the expense of the state (Caldwell, 1980, p. 240). Instead, these primers told stories of children with African names who lived in nuclear families, played with toys, went to school, and performed household or farm chores not as duties but as favors to their parents. Arranged marriages were portrayed as legalizing love matches already underway. Put otherwise, the third-world school transmits Western technical knowledge through Western cultural vehicles which incorporate the nuclear-family concept.

Formal schooling can reduce the productivity of children in the family economy by shortening the time when they are home and available to work. The composition of chores can change so that the children can spend more energy on succeeding at school (Caldwell, 1980, p. 227). Also, education can raise the price of children in direct ways through tuition, uniforms, and stationery, and in indirect ways through other expenditures (e.g., shoes and satchels) so that they will appear no worse than their classmates (p. 227). By familiarizing children with an outside material world, schooling can encourage them to demand more expenditures from their parents. But these child-favoring effects on intergenerational wealth flows may last only as long as the child is in school. For Caldwell, the crucial fact making these changes permanent is the school-transmitted Western concept of the child-centered nuclear family.

At least two implications follow. One is that family morality will probably not yield to community morality until mass primary-school education [liberally defined by Caldwell (1980, p. 233) as the attendance of primary school by most children at least irregularly] has been achieved. Another is that fertility decline can precede economic development if mass primary-school education does so. Examples of this latter phenomenon are Sri Lanka and Kerala State (India) (Caldwell, 1980, p. 227).

Madigan (1977) rejected the thesis that Western cultural diffusion can account for fertility decline in the Philippines. Since the Philippines was a Spanish colony from 1565 to 1898 and an American protectorate from 1898 to 1946, Madigan argued that Filipino fertility should have begun to decline well before the actual onset in the 1970s, if the thesis were correct (7).   However, mass primary-school education was never achieved in the Spanish colonial period.   Schooling was reserved for the elite: Spanish colonialists, their children, and the few Filipinos entering the Roman Catholic clergy (Hunt and McHale, 1965).   Census materials showed that as late as 1903, the literacy rate was only 20 percent.   But during the first decade of the twentieth century, the American colonialists expanded the number of primary schools, imported thousands of American teachers, and instituted English as the language of the classroom.   Largely as a result of these efforts, the literacy rate rose to 60 percent by 1948 (Hunt and McHale, 1965, p. 68).   While the sex differential in educational attainment was substantial at the start of the century, it had disappeared by the early 1950s (Smith and Cheung, 1981).   In contradiction to Madigan, Western cultural diffusion does appear to have brought on a decline in Filipino fertility but only after mass primary education became a reality during American rule.

Caldwell's theory, cast with reference to contemporary developing countries, nevertheless sheds light on why marital fertility declined before urban industrialization in eighteenth-century France and nineteenth-century America.   In both countries, the majority of the populations owned and operated farms, where the inheritance pattern was joint heirship rather than primogeniture and where land ownership was a prerequisite for the marriage.   The absence of pronounced urban industrial growth in eighteenth-century France meant that rural-urban migration did not offer an alternative livelihood to family-farm production.   Since the rural French population was growing due to declining mortality, farm couples had no choice but to contracept (probably by coitus interruptus) if they were to avoid an uneconomic subdivision of farmland among a large number of heirs (Goldscheider, 1971, p. 156).   While urban industrialization was more significant in nineteenth-century America, it apparently cannot account for the fertility decline which began first in older (eastern) farm areas and then extended to newer (western) ones (Petersen, 1975).   Rather, land scarcity probably raised the price of procuring farmland for all children when they reached adulthood (Easterlin et al., 1978).   Since land access became problematic first in older farm areas, the rural fertility decline was initiated there.   In both the cases of France and America, marital fertility declined on rural farms because the intergenerational transmission of wealth favored children and because land scarcity threatened to interrupt that flow.

MODERN RURAL DEVELOPMENT POLICY AND THE VALUE OF CHILDREN

Access to the means of family-farm production affects the magnitude, if not the direction, of intrafamilial wealth flows.   A reduction in magnitude below a socially acceptable level requires a reduction in the number of recipients or an increase in the number of donors.   Since children were wealth recipients in pre-twentieth-century France and America, land scarcity meant fertility decline.   Since children are wealth givers to the patriarchs on contemporary third world farms, it is logical to inquire whether economic development policies granting wider-scaled access to farmland might be pronatalist (see Chapter 10).

Land Ownership

There are at least two ways in which farmland can affect the net wealth flow from children to patriarchs in the third world. One is the institutional mechanisms distributing access to land. Caldwell (1978) argued that communally owned lands used for hunting, gathering, nomadic pastoralism, or shifting cultivation might encourage higher fertility than private ownership. In familial modes of subsistence production, land and children are the only two investment avenues; and most households diversify their investment profiles (p. 342). Where private ownership of land is not practiced, "the only real investment may be in reproducing labor" (Caldwell, 1983, p. 373). Accordingly, Ware (1978, p. 6) argued that communal ownership of land enhanced the material benefits of children in Upper Volta and Sudan, where usufructary rights are based on the size of the household labor force.

In Bangladesh, where private land ownership is practiced, landless farm laborers apparently have lower fertility than do landed agriculturalists. The landless in Bangladesh face longer periods of spousal separation due to the employment of husbands as migrant farm laborers. Perhaps because of undernutrition, landless farm women may suffer a higher incidence of involuntary subfecundity and spontaneous abortion (Stoeckel and Chowdhury, 1980). Likewise, child mortality rates have been found to be higher among the landless than among the landed in Bangladesh (Cain, 1978, p. 434). In other words, in subsistence agriculture based on private land ownership, landlessness can reduce the supply of children by lowering pregnancy and survivorship rates.

Land ownership in Bangladesh is a lever of social control through which a farm owner is better able to influence his children's labor and to profit from it (Cain, 1978, p. 435; Caldwell et al., 1980). Sons of landed farmers in Char Gopalpur begin plowing, weeding, transplanting, harvesting, and threshing rice, cutting and washing jute, picking chillies, and digging potatoes at much younger ages than do sons of landless farm laborers (Cain, 1977). A Bangladeshi farm owner can increase his returns from child labor by delaying the departure of adult sons from the natal household. A son is unlikely to demur, for rebellion could jeopardize his inheritance, particularly when there are brothers with whom to share patrimony. Thus, Cain (1978, p. 436) found that the age of a son's departure from the parental household in Char Gopalpur was lowest (22.3 years) when the father had no de facto access to farmland (by squatting, lease, purchase, or inheritance) and varied directly with the size of holding when the father had such access. A departing son is granted usufruct rights to some farmland when his father owns any, but the father retains legal title until death as a way of expropriating future returns to the land (Cain, 1978, p. 436; 1982, p. 171). In these ways, land ownership can increase the demand for child labor in subsistence agriculture.

Land is the material base of not only paternal control over children but also male domination over females in Bangladesh. Women are denied physical access to the rice and jute paddies since fieldwork would expose them to view and violate the tradition of purdah. Women are not denied legal access to the land, since Muslim law allows them to inherit it from their fathers. But the law limits their patrimony to half what their brothers receive. Moreover, exogamy and patrilocal residence move married daughters some distance away from their father's land so that they are often powerless to protect their share from poachers and thieves. Even when a married daughter successfully claims her inherited land, her husband seizes managerial control as if the land were his own (see Cain et al., 1979).

Bangladeshi daughters have not received an education as a substitute form of patrimony. Education is rendered difficult by purdah, which restricts women's travel outside the family compound and forbids them to speak in the presence of strangers. While mass primary education does not yet exist for either sex, females are less than half as likely as males to be able to read and write (8). In the absence of an educational ladder, land is the only potential source of economic mobility in Bangladesh. Therefore, the institutions of purdah, kinship, and Muslim law preserve the gender inequalities of family production by granting women access to land only through men.

Given the importance of land for the creation of wealth in Bangladesh, several land reform laws have been enacted since World War II to increase the extent of ownership. This legislation has failed in that purpose for several reasons. First, the law set a limit on farm sizes at 33 acres in 1950, changed it to 125 acres in 1961, and reverted it to 33 acres in 1972. The fact that the median farm size in Cain's (1981) typical study village was only 0.7 acre suggests the legal ceiling was set too high to have much effect. However, many of the wealthy owners whose land size exceeded the limit apparently evaded the law by retitling property in the names of sons or other close relatives (Cain, 1981, p. 449). Further concentration of farmland into the hands of a few has been accomplished by poaching land or forging titles, since the legal and police systems of Bangladesh are weak (Cain, 1981). As a result, the land reform laws have failed to prevent a further decline in ownership and size of farm holdings in Bangladesh.

As was the case in Bangladesh, Schutjer et al. (1980) reported a positive relationship between land ownership and human fertility in 68 rural barrios of Cavite Province, Philippines. However, land ownership was also associated with higher female education and better quality housing (i.e., more sanitary toilet facilities), all of which has a negative association with human fertility. Since the associations of land ownership on human fertility through female education and housing were stronger than was the direct effect, the net balance of land ownership was antinatalist. Although the cross-sectional data used in this study could not confirm the hypothesized time-series relationships, it is likely that land ownership is heightening female education and depressing fertility in the younger Filipino generation. Because of the bilateral nature of inheritance in the Philippines and the expansion of school systems in the American colonial period, land ownership has contributed to the mass education of women. Farm daughters have increasingly taken their share of patrimony in the form of higher schooling, while their brothers have taken the land (Smith and Cheung, 1981, p. 43).

In contrast to Bangladesh, the land reform in Karnataka, Andhra Pradesh, and Maharashtra, India, has been a limited success (Caldwell et al., 1982b). A key difference has been the inability of Bangladesh to enforce any kind of legislation (Cain, 1981, p. 450). As in Bangladesh, many Indian owners of large or irrigated farms avoided losing acreage above the ceiling by deeding it to sons as a form of ante mortem inheritance. But while the reform law in these three Indian states may not have resulted in much loss of land by big owners, it probably discouraged further accumulation by the rich (Cain, 1981).

The case of Karnataka is illustrative. Farm owners, apprehensive that their land be subdivided by the State with future legislation, moved some of their sons into nonagricultural employment and increasingly invested in sons' education. Primary education (ages 6 to 11) is now universal for boys but not yet for girls (Visaria and Visaria, 1981, p. 35). Daughters have profited educationally, however, the better to attract educated sons-in-law and to reduce the risk that married daughters would return destitute to the parental household (Caldwell et al., 1982b). As such, consequences of the land reform have been a large rise in male and a smaller rise in female education and some geographic dispersal of the extended family.

While land generates larger income streams for males than females in Indian agriculture, female access to land income is not totally through husbands or patriarchs. Indian females can cultivate their own holdings or sell their labor in the agricultural work force. Preparing seed beds, transplanting, and weeding rice are exclusively female tasks; but both men and women can harvest and thresh (Cain, 1981, p. 457). Therefore, the limited success of land reform in Karnataka, Andhra Pradesh, and Maharashtra has benefited women financially and may partially account for the lower fertility in these states than in Bangladesh.

Land Size

A second way in which farmland can structure wealth flows from children to patriarchs is through the absolute size of cultivated holdings. Farms that are too fragmented to produce a subsistence for the operator's household require a supplementation with other income sources such as fishing, petty trading, or wage labor. The uncertainty or the sporadic nature of these latter sources may lead to poorer nutrition and medical care for women and children and to higher rates of male labor migration. Thus, fertility may be lower among the cultivators of small holdings due to lower pregnancy rates and higher rates of subfecundity, intrauterine mortality, and child mortality. Larger-sized plots may also enhance the productive utility of farm children in labor-intensive subsistence agriculture. Cain (1977, p. 218) found that sons of large farmers in Bangladesh were more likely to engage in crop production and less likely to perform wage labor than were sons of small cultivators. Perhaps for these reasons, the size of cultivated holdings was found to be positively related to human fertility in Bangladesh (Stoeckel and Chowdhury, 1980), the Philippines (Hawley, 1955), and India (Driver, 1963).

Nevertheless, land reform laws have resulted in nonpositive relationships between farm size and human fertility in Japan and Taiwan. In Japan and China before the late 1940s, farmland was viewed as the communal property of the ancestors and, thus, a legacy to be held in trust. Because land inheritance was from father to eldest son, it reinforced the inequalities by age and sex on which wealth flows in familial production are based. The farm was the site of the family shrine and a burial place of the ancestors. A responsibility of the heir was to supply the shrine with offerings and to safeguard the tablets of family descent. When ancestral property was large, Japanese farmers founded branch families by dividing the land among several sons. Because the eldest son was culturally designated as the sole beneficiary, younger sons of wealthy farmers had to earn the privilege of heading branch families by working on their father's farm longer until marriage; and in this way, large landowners could extract additional labor from their younger sons (Dore, 1953). Landowners who established branch families wielded considerable political power in life and guaranteed themselves many more descendants who would keep shrines for their spirit after death. Consequently, land bequests were not interpreted as a wealth flow from father to son(s) because the heir was seen as a custodian rather than a private owner. The rites of ancestor worship for which he was responsible symbolized a perpetual wealth flow from the younger generation to the older patriarch. Before the postwar land reform, the 1940 Census of Japan showed a positive relationship between human fertility and farm size (Dore, 1953, p. 86).

After World War II, however, the land reform laws in Japan (1947) and Taiwan (1949) limited each farm to a maximum of about seven acres and required equal division of this property among all surviving children of both sexes at the owner's death. By denying sole heirship to eldest sons, the new laws eroded age and sex as the bases of economic and family prerogative. The scarcity of reclaimable land and the threat of fragmentation encouraged the adoption of such labor-intensive technologies as irrigation, chemical fertilizers, and high-yield varieties of rice. These capital inputs increased the yield per acre, the possible number of crop cycles, and, thus, the demand for farm labor. Nevertheless, children did not supply this demand because of new compulsory education laws which virtually eliminated gender differences in primary schooling (on Japan, see Dore, 1953; on Taiwan, see Chaffee et al., 1969). The farm cooperatives that were organized to meet the new farm-labor demands initiated a nonfamilial mode of agricultural production, which reduced the economic rewards of high fertility to the patriarch. Land reform also replaced the concept of ancestral ownership of land with the notion of personal ownership. The relationship between human fertility and landholding size had become U-shaped in Japan by the late 1940s (Dore, 1953, p. 86) and inverse in Taiwan by the early 1960s (Hermalin and Lavely, 1979).

CONCLUSION

Land ownership and land size change the magnitude, not the direction, of wealth flows internal to farm families. In Bangladesh, the Philippines, and India, where farm children and women generate income streams toward men, the direct effects of ownership or size of land are positively associated with human fertility. Therefore, in order for land reform to be antinatalist, it is necessary that land-reform legislation redirect wealth flows to favor women or children. For example, a land reform could create wealth flows toward women by making it legally possible for them to inherit land on parity with their brothers and to obtain credit for land purchases. Labor laws could require equal pay to men and women hired for the tasks (e.g., in India, where both men and women harvest and thresh). Removal of gender barriers to land ownership and land income would increase the magnitude of women's wealth and the socially constructed value of women's farm production. Since patriarchal authority originates in a disvaluation of women's work, a basis would have been laid for a redirection of wealth flows within the farm family.

The lessons of the Philippines, Japan, and Taiwan are that compulsory education laws which result in universal primary schooling for both sexes are one means to accomplish this aim. Primary school attendance lowers the productive value of children by reducing the time they are available to work on the farm. Schooling raises the direct cost of children through uniforms, tuition, and stationery. But more fundamentally, the third-world school is a medium of Western cultural diffusion. It introduces the child to the concept of the nuclear family in which children are seen as immature dependents whose potentialities must be developed slowly through instruction. Caldwell (1980) claimed that the nuclear family concept was pivotal in redirecting wealth flows from the older to the younger generation.

Yet, mass primary-school education has different social and economic consequences for males than for females in a pre-transitional society. As in India, males are probably the first to achieve mass primary education. An immediate consequence of this timing is more frequent heterogamous marriage. The male educational advantage can enable him to establish a two-tiered production system in which he sells his labor in a capitalist market while presiding over a family economy in which his wife and children participate. The male age at marriage may decline, as is happening in Karnataka (Caldwell et al., 1982, p. 710), because educated males attract higher dowries and more offers. The result may be a rise in marital fertility because of the younger male age at entry into sexual unions and because wealth flows from wives and children still favor males.

Another consequence of the earlier timing of mass education for males vis-a-vis females is probably a rise in the consumption utility of educated wives and daughters. One impetus for educating women is their entertainment value: "educated husbands want to talk to educated wives . . . and educated fathers want to talk to educated daughters" (Caldwell, 1978, p. 570). Educating daughters, whose services will not benefit the paternal household, can bring status to their father as conspicuous consumption or as dowry to befit them for a wealthy marriage. The education of daughters can also be a patriarch's way of investing in his own future: their marriages can fetch him valuable affinal ties (an advantage now appreciated by patriarchs in Karnataka) (Caldwell et al., 1982b). Thus, the social value of female education to men probably leads to universal female schooling.

Caldwell (1980, p. 248) argued that it is the females to whom the school must teach the Western nuclear-family model, since it is they who must implement it. A source of stability in the patriarchal family structure is the tension between matriarch and daughter-in-law (p. 563), for female rivalry strengthens male authority. Thus, the Western nuclear-family model should appeal to the daughter-in-law as an escape route from the tyranny of the matriarch. Because of the higher social status conferred on the educated, schooling emboldens the daughter-in-law to prevail on her husband to leave the joint family for a two-generation (nuclear) residence. By invoking Western notions of romantic obligation, the educated daughter-in-law can also compete against her mother-in-law for withdrawals from the husband-son's purse. For these reasons, Caldwell concluded that mass primary-education for females destabilizes the patriarchal family by changing power relationships and wealth flows between matriarch and daughter-in-law and, hence, from older to younger generations.

While compulsory education does require child-favoring flows of intrafamily wealth, it does not require that these occur in nuclear families. Universal primary education has been achieved for both boys and girls in Taiwan, where parents view education as an investment to increase their post-retirement receipts from children. Yet the nuclear family is rare. As late as 1973, over 80 percent of elderly parents resided with a married son; and other sons were expected to send money (Freedman, 1979, p. 7). But in the same year, wives under age 35 averaged only 2.6 living children (Wu, 1977, p. 74). The lesson of Taiwan is that the nuclear family is not a necessary condition for child-favoring wealth flows or for lower fertility.

Primary education does not invariably result in lower fertility. In Indonesia, high-status wives are strongly pressured to withdraw from food- or income-producing activities as a sign of family prestige (Hull, 1976). The resultant low opportunity costs of childbearing to such women may partly explain the higher fertility among Indonesian women with some primary schooling than among the less educated (Hull and Hull, 1977b). In Bangladesh, where purdah blocks most farm women, irrespective of education, from any food- or income-generating labor, women with some primary schooling have similar fertility to women without schooling (5.7 children ever born to women aged 30 to 34; see Lightbourne et al., 1982, p. 22). The nuclear family is the modal type in Indonesia and Bangladesh (Geertz, 1961, p. 31; Caldwell et al., 1982a), but total fertility rates remain extremely high by world standards (see note 5). Therefore, Indonesia and Bangladesh show that the nuclear family is an insufficient condition to produce a major fertility decline, especially when educated women face social barriers to income-generating labor.

The Western message to third-world women central for fertility and wealth flow change is not the nuclear family, as Caldwell contended, but gender equality instead. Caldwell's acknowledged failure to examine cross-sex wealth flows (1978, p. 244; 1980, p. 248) resulted from his interest in parent-child wealth flows and from his tacit assumption that these were in the same direction for mothers and fathers. In other words, Caldwell implied that in the pre-transitional society, children generated net wealth flows toward both mothers and fathers.

This assumption fails to recognize that wealth flows produced by women of all ages favor children in both kinds of society in that women are the primary providers of home maintenance and child care. Thus, time-use studies in Java, Bangladesh, and Nepal showed that housework and child care resulted in much longer total working hours each day for women aged 20+ than for men of the same age or for younger boys and girls (White, 1975; Cain, 1977; Nag et al., 1978). Child care duties are important even for the matriarch. As such, in Nigeria, the Philippines, the People's Republic of China, and perhaps Taiwan, sexual relationships with spouses permanently cease at the birth of the wife's first grandchild "so as to avoid the social and psychological tension arising from competing *maternal* and *grand-maternal obligations*" (emphasis added) (Caldwell, 1976, p. 345). In India, widow remarriage is tabooed "partly because of the conflicting claims of children from two marriages. . ." (Caldwell et al., 1982b, p. 695). In Karnataka State and sub-Saharan Africa, joint families weaken the mother-child bond by delegating some or most child care to the grandmother (a factor which could contribute to the traditional rivalry between these two women) (see Caldwell, 1977a; Caldwell et al., 1982b). But these examples illustrate that in patriarchal societies, women of all ages are expected to have stronger emotional bonds with children than men are, with a net wealth flow from women to children being implied (9).

In pre-transitional societies, women's emotional bonds with children or grandchildren are more intense than with their husbands. Gore (1968, p. 22) observed that in India, the conjugal bond is weakened by a cultural emphasis on the wife's maternal duties. A survey of Yorubaland found that only a third of the wives normally slept in the same room or ate at the same able with their husbands; and few expressed regret about the loss of sexual intercourse during the lengthy period of breastfeeding (Caldwell, 1977a, p. 11). Indeed, Caldwell himself (1978, p. 566; 1982, p. 230, 344) acknowledged the aloofness of the patriarch toward the wife and children and interpreted it as an elusion of the challenges to his claim over the means of family production.

The message of gender equality can reduce the net wealth flow from women to men in at least three ways. One way is by increasing the egalitarianism of the husband-wife bond. Illiterate parents may be disadvantaged in planning the match of an educated daughter so that she must arrange it herself on terms more favorable to her. Also, literacy introduces women to Western books and magazines extolling the pleasure of sexual gratification (Caldwell, 1976, p. 354; 1977a, p.

15). Conjugal sexual gratification will likely intensify the conjugal emotional bond and result in a more balanced wealth exchange between males and females.

A second way in which education reduces the wealth flow from women to men is through transmitting the technical knowledge of non-familial production and in preparing women to be decision makers in the capitalist or socialist sector. By raising the socially constructed value of women's labor, education legitimates their claim to a larger share of their produce and, in this way, reduces the wealth flow to husbands and parents-in-law. In either case, the increased wealth of the woman is bound to benefit her children, since their status can not reflect unfavorably on her own.

Third, the reevaluation of women's labor should create a more adequate recognition of the net wealth they generate toward children. The discrepancy with the child-directed wealth flows from men should turn the net wealth flow from children to males downward, with a concomitant strengthening of the emotional bond between father and children. Thus, a recent U.S. survey found that a majority of fathers most often cited love, companionship, and stimulation as the important values of children (Fawcett, 1978; Hoffman et al., 1978). Because net wealth flows are transmitted from women to children in both pre-transitional and transitional societies, mass education can raise the dependency of children by lowering the dependency of women.

This revision of the wealth-flows theory implies that in pre-transi-tional societies, husbands and wives have competing interests in marital fertility regulation. To wit, since children create net wealth flows to the father, it is economically rational for him to have an unlimited number of offspring; yet since they create net wealth drains from the mother, it is economically rational for her to be childless. That she is not results from the patriarch's material advantage, which allows him to assert his class interests. Thus, in such patriarchal societies as Bangladesh, Nepal, Indonesia, and Karnataka State, only a small per-centage of married couples ever use contraception (15, 4, 38, and 33 percent, respectively); and most of them adopt it near the wife's meno-pause (Caldwell et al., 1982b; Mamlouk, 1982, p. 33). This explains the pronounced reliance in Bangladesh, Nepal, and Karnataka on methods requiring male cooperation (abstinence, withdrawal, rhythm, and con-doms) or resulting in irreversible sterility (vasectomy, tubal ligation). As such, the discrepancy in desired and actual number of children often stated by third-world wives in KAP surveys may reflect not irrational-ity but the contradiction of husband/wife economic interests in repro-ductive behavior.

The reproductive decision makers in a pre-transitional society are not at first the biological married couple but the husband's father (Caldwell, 1982). On his behalf, the mother-in-law in the joint house-hold can regulate the frequency of intercourse between son and daugh-ter-in-law by controlling the use of house space and the privacy it affords. Joint residence thus enables the matriarch to enforce sexual abstinence on the lactating wives in her charge. Indeed, a son attempting to usurp reproductive decision-making power is likely to confront a coalition of his mother and brothers (Caldwell, 1978, p.

566). Consequently, a shift in reproductive decision-making power from the patriarch to the son is likely to occur late in the daughter-in-law's fecund life cycle if she lives in a joint household. But even in Karnataka State, sons and daughters-in-law are never sterilized without first consulting their patriarch and matriarch (Caldwell et al., 1982b).

Gender inequality of production and reproduction in the pre-transitional society implies that the benefits of children as perceived by the childbearer should be different for higher-order than lower-order births, since the influence of the patriarch wanes. In the early stages (low birth orders) of childbearing, the prime values of children as reported by the childbearer should be more likely to reflect the interests of the father-in-law: viz., the assurance of intergenerational continuity of her bloodline and recruitment of new family members to fill sex-specific tasks. In the later stages (high-birth orders), the main values of prospective births as anticipated by the childbearer should more nearly mirror her husband's own economic interests: e.g., the productive rewards of children or their help in old age. This profile of parity-specific values has been reported in some transitional societies (the Philippines and The Republic of Korea; Bulatao, 1981) and should be even more salient in pre-transitional ones, although comparative studies of this issue are lacking. Research directed at these issues would aid our understanding of why high fertility often persists in the presence of forces which could be expected to lead to a fertility decline, and why fertility is sometimes lower than objective levels of development might suggest.

NOTES

1. This research was supported by Michigan Agricultural Experiment Station Project No. 3243S and is Journal Article No. 10953.
2. The low level of investment in children and wives can be seen in their relative levels of mortality. In India and Bangladesh, infant mortality is high; and females have shorter life expectancies than do males (see D'Souza and Chen, 1980; Visaria and Visaria, 1981; D'Souza and Bhuiya, 1982).
3. Nepalese children of both sexes worked longer hours in both maintenance and directly productive activities during the average day than did their counterparts in Java (Nag et al., 1978). The greater economic value of young children in Nepal than in Indonesia may partially account for the higher fertility rate in the former country. The total fertility rate is 6.5 in Nepal and 4.4 in Indonesia (Kent, 1983).
4. The average age at marriage of those marrying by age 50 in Bangladesh is 16.3 years for females and 24.0 years for males (Durch, 1980, p. 11).
5. The total fertility rate implies 6.2 live births to women by age 49 in Bangladesh and 4.4 in Indonesia (Kent, 1983).
6. For a description of the economic activities of children in Nigeria, see Caldwell (1977a); in Ghana, see Oppong (1973).
7. For a description of the recent fertility decline in the Philippines, see Reyes (1981).

8. The literacy rates in Bangladesh are 20 percent for females and 44 percent for males (Durch, 1980, p. 28).
9. Geertz (1961, p. 121) noted that patriarchal aloofness in Java becomes manifest in late childhood, when a boy must never again speak to his father unless necessary or eat at the same table with him. In contrast, children's relationship to their mother remains "strong and secure. . . throughout the individual's life" (Geertz, 1961, p. 107).

REFERENCES

Arnold, F., R.A. Bulatao, C. Burapakdi, B.J. Chung, J.T. Fawcett, T. Iritani, S.J. Lee, T.S. Wu. 1975. The Value of Children: A Cross-National Study. Vol. 1, Introduction and Comparative Analysis. Honolulu: East-West Population Institute.

Briscoe, J. 1979. Energy use and social structure in a Bangladesh village. Population and Development Review 5:615-642.

Bulatao, R.A. 1981. Values and disvalues of children in successive childbearing decisions. Demography 18:1-26.

Cain, M.T. 1977. The economic activities of children in a village in Bangladesh. Population and Development Review 3:201-228.

_____ 1978. The household life cycle and economic mobility in rural Bangladesh. Population and Development Review 4:421-438.

_____ 1981. Risk and insurance: Perspectives on fertility and agrarian change in India and Bangladesh. Population and Development Review 7:435-474.

_____ 1982. Perspectives on family and fertility in developing countries. Population Studies 36:159-175.

_____, S.R. Khanam, and S. Nahar. 1979. Class, patriarchy, and women's work in Bangladesh. Population and Development Review 5: 405-438.

Caldwell, J.C. 1976. Toward a restatement of demographic transition theory. Population and Development Review 2:321-366.

_____ 1977a. The economic rationality of high fertility: An investigation illustrated with Nigerian survey data. Population Studies 31:5-27.

_____ 1977b. The Persistence of High Fertility. Canberra: Australian National University.

_____ 1978. A theory of fertility decline: From high plateau to destabilization. Population and Development Review 4:553-578.

_____ 1980. Mass education as a determinant of the timing of fertility decline. Population and Development Review 6:225-256.

_____ 1982. Theory of Fertility Decline. New York: Academic Press.

_____ 1983. Direct economic costs and benefits of children. In: R.A. Bulatao and R.D. Lee (eds.) Determinants of Fertility in Developing Countries: A Summary of Knowledge, Part A, pp. 370-379. Washington, D.C.: National Academy Press.

_____, A.K.M. Jalaluddin, P. Caldwell, and W. Cosford. 1980. The Control of Activity in Bangladesh. Working Paper No. 12. Canberra: Department of Demography, Australian National University.

————, G. Immerwahr, and L.T. Ruzicka. 1982a. Illustrative Analysis: Family Structure and Fertility. Scientific Report No. 39. London: World Fertility Survey.

————, P.H. Reddy, and P. Caldwell. 1982b. The causes of demographic change in rural south India: A micro approach. Population and Development Review 8:651-688.

Chaffee, F.H., G.E. Aurell, H.A. Barth, E.C. Betters, A.S. Cort, J.H. Dombrowski, V .J. Fasano, and J.O. Weaver. 1969. Area Handbook for the Philippines. Washington, D.C.: U.S. Government Printing Office.

Chen, L., E. Huq, and S. D'Souza. 1981. Sex bias in the family allocation of food and health care in rural Bangladesh. Population and Development Review 7:55-70.

Darroch, R.K., P.A. Meyer, and M. Singarimbun. 1981. Two are not enough: The value of children to Javanese and Sundanese parents. Paper No. 60-D. Honolulu: East-West Population Institute.

Dore, R.P. 1953. Japanese rural fertility: Some social and economic factors. Population Studies 7:62-88.

Driver, E. 1963. Differential Fertility in Central India. Princeton: Princeton University Press.

D'Souza, S. and A. Bhuiya. 1982. Socioeconomic mortality differentials in a rural area of Bangladesh. Population and Development Review 8:753-769.

D'Souza, S. and L.C. Chen. 1980. Sex differentials in mortality in rural Bangladesh. Population and Development Review 6:257-270.

Durch, J.S. 1980. Nuptiality Patterns in Developing Countries: Implications for Fertility. Reports of the World Fertility Survey, No. 1. Washington, D.C.: Population Reference Bureau.

Easterlin, R.A., G. Alter, and G.A. Condran. 1978. Farms and farm families in old and new areas: The northern states in 1860. In: T.K. Hareven and M.A. Vinovskis (eds.) Family and Population in Nineteenth-Century America, pp. 22-84. Princeton: Princeton University Press.

Fawcett, J.T. 1978. The value and cost of the first child. In: W.B. Miller and L.F. Newman (eds.) The First Child and Family Formation, pp. 244-265. Chapel Hill: Carolina Population Center.

Freedman, R. 1963. Norms for family size in underdeveloped areas. Proceedings of the Royal Society 159:220-245.

———— 1979. Theories of fertility decline: A reappraisal. Social Forces 58:1-17.

Geertz, H. 1961. The Javanese Family. New York: The Free Press of Glencoe, Inc.

Goldscheider, C. 1971. Population, Modernization, and Social Structure. Boston: Little, Brown.

Goody, E.N. 1973. Contexts of Kinship: An Essay in the Family Sociology of the Gonja of Northern Ghana. Cambridge: Cambridge University Press.

Gore, M.S. 1968. Urbanization and Family Change. Bombay: Popular Prakashan.

Hawley, A. 1955. Rural fertility in central Luzon. American Sociological Review 20:21-27.

Hermalin, A.I. and W.R. Lavely. 1979. Agricultural development and fertility change in Taiwan. Paper presented at the annual meetings of the Population Association of America, Philadelphia, Pennsylvania.

Hoffman, L.W. and M.L. Hoffman. 1973. The value of children to parents. In: J.T. Fawcett (ed.) Psychological Perspectives on Population, pp. 19–76. New York: Basic Books.

Hoffman, L.W., A. Thornton, and J.D. Manis. 1978. The value of children to parents in the United States. Journal of Population 1:91–131.

Hull, T.H. and V.J. Hull. 1977a. Indonesia. In: J.C. Caldwell (ed.) The Persistence of High Fertility, pp. 829–894. Canberra: Australian National University.

_____ 1977b. The relation of economic class and fertility: An analysis of some Indonesian data. Population Studies 31:43–57.

Hull, V.J. 1976. Women in Java's rural middle class: Progress or regress? Paper presented at Fourth World Congress of Rural Sociology, Torun, Poland.

Hunt, C.L. and T.R. McHale. 1965. Education and Philippine economic development. Comparative Education Review 9:63–73.

Johnson, N.E. and J.A. Beegle. 1982. The rural American people: A look backward and forward. In: D.A. Dillman and D.J. Hobbs (eds.) Rural Society in the U.S.: Issues for the 1980s, pp. 58–68. Boulder, Colorado: Westview Press.

Kent, M.M. 1983. 1983 World Population Data Sheet. Washington, D.C.: Population Reference Bureau.

Lieberman, S.S. 1980. Rural development and fertility transition in South Asia: The case for a broad-based strategy. Social Research 47:305–338.

Lightbourne, R., Jr., S. Singh, and C.P. Green. 1982. The world fertility survey: Charting global childbearing. Population Bulletin 37:1–54.

Madigan, F. 1977. Transition from the demographic transition: Perspective from the Philippines. In: J.C. Caldwell (ed.) The Persistence of High Fertility, pp. 765–783. Canberra: Australian National University.

Mamlouk, M. 1982. Knowledge and Use of Contraception in Twenty Developing Countries. Report No. 3 of the World Fertility Survey. Washington, D.C.: Population Reference Bureau.

Mueller, E. 1976. The economic value of children in peasant agriculture. In: R. Ridker (ed.) Population and Development: The Search for Selective Interventions, pp. 98–153. Baltimore: Johns Hopkins University Press.

Nag, M., B.N.F. White, and R.C. Peet. 1978. An anthropological approach to the study of the economic value of children in Java and Nepal. Current Anthropology 19:293–306.

Notestein, F.W. 1945. Population: The long view. In: T.W. Schultz (ed.) Food for the World, pp. 36–57. Chicago: University of Chicago Press.

_____ 1953. Economic problems of population change. In: Eighth International Conference of Agricultural Economists, pp. 15–18. London: Oxford University Press.

Oppong, C. 1973. Growing Up in Dagbon. Accra: Ghana Publishing Co.

Petersen, W. 1961. Population. New York: Macmillan.
_____ 1975. Population (3/e). New York: Macmillan.
Reyes, F. 1981. Evaluation of the Republic of the Philippines Fertility Survey 1978. Scientific Report No. 19. London: World Fertility Survey.
Schutjer, W.A., C.S. Stokes, and G. Cornwell. 1980. Relationships among land, tenancy, and fertility: A study of Philippine barrios. Journal of Developing Areas 15:83-96.
Smith, P.C. and P.P.L. Cheung. 1981. Social origins and sex-differential schooling in the Philippines. Comparative Education Review 25:28-44.
Stoeckel, J. and A.K.M. Alauddin Chowdhury. 1980. Fertility and socio-economic status in rural Bangladesh: Differentials and linkages. Population Studies 34:519-524.
Visaria, P. and L. Visaria. 1981. India's population: Second and growing. Population Bulletin 36:1-56.
Ware, H. 1978. The Economic Value of Children in Asia and Africa: Comparative Perspectives. Paper No. 50. Honolulu: East-West Population Institute.
White, B. 1975. The economic importance of children in a Javanese village. In: M. Nag (ed.) Population and Social Organization, pp. 127-146. The Hague: Mouton.
Williamson, N. 1978. Boys or girls? Parents' preferences and sex control. Population Bulletin 33:1-35.
Wu, T.S. 1977. The Value of Children: A Cross National Study. Volume 5, Taiwan. Honolulu: East-West Population Institute.

PART III
Policies for Rural Development: Impacts on Fertility

CHAPTER 10

Access to Land and Fertility in Developing Countries

C. Shannon Stokes and Wayne A. Schutjer

The distribution of landholdings and patterns of land tenure are fundamental to the economic and social organization of rural societies throughout the world. Rural stratification systems which determine the allocation of power, status, and wealth depend largely upon the land system, in contrast to urban hierarchies which lean more heavily on occupational position. Consequently, analyses of rural development and human fertility must confront this basic rural institution.

The importance of the land system to rural social and economic structure is reflected in rural development and technical change models. However, given the importance of high fertility and rural population growth for many developing nations, regions and total world growth, it is somewhat surprising that more attention has not been given to the relationship between access to land and human fertility. There exists scattered and fragmentary evidence that relates land and fertility, but in most of the research, land is of secondary importance and most interpretations of its effect are post factum in nature and lack any theoretical base.

This chapter offers a theoretical framework within which to view connections between land and human fertility. The available literature is reviewed within that context, and some encouraging uniformities are observed. Finally, although current knowledge is deemed inadequate to formulate fertility–sensitive land reform policy, it is highly suggestive of potentially important connections between land and fertility. These relationships point to possible policy alternatives for linking rural

195

development and population policy and identifying salient areas for further research.

Before presenting a framework within which to view land-fertility connections, the broader context from which such relationships emerge must be noted. An important part of that context is the recognition that fertility decisions and behavior occur within local institutional settings which mediate the impact of larger social and economic structures. Although land-related institutions are an important component of most rural environments, a focus on the relationship between land and fertility necessarily abstracts a single dimension from the larger institutional context. Thus, while land distribution and tenure are undeniably important to most aspects of rural social and economic structure, including childbearing, there is the danger of oversimplification in focusing on one dimension to the exclusion of others. Similarly, the potential impact on fertility of rural development strategies requiring land redistribution or tenure reform is difficult to specify apart from the specific geographic, cultural, socioeconomic, and institutional environments in which they occur. Thus, although theoretical relationships may be identified, their application to specific locales and environmental settings undoubtedly will require modification.

Access to land is pervasive in its effects within the rural sector, with the result that its potential role in rural development policy is sizable, as are the potential fertility implications (International Bank for Reconstruction and Development, 1975). It is important to recognize, however, that demographic considerations, including a fertility reduction strategy, are not likely to rank very high in the decision to initiate rural development programs such as land reform. Political and economic factors undoubtedly hold sway in such decisions (McNicoll and Nag, 1982). Several recent analyses of fertility determinants point to the need for expanding our knowledge about the institutional settings which lead to higher or lower fertility. Prominent among those factors identified as deserving special attention are those institutional factors that affect the economic contributions of children, including land ownership and size of holding (Committee on Population and Demography, 1982). Development programs such as land reform and guaranteed employment schemes which are hypothesized to influence fertility through changing the rural institutional system have also been singled out for attention (Population Council, 1981).

Finally, it is important to realize that most institutional arrangements that influence fertility are at least one step removed from those factors which immediately determine the level of fertility in a group or society. Figure 1 suggests an ordering of factors influencing fertility beginning with the proximate determinants (Bongaarts, 1978), and moving outward toward increasingly more distant fertility determinants. Within this framework, each succeeding level may influence the proximate determinants of fertility directly or through mediating factors. The influence of land systems on fertility in such a scheme may be seen through their impact on the economic contributions of children, alterations in the decision-making processes of parents (including changes in the perceived costs and benefits of children), and directly on the proximate determinants of fertility. The effects of landholdings on the proximate determinants suggest that variations in access to land

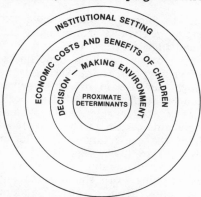

Figure 1. A classification of fertility determinants suggesting proximate and secondary influences on fertility. Source: based on an ordering of fertility determinants suggested by The Population Council (1981, p. 318).

may not only operate by altering the demand for children, but also by changing the supply of surviving children among households of different landholding and tenure statuses. This chapter focuses primarily on the effects of land on the demand for children, although some tentative observations on supply are advanced.

LAND AND FERTILITY: A FRAMEWORK FOR ANALYSIS

At least two dimensions of land appear to be important for fertility behavior. One dimension is the size of landholdings to which a household has access for cultivation purposes. A second dimension is land ownership, including all legal and institutional arrangements that specify how land is to be used and how produce from the land is to be distributed (Stokes and Schutjer, 1983; Schutjer et al., 1983).

The two dimensions are distinct in that an individual, family, or household may have use rights (usufruct), but not ownership rights. Equally important, the two dimensions lead to different streams of income. Individuals or households with use rights (renters, sharecroppers, leasees, etc.) receive a management return for managing the agricultural production processes on the land. Owners of agricultural land receive returns to equity based on their investment. A third income stream is generated by the labor input to the agricultural production process. For the landless laborer this is typically the entire return. Owner-operators are the only households which can capture all three types of return: labor, management, and equity. Tenants of various types may receive a management and labor return, but regardless of how secure their use-rights, they do not receive returns to equity. The two dimensions of land and the alternative income streams have disparate implications for fertility.

The size of holding to which a household or family has access for cultivation purposes is hypothesized to influence fertility through altering the economic contributions of children. Stated simply, farm

households with access to larger holdings have greater labor requirements, are able to employ profitably more family labor, and this incentive encourages continued high fertility (1).

Land ownership, on the other hand, is hypothesized to have negative
long-term effects on fertility, operating through the income returns to
equity and the resulting increase in old-age security. Land ownership
can guarantee an income stream beyond the period during which an
individual is able to work and/or manage an agricultural operation and
earn a labor or management return. Thus, at least theoretically, land
ownership should reduce the importance of children as sources of old-
age security and contribute to lower fertility.

Size of holdings and land ownership can be viewed theoretically as
influencing fertility by altering both the demand and supply of children.
Demand considerations have been given precedence in most of the
empirical and theoretical literature (White, 1973, 1975; Yengoyan, 1974;
Nag, 1976; Mueller, 1976; Cain, 1977;, Nag et al., 1978). However, a
case can be made that differences in size of landholdings and ownership
may also influence natural fertility and the number of surviving
children.

Agricultural households with higher incomes, i.e., those with larger
size holdings and landowners, are more likely to survive difficult
periods without losing members to death prematurely. One study in
Bangladesh reports that death rates in a famine year among children
aged one to four in landless households were over four times those of
landed families with more than 1.2 hectares (Arthur and McNicoll,
1978, p. 51). While differential mortality was greatest between the
landless and those with more than 1.2 hectares, noticeable differences
were also reported for the various size of landholding classes.

Some evidence suggests that the differences in childhood and adult
mortality found among agricultural households in Bangladesh may be
paralleled by differences in involuntary fetal mortality, secondary
sterility, and fecundity impairments. Hull (1978, p. 301) reports that in
rural Java ". . . the fertility of the poor is more restricted than that
of the rich by such indirect or involuntary factors as infecundity, divorce, and pregnancy losses. Poor people also breast-feed and abstain
from sex for longer periods following a birth." Further, women from
lower-income groups complete their reproductive lives earlier than
those from higher income groups (Hull and Hull, 1977). Huffman et al.
(1978) report related findings showing that richer women in Bangladesh
and those using better supplementary feeding for infants were more
likely to have resumed menstruation than other women in the same
postpartum interval. Although such evidence is fragmentary and available only for selected nations and areas, it suggests that studies of
land-fertility connections should include factors affecting natural
fertility and the supply of surviving children.

What evidence is available on the relationship of size of holdings and
land ownership to fertility? Do macro- and micro-level studies reveal
consistent results on the effects of landholdings and tenure? Finally,
what are the implications of such work for further research and for the
design of fertility-sensitive land policy? These questions are addressed
in the remaining sections of this chapter.

SIZE OF LANDHOLDINGS AND FERTILITY

The literature reviewed in this section focuses primarily on the effects of size of holdings on marital fertility. Access to land and land availability have been demonstrated to influence family formation and fertility in a large number of historical studies in the United States, Canada, and Western Europe (Yasuba, 1962; Connell, 1965; Demeny, 1968; Forster and Tucker, 1972; Easterlin, 1976a,b; Leet, 1976; McGinnis, 1977; Laidig et al., 1981; Shapiro, 1982). Most of this research emphasizes the fertility impacts of land availability on age at marriage and proportions married, rather than on marital fertility (Guest, 1981). Since much of this material is discussed in Chapter 5, it is not included here. Further, Coale (1975) has argued that couples marry earlier or later within socially accepted ages for marriage depending upon their ability to meet such marriage requirements as income and land ownership. They do not marry one year earlier or later on the basis that they will have one child more or less. Thus, the voluntary limitation of births within a marriage, which is of primary concern here, is viewed as responding to a different set of forces.

The available research on size of holdings and fertility is characterized by a number of empirical and conceptual problems. At an empirical level, most studies that include data on size of landholdings and fertility are not primarily directed at estimating or understanding this relationship, but use land as a measure of socioeconomic status, wealth, or involvement in the agricultural sector. The interpretation given to such findings as do emerge is largely ad hoc in nature. Further clouding the meaning of relationships is the absence of adequate controls for other theoretically important factors including such straightforward variables as age at marriage or duration of marriage.

Conceptually, questions may be raised as to the causal direction of the effect. While most writers argue as we have that size of holdings affects fertility by increasing the economic contributions of children, and thus influences demand, others posit reverse causality, hypothesizing that children represent a means of acquiring, retaining, and improving land (Mamdani, 1972; Mazur, 1975; McGinnis, 1977). The cross-sectional nature of most research precludes a choice among these alternatives. Moreover, both of these perspectives largely ignore the effects of larger holdings which might operate to increase natural fertility and the number of surviving children. Interpretation of the studies reviewed must be made with these limitations in mind.

Micro-Level Studies

Much of the research on land and fertility stems from the work of Stys (1957) on fertility among two generations of Polish peasants. Stys presented data showing that richer peasant girls from families with larger landholdings married earlier, initiated childbearing sooner, and bore children more frequently and to a later age than women from families with smaller holdings. His data also indicated higher child mortality among the landless and those with small holdings. Thus larger farm size may be seen to influence higher fertility through both the economic value of children and through the number of surviving children.

Early studies of land and fertility in Bangladesh report conflicting results. Stoeckel and Choudhury (1969) report landholdings to be negatively related to total marital fertility, yet desired family size was slightly larger among landholders than among the landless (Mosena and Stoeckel, 1972). In a related vein, Latif and Chowdhury (1977) report land to be significantly related to the number of live births and number of surviving children among a northern village sample, but unrelated in a southern village. The authors note the small sample size used in the study, but do not offer an explanation for the inconsistent results.

More recent research in Bangladesh using a very large sample of women reports a positive relationship between size of holdings and fertility. The authors suggest that since less than five percent of the population at the time of the survey was using contraception, and the incidence of abortion was negligible, higher fertility among larger landholders was primarily a result of differences in involuntary fetal mortality, infecundity due to involuntary causes, and voluntary and involuntary abstinence (Stoeckel and Chowdhury, 1980, p. 522). This study is notable in that it represents one of the few attempts to address the potential impact of size of holdings on natural fertility and the supply of children. The interpretation is quite different from that of Mahmud and McIntosh (1980) who argue for the importance of children (sons) in obtaining access to land. Regardless of the theoretical explanation offered, both studies report positive relationships between fertility and size and holdings.

In an analysis of economic and fertility behavior in rural Thailand, Prasithrathsin (1971, p. 270) reports ". . . positive relationship(s) between size of landholding and fertility, whether fertility is measured by pregnancies, live births, living children or ideal family size." These findings were not statistically significant once age was controlled, a result the author attributed to the small sample sizes involved in the comparisons. In contrast, a multiple regression analysis involving size of holding and fertility in the central plains of Thailand found a significant positive effect with relevant sociodemographic factors included (Chalamwong et al., 1979).

Evidence supporting the notion that farm size is related to parental perceptions of the economic value of children is given by attitudinal data gathered in the 1975 Survey of Fertility in Thailand (Arnold and Pejaranonda, 1977). When respondents were asked about the need for children's help in a family enterprise, the percentage mentioning help from children as an advantage of a large family varied from 4 percent among those with no farm or business to 50 percent of those with larger landholdings (21 rai or more). Farmers with hired employees were slightly less likely to mention children's help as an advantage of a large family, suggesting that hired labor can substitute for that of children.

Hawley (1955) found that fertility varied directly with size of farm among Filipinos residing in central Luzon. This finding remained when controls for age and education were instituted. Driver (1963) found a similar pattern in central India, although controls for wife's age and age at marriage revealed slightly lower fertility for the smallest landholding class than for landless households. A study in Nepal found a "pattern of increasing fertility with landholding in the older age groups . . . suggest[ing] that larger families are still valued for the labour they contribute" (Tuladhar et al., 1982, p. 85).

Several studies in Iran show positive relationships between size of landholdings and fertility (Ajami, 1969, 1976; Aghajanian, 1978). The number of children ever born and the number living at time of interview were both positively and significantly related to size of holding (Ajami, 1976). Landless households desired slightly fewer children than those with land, but differences in desired number of children were not statistically significant. The lack of appropriate controls for age at marriage and marital duration, as well as other socioeconomic factors, limit the interpretation of these findings.

Using micro-level data from Lower Egypt, we estimated a model in which children ever born was viewed as a function of size of holdings, land ownership, age at marriage, current age, and a series of additional socioeconomic factors (Schutjer et al., 1983). The findings suggest that other than the woman's age, the size of holdings cultivated was the strongest predictor of children ever born. The positive coefficient associated with size of holdings was interpreted as supporting the value of child labor for households with larger holdings. Interestingly, the effect of land ownership was negative in sign, suggesting that ownership was associated with lower fertility. These findings are discussed more fully in the section on land ownership.

Finally, an anthropological field study and survey in Guatemala revealed that farmers with irrigated land had significantly higher fertility than basketmaking families and slightly higher fertility than farmers of rainfed land (Odell, 1982). These differences were attributed to the greater labor demands among farmers who irrigated and engaged in multiple cropping. This example points to the potential difference in labor demands for land of varying quality—irrigated land generally being of higher quality (2).

The micro-level studies reviewed tend to be fairly consistent in showing the expected positive association between size of holding and fertility. Methodological and conceptual problems plague much of the extant literature and permit only cautious generalizations. Nonetheless, the consistency of the findings is encouraging. The examination of macro-level studies provides additional evidence on this relationship.

Macro-Level Studies

Aggregate level analyses which typically employ village, district, or regional level data should be separated analytically from farm-level studies. At the individual farm level, the relation between farm size and fertility, as noted previously, may be reciprocal, in which case farm size may be viewed as adapting to family size (fertility) as well as the reverse. As Firebaugh (1982, p. 485) notes, this type of effect is (usually) not possible at the village level because village land is fixed. In addition to this issue, problems of ecological inference limit generalization of macro-level research to its farm-level analogue. Of particular importance here is the difficulty in interpreting effects of observed relationships between land distribution or size of holdings and fertility at the macro-level. Fundamental theoretical questions include issues such as: Is the observed relationship due to behavioral adjustments of the population to differences in the economic value of children? or how much is a result of income related differences in natural fertility and survival prospects of children? Further, to what extent do opportunities for outmigration influence empirical findings?

Merrick's work on fertility in various regions of Brazil reflects a sensitivity to demand and supply considerations in relating land availability and fertility. In more developed regions such as South-Central Brazil where fertility differences among micro-regions are thought to reflect differences in fertility control (Merrick, 1978, p. 327), his analysis emphasizes demand factors such as the value of children, the bequest hypothesis of Easterlin (1967a,b), and female literacy. Land scarcity and a measure of subsistence farming, both thought to influence the economic contributions of children, were significantly related to fertility within the 155 micro-regions examined. As expected, land scarcity was negatively related to fertility, while greater subsistence farming had pronatalist effects.

In contrast to the demand-oriented model in South-Central Brazil, the Amazon and Northeast regions are characterized by the virtual absence of fertility control within marriage, justifying the assumption "that differences in the number of surviving children reflects variation in supply . . ." (Merrick, 1981, p. 105). Median size of farm within micro-regions was positively related to children ever born and surviving children, consistent with the notion that increased size of holdings may operate on the supply of children through a higher standard of living among larger landholders. However, Merrick notes that observed differences in the supply of children does not mean there is no variation in demand for children. Limitations of data reflecting micro-region averages, rather than individual household variation, are singled out as problems in addressing demand considerations. Nonetheless, further macro-level analyses of child labor, schooling, and farm equipment yield findings consistent with microeconomic theory. While aggregate level data are not adequate substitutes for individual household studies, careful work at the macro-level can be fruitful.

A demand-oriented model of fertility was developed by Hicks (1974) to explain fertility in 31 rural areas in Mexico. A negative effect of size of holdings was posited on the basis that "if the average size of holdings is small, there is an incentive to limit fertility within marriage to prevent further fragmentation of holdings and a further decline in the marginal productivity of labor" (Hicks, 1974, p. 409). Although size of holdings could not be directly measured for the areas in question (a common problem of macro-level research), a measure of arable land per agricultural worker was positively related to cohort fertility, suggesting that benefits from children increase directly with the land/man ratio.

Beaver (1975) similarly incorporated a measure of land availability in his cross-national analysis of fertility and demographic transition between 1950 and 1969 in 24 nations of Latin America. While the measure of land availability used was not a direct measure of size of holdings, it did reflect the land/man ratio within rural areas of the countries considered. Land availability was second in importance only to urbanization in accounting for variance in age-sex standardized birth rates, findings Beaver termed "strikingly confirmatory" (1975, p. 130). The interpretation due such results, however, is clouded by the extreme inequality of land distribution in Latin America. Thus, while Beaver, Merrick, and others have suggested that access to land is important for fertility in the region, little direct evidence on the relationship of land and fertility is available at the household level for Latin America (Durham, 1977; Karush, 1978).

Average size of holdings and fertility has been studied among districts in rural India. Kleinman (1973) found that cultivated acreage per agricultural household was the most important predictor of general fertility among 315 districts. Larger average holdings within a district were associated with higher fertility, while land concentration had a negative impact. These relationships remained strong even when controls for selected intermediate variables measuring supply factors were introduced.

A more formal model of the economic contribution of children and fertility in India reported similar findings (Rosenzweig and Evenson, 1977). Land size, which was assumed to be complementary with child labor, was found to have a positive and significant impact on two measures of the child-woman ratio. A measure of land concentration, on the other hand, exerted a negative influence on fertility. The authors take these findings to mean that ". . . a land redistribution program aimed at promoting equality, unaccompanied by other changes, would both increase fertility and depress school enrollment rates" (Rosenzweig and Evenson, 1977, p. 1078). That interpretation was rejected by Repetto (1979, p. 140) who argues that the effects of land redistribution would be negative. The effect of a land redistribution program on the supply of children is largely ignored by both of these interpretations, as is the potentially negative impact of increasing land ownership. Resolution of these conflicting views requires a more fully specified model including both supply and demand factors, land ownership, and preferably, household level data.

LAND OWNERSHIP AND FERTILITY

The evidence on the relationship of land ownership and fertility is less complete and more problematic than that on size of holdings. Most research which relates landholdings to fertility does not distinguish between the size of holdings to which a household has access for cultivation purposes, and the amount of land that is owned. Instead, cross-tabulations, or even more elaborate multivariate models, typically relate fertility to landholdings, presumably referring to the size of area cultivated, regardless of ownership status.

Ownership of landholdings varies from full-owners who own all the land they cultivate (including some who own more than they cultivate, i.e., landlords), part-owners who rent some land and own some, to full-tenants, sharecroppers, and renters who may own none of the land they farm.   Landless agricultural laborers remain outside this system and must rely solely on returns to their labor in agricultural production for income.   The argument advanced here is that the income stream associated with ownership of land has a distinct and separate impact on fertility.   The return to equity which only owners receive, provides an alternative source of old-age security, and thus reduces one incentive for continued high fertility.   However, not only does land ownership provide long-term security as an alternative source of income beyond the period when a person can work or manage an agricultural operation, it may also provide a form of social insurance against risk and adversity in the short run (Cain, 1981).   Where formal capital markets exist, land can serve as collateral for loans during periods of extreme adversity.   Without such markets, even ownership of land may not provide enough of a buffer for periods of severe hardship.

Land ownership as old-age security is viewed as altering the long-run economic contributions of children and thus affecting demand.   Since landowners typically have higher incomes than partial- or full-tenants, the resulting higher standard of living may also result in an increase in the supply of children.   In this regard, the supply effect of land ownership is identical to the supply effect of size of holdings.   Higher incomes may be expected to increase natural fertility and the number of surviving children.   Such an effect may be offset by the decrease in demand arising from the greater security of landowners.   In addition, the higher incomes of landowners may result in greater aspirations and investments such as child schooling and health, resulting in the hypothesized quality-quantity tradeoff of microeconomic theory.

On balance, it appears that where methods of fertility limitation are widely known and practiced, the effects of land ownership should operate through the demand for children to reduce fertility.   Under conditions approximating a natural fertility regime with little deliberate control of fertility, the higher incomes of landowners likely would work through the supply side to increase fertility, at least in the short run.   Consequently, the effects of increasing land ownership may be expected to vary with the stage of economic and demographic development of a society and of subgroups within a society (Tabbarah, 1971; Easterlin, 1975, 1978).   The following studies are reviewed with these issues in mind.

In a recent review of agricultural policies and human fertility, we argue for the important contribution of increasing land ownership to fertility reduction (Schutjer and Stokes, 1982).   The emphasis in that paper, and in much of the extant research, is on the effects of ownership in reducing the dependence of parents on children as sources of security in old age.   The limited evidence on the effects of ownership is generally consistent with that perspective.

Prasithrathsin (1971, p. 278) shows cross-tabulations of ideal number of children and live births for owners, part-owners, and landless laborers in rural Thailand.   His findings reveal that part-owners had the lowest ideal and actual fertility, landless laborers and full-tenants had the highest, with full-owners in an intermediate position. The lower ideal and actual fertility of part-owners is attributed to their "enterprising attitude," but little else is offered to explain the observed differences.

By contrast, Chalamwong et al. (1979) estimated an eight-variable regression model of selected socioeconomic and demographic variables on children ever born for a sample of households in the central plains of Thailand. With size of cultivated area, income, female education, and appropriate demgraphic control variables included in the model, land ownership was significantly and negatively related to children ever born.

Three studies of fertility involving land ownership have been reported for the Philippines. The work of Hawley (1955) in Central Luzon, discussed in the section on size of holdings, also examined data on land tenure and fertility. The highest fertility observed was among farm tenants, with farm owners and farm laborers exhibiting similar levels. Hawley did not offer an explanation for these patterns. Hiday (1978) reports similar findings for two rural Philippine communities, suggesting that the negative effect of land tenure operated through age at marriage.

A path analysis of village-level data from the Philippines found that the direct effect of land ownership on fertility was positive (Schutjer et al., 1980). The indirect effects, however, were negative and larger, resulting in a negative total effect. While the three Philippine studies were conducted with different objectives in mind and with quite varied data sets, all show a connection between tenure status and fertility.

An analysis of social status and fertility in Iran affords more insight into the dynamics of how land ownership might influence fertility. Good et al. (1980) use individual level data from one town and three villages in northwestern Iran to examine the differential effects of various measures of social status on fertility in both urban and rural settings. Instead of focusing on size of landholdings, they classify rural villagers into those who own land and those who do not. With age of women controlled, landowners were found to have a significantly lower ideal family size and lower numbers of children ever born. In addition, wives of landowners had a significantly lower average age at marriage and were more likely to report having used contraception.

These findings illustrate the difficulty of disentangling the effects of land ownership on fertility. A lower average age at marriage is generally associated with higher fertility, and if land ownership has a negative effect on fetal wastage, infecundity, and length of postpartum amenorrhea as has been suggested, these factors should operate to increase natural fertility and the number of surviving children. On the other hand, the lower ideal family size and greater contraceptive use of landowners apparently outweighs the potential increase in the supply of children and results in lower actual fertility. Whether the greater security associated with land ownership contributes to these findings cannot be inferred, but it does appear that factors affecting the demand for children are increasingly important in determining fertility in rural Iran.

In an analysis of fertility in rural lower Egypt, we recently estima-ted a model incorporating both land ownership and size of holdings, as well as a number of socioeconomic and demographic variables (Schutjer et al., 1983). For the sample as a whole, slightly less than half of the agricultural land was owned by the households cultivating it. Income and ownership were positively related to size of holdings as expected. More importantly, the signs for the ownership and size of cultivated holdings variables were consistent with theoretical expectations and both were statistically significant. Size of cultivated holdings was positively related to children ever born and was second in importance only to current age of women in predicting fertility. Land ownership exerted a negative influence and the coefficient was comparable in size to that of age at marriage.

While the findings relating land and fertility are consistent with the theoretical perspective we have advanced here, further work is re-quired to specify the mechanisms through which ownership and size operate. Our preliminary work suggests that both demand and supply forces operate. For example, land ownership in rural Egypt is signifi-cantly related to lower levels of infant mortality, but positively associated with the school enrollment rates of children (unpublished data). As has been noted previously, it is those households with slightly higher incomes who feel obligated to give school attendance precedence over children's help in the fields (Nag, 1976, p. 11). We view these findings as encouraging of further work, given that less than 20 percent of the women reported ever using contraception. The im-portance of factors influencing the demand for children should increase as rural Egyptian women increasingly limit fertility within marriage (Stokes et al., 1983).

Evidence that land ownership may be one mechanism linking old-age security and fertility in India is provided by Vlassoff and Vlassoff (1980). Their work questions the importance of old-age security pro-vided by children (sons) as a motivation for high fertility, instead pointing to the importance of economic assets, primarily land. An examination of optimistic and pessimistic attitudes to old age in Maha-rashtra State revealed that respondents with optimistic attitudes owned on average almost twice as much land as those with more pessimistic outlooks.

An aggregate level study of fertility in Mexico suggests that the negative relationship between land ownership and fertility can be offset by pronatalist restrictions governing ownership (DeVany and Sanchez, 1977, 1979). The Mexican "ejido" system in which rights to land (usu-fruct) are granted on an individual basis is seen as creating a series of pronatalist incentives. Prominent among these incentives are the desire of households to retain rights to the land and to utilize child labor to augment or substitute for adult labor. They also note:

> The uncertainty of rights in the land, including the lack of salability, limits the degree to which the family will depend upon investment in its farm of in crops and other assets tied to the land as a means of distributing present production for-ward to the future. In addition, this uncertainty will make

lenders reluctant to lend to ejidatarios (members of the collective), since the loan cannot be secured by the land, and
so the ejidatario is somewhat restricted in his ability to
reallocate future resources back to the present for consumption. In this setting children become a form of security or
investment for effectuating intertemporal allocation (DeVany
and Sanchez, 1977, p. 744).

The empirical findings supported the fertility-enhancing effect of the
ejido system, in comparison to private farmers or paid agricultural
workers. DeVany and Sanchez suggest that reducing the uncertainty
associated with ejido land, improving markets, and restoring the land
market should reduce the incentives to high fertility. This study points
to the potentially important role that land-tenure reform might have in
a fertility-reduction strategy. Although as we noted earlier, it is
unlikely that demographic considerations would weigh heavily in the
decision to initiate such a reform, nations which ignore the demographic implications of land policies do so at the risk of creating conflict
between their land reform policies and population policies.

Seligson (1979) identifies just such potential conflict between family
planning policy and agrarian policy in Costa Rica. Noting higher
fertility among landed peasants than among landless ones, he suggests a
communal land reform (not to include ownership) as a solution to the
policy conflict. Landed peasants in his research included landowners,
squatters, renters, and sharecroppers, and the study did not examine
fertility differences by land ownership status or size of holding. Consequently, while we support the general conclusion of Seligson on the
need to coordinate public policies on land reform and population,
further research is needed on the process through which such policies
influence fertility (Stokes and Schutjer, 1983).

CONCLUSIONS

The argument has been advanced that land ownership and size of
landholdings have opposite effects on human fertility. The size of holding to which a family has access is hypothesized to influence fertility
primarily through the economic contributions of children. Families with
access to larger holdings can more profitably use additional labor and
this provides an incentive for continued high fertility or, at a minimum,
offers less incentive for practicing contraception. Land ownership, in
contrast, is thought to have negative effects on fertility by altering
the dependence of parents on children for old-age security, and perhaps
even by providing additional protection against risk during the productive years. Both factors may also influence natural fertility and the
supply of surviving children by increasing income.

Studies of the relationship between size of landholdings and fertility
are surprisingly consistent. Despite differences in methodology, theoretical approaches, or level of aggregation, larger size holdings are
associated with higher fertility. Such results have been taken by a
number of writers to indicate that a land redistribution program would

result in increased fertility, at least in the short run (Chaplin, 1971, p. 227; Rosenzweig and Evenson, 1977; Simon, 1977, p. 371; Mackay, 1979). From the studies reviewed here, an increase would appear likely for two reasons. First, families who experience increases in the size of their holdings under a redistribution program could more profitably utilize child labor on their increased holdings. Secondly, the higher incomes associated with larger holdings could be expected to increase natural fertility and the survival prospects of children.

This interpretation appears accurate for the short-term response of fertility to a land redistribution program, but is not likely to hold over the long term, particularly if rising incomes alter educational expectations for children. Moreover, redistribution programs rarely take place in the absence of some type of tenurial reform. Our reading of the literature on land ownership indicates that if a land redistribution program were accompanied by changes in land ownership, the pronatalist impact of the redistribution program may be partially or totally offset. In short, the negative effects of land ownership may be expected to counteract any increase in the supply of surviving children due to an improved standard of living. Similarly, lower levels of infant and childhood mortality should also exert a downward force on fertility.

Even in countries where effective land reforms have been shown to decrease fertility, the initial effect of the reform may have been to increase reproduction. Kocher (1973) and Rich (1973) both argue convincingly for the fertility-reducing impact of land reform (which included major changes in tenure) in Taiwan. Yet Liu and Lu (1979, p. 18) state that: "Tenants who benefited [from the reform] tended to have an increase in fertility because of improvements in their living standard in the beginning, but soon the *owner-farmers* of small holdings were conscious of the economic consequences of having large families" (italics added). Average fertility during the period 1951 to 1955, during and immediately after the land reform, was the highest level recorded in Taiwan during this century.

The potential impact of land redistribution on rural development and fertility is sharply limited by the supply of available land for redistribution. In some areas, such as much of Asia, the physical availability of land provides the constraint. Where population pressure on the land is highest, a forced redistribution would likely result in a large number of uneconomic and nonviable holdings (Sinha, 1975). In such cases, alternative strategies such as guaranteed employment schemes have been suggested to influence the economic conditions and fertility of landless laborers (Lieberman, 1980). In other areas of the world land is not in short supply, but political factors prevent its redistribution. Thus, even in many nations where laws on ceilings for landholdings have been enacted, progress in redistributing land has been slow.

Opportunities for reform of ownership patterns or tenancy arrangements exist even where land distribution is not possible. The evidence suggests that increased ownership is likely to depress fertility as land substitutes for children as the primary source of security in old age. Further, the higher incomes associated with ownership or improved tenancy arrangements may be expected to lead to greater investments in child quality, particularly additional schooling. The negative impact of ownership may be offset if pronatalist incentives surround the conditions under which land is held. Knowledge of these conditions is best described as rudimentary, but the available evidence suggests that careful attention be given to the conditions under which a land redistribution or tenure reform program is carried out.

Additional research is needed on both dimensions of land. The range and magnitude of the effects of farm size and land ownership need to be specified in different institutional settings. For example, are the effects complementary in some cases, but work at cross-purposes in others? Descriptive work which would lead to comparisons of differences in tenure and size and their relation to fertility is required.

Identification of the mechanisms by which land size and ownership operate is crucial. Effects on the proximate determinants, the economic contributions of children, the intermediate variables, and the decision-making environment are important issues for further research. Studies of land-fertility relationships at the individual level should include data on the timing and means of land acquisition, e.g., holdings at time of marriage, inherited land, purchased or rented land, and land lost. Such data would in principle permit a sorting out of the direction of influence—that is, whether those with larger holdings have higher fertility, or those with high fertility are able to acquire access to more land.

Finally, research on agricultural mechanization policy as a mitigating factor between land and fertility is needed. The potential increase in the economic contributions of children could possibly be offset through mechanization policy aimed at the type of family labor which children can provide. Conversely, certain technology packages can increase labor demand (Schutjer and Van der Veen, 1975).

Land settlement, reclamation, and colonization projects represent one set of opportunities to gain insight into the effects of land policies on fertility. These projects must be viewed within the institutional environments in which they operate. Waterbury (1971) notes that most such projects in north Africa are based on pronatalist criteria, but little is known of their demographic (fertility) impacts. Similarly, pronatalist factors have been identified in the use of communally owned land in tropical Africa (Ware, 1978).

A related development in the People's Republic of China is the growing use of private agricultural plots. In an attempt to encourage adoption of the one-child norm, an only child counts as 1.5 to 2 persons in the allocation of private farming plots in rural communes (Chen and Kols, 1982). This scheme, coupled with implementation of the full responsibility system in which individual households or small production teams are allowed to keep any agricultural surplus above a fixed quota, appears to have raised the economic value of children as productive assets in rural areas. Concern is now being expressed about conflict between the new agricultural policies and the birth planning effort, with reports that the birth rate has increased in some areas (Goodstadt, 1982, p. 52).

Improved knowledge on the connections between land and fertility is unlikely to provide facile solutions to the difficult question as to how nations might rapidly lower their fertility and slow population growth.

Certainly in the short run programs of family planning and other approaches which directly influence the proximate determinants of fertility are more likely to yield impressive results. In the long run, however, changes in basic institutional arrangements such as those governing access to land may provide the necessary base for a sustained fertility decline and genuine improvement in the lot of the rural poor.

NOTES

1. The phrase "continued high fertility" is used deliberately. We are not suggesting that couples rationally weigh agricultural labor requirements when making fertility decisions. As Masnick has observed (1978, p. 303): "As long as drives to mate and attain adult status motivates couples to pair off and begin family formation . . . reproduction is assured. Only an active role in preventing births . . . will result in lowered fertility. If the social structure allows economic value to accrue to children, it is all the more unlikely that birth control will be practiced effectively, and high fertility will result. This is not to say that high fertility is an economic goal; rather, it is a consequence of forces that are primarily sociological and biological."

2. We have argued previously for the distinction between land quantity and land quality (Stokes et al., 1979a,b), although the theoretical effect on fertility should be similar. That is, land of higher quality should be able to absorb additional labor to a greater extent than an equal size plot of lesser quality. However, since we are aware of but one study which relates land quality to fertility (Rosenzweig and Evenson, 1977), and our attempts at estimating effects of this dimension have been inconclusive (Laidig et al., 1981), we have not included a discussion of this dimension.

REFERENCES

Aghajanian, A. 1978.   Fertility and family economy in the Iranian rural communities.   Journal of Comparative Family Studies 9:119-127.

Ajami, I. 1969.   Social class, family demographic characteristics and mobility in three Iranian villages.   Sociologia Ruralis 9:62-70.

_____ 1976.   Differential fertility in peasant communities: A study of six Iranian villages.   Population Studies 30:453-463.

Arnold, F. and C. Pejaranonda. 1977.   Economic Factors in Family Size Decisions in Thailand.   Bangkok: Institute of Population Studies, Chulalongkorn University, National Statistical Office, and East-West Population Institute.

Arthur, W.B. and G. McNicoll. 1978.   An analytical survey of population and development in Bangladesh.   Population and Development Review 4:23-80.

Beaver, S.E. 1975.   Demographic Transition Theory Reinterpreted. Lexington, Massachusetts: Lexington Books.

Bongaarts, J. 1978. A framework for analyzing the proximate determinants of fertility. Population and Development Review 4:105–132.

Cain, M.T. 1977. The economic activities of children in a village in Bangladesh. Population and Development Review 3:201–227.

―――― 1981. Risk and insurance: Perspectives on fertility and agrarian change in India and Bangladesh. Population and Development Review 7:435–474.

Chalamwong, Y., M. Nelson, and W.A. Schutjer. 1979. Variation in land availability and human fertility among Thai rice farmers. Paper presented at annual meeting of the Population Association of America, Philadelphia.

Chaplin, D. 1971. Some institutional determinants of fertility in Peru. In: D. Chaplin (ed.) Population Policies and Growth in Latin America, pp. 223–230. Lexington, Massachusetts: D.C. Heath and Co.

Chen, Pi-chao and A. Kols. 1982. Population and birth planning in the People's Republic of China. Population Reports 10:577–618.

Coale, A.J. 1975. The Demographic Transition. The Population Debate, Vol. 1. New York: United Nations.

Committee on Population and Demography. 1982. Determinants of Fertility in Developing Countries: An Overview and Research Agenda. Report No. 16. Washington, D.C.: National Academy Press.

Connell, K.H. 1965. Land and population in Ireland: 1780–1845. In: D.V. Glass and D.E.C. Eversley (eds.) Population in History, pp. 423–433. Chicago: Aldine.

Demeny, P. 1968. Early fertility decline in Austria-Hungary: A lesson in demographic transition. Daedulus 97:502–522.

DeVany, A. and N. Sanchez. 1977. Property rights, uncertainty and fertility: An analysis of the effect of land reform on fertility in rural Mexico. Weltwirtschaftliches Archiv 113:741–764.

―――― 1979. Land tenure structures and fertility in Mexico. Review of Economics and Statistics 61:67–72.

Driver, E. 1963. Differential Fertility in Central India. Princeton: Princeton University Press.

Durham, W.H. 1977. Land tenure and population policy in El Salvador: An ecological perspective. Paper presented at the Joint National Meeting of the Latin American Studies Association and the African Studies Association.

Easterlin, R.A. 1975. An economic framework for fertility analysis. Studies in Family Planning 6:54–63.

―――― 1976a. Population change and farm settlement in the northern United States. Journal of Economic History 36:45–75.

―――― 1976b. Factors in the decline of farm family fertility in the United States: Some preliminary research results. Journal of American History 63:600–614.

―――― 1978. The economics and sociology of fertility: A synthesis. In: C. Tilly (ed.) Historical Studies of Changing Fertility, pp. 57–133. Princeton: Princeton University Press.

Firebaugh, G. 1982. Population density and fertility in 22 Indian villages. Demography 19:481–494.

✳ Forster, C. and G.S.L. Tucker. 1972. Economic Opportunity and White American Fertility Ratios, 1800–1860. New Haven: Yale University Press.

Good, M.D., G.M. Farr, and B.J. Good. 1980. Social status and fertility: A study of a town and three villages in northwestern Iran. Population Studies 34:311–319.

Goodstadt, L.F. 1982.   China's one-child family: Policy and public response. Population and Development Review 8:37–58.

Guest, A.M. 1981.   Social structure and U.S. inter-state fertility differentials in 1900. Demography 18:465–486.

Hawley, A.H. 1955. Rural fertility in Central Luzon. American Sociological Review 20:21–27.

Hicks, W.W. 1974. Economic development and fertility change in Mexico, 1950–1970. Demography 11:407–421.

Hiday, V.A. 1978. Agricultural organization and fertility: A comparison of two Philippine frontier communities. Social Biology 25:69–79.

Huffman, S.L., A.K.M. Allauddin Chowdhury, and W.H. Mosley. 1978. Postpartum amenorrhea: How is it affected by maternal nutritional status? Science 200:1155–1157.

Hull, T.H. 1978. Comments on an anthropological approach to the study of the economic value of children in Java and Nepal. Current Anthropology 19:301–302.

_____ and V.J. Hull. 1977. The relation of economic class and fertility: An analysis of some Indonesian data. Population Studies 31:43–57.

International Bank for Reconstruction and Development. 1975. The Assualt on World Poverty. Baltimore: Johns Hopkins University Press.

Karush, G.E. 1978. Plantations, population, and poverty: The roots of the demographic crisis in El Salvador. Studies in Comparative International Development 13:59–75.

Kleinman, D.S. 1973. Fertility variation and resources in rural India. Economic Development and Cultural Change 21:679–696.

Kocher, J.E. 1973. Rural Development, Income Distribution, and Fertility Decline. New York: The Population Council.

Laidig, G.L., W.A. Schutjer, and C.S. Stokes. 1981. Agricultural variation and human fertility in antebellum Pennsylvania. Journal of Family History 6:195–204.

✳ Latif, A. and N. Chowdhury. 1977. Land ownership and fertility in two areas of Bangladesh. Bangladesh Development Studies 5:239–246.

Leet, D.R. 1976. The determinants of the fertility transition in antebellum Ohio. Journal of Economic History 36:359–377.

Lieberman, S.S. 1980. Rural development and fertility transition in South Asia: The case for a broad-based strategy. Social Research 47:305–338.

Liu, P.K.C. and G.L.T. Lu. 1978. Projections of agricultural population in Taiwan, ROC, 1975–1990. Taipei: Joint Commission on Rural Reconstruction.

Mackay, B. 1979. The effects of socialist transformation on the fertility of the rural population of Ethiopia. Ethiopian Journal of Developmental Research 3:55–64.

Mahmud, S. and J.P. McIntosh. 1980. Returns to scale to family size—Who gains from high fertility? Population Studies 34:500–506.

Mamdani, M. 1972. The Myth of Population Control: Family, Caste, and Class in an Indian Village. New York: Monthly Review Press.

Masnick, G.S. 1978. Comments on an anthropological approach to the study of the economic value of children in Java and Nepal. Current Anthropology 19:303.

Mazur, D.P. 1975. The influence of human fertility on the economic conditions of the rural population in Poland. Population Studies 29: 423-438.

McGinnis, R.M. 1977. Childbearing and land availability: Some evidence from individual household data. In: R.D. Lee (ed.) Population Patterns in the Past, pp. 201-227. New York: Academic Press.

McNicoll, G. and M. Nag. 1982. Population growth: Current issues and strategies. Population and Development Review 8:121-139.

Merrick, T.W. 1978. Fertility and land availability in rural Brazil. Demography 15:321-336.

———— 1981. Land availability and rural fertility in northeastern Brazil. Research in Population Economics 3:93-121.

Mosena, P.W. and J. Stoeckel. 1972. Correlates of desired family size in a rural area of Bangladesh. Journal of Comparative Family Studies 3:207-216.

Mueller, E. 1976. The economic value of children in peasant agriculture. In: R.G. Ridker (ed.) Population and Development: The Search for Selective Interventions, pp. 98-153. Baltimore: Johns Hopkins University Press.

Nag, M. 1976. The economic view of children in agricultural societies: A review and proposal. In: J.F. Marshall and S. Polgar (eds.) Culture, Natality, and Family Planning, p. 3-23. Chapel Hill: Carolina Population Center.

————, B.N.F. White, and R.C. Peet. 1978. An anthropological approach to the study of the economic value of children in Java and Nepal. Current Anthropology 19:293-306.

Odell, M.E. 1982. The domestic context of production and reproduction in a Guatemalan community. Human Ecology 10:47-69.

Population Council. 1981. Research on the determinants of fertility: A note on priorities. Population and Development Review 7:311-324.

Prasithrathsin, S. 1971. Economic and Fertility Behavior of Rural People in Thailand. Unpublished Ph.D. Dissertation, Brown University.

Repetto, R. 1979. Economic Equality and Fertility in Developing Countries. Baltimore: Johns Hopkins University Press.

Rich, W. 1973. Smaller Families Through Social and Economic Progress. Washington, D.C.: Overseas Development Council.

Rosenzweig, M.R. and R. Evenson. 1977. Fertility, schooling, and the economic contributions of children in rural India: An econometric analysis. Econometrica 45:1065-1079.

Schutjer, W.A. and C.S. Stokes. 1982. Agricultural policies and human fertility: Some emerging connections. Population Research and Policy Review 1:225-244.

Schutjer, W.A. and M. Van der Veer. 1975. Economic Constraints on Agricultural Technology Adoption. Occasional Paper No. 5, Economics and Sector Planning Division, Office of Agriculture, Technical Assistance Bureau, U.S. Agency for International Development.

Schutjer, W.A., C.S. Stokes, and G. Cornwell. 1980.   Relationships among land, tenancy, and fertility: A study of Philippine Barrios. Journal of Developing Areas 15:83-96.

Schutjer, W.A., C.S. Stokes, and J.R. Poindexter. 1983.   Farm size, land ownership, and fertility in rural Egypt.   Land Economics 59:393-403.

Seligson, M.A. 1979.   Public policies in conflict: Land reform and family planning in Costa Rica.   Comparative Politics 12:49-62.

Shapiro, M.O. 1982.   Land availability and fertility in the United States, 1760-1870.   Journal of Economic History 42:577-600.

Simon, J.L. 1977.   The Economics of Population Growth.   Princeton: Princeton University Press.

Sinha, J.N. 1975.   Population and agriculture.   In: L. Tabah (ed.) Population Growth and Economic Development in the Third World, pp. 251-305.   Liege: International Union for the Scientific Study of Population.

Stoeckel, J. and M.A. Choudhury. 1969.   Differential fertility in a rural area of East Pakistan.   Milbank Memorial Fund Quarterly 47:189-198.

Stoeckel, J. and A.K.M. Alauddin Chowdhury. 1980.   Fertility and socio-economic status in rural Bangladesh.   Population Studies 34:519-524.

Stokes, C.S. and W.A. Schutjer. 1983.   A cautionary note on public policies in conflict: Land reform and human fertility in rural Egypt. Comparative Politics 16:97-104.

Stokes, C.S., W.A. Schutjer, T.L. McCoy, and C.H. Wood. 1979a.   Rural Development, Land, and Human Fertility: A State-of-the-Arts Paper. Washington, D.C.: U.S. Agency for International Development.

Stokes, C.S., W.A. Schutjer, and M.R. Nelson. 1979b.   Land and human fertility: Toward a synthesis of agricultural and demographic development policy.   Unpublished paper. Pennsylvania State University.

Stokes, C.S., W.A. Schutjer, and J.R. Poindexter. 1983.   A note on desired family size and contraceptive use in rural Egypt.   Journal of Biosocial Science 15:59-65.

Stys, W. 1957.   The influence of economic conditions on the fertility of peasant women.   Population Studies 11:136-148.

Tabbarah, R.B. 1971.   Toward a theory of demographic development. Economic Development and Cultural Change 19:257-276.

Tuladhar, J.M., J. Stoeckel, and A. Fisher. 1982.   Differential fertility in rural Nepal.   Population Studies 36:81-85.

Vlassoff, M. and C. Vlassoff. 1980.   Old age security and the utility of children in rural India.   Population Studies 34:487-499.

Ware, H. 1978.   The economic value of children in Asia and Africa: Comparative perspectives.   Paper No. 50.   Honolulu: East-West Population Institute.

Waterbury, J. 1971.   The Cairo workshop on land reclamation and resettlement in the Arab world.   American Universities Field Staff Report.   Northeast Africa Series 17:1-14.

White, B. 1973.   Demand for labor and population growth in colonial Java.   Human Ecology 1:217-236.

_____ 1975.   The economic importance of children in a Javanese village.   In: M. Nag (ed.) Population and Social Organization, pp. 127-146.   The Hague: Mouton.

Yasuba, Y. 1962. Birth Rates of the White Population in the United States, 1800–1860. Baltimore: Johns Hopkins University Press.

Yengoyan, A.A. 1974. Demographic and economic aspects of poverty in the rural Philippines. Comparative Studies in Society and History 16:58–72.

CHAPTER 11

Income Distribution and Fertility

James E. Kocher

This chapter addresses two major questions. First, in the course of socioeconomic development and increases in per capita income, are changes in the overall fertility rate affected by the distribution of income in the country? Second, if there is a relationship between fertility and the distribution of income, what is the nature of the relationship and what are the causal mechanisms? We shall answer these questions in this chapter by concluding that under conditions of significant aggregate economic growth and development, the more equitable the distribution of income, the more rapid the rate of overall fertility decline will be. There are, however, caveats to this general statement, and we shall discuss these later.

The relationships between the distribution of income and resources within developing country populations and the fertility of those populations are observed at the macro-level. However, an analysis of the relationship between the distribution of income and fertility requires more than simply knowing aggregate-level characteristics, e.g., per capita gross domestic product, the Gini coefficient or other measures of income distribution, and the crude birth rate or other aggregate-level fertility measures. It also requires more than an understanding of the determinants of fertility at the micro-level, although this is also necessary and will be discussed in some detail later. Specifically, aggregate-level data may mask significant subaggregate differences. If different groups of a population are experiencing different socioeconomic and cultural (and possibly biological) fertility-affecting processes, the fertility effects at the aggregate-level will be the product of the fertility effects in each group weighted by the relative proportions of the population found in each of the groups. This is a simple and apparently obvious point, but it seems to be often overlooked or misunderstood. Analysis of subaggregate developmental and demographic data is essential for an appropriate analysis of the role of the distribution of incomes and resources and their associations with aggregate fertility.

The foundation for analysis of aggregate and subaggregate relationships and policy issues and options must be an adequate understanding of the determinants of human fertility at the micro-level. It is therefore necessary to review briefly relevant aspects of the determinants of human fertility before proceeding to a discussion and analysis of possible macro-level relationships as well as implications, if any, for policies intended to influence income distribution. The so-called Easterlin Framework of the determinants of human fertility is reviewed in the next section.

The definition of what constitutes family income is important to the consideration of the income-fertility relationship. The case is made in this chapter that "income" needs to be defined in a full or functional way rather than in the conventional narrow sense. Full income refers to the total resources available to the households (Birdsall et al., 1979). It includes (a) personal disposable income from personal assets (labor and capital), and (b) returns to the use of time in home production, leisure, study, and use of health care services. That is, included among family resources are access (or lack of access) to human capital-creating resources including public goods such as schooling, skill training, health care services, water and sanitation services, labor-productivity enhancing inputs, and access to markets. This is elaborated more fully in this chapter.

Income distribution data are notoriously imprecise and difficult to interpret. Major problems include not only defining the appropriate income concept (Birdsall et al., 1979; Deaton, 1982; Fields, 1980a; Kusnic and DaVanzo, 1982), but also in defining the appropriate recipient unit (Ben-Porath, 1982; Greenhalgh, 1982; Kuznets, 1976), identifying the most appropriate measures of income distribution (Fields, 1980a; Visaria, 1979), dealing with the complications caused by variations in household size and composition, understanding the effects of different stages in life cycles (Meesook, 1982), and, of course, measurement problems and errors. Since this chapter attempts to identify and assess general relationships and does not undertake a statistical analysis, only the issues of the concept and definition of income are addressed.

The effects of the distribution of rising income on the determinants of the supply of and demand for surviving children as well as relationships between income distribution and the costs of fertility regulation are also discussed in this chapter. It is shown that in some circumstances a more egalitarian distribution of increases in full income will result in a fertility rise. However, if, as is generally believed, fertility is negatively related to income over most of the relevant income range, but becomes increasingly less income-sensitive after some income level, then a more egalitarian distribution of rising full incomes will speed the process of overall fertility decline regardless of the initial effect on aggregate fertility.

The question, "has experience been reasonably consistent with the above analysis and conclusions?" is also addressed. It is concluded that although the experiences of developing countries have been complex and widely varied, they appear to have been generally consistent with what the preceding analysis suggests.

Implications for policies intended to improve income distribution are discussed briefly at the end of the chapter, together with observations on the conditions necessary for successful policy implementation. It is observed that, in virtually all countries, policies directed toward effecting a more egalitarian distribution of full incomes are likely to be effective only if significant aggregate economic growth is occurring simultaneously. Policies recommended for their favorable distributional effects are the following: (a) priority on commitment of public resources to basic schooling (especially up to secondary level, and especially for girls), technical training, health care, and family planning services; (b) development strategies which favor labor-intensive sectors and investments; and (c) technology development, promotion, and adoption strategies that favor technologies that complement rather than displace labor, in both the urban and rural sectors.

THE MICRO-LEVEL THEORY OF THE DETERMINANTS OF FERTILITY

In order to know in what ways, if any, the distribution of income affects fertility and fertility decline, it is first necessary to have an adequate understanding of the determinants of fertility. Among students of population change, the so-called Easterlin Framework is currently perhaps the most widely accepted conceptual approach to the determinants of human fertility (1). This framework has three central components: (a) the supply of surviving children, defined as the number of children who would survive to adulthood in the absence of efforts to deliberately limit family size; (b) the demand for surviving children, i.e., desired number of children; and (c) the costs of fertility regulation. In circumstances where demand for surviving children exceeds supply, parents will be motivated to have additional births. Only where the number of surviving children exceeds (or is expected by parents to exceed) the number desired will parents be motivated to limit fertility. Whether in fact they actually do limit their fertility will depend primarily on the perceived costs of doing so.

An important implication of this framework is that motivation for fertility control will increase as the result of either increases in the supply of surviving children, through either rising fertility or rising infant and child survival rates, or reductions in demand for surviving children, i.e., the number of surviving children desired.

For this chapter, the key questions therefore become, first, what are the major determinants of (a) the rising supply of surviving children, (b) a declining demand for surviving children, and (c) the costs of fertility regulation, and second, of these, which are affected—and how—by the distribution of incomes and changes in that distribution?

Determinants of Supply

The supply or potential output of children is defined as the number of surviving children a couple would have if family size were not deliberately limited. Thus, "supply" is the result of natural fertility as reduced by infant and child mortality. The principal proximate determinants of natural fertility are as follows: (a) age at marriage (or age at onset of exposure to intercourse), (b) spontaneous intrauterine mortality, (c) postpartum infecundability, (d) the waiting time to conception, (e) marital disruption, and (f) the onset of permanent sterility (adapted from Bongaarts, 1978, 1981, 1983).

As Bongaarts and Menken (1983) show, age at marriage and postpartum infecundability have by far the largest impact on natural fertility. Postpartum infecundability primarily reflects breastfeeding practices and in some (particularly African) cultures, prolonged periods of postpartum sexual abstinence. As a general rule, each additional month of breastfeeding increases the postpartum infecundability period by over half a month. The overall impact on natural fertility can be significant. If, over a period of time, prolonged breastfeeding is largely abandoned without being replaced with use of modern contraceptives, total natural fertility could be expected to double from about five or six to about ten (CPD, 1982).

Increases in child survival can have an equally dramatic impact on the number of surviving children. The combined effects of a significant increase in natural fertility together with a large increase in child survival rates can produce roughly a fourfold increase in the supply of surviving children (CPD, 1982). This could radically alter the relationships between the number of surviving children desired (demand) and the actual number of surviving children (supply).

Therefore, although the supply of children can be influenced by a number of factors, including the nutritional and health status of mothers, supply in high fertility populations is primarily determined by age at first marriage (or the onset of frequent sexual intercourse), the duration of postpartum infecundability, and levels and changes in infant and child survival rates.

Determinants of Demand

Bongaarts (1982) also shows that only four intermediate fertility variables are important in determining actual fertility, in any population. They are proportion married, contraception, induced abortion, and postpartum infecundability (due mostly to breastfeeding). In a study of 41 populations, these four variables accounted for 96 percent of the variance in total fertility rates. Yet total fertility rates in these populations ranged from less than two to over seven.

Parents will not be motivated to restrict fertility until their demand for surviving children is less than their supply. World Fertility Survey data suggest that, in many parts of the developing world, the supply of surviving children now exceeds demand. This does not appear to be the case in Africa, however, where demand is still fairly high; the preferred number of children per woman is between six and nine in African countries included in the WFS (Lightbourne et al., 1982). In some developing countries demand apparently declined very rapidly over a short period of time. For example, in Taiwan the preferred number of children declined from 4.0 in 1965 to 2.5 in 1980; in Korea ideal family size declined from around five in 1960 to approximately 2.5 in 1980 (CPD, 1982).

There are four major distinct categories of determinants of parental demand for children: (a) the direct costs and benefits of children, (b) the opportunity costs of children, (c) the family's income and wealth, and (d) family tastes and norms. In general, research and analyses suggest that during the course of socioeconomic modernization, both the net direct costs (direct economic returns less direct costs of children) and the opportunity costs (time costs) of children rise, thereby reducing the number of surviving children desired (demand). As family income/wealth increases, the expected increase in demand for children usually appears to be expressed as a desire for higher quality children rather than for more children (Schultz, 1979). "Higher quality children" usually are more costly, so that the net effect of increases in income/wealth is probably a reduction in the number of children desired.

It is worth recalling that one of the necessary preconditions for a decline in marital fertility is that the family or household concerned must perceive fertility control to be advantageous to them (Coale, 1973). That is, they must perceive that they would be better off with fewer children than they would be without any deliberate action to limit fertility.

Costs of Fertility Regulation

Parents will not take deliberate actions to limit fertility unless they expect that the benefits will exceed all costs to them of doing so. Fertility regulation costs are of two broad types: (a) costs of access to the means of fertility control and (b) costs of actually using contraceptives or abortion services, including both psychosocial and health costs. Although direct use costs are often high in relative terms, they usually do not appear to be a significant obstacle to actual use (CPD, 1982). Typically, costs of access to services are relatively high when the number of users in a given locale is small, and costs decrease as the number of users increases. Costs are correspondingly lower where there is relatively low cost and widespread access to public goods and services, including government health and family planning services, schooling, information on health and family planning, and transportation services. However, psychosocial costs, although very difficult to measure, do often appear to be important obstacles to the use of fertility regulation methods.

INCOME: A DEFINITION, AND ITS DISTRIBUTION

Definition of Income

In this chapter, the word "income" is used in a full or functional sense to include both economic returns to factors of production, as well as benefits to individuals from access to and utilization of human capital-creating resources. These include schooling, skill training, health care and family planning services, water and sanitation, transportation, and productive inputs and markets (see Birdsall et al., 1979). In this loose, nonrigorous sense, the meaning of "income" corresponds more closely to the more general term "levels of living." Therefore, in this chapter the term "distribution of income" will mean "distribution of levels of living." The reasons behind the use of this broad definition are described below.

"Income" is conventionally defined by economists as personal income which accrues to the owners of factors of production: land, labor, and capital. Though often not specified, this conventional definition usually also means only "monetary income," although it should also include income in kind. At the aggregate national level, this becomes gross domestic product (GDP) or, at the per capita level, per capita income or per capita GDP. Although per capita income or per capita GDP have been the most common single measures of economic well-being and levels of living, their inadequacy for measuring and comparing levels of living and changes therein in developing countries is widely acknowledged (e.g., McGreevey, 1980) (2).

The conceptual limitations imposed by a strict definition of income limits its usefulness for an analysis of relationships between changes in levels of living and fertility. Two major reasons why the narrow definition of income is inadequate for analyzing relationships between income and fertility are: (a) research and development experiences have shown that there are potentially important fertility/levels of living relationships that are not captured by income alone; and (b) some of the components of "levels of living" can, and often are, altered for some subaggregate populations through government policies and programs, thereby altering the distribution of levels of living within the population over time, and this may very well have fertility effects for the affected groups and therefore for the total population.

Key components of this broad and more functional definition of income have much in common with the now somewhat faded concept of "basic needs" (3). Specific components include basic schooling, technical training, improved health through appropriate public health measures (water, sanitation, etc.), health care services, improved nutrition, and access to family planning services.

Although these are important additional components of a functional definition of income, they obviously cannot fully substitute for personal discretionary income. The point is that access to the above goods and other services and resources can increase both real and psychic income.

Existing Income Distributions

Although the existing distribution of incomes is important for an analysis of current and recent fertility and fertility change, the focus of this chapter is primarily on the distribution of increases in national income over time and its impact on fertility. Nearly all cross-national studies of income distributions and changes over time have used a conventional and not a full income concept. Nevertheless, the results of those studies are instructive and show that the existing distribution of assets and resources is highly unequal and varies considerably across countries.

As one illustration, income recipients in the richest 5 percent of developing country populations typically receive over 20 times as much income as those in the bottom 20 percent (Fields, 1980b). In a World Bank study of the existing income distributions of about 45 developing countries, the proportion of total national income received by the poorest 40 percent of the population ranged from 6.5 percent to over 20 percent. From 40 to over 70 percent of national income accrued to the top 20 percent of income recipients (Ahluwalia, 1974).

On the distribution of the growth in national income, Chenery (1980) summarizes another World Bank study that found large variation in the proportion of income growth that went to various income groups of each total population in eleven developing countries. Less than 20 percent of the growth in aggregate income went to the poorest 60 percent of the population in Brazil, Mexico, and Peru. Between 20 and 30 percent of aggregate income growth went to the poorest 60 percent of the population in India, the Philippines, Turkey, and Columbia, while over 30 percent of the increase in aggregate national income went to the poorest 60 percent of the population in Taiwan, Yugoslavia, Sri Lanka, Korea, and Costa Rica.

It is important to note again that the issue in this instance is not income redistribution. Rather, it is both the existing distribution as well as the distributional pattern of increases in aggregate and per capita living conditions over time. The latter has been referred to as "redistribution with growth" (Chenery et al., 1974), although in the real world such redistribution with growth is probably more likely to produce a less egalitarian distribution than a more egalitarian one (Ahluwalia, 1974; Kuznets, 1979).

The essential question is, over time what segments of the population experience significant improvements in their levels of living? Are improvements basically limited to a small elite, or are they shared by a large proportion of the population?

INCOME DISTRIBUTION AND THE DETERMINANTS OF FERTILITY

Fertility is generally negatively related to income, but most studies show that the relationship is not linear. Moreover, at very low levels of income, as income increases fertility may also increase before it starts to fall (4).   However, as income continues to rise, fertility begins to fall at some point and continues falling until a relatively low-level plateau is reached even if incomes continue to increase.

The critical questions are, where along this income-fertility curve are various segments of the population located, and what are the relative sizes of the population groups located along various portions of this curve?   If a large proportion of the population has very low incomes which are positively associated with their fertility, and if their incomes rise, their fertility will also rise and this will probably produce a rise in overall national fertility.   However, if the income levels of all significant population groups are in the middle income range where fertility is inversely related to income, then the net effects of rising income on national fertility will depend on the relative income sensitivity of the fertility of each of the groups as well as their sizes relative to each other.   Micro-level processes are elaborated further below.

Supply Effects

In early stages of socioeconomic development, increases in full income typically increase the supply of surviving children.   This is because the following are usually associated with rising levels of living: (a) The period of postpartum infecundability declines, due to substantial declines in the duration and intensity of breastfeeding and abandonment of the practice of long periods of postpartum sexual abstinence (where this had been common).   The result is substantially shorter average birth intervals over the full reproductive period.   (b) This may be partially offset by a rise in the age at first marriage which would independently reduce fertility.   (c) However, typically taking place concurrently, there is a significant decline in infant and child mortality, thereby producing a substantial increase in the proportion of children born who survive to adulthood.   The net effect, for those families experiencing substantial improvements in living conditions, is usually a sizable increase in the number of surviving children, unless offset by a reduction in fertility resulting from a significant increase in the effective use of modern contraceptives in response to lower demand.   The independent "supply effect" of improved living conditions is therefore likely to be rising fertility.

If income gains are concentrated among a relatively small proportion of the population, then these substantial "supply effects" are likely to be limited to this same relatively small proportion of the population, and therefore the impact on overall fertility will probably be small. However, if income gains are widely shared by a large proportion of the total population, "supply effects" can also be expected to be widespread.   This same relatively large proportion of the population can be expected to experience rising fertility if their incomes are initially quite low, and in this case there would probably be a substantial increase in overall (aggregate or national level) fertility.

This appears to be the explanation for the rise in overall fertility in Kenya from a total fertility rate of about 6.6 in 1967 to a total fertility rate of over 8 in 1980 (Mott and Mott, 1980). That is, gains in income (broadly defined to include education, access to health, and other services) were shared fairly widely in Kenya. This resulted in shorter birth intervals and increases in infant and child survival rates among a fairly large proportion of the population. The increases in infant/child survival rates (during this period infant mortality is estimated to have declined from about 120 to about 80 per 1000 births) together with rising total fertility produced a very large increase in the average number of surviving children per woman. Declines in duration of breastfeeding and postpartum sexual abstinence were obviously not fully compensated by the increased use of effective modern contraceptives. Had these broad gains in income been concentrated among only the small proportion of Kenya's population with relatively high incomes, it seems likely that the impact on overall fertility (and probably also overall infant/child survival rates) would have been much smaller.

Demand Effects

Parents will only be motivated to limit fertility if they perceive it is advantageous to them to do so, and if the expected costs (of all types) incurred in limiting fertility are less than the expected benefits to them from doing so. This is more likely to happen if the number of surviving children they want (demand) is substantially less than the number they have (supply) or expect to eventually have. This is also more likely to happen if demand is declining over time.

Under some circumstances, parents may be motivated to try to limit fertility even without a reduction in demand. This could happen in the following situations: (a) where existing demand is already well below supply; (b) where parents want to exceed a certain minimum interval between births even though existing demand is equal to or greater than the supply or expected supply; and (c) where the supply of surviving children increases, even with demand unchanged, to the point where the level of excess supply is greater than the perceived costs of taking action to regulate fertility.

However, as described earlier, during the course of socioeconomic development those families that experience substantial improvements in living conditions usually also desire fewer surviving children than was the case for the previous generation or for their lower-income contemporaries. That is, many of the improvements in levels of living and related cultural and social/psychological changes which result in a rising supply of surviving children also contribute to a decline in the number of children desired.

Costs of Fertility Regulation

"Full income" means all the household's resources including services to which members have access. Access to knowledge and information about family planning as well as convenient access to family planning services would be included as part of full income. Rising monetary incomes, even if relatively egalitarian in distribution, do not assure increased access to family planning knowledge, information, and services. However, an effective government commitment to making family planning information and services readily available to the bulk of the population would contribute to a more egalitarian distribution of full income. It would also substantially reduce the costs of regulating fertility for a large share of the population and would thereby speed the process and pace of aggregate fertility decline.

"Net" Fertility Effects

If the relationship between income and fertility is not under all circumstances negative and linear, then any observed relationship between rising per capita income and aggregate fertility may be a poor indicator of the income-sensitivity of fertility at various income levels. For some population groups, income may be rising; for others, it may be falling at various rates; and for some, it may be beginning to fall after a period in which it had been rising or unchanged. The "net" effect on national-level fertility of such a variety of subaggregate fertility effects will be the product of the fertility effects in each group weighted by the relative proportions of the population found in each of the groups.

This is a compelling reason to study fertility trends and processes and associated socioeconomic characteristics among important groups of any aggregate population of interest, and it is the relationships between socioeconomic development and fertility (not population growth rates) that should be analyzed. Although the population growth rate is important, it is not the appropriate demographic variable for most studies since, as simply the fertility and mortality residual, it frequently masks information on the real variables of interest: fertility and mortality.

WHAT DOES EXPERIENCE SHOW?

In recent years a number of studies, including both country-specific micro-level as well as multicountry cross-sectional analyses, have concluded that lower fertility and more rapid fertility decline are generally associated with more egalitarian distributions of income and relatively greater access to education, employment, and health and social welfare services (Birdsall, 1980; Bhattacharyya, 1975; Flegg, 1979; Kocher, 1973; Moravetz, 1978; Repetto, 1978, 1979, 1982; Rich, 1973; Ridker, 1976; Yotopoulos, 1977). Other researchers have expressed skepticism about the existence and identification of a relationship between the distribution of income and fertility, but the skepticism has primarily focused on questions about the adequacy of the data for identifying such associations and the interpretations of analyses of the relationships (e.g., Boulier, 1982; Cassen, 1978; Mauldin, 1982; Simmons, 1979).

The experiences of a number of developing countries are consistent with the empirical observation that fertility is related to the level of income, particularly the level of full income.   What is not known is whether the shares of income going to particular socioeconomic classes, independent of the absolute levels of income going to each class, also have an independent effect on the fertility of each class (Birdsall, 1980).   Although it would be helpful to know the latter, it is not the central issue.

The central issue can be summarized as a series of propositions: (a) Aside from some special circumstances, increases in income are associated with declines in fertility.   (b) Among relatively low-income households, increases in income are generally associated with relatively large decreases in fertility, i.e., once fertility has begun to decline.   Equivalent increases in absolute income in relatively high-income households produce little or no fertility decline because fertility in most cases is already fairly low.   (c) Of principal interest is the relationship between growth of income, including its distribution, over time as associated with fertility.   Since increases in incomes among low income recipients are associated with greater fertility declines than are equivalent increases among higher income recipients, the larger the proportion of total national income growth that accrues to the poorer segments of the population (implying relatively less income inequality), the greater will be the overall fertility decline.

Broad Types of Demographic Transition Experiences to Date

Aggregate-level fertility decline experiences in countries or among large subnational populations can be broadly categorized as: (a) those where fertility decline has been widespread and generally rapid;   (b) those where fertility decline has been highly varied and usually slow overall;   (c) some combination of these two;   and (d) those where overall fertility has not declined to date.

Widespread Fertility Decline

In most cases, widespread and usually rapid fertility decline has occurred where the socioeconomic development process has been broadly participatory.   That is, in these situations, improvements in living conditions by and large have resulted in a desire to limit fertility. Because the distribution of these improvements has been relatively egalitarian, both improvements in living conditions and fertility decline have been widely spread across regions and classes.   Populations in this category include China, Taiwan, Korea, Sri Lanka, Kerala, Costa Rica, postrevolutionary Cuba, and perhaps Thailand.   Japan, and the white population of the United States should probably also be included here (or in the third category below).   In some settings cultural/social homogeneity, provided it has not been unduly at odds with emerging aspirations for small families, has facilitated the rapid overall fertility decline process.   However, where there is considerable cultural/religious homogeneity which is pronatalist (e.g., fundamentalist Islamic societies and, for extended periods of time, some predominantly Catholic countries), such homogeneity may substantially delay fertility decline (Lesthaeghe, 1980).

Highly Differentiated and Usually Slow Overall Fertility Decline

This is the opposite extreme. Countries in this category have generally experienced highly differentiated, "trickle-down" socioeconomic development, with highly skewed distributions of improved living conditions. Brazil, a country of socioeconomic extremes, is one example. Overall fertility in Brazil has declined considerable but is still moderately high (the current total fertility rate is about 4.5). However, some segments of the Brazilian population now have quite low fertility. Fertility of women in the higher income groups is only about half as high as fertility of low-income illiterate women.

India is also in this category. In the past 20 years India has experienced substantial socioeconomic development, and overall fertility has declined by 15 to 20 percent, and the total fertility rate is now under five. However, the benefits of development have been highly concentrated by region and class. In those regions where the benefits of development have been fairly widely shared, substantial overall fertility decline has occurred. In other areas, particularly the densely populated, economically depressed and highly economically and socially differentiated north central states, overall fertility has declined very little. India might also be classified in the following group.

Mix of Widespread and Highly Differentiated Fertility Decline

There are countries between these two extremes in which socioeconomic development has been neither extremely skewed nor very egalitarian. Overall fertility has declined, usually with moderate speed, but significant fertility differentials remain; fertility decline lags for a sizable proportion of the population. Countries in this group probably include Indonesia, Colombia, and perhaps Mexico, although Mexico also has important elements of the second category.

No Overall Fertility Decline to Date

There are two major categories of countries in this group: Sub-Saharan African countries and revivalist/fundamentalist Islamic countries. Both are interesting cases from a distributional perspective. Since fertility has yet to decline in these countries, the following speculative comments are offered.

In these countries demand for children remains high; children are highly valued. This probably primarily reflects economic conditions and relationships, i.e., Caldwell's (1976) "intergenerational flow of wealth." Micro-level economic conditions are strongly reinforced by cultural values associated with continuation of the family and lineage, naming customs, and political control and power of male elders.

Moreover, in traditional African societies fertility has been principally limited by the length of birth intervals, typically three to four years or more. Long birth intervals resulted primarily from long breastfeeding and long periods of postpartum sexual abstinence. As Lesthaeghe (1980, p. 531) shows, not only did these practices have beneficial effects for birth intervals and child mortality, long postpartum sexual abstinence is also important in "maintaining the grip of the lineages on their members and, particularly through its link with polygyny, it serves as an element of male gerontocratic control."

What is likely to happen when this cultural code erodes (as it is in many parts of Africa) through socioeconomic improvements, educational gains, and rapidly rising aspirations? Birth intervals will decline and fertility will rise. This is what has happened in Kenya; it is happening in at least some parts of Nigeria (Caldwell and Caldwell, 1981; Dow, 1977; Lesthaeghe et al., 1981b; Orubuloye, 1981; Rehan and Abashiya, 1981), and it is probably happening (largely undocumented to date) throughout Africa. In this situation, the more widespread these processes and the more homogeneous the cultural values, the larger and more rapid the (probable) fertility rise will be. Fertility decline will await the stresses produced by these processes: rapidly rising aspirations and the perception of increases in costs of living will inevitably clash with close birth intervals and large numbers of surviving children. In such settings, when the desire for fertility limitation finally takes root, it is also likely to be widespread. It is therefore possible that the subsequent fertility decline in these populations will be widespread and perhaps fairly rapid.

In revivalist/fundamentalist Islamic countries, "keeping women in their place" is an important part of the religious/cultural code. Although contradictions inevitably emerge as incomes and aspirations rise and confront religious/cultural values, it does not appear inevitable that traditional values will succumb to income-related aspirations. To the contrary, since in these settings men continue to monopolize all important elements of political and religious life, rising incomes may make it somewhat easier for them to keep their women sheltered and to maintain traditional social and family values. These values will likely include large families. If over time men begin to perceive that they would be better off if women limited fertility somewhat, it seems inevitable that eventually some private compromises will be made with the cultural/religious code, and fertility limitation will be practiced on a significant scale. However, the strength of the prevailing cultural/ religious code and the relative homogeneity of these populations (in terms of value systems) suggests that in these countries the cultural/ religious code will prove to be quite resilient, and overall fertility decline is likely to be delayed for quite some time.

In these settings, it seems likely that a more egalitarian distribution of income (and/or greater homogeneity in the cultural/religious code) would not produce early and rapid fertility decline; to the contrary, it might help overwhelm whatever latent social/cultural/religious deviations exist in the society. However, once people do begin to limit fertility, more equitable incomes and homogeneous cultural/religious conditions may contribute to more rapid fertility decline.

Other Important Issues

Other points should be made here, not all of which may be fully evident in the preceding review. The demographic transition, and particularly sustained fertility decline, is a complex process. There will frequently be long lag periods between socioeconomic/cultural changes which ultimately have important effects on fertility and the resultant fertility change. As described above for Kenya and Nigeria, the fertility decline transition may initially result in fertility rise, and this may be an unavoidable phase prior to the onset of fertility decline. There may be some segments of the population that are experiencing rising fertility, others experiencing declining fertility, and others essentially unchanged fertility. It may be difficult or impossible to identify these important variations from aggregate level data.

If there is an emerging desire on the part of a large proportion of reproductive age parents to limit fertility, the fertility decline process will be greatly facilitated and speeded through relatively easy and low cost access to modern means of fertility control. Otherwise, fertility decline is likely to be slowed because the private costs (of regulation) remain unnecessarily high. This, too, is an important element of income distribution as defined in this chapter.

POLICY IMPLICATIONS

Finally, a few observations may be made about the policy implications of the relationship between the distribution of income and fertility. The most important question is, what genuine options are available for altering the existing distribution of productive assets and resources and returns thereto?

In most developing countries, those in power belong to the highest income class in the country, and therefore they are not likely to support government policies or programs which would reduce the income and wealth of the highest income class and redistribute it to the poorer classes. In nearly all countries, if there is to be genuine commitment by the ruling class to increasing the share of national income which goes to the low income majority of the population, commitment would be limited to the distribution of increases in national income.

Genuine options for government policies and programs are limited but nevertheless significant. The following three categories of policies can, over a period of perhaps two or more decades, have a significant impact on the level of full income accruing to the low income majority (Schultz, 1979, 1981; World Bank, 1981): (a) major commitment of public resources to basic schooling, especially primary schooling up to secondary level, and especially for girls, technical training, and the provision of health care and family planning services; (b) adoption of development strategies which give strong emphasis to policies and investments which stimulate labor-intensive sectors; and (c) technology development, promotion and adoption strategies which emphasize technologies which complement rather than displace labor, in both the urban and rural sectors.

If the commitment of development resources is consistent with the above guidelines, their impacts individually and in combination will increase the resources (full income) available to low income families and particularly the human capital of low-income individuals and families.   This in turn will, over time, enable these individuals and families to become more productive and to further increase their incomes in future years.   Since most of these families will be in the highly income-sensitive portion of the fertility decline curve or, if not yet there, will shortly enter that phase as their incomes continue to rise, the overall fertility decline effects will be greater than would occur if these development resources were directed to other areas.

NOTES

1. This conceptual framework was utilized by the National Academy of Sciences' Committee on Population and Demography in its recent review of the determinants of human fertility (e.g., CPD, 1982). The framework is described in some detail in Easterlin (1975, 1978, 1983).   A similar approach, but directed more specifically toward African populations, is presented in Kocher (1977, 1979, 1983), and in Lesthaeghe et al. (1981a).
2. Over the years several alternative indices of "levels of living" have been constructed.   Two which emerged in the late 1970s were PQLI (physical quality of life index) and a purchasing power adjusted index of per capita income.   The PQLI is a composite of infant mortality, life expectancy at birth, and literacy rate (see Morris, 1979).   The purchasing power index is an attempt to construct internationally comparable adjustments in per capita incomes which reflect purchasing power equivalents across countries (see Kravis et al., 1975, 1978, 1982).
3. See, for example, Streeten (1982).
4. Although this initial rise in fertility may reflect a rising demand for children, it is more likely to be a response to changes in determinants of the supply of surviving children, which is associated with rising income.

REFERENCES

Ahluwalia, M.S. 1974.   Income inequality: Some dimensions of the problem.   In: H. Chenery, M.S. Ahluwalia, C.L.G. Bell, J.H. Duloy, and R. Jolly (eds.) Redistribution with Growth, pp. 3-37.   New York: Oxford University Press.

Ben-Porath, Y. 1982.   Individuals, families, and income distribution.   In: Y. Ben-Porath (ed.) Income Distribution and the Family, pp. 1-13. Population and Development Review 8:Supplement.

Bhattacharyya, A.K. 1975. Income inequality and fertility: A comparative view. Population Studies 29:5-19.

Birdsall, N. 1980. Population and Poverty in the Developing World. World Bank Staff Working Paper No. 404.

_____, J. Fei, S. Kuznets, G. Ranis, and T.P. Schultz. 1979. Demography and development in the 1980s. In: P. Hauser (ed.) World Population and Development: Challenges and Prospects, pp. 211-295. New York: Syracuse University Press.

Bongaarts, J. 1978. A framework for analyzing the proximate determinants of fertility. Population and Development Review 4:105-132.

_____ 1981. The impact on fertility of traditional and changing child-spacing practices. In: H.J. Page and R. Lesthaeghe (eds.) Child-spacing in Tropical Africa: Traditions and Change, pp. 111-129. New York: Academic Press.

_____ 1982. The fertility-inhibiting effects of intermediate fertility variables. Studies in Family Planning 13:179-189.

_____ 1983. The proximate determinants of natural marital fertility variables. Studies in Family Planning 13:179-189.

_____ and J. Menken. 1983. The supply of children: A critical essay. In: R.A. Bulatao and R.D. Lee (eds.) Determinants of Fertility in Developing Countries: A Summary of Knowledge, pp. 22-49. Washington, D.C.: National Academy Press.

Boulier, B.L. 1982. Income redistribution and fertility decline: A skeptical view. In: Y. Ben-Porath (ed.) Income Distribution and the Family, pp. 159-173. Population and Development Review 8:Supplement.

Caldwell, J.C. 1976. Toward a restatement of of demographic transition theory. Population and Development Review 2:321-366.

_____ and P. Caldwell. 1981. Cause and sequence in the reduction of postnatal abstinence in Ibadan City, Nigeria. In: H. Page and R. Lesthaeghe (eds.) Child-spacing in Tropical Africa: Traditions and Change, pp. 181-199. New York: Academic Press.

Cassen, R.H. 1978. India: Population, Economy, Society. New York: Holmes and Meier.

Chenery, H.B. 1980. Poverty and progress: Choices for the developing world. Finance and Development 17:12-16.

_____, M.S. Ahluwalia, C.L.G. Bell, J.H. Duloy, and R. Jolly. 1974. Redistribution with Growth. New York: Oxford University Press.

Coale, A.J. 1973. The Demographic Transition. Proceedings of the IUSSP Conference. Liege: Ordina Editions.

Committee on Population and Demography (CPD). 1982. Determinants of Fertility in Developing Countries: An Overview and a Research Agenda. Washington, D.C.: National Academy Press.

Deaton, A. 1982. Inequality and Needs: Some experimental results for Sri Lanka. In: Y. Ben-Porath (ed.) Income Distribution and the Family, pp. 35-49. Population and Development Review 8:Supplement.

Dow, T.E., Jr. 1977. Breast feeding and abstinence among the Yoruba: Demographic and contraceptive patterns among Kenya women. Studies in Family Planning 13:12-23.

Easterlin, R.A. 1975. An economic framework for fertility analysis. Studies in Family Planning 6:54-63.

232   Policies for Rural Development: Impacts on Fertility

_____ 1978. The economics and sociology of fertility: A synthesis. In: C. Tilly (ed.) Historical Studies of Changing Fertility, pp. 57–133. Princeton: Princton University Press.

_____ 1983. Modernization and fertility: A critical essay. In: R.A. Bulatao and R.D. Lee (eds.) Determinants of Fertility in Developing Countries: A Summary of Knowledge, pp. 971–991. Washington, D.C.: National Academy Press.

Fields, G.S. 1980a. Assessing progress toward greater equality of income distribution. In: W.P. McGreevey (ed.) Third–World Poverty: New Strategies for Measuring Development Progress, pp. 47–81. Lexington, Massachusetts: Lexington Books.

_____ 1980b. Poverty, Inequality, and Development. Cambridge: Cambridge University Press.

Flegg, A.T. 1979. The role of inequality of income in the determination of birth rates. Population Studies 33:457–473.

Greenhalgh, S. 1982. Income units: The ethnographic alternative to standardization. In: Y. Ben–Porath (ed.) Income Distribution and the Family, pp. 70–91. Population and Development Review 8:Supplement.

Kocher, J.E. 1973. Rural Development, Income Distribution and Fertility Decline. New York: The Population Council.

_____ 1977. Socioeconomic development and fertility change in rural Africa. Food Research Institute Studies 16:63–75.

_____ 1979. Rural Development and Fertility Change in Tropical Africa: Evidence from Tanzania. African Rural Economy Paper No. 19. East Lansing: Michigan State University.

_____ 1983. Supply-demand disequilibria and fertility change in Africa: Toward a more appropriate economic approach. Social Biology 30:41–58.

Kravis, I.B. 1982. Phase III: World Product and Income: International Comparisons of Real GDP. Baltimore: Johns Hopkins University Press.

_____, Z. Kennessey, A. Heston, and R. Summers. 1975. Phase I: A System of International Comparisons of Gross Product and Purchasing Power. Baltimore: Johns Hopkins University Press.

_____, A. Heston, and R. Summers. 1978. Phase II: International Comparisons of Real Product and Purchasing Power. Baltimore: Johns Hopkins University Press.

Kusnic, M.W. and J. DaVanzo. 1982. Who are the poor in Malaysia? The sensitivity of poverty profiles to definition of income. In: Y. Ben–Porath (ed.) Income Distribution and the Family, pp. 17–34. Population and Development Review 8:Supplement.

Kuznets, S. 1976. Demographic aspects of the size distribution of income: An exploratory essay. Economic Development and Cultural Change 25:1–94.

_____ 1979. Growth, Population, and Income Distribution: Selected Essays. New York: W.W. Norton and Co.

Lesthaeghe, R. 1980. On the social control of human reproduction. Population and Development Review 6:527–548.

_____, P. Ohadike, J.E. Kocher, and H.J. Page. 1981a. Child-spacing and fertility in sub-Saharan Africa: An overview of issues. In: H.J. Page and R. Lesthaeghe (eds.) Child-spacing in Tropical Africa: Traditions and Change, pp. 2–23. New York: Academic Press.

_____, H.J. Page, and O. Adegbola. 1981b. Child-spacing and fertility in Lagos. In: H.J. Page and R. Lesthaeghe (eds.) Child-spacing in Tropical Africa: Traditions and Change, pp. 147-179. New York: Academic Press.

Lightbourne, R., Jr., S. Singh, and C.P. Green. 1982. The World Fertility Survey: Charting Global Childbearing. Population Bulletin 37.

Mauldin, W.P. 1982. The determinants of fertility decline in developing countries: An overview of the available empirical evidence. International Family Planning Perspectives 8:116-122.

McGreevey, W.P. 1980. Measuring development performance. In: W.P. McGreevey (ed.) Third-World Poverty: New Strategies for Measuring Development Progress, pp. 1-46. Lexington, Massachusetts: Lexington Books.

Meesook, O.A. 1982. A note on income distribution and the life cycle of individuals. In: Y. Ben-Porath (ed.) Income Distribution and the Family, pp. 151-156. Population and Development Review 8:Supplement.

Moravetz, D. 1978. Basic needs policies and population growth. World Development 6:1251-1259.

Morris, M.D. 1979. Measuring the Condition of the World's Poor: The Physical Quality of Life Index. Washington, D.C.: Overseas Development Council.

Mott, F.L. and S.H. Mott. 1980. Kenya's Record Population Growth: Dilemma of Development. Population Bulletin 35.

Orubloye, I.O. 1981. Child-spacing among rural Yoruba women: Ekiti and Ibadan division in Nigeria. In: H.J. Page and R. Lesthaeghe (eds.) Child-spacing in Tropical Africa: Traditions and Change, pp. 225-236. New York: Academic Press.

Rehan, N. and A.K. Abashiya. 1981. Breastfeeding and abstinence among Hausa women. Studies in Family Planning 12:229-232.

Repetto, R. 1978. The interaction of fertility and the size distribution of income. Journal of Development Studies 14:22-39.

_____ 1979. Economic Equality and Fertility in Developing Countries. Baltimore: Johns Hopkins University Press.

_____ 1982. A reply. In: Y. Ben-Porath (ed.) Income Distribution and the Family, pp. 174-178. Population and Development Review 8:Supplement.

Rich, W. 1973. Smaller Families through Social and Economic Progress. Monograph No. 7. Washington, D.C.: Overseas Development Council.

Ridker, R.G. (ed.). 1976. Population and Development: The Search for Selective Interventions. Baltimore: Johns Hopkins University Press.

Schultz, T.W. 1979. Investment in population quality throughout low-income countries. In: P. Hauser (ed.) World Population and Development: Challenges and Prospects, pp. 339-360. Syracuse, New York: Syracuse University Press.

_____ 1981. Investing in People: The Economics of Population Quality. Berkeley: University of California Press.

Simmons, G.B. 1979. Family planning programs or development: How persuasive is the new wisdom? International Family Planning Perspectives 5:101-110.

Streeten, P. 1982.   First Things First: Meeting Basic Needs in Developing Countries.   New York: Oxford University Press.
Visaria, P. 1979.   Demographic factors and the distribution of income: Some issues.   In: Economic and Demographic Change: Issues for the 1980s.   Proceedings of a Conference, Vol. 1, pp. 289-320.   Liege: IUSSP.
World Bank. 1981.   Accelerated Development in Sub-Saharan Africa: An Agenda for Action.   Washington, D.C.: The World Bank.
Yotopoulos, P.A. 1977.   The population problem and the development solution.   Food Research Institute Studies 16:1-131.

CHAPTER 12

Food Policy, Human Nutrition, and Fertility

Per Pinstrup-Andersen and Shubh K. Kumar

Food policy may influence human fertility through its impact on the nutritional status of women and children and through changes in other fertility-related factors. Although the influence may be important, it is usually indirect and operates through a number of interrelated factors. This suggests that the relationship between food policy and fertility may be difficult to observe directly. It also implies that efforts to improve the understanding of how various food policy measures affect or might be expected to affect fertility should focus on: (a) identification of the factors involved and the paths through which such effects might occur, and (b) estimation of the coefficients that in a causal way link the factors within each path. Such an approach would provide guidelines for the design of food policy that would be more useful than those provided by the common comparisons of fertility and selected socioeconomic variables, the correlates of fertility. Such correlates frequently do not identify the direction of causality and usually ignore the mechanisms by which the impacts occur.

This chapter attempts to identify the most important paths and intervening variables that determine the impact of food policy on fertility for the purposes of: (a) developing a conceptual model useful for thinking about and assessing the impact of food policy measures on fertility; (b) identifying, on the basis of existing evidence, the aspects of food policy that appear to be of particular importance from the point of view of fertility; and (c) identifying critical knowledge gaps and research needs.

235

Although the most important impact is likely to operate through changes in the nutritional status of women and children, food policy may also influence fertility through other mechanisms.   Each of three sets of relationships are discussed in a separate section, beginning with the impact of food policy on nutrition, followed by the impact of changes in nutritional status on fertility, and finally, by the direct impact of food policy on fertility excluding the effects operating through nutrition.   The last section of the chapter highlights the implications for food policy and proposes ways in which food policies may be designed to better meet fertility and population growth goals.

FOOD POLICY AND NUTRITION

Food policy influences human nutrition through a number of intermediate factors.   These factors must be identified and the process by which they operate must be understood in order to predict effectively how alternative policy formulations will influence nutrition.   Figure 1 presents a schematic overview of the principal intermediate variables and causal links between food policy and nutrition.

The principal factors determining the effect of food policy on nutrition are: (a) the ability of the household to acquire food; (b) the extent to which this ability is actually translated into food acquisition and the type of food acquired (household food acquisition behavior); (c) the distribution of food among household members; and (d) the physiological utilization of food by individual household members.   Food policy may influence nutrition through any of these factors.   Poverty and high food prices (relative to income) are the most important

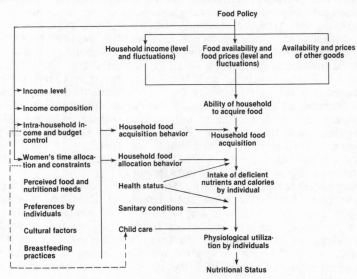

Figure 1.   The causal relationships between food policy and nutritional status.

reasons for insufficient food acquisition to meet nutritional needs, and the principal nutritional impact of food policies occurs through changes in the real income and purchasing power of households and the prices of basic goods.

Incomes of malnourished households may be affected by food policy through several mechanisms. One possibility is through income generation, e.g., policies related to technological change in agriculture and food-for-work programs. Secondly, income transfers may be in the form of cash or redeemable coupons (e.g., food stamp programs), or in food (e.g., food supplementation schemes of various types). Finally, food price policies represent yet another alternative. Food price policies may also change the price of one or more foods relative to other foods and to other goods. Thus, in addition to the effect of real incomes embodied in price changes, these policies may influence household budget allocations to individual foods and between food and other goods, and thus influence food consumption and nutrition.

Estimates of the adjustments low-income households make in their food acquisition in response to changes in income cover a wide range. The adjustment in total calorie consumption among low-income households is usually larger than that made by higher-income households. It is not uncommon to find that the very poor spend as much as 70 percent of additional income on food, although some may spend as little as 20 percent. The various reasons for the apparent limited emphasis on food by some low-income households are discussed elsewhere and are not repeated here (Pinstrup-Andersen, 1982a,b).

Empirical evidence on the adjustment in food acquisition which the poor make in response to changes in the prices of food commodities is much more limited. The available evidence does, however, indicate that the poor are in general more responsive to price changes than are better-off population groups. Price elasticities of demand for staple foods around -0.7 for the poor, and -0.2 for the better-off households are not uncommon, although the magnitude of these elasticities varies considerably from one location to another (1).

The composition of household income may also be important for nutrition. According to neoclassical demand theory, the effect of changes in household real income on food consumption is independent of income type and source, i.e., it does not matter whether additional income is received in the form of food or cash, as long as the receipt of food is inframarginal (less than the amount that the household would acquire in the absence of the additional income) and all income is considered permanent rather than transitory. Many nutritionists, on the other hand, assume that inframarginal food transfers to malnourished households result in a larger addition to household food consumption than a transfer of an equal amount of cash income. In fact, this assumption seems to underlie a great deal of past and ongoing inframarginal food supplementation schemes. However, there is only limited empirical evidence available regarding this issue. For example, there is some evidence that real income in the form of food from household production (home gardens or semisubsistence farming) contributes more to food consumption than an equal amount of cash income (Kumar, 1977). Furthermore, there is reason to believe that the nutrition effect of real income expansion, whether in money, in kind, or through price decreases, may depend on who in the household controls such income expansions and who decides what should be the appropriate adjustments in household consumption patterns.

A large part of existing calorie/protein deficiencies among the rural poor appear to be the result of seasonal or irregular fluctuations in food prices, income, and food availability—in other words, fluctuations in the ability to acquire food.   Thus, policies affecting these fluctuations such as storage, transportation, foreign trade, and crop insurance policies, may have significant nutritional implications.

While changes in food prices and income influence the ability of households to acquire food, household food acquisition behavior determines the extent to which changes in the ability to acquire food result in actual alterations in household food acquisition.   As shown in Figure 1, food policies may influence ability as well as behavior.   The impact of consumer-oriented food price policies, food-linked income transfers, and food transfer programs occurs primarily through changes in the households' ability to acquire food.   The impact of food policy on behavior and intrahousehold food allocation through changes in income composition, intrahousehold income and budget control, and women's time allocation, is also likely to be important in many cases although empirical evidence on this matter is very limited.

The discussion presented in this section was purposely kept brief to avoid repetition of other work recently completed and available.   A more detailed discussion of the conceptual relationships may be found in Pinstrup-Andersen (1982a,b); the nutritional effects of food policies and nutrition programs are analyzed by Kennedy and Pinstrup-Andersen (1983).

NUTRITION AND HUMAN FERTILITY

The discussion of possible nutrition effects on fertility is focused narrowly on the intermediate biological factors that are influenced by changes in nutritional status.   In general, when nutritional status improves, it is assumed that the biological capacity for a wide range of activities increases, including fecundity.   In addition to influencing reproductive capacity, nutritional improvements also contribute to lower mortality across all ages.   This effect can be postulated to influence fertility through two main mechanisms: increasing life expectancy of adults raises fertility, and increasing the survival probability of infants decreases fertility.   These biological tendencies may be substantially influenced by behavioral factors, and to the extent possible, it is desirable to separate the two.   Among the set of possible biological mechanisms are (see Figure 2): (a) an extension of reproductive age at both ends of the child-bearing years, earlier onset and later conclusion; (b) increased fecundity during the reproductive ages, including the joint effects of postpartum sterility and conception probabilities; and (c) a reduction in mortality rates of adults and children.

These mechanisms are discussed and available evidence is used to illustrate the main conclusions that can be derived at the present time.

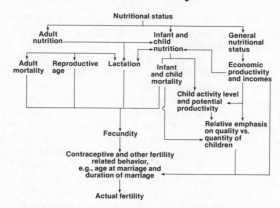

Figure 2. The principal factors and relationships determining the impact of nutritional status on fertility.

Seasonal patterns of vital elements and their possible links with nutrition and health, the influence of male nutritional status on fertility, and the prevalence of permanent sterility are not addressed because of the relatively limited information available.

While the biological basis for the nutritional impact on fertility is limited to fecundity, actual fertility is mediated substantially by behavioral factors, most of which are nonnutritional in origin (see the discussion of Figure 3 in the Food Policy and Fertility section of this chapter). Thus, fecundity may be viewed as the potential "supply" of children, what is biologically possible, while behavioral factors reflecting the desire to have children may be viewed as the "demand" for children. Interaction between supply and demand results in actual fertility. There may be, however, some basis for modification in fertility behavior or the demand for children as a result of nutritional change. This would stem from reduction in child mortality and possible improvements in the productivity potential of children. Reduction in child mortality would reduce the cost of raising additional children to adulthood, whereas improvement in productivity potential would reduce the net cost of investing in child quality (nutrition, health, and education). The realization of this productive potential would occur under a favorable employment and wage environment. The result would be a reduction in the cost of both child numbers and quality and a consequent increase in the demand for both. On balance, the net behavioral effect would be determined by the relative price elasticity of child numbers and quality, the magnitude of reduction in cost of child numbers and quality, and the elasticity of substitution between numbers and quality of children.

Influence of Nutrition on Reproductive Age

The start of a women's reproductive age at menarche is one of the biological factors that has been most clearly shown to be nutrition related.   The empirical basis is provided by both time-series and cross-sectional data on age at menarche in individual countries.   Longitudinal data available from developed countries with historical records indicate that a substantial decline in age at menarche occurred during the first half of this century.   Since levels of living, health standards, and nutrition were rising during this period, it was postulated that nutrition was related to the earlier start of the reproductive age.   Cross-sectional data from both developed and developing countries have also linked the lower age at menarche to higher socioeconomic status, the dietary intake of girls, and anthropometric indicators of nutritional status. Bongaarts (1980) reviews studies on each of these aspects.

While this is one area in which data available from longitudinal and cross-sectional measures have helped to clarify the relationship between fertility and improved nutrition, it also serves to highlight the deficiencies in making prima facie use of cross-cultural comparisons.   Thus, age at menarche is reported to be 13 to 14 years in India and about 13 years in present Western societies, but within each group, differences in diet and nutritional status can account for up to two years of variation in the onset of puberty.

As stated previously, nutrition-related biological factors such as the age at menarche can influence the level of fecundity.   For elucidating the effect of nutrition on actual fertility, behavioral factors must be considered and they may be more important than biological factors in explaining observed changes.   If improvement in nutrition and reduced age at menarche are not accompanied by a substantial reduction in age at marriage, this factor may not greatly increase fertility (2).   Ultimately, however, it is the age at marriage (or initiation of sexual intercourse) and not the onset of puberty which is the determining factor in fertility.

The influence of nutrition on the onset of menopause is not as clear-cut as the influence on age at menarche.   Most empirical evidence employs retrospective data.   There seem to be enormous methodological problems in obtaining accurate age information, and research is also complicated by the fact that menopause is a gradual phenomenon and not as well defined as menarche.

There is some variation in the interpretation of available data on nutrition and age of menopause.   According to Bongaarts (1980, p. 566): "No conclusive evidence regarding nutritional variation in age at menopause is provided in these studies."   On the other hand, Frisch (1978, p. 25) concludes that there is a time trend discernible for Western populations, and states that: "The average age of menopause in about 1850 was between 45 and 50 years. [Further] the average age of menopause for present-day women is about 50 years or more." However, the demographic significance of age at menopause is questionable since it does not coincide with differences in age at last birth. Thus while the age at menopause is reported to be higher in present-day Hutterite women than the average in 1850 (Frisch, 1978), the mean age at last birth is 40.9 years among the well-nourished present-day Hutterites, but was slightly higher at 41.7 years in a poorly nourished mid-nineteenth century English population (Bongaarts, 1980).

Adult Mortality

Rates of adult mortality have traditionally been high for populations with poor health facilities. Improvements in health services help to reduce birth complications and maternal mortality as well as improve general life expectancy. When rates of' maternal mortality are high and life expectancy is low, such improvements would increase the reproductive life of men and women and, thus, potentially increase fertility. Nutrition is only an indirect factor here. The highest incidence of maternal mortality occurs when health services and the sanitary environment are poor and parity is high. However, the nutritional depletion of women tends to increase with increasing numbers of children in conditions of chronic undernutrition. This would be especially pronounced, as is the case for many areas of South Asia, where there is an intrahousehold maldistribution of resources away from female members.

This factor is likely to influence fertility rates only at very low levels of life expectancy for women below 40 years, but to higher ages for men. As in other cases, however, behavioral modifications, whether a result of the process by which improvements in health or nutrition take place, or caused by other factors, determine the actual fertility change that takes place.

Fecundity

LACTATIONAL AMENORRHEA OR POSTPARTUM STERILITY. It is well accepted that breastfeeding is a principal factor in determining the duration of postpartum sterility. Characteristics of breastfeeding that are considered important in this regard include the length of the breastfeeding period, demand versus scheduled feeding, as well as frequency of suckling and the degree to which breast milk is supplemented with other foods. In addition to breastfeeding, maternal age and parity are found to be positively correlated with duration of lactational amenorrhea.

The biological basis for amenorrhea during breastfeeding is currently understood to be the product of several hormonal changes. Breast milk is produced by the action of the hormone prolactin and elevated levels of this hormone in the bloodstream of postpartum women delays the onset of ovulation. Cells producing the hormone are located in the pituitary gland and these multiply during pregnancy (Noel et al., 1974). Following birth when estrogen levels fall, the elevated prolactin can stimulate milk secretion (Guyton, 1971). However, the maintenance of high prolactin secretion seems to occur through a neurogenic feedback mechanism which is triggered by suckling. It appears that at least two hormones may be associated in the stimulation of prolactin by breastfeeding. First, the hormone prolactin is secreted by the anterior pituitary gland and stimulates synthesis of large quantities of fat, lactose, and casein (i.e., milk) by the mammary glandular cells; and second, the hormone oxytocin and to a lesser extent, vasopressin is secreted by the hypothalmus directly in response to the suckling. The oxytocin causes contraction of cells in the walls of the milk containing alveoli, thereby secreting milk (Guyton, 1971). It is not clear from the literature whether it is the levels of oxytocin itself, or the sensory impulses of suckling that stimulates the prolactin secretion that is associated with breastfeeding.

An examination of the neuroendocrine control of lactation and gonadotropin (3) secretion shows that the pattern of nursing is impor- tant in inhibiting the secretion of the gonadotropin-releasing factor and suppressing ovulation (Tyson and Perez, 1978). Since the gonadotropin- releasing factor is produced by the hypothalamus, which also produces oxytocin in response to suckling, this may also provide a link for reduced gonadotropin production during lactation. It also appears that the production of milk and prolactin stimulation may be connected via a negative feedback mechanism such that presence of unutilized milk in the mammary glands suppresses prolactin, whereas its evacuation stimu- lates the release of the hormone into the bloodstream.

Earlier cross-cultural and historical data on duration of lactational amenorrhea, e.g., comparing Hutterite women and women from low- income countries, led to the hypothesis that malnutrition influences the period of postpartum sterility. Recent more careful investigation in Bangladesh and Guatemala (Huffman et al., 1978; Bongaarts and Del- gado, 1979) has shown that differences in maternal weight and weight for height has no significant impact on the duration of postpartum sterility. Extreme variation in caloric intake also had no significant impact on duration of postpartum sterility in Guatemala (Delgado et al., 1978). Cross-cultural comparisons in a study of data from nine coun- tries has also shown that postpartum variation in the proportion of women breastfeeding, explained about 85 percent of variation in the proportion of menstruating women (Chowdhury, 1978). While differences in women's nutrition can explain some of the variation in length of postpartum amenorrhea, according to Bongaarts (1980, p. 567):

> The small differences between nutritional status groups in duration of amenorrhea are not necessarily caused by a direct physiological effect of malnutrition on the mother. . . . For example, if malnourished mothers have less food available for supplementing infant diets, or late in introducing supplementa- tion, their infants will suckle more and thus prolong amenor- rhea.

However, prolonging amenorrhea by this means is hardly desirable. If children of malnourished mothers need to suckle more because their mother's milk is inadequate to meet their growing needs, and supple- mentary foods are not available, it is likely to have adverse nutritional implications. It has been shown that the volume of milk production declines more rapidly in malnourished mothers, and may be inadequate as the sole source of nutrients for the growing child after the first three to four months of age. Children of these mothers are not only exposed to malnutrition through inadequate breastmilk in early infancy, but if supplements are used, they also face the hazard of contaminated supplements.   It is well established that malnourished infants face a higher risk of mortality.   Thus, if the choice is between earlier diet supplementation of children, or improving mothers' nutritional status, clearly the choice should be for improving maternal nutrition.

CONCEPTION RATES.   Conception rates among menstruating women are often used to estimate the underlying fecundity level of a population.   Also known as waiting time, conception rates measure the number of months between the occurrence of the first postpartum menses and the next conception.   Together with lactational amenorrhea and the pregnancy period it constitutes birth intervals, which determine fertility levels in a population.

Two of the studies reported earlier which looked at postpartum amenorrhea in relation to nutrition in Bangladesh and Guatemala have also examined the waiting time to conception in the same group of women.   In both cases there was no significant association between nutritional status and waiting time to conception.

FECUNDITY AND FERTILITY UNDER EXTREME FOOD SCARCITY. Numerous observations have been made on fertility during periods of famine, starvation, and other types of severe socioeconomic stress, such as wars and mass migrations.   Since amenorrhea is reported in many of these instances, an impairment in fecundity appears to be involved. Before examining the possible bases for observed impairments in fecundity, it should be noted that such events rarely manifest themselves simply in the form of food shortages alone.   They are usually accompanied by severe economic hardships, loss of lives and assets, epidemic disease, departure of able-bodied men to war or in search of work, and other stressful situations.

Studies of human biological response in moderate to severe protein-caloric malnutrition shows that many components of the endocrine systems are sensitive to nutritional status.   In a systematic analysis of existing information, Brasel (1978) has shown that in protein malnutrition, when protein synthesis is generally reduced, the gonadotropin and growth hormones are synthesized and secreted in increased amounts. Since gonadotropin is responsible for stimulating ovarian hormones and ovulation, it does not appear that fecundity would be influenced by protein-caloric deficiency.   Anorexia nervosa, a disease related to mental stress, has been associated with amenorrhea.   The author concludes, however, that endocrinology of anorexia nervosa cannot be equated with imposed caloric or protein malnutrition.

Stress-related amenorrhea is also known to occur in a wide range of circumstances.   Similarly, psychic disturbances in the human female can greatly alter the periodicity of monthly cycles, as well as the character of the cycle (Guyton, 1971) (4).   It seems plausible, therefore, that famine-related infecundity and amenorrhea may be better characterized as stress-induced, rather than nutritionally induced.

Many of the body's responses under extreme stress are geared to preserving life itself and even preserved functions such as procreation

are relinquished.   When populations undergo such severe deprivations
that large numbers are decimated, an examination of the short-run
fecundity implications seems to have limited practical usefulness.

Infant and Child Mortality

Food policies can have an impact on infant and child mortality rates
by improving the general nutrition level and through improvements in
maternal and child nutrition.   Maternal nutrition bears a strong association with nutrition of the newborn infant when it is totally dependent
on the mother for its nutrient supply.   A recent review by Zeitlin et
al. (1982) examines the available literature on this issue.   Evidence
points to the association between poor maternal nutrition, low birthweight, and prematurity, and to low birthweight and prematurity as
causes of high infant mortality.

Infant and child mortality can influence fertility in two ways.   The
first influence on fertility is through the biological response of shortening postpartum amenorrhea among lactating mothers whose infants die.
Thus, shorter birth intervals result, with adverse consequences for both
fertility and maternal nutrition status.

The second influence of changes in infant and child mortality is on
the demand for children operating through behavioral factors linking
child mortality and the number of children desired by a household.
There is evidence to show that improvement in the probability of child
survival leads to curtailment in fertility by childbearing couples
(Preston, 1978; Schultz, 1976; Wray, 1975).   The reduction in fertility,
however, is generally smaller than the additional number of surviving
children (Cochrane and Zachariah, 1983).   A discussion of the behavioral factors which explain this relationship is beyond the scope of this
chapter, but lucid expositions may be found in Preston (1978) and
Schultz (1974).

In many societies parents have a strong preference for male children
because they are more likely to bring economic returns and security to
the family.   In these circumstances desired family size is likely to
decrease relatively slowly with reductions in the mortality rate.
However, where strong sex preferences exist, there may be selective
reduction in male mortality.   Neglect, malnutrition, and even female
infanticide have been reported in many parts of the world as ways of
reducing family size, while retaining the desired number of male children.   Improvements in the status of women and their income-earning
ability would assist in reducing the magnitude of this problem and in
reducing actual fertility (Rosenzweig and Schultz, 1983).

FOOD POLICY AND FERTILITY

Excluding the impact of food policy that operates through nutrition,
which was discussed in an earlier section, food policy may influence
human fertility through changes in household income, the demand for
and shadow cost of women's time, intrahousehold income and budget

control, and the demand for and shadow cost of children's time (Figure 3). This section discusses how each of these factors is influenced by food policy and how they, in turn, influence fertility.

HOUSEHOLD INCOMES. The impact of various food policy measures on household income was discussed in an earlier section. Changes in income may influence fertility through changes in maternal and child health which, in turn, lead to changes in fecundity and child mortality. Changes in income influence the relative emphasis that a household places on the quality versus the quantity of children. The latter influence is closely linked with the shadow cost of women's time, as well as the potential economic productivity of children, variables which themselves are influenced by changes in household income. Thus, the income-fertility relationship is complex and has been subject to considerable attention by researchers.

Since the impact of income changes on the quality and quantity of children is treated in detail elsewhere in this volume, no attempt is made to summarize the state-of-the-art regarding both theoretical and empirical findings. It should be noted that the impact is likely to depend on how the demand for and the shadow cost of time of women and children are affected, whether the income change is perceived to be permanent or transitory, and who controls the income within the household. Although opposing causal effects appear to exist, current empirical evidence supports the hypothesis that increasing income results in reduced fertility, although the immediate effect of a rise in income in traditional subsistence agriculture may be to increase fertility (Simon, 1976).

DEMAND FOR AND SHADOW COST OF WOMEN'S TIME. Food policy may influence the demand for and the economic productivity of women's time in food production, processing, marketing, and consumption-related

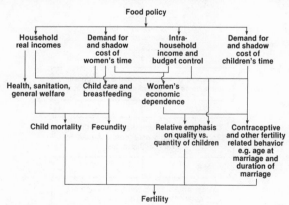

Figure 3. Paths through which food policy may affect human fertility excluding paths operating through nutrition.

activities.   Such influences have repercussions for fertility in various
ways.   The immediate impact may occur through changes in the time
women   allocate   to   child   care,   including breastfeeding.   Thus,   an
increasing demand for time in food-related activities, and/or higher
earning opportunities compete with child care for time and the result
may be reduced child care and increasing child mortality.   The longer-
run effect of expanding opportunities is likely to be a reduction in the
desired number of children.   Such a causal effect is likely to be
strongest in cases where the additional employment does not permit
women to tend simultaneously to their children (Rosenzweig, 1978).

Evidence on the relationship between the value of time and fertility
is summarized by Nerlove (1974, p. S217):   "The increased value of
human time results in fewer children per household, with each child
embodying greater investments in human capital which in turn result in
lower mortality and greater productivity in the economically active
years."

Increasing the economic productivity of women's time may also lead
to greater decision making power for women within the household.
Since women and men are affected differently by changes in fertility,
changes in the relative power of decision making is likely to influence
desired family size.   The relevant processes are complex and not fully
understood.   Figure 4 illustrates the causal sequence proposed by Dixon
(1978).

INTRAHOUSEHOLD INCOME AND BUDGET CONTROL.   There is
very little empirical evidence on how household food acquisition and
nutrition are influenced by changes in intrahousehold income and budget
control.   Similarly, it is not clear whether there is a fertility impact
of changes in income control except as they affect the value of time of

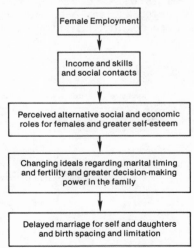

Figure 4.   Hypothesized effects of female employment on age at marriage, fertility regulation, and fertility.

individual household members. Although the empirical evidence is limited, anecdotal evidence from various countries suggests that the proportion of additional household income spent on food and child care tend to be larger if the income is controlled by women instead of by men. While this may be accepted as a working hypothesis, more research is needed to provide empirical evidence. Similarly, there is a need for more work on the impact of the intrahousehold distribution of income control on decisions regarding quality and quantity of children. The theory of household economics as it currently stands has little to offer on this question because it is based on a single household utility function.

DEMAND FOR AND SHADOW COST OF CHILDREN'S TIME. Children's labor may provide an important source of income for low-income rural households. Thus, food policy which increases the demand for and the economic productivity of children's labor would be expected to induce households to have more children. Empirical evidence supports this expectation. Rosenzweig and Evenson (1977) found a significant positive relationship between the wage rates of children and fertility in rural India. Similar findings resulted from work in the Philippines (Rosenzweig, 1978). Other related findings are reviewed by Schutjer and Stokes (1982).

SUMMARY AND POLICY IMPLICATIONS

The impact of food policy on fertility is largely indirect and operates through a number of intervening factors. Thus, for the purpose of incorporating fertility concerns into policy design and modification, it is important to identify the paths and factors most important within the relevant socioeconomic environment. Since food policy does not affect fertility directly, but through intermediate factors, the challenge is to identify the factors through which food policy is likely to have the greatest impact on fertility (positive or negative), and to estimate the effect on these factors of the various policy options which may be considered in a particular case.

Two of the factors which are directly influenced by food policy are of great importance for fertility: (a) the level and stability of real income of low-income households, and (b) the demand for and shadow cost of women's time. Food policies which affect the level and stability of real income in low-income households influence maternal and child nutrition and child mortality, all of which influence fertility. Similarly, such policies can affect the relative emphasis on quality and quantity of children in low-income households, and the nutritional status of others which influences productivity and income-earning capacity. Food policies that result in permanent improvements in real income of the poor are likely to result in greater reductions in fertility than food policies which produce transitory gains in income. Thus, real income changes embodied in food transfer programs or food price subsidies are likely to have a more limited effect on fertility than real income changes which result in the transfer of income-earning resources to the poor, simply because the former may be discontinued more easily than the latter, or at least are perceived as such.

Changes in the demand for and shadow cost of women's time influences child care and breastfeeding in the short run, and desired family size in the longer run. Food acquisition behavior is also likely to be affected. Thus, the short-run impact of increasing the shadow cost of women's time may include: (a) reduced child care because of stronger competition for the mother's time; (b) reduced nutritional status of infants and children due to the shorter duration of breastfeeding and shifts towards more costly foods in order to save time in food preparation; and (c) increases in infant and child morbidity and mortality leading to increased fertility. In the longer run, however, increased shadow costs of women's time are likely to lead to a desire for fewer children. The interaction between the demand for and the shadow cost of women's time and the economic contribution of children may be important in this context. As the demand for women's time increases, a number of the activities performed by women may be taken over by older children, thus increasing their shadow cost. This relationship may dampen the fertility reduction although probably not to any great extent.

Food policy may also influence the potential economic contribution of children directly. However, while there is evidence of a positive correlation between both the demand for and the economic contribution of child labor, and the number of children in the family, such evidence is based on cross-sectional data and should probably be interpreted to mean that the demand for child labor may inhibit fertility reductions in the short run. In the longer term, however, it is more difficult to visualize an increase in fertility due to an increase in the demand for child labor.

There are a number of other ways in which fertility may be influenced by food policy. The importance of factors such as changes in intrahousehold income and budget control, are not known, while others appear to be much less important than previously expected. Among the latter is the fertility impact of food policy operating through improved fecundity and longer reproductive periods of women brought about by improved nutrition. While the impact of food policy on maternal nutrition is an important consideration, the hypothesis that improved maternal nutrition greatly increases fertility is not supported by available evidence. Similarly, there is little evidence in support of the argument that improved infant and child nutrition will lead to increased fertility. On the contrary, to the extent that such nutritional improvements are reflected in higher perceived survival rates for children, fertility is likely to decline.

The potential impact of food policy on the demand for children appears to be much more important than the impact on supply. If this conclusion is correct, food policy need not lead to a conflict between the goals of improved nutrition and reduced fertility. To those responsible for food policy, this suggests that fertility as well as nutritional goals are best achieved through the design of policies which result in the largest self-sustained economic benefits for low-income households, and for the most disadvantaged within such households, especially women and children.

NOTES

1. Price elasticity is defined as the percentage change in the quantity demanded associated with a one percent change in the price.

2. Bongaarts (1980) has calculated that a one year decline in age at marriage from 17 to 16 years in response to reduced age at menarche would increase fertility by about five percent.

3. The gonadotropins comprise three hormones released by the pituitary gland. Of these, two, namely the follicle stimulating hormone (FSH) and leutimizing hormone (LH) are responsible for stimulating production of ovarian hormones; estrogen and progesterone and together cause ovulation. These ovarian hormones inhibit the release and action of prolactin.

4. This appears related to the role of the hypothalamus in producing gonadotropin stimulating hormones, as well as its role in producing ACTH which is sharply elevated during stress.

REFERENCES

Brasel, J. 1978. Impact of malnutrition on reproductive endocrinology. In: W.H. Mosely (ed.) Nutrition and Human Reproduction, pp. 29–60. New York: Plenum.

Bongaarts, J. 1980. Does malnutrition affect fecundity? A summary of evidence. Science 208:564–569.

———— and H. Delgado. 1979. Effects of nutritional status on fertility in rural Guatemala. In: H. Leridon and J. Menken (eds.) Natural Fertility, pp. 107–133. Liege: Ordina Editions.

Chowdhury, A. and K.M. Alauddin. 1978. Effect of maternal nutrition on fertility in rural Bangladesh. In: W.H. Mosely (ed.) Nutrition and Human Reproduction, pp. 401–410. New York: Plenum.

Cochran, S.H. and K.C. Zacariah. 1983. Infant and Child Mortality as a Determinant of Fertility. Staff Working Paper No. 556. New York: World Bank.

Delgado, H., A. Lechtig, E. Brineman, R. Martorell, C. Yarbrough, and R. Klein. 1978. Nutrition and birth interval components: The Guatemalan experience. In: W.H. Mosely (ed.) Nutrition and Human Reproduction, pp. 385–399. New York: Plenum.

Dixon, R.B. 1978. Rural Women at Work. Baltimore: Johns Hopkins University Press.

Frisch, R.E. 1978. Population, food intake, and fertility. Science 199: 22–30.

Guyton, A.C. 1971. Textbook of Medical Physiology, 4th ed. Philadelphia: W.B. Saunders.

Huffman, S.L., A.K.M.A. Chowdhury, J. Chakroborty, and W.H. Mosley. 1978. Nutrition and postpartum amenorrhea in rural Bangladesh. Population Studies 32:251-260.

Kennedy, E.T. and P. Pinstrup-Andesen. 1983. Nutrition Related Policies and Programs: Past Performances and Research Needs. Washington, D.C.: International Food Policy Research Institute.

Kumar, S. 1977. Role of the Household Economy in Determining Child Nutrition at Low-Income Levels: A Case Study in Kerala. Occasional Paper No. 95. New York: Cornell University, Department of Agricultural Economics.

Nerlove, M. 1974. Household and economy: Toward a new theory of population and economic growth. Journal of Political Economy 82: S200-S218.

Noel, G.L., H.R. Suh, and A.G. Frantz. 1974. Prolactin release during nursing and breast stimulation in post-partum and non-post-partum subjects. Journal of Clinical Endocrinology and Metabolism 38:413-423.

Pinstrup-Andersen, P. 1982a. Food policy and human nutrition. Paper presented at workshop on The Interfaces Between Agriculture, Food Science and Human Nutrition in the Middle East, Aleppo, Syria.

_____ 1982b. An Analytical Framework for Assessing the Nutrition Effects of Policies and Programs. Paper presented at Rockefeller Foundation Workshop on Strengthening National Food Policy Capabilities, Bellagio, Italy.

Preston, S.H. (ed.). 1978. The Effects of Infant and Child Mortality on Fertility. New York: Academic Press.

Rosenzweig, M.R. 1978. The value of children's time, family size and non-household child activities in a developing country: Evidence from household data. Research in Population Economics 1:331-347.

_____ and R. Evenson. 1977. Fertility, schooling, and the economic contribution of children in rural India: An econometric analysis. Econometrica 45:1065-1079.

_____ and T.P. Schultz. 1983. Consumer demand and household production: The relationship between fertility and mortality. American Economic Review 73:38-42.

Schultz, T.P. 1976. Interrelationships between mortality and fertility. In: R.G. Ridker (ed.) Population and Development, pp. 239-289. Baltimore: Johns Hopkins University Press.

Schultz, T.W. 1974. Economics of the Family. Chicago: University of Chicago Press.

Schutjer, W.A. and C.S. Stokes. 1982. The Human Fertility Implications of Food and Agricultural Policies in Less-Developed Countries. College of Agriculture, Bulletin 835. University Park: Pennsylvania State University.

Simon, J.L. 1976. Income, wealth, and their distribution as policy tools in fertility control. In: R.G. Ridker (ed.) Population and Development, pp. 36-76. Baltimore: Johns Hopkins University Press.

Tyson, J.E. and A. Perez. 1978. The maintenance of infecundity in post-partum women. In: W.H. Mosely (ed.) Nutrition and Human Reproduction, pp. 11-27. New York: Plenum.

Wray, J.D. 1975.   Will better nutrition decrease fertility?   In: Proceedings of the 9th International Congress of Nutrition, Vol. 2, pp. 16-31.   Mexico: Karger, Basel.

Zeitlin, M.F., J.D. Wray, J.B. Stanbury, N.P. Schlossman, M.J. Meurer, and P.J. Weinthal. 1982.   Nutrition and Population Growth: The Delicate Balance.   West Germany: Oelgeschlager, Gunn and Hain.

CHAPTER 13
Agricultural Mechanization Policy and Human Fertility

E. Kwan Choi and W. Whitney Hicks

The mechanization of agriculture has been associated with increased output and rising agricultural productivity in most nations experiencing agricultural development. In these nations, farm mechanization has been a relatively slow process of introducing tools, machinery, and equipment into the production system. In an attempt to expedite the mechanization process, governments frequently resort to the preferential allocation of capital. The net result is the distortion of factor prices which subsequently influences the choice among alternative strategies of mechanization. Thus Merrill (1975, p. 6) noted that "the decision to substitute machinery for labor . . . may be a response to changes in the relative price of inputs (i.e., labor and capital)." Lowering the price of capital (interest rates) relative to the price of labor (wage rates) will encourage the substitution of machinery for labor.

Many researchers have cautioned against the premature mechanization of the agricultural sector. Merrill (1975, p. 8) noted that "during the early stages of mechanization most new machines have little effect on yields" and attributed yield increases to other changes which frequently occur simultaneously with, but independent of, mechanization, such as intensive use of fertilizer, better water control, and improved cultivation practices.

The available evidence indicates the danger inherent in the various attempts to shortcut the slow process of economic development. Policy makers tend to seek simple answers to difficult economic problems, ignoring the secondary impacts of proposed policies. The temptation is to set factor prices and influence income distributions dramatically, rather than to allow factor prices to be determined by market forces. The anomaly lies in how long it has taken to learn that factor price distortion is no shortcut to the economic development process (see Timmer, 1982, p. 6). de Janvry (1978, p. 311) argues further that policies which distort factor prices, coupled with the failure to pursue technological research appropriate to the country's resource endowment, often reflect the ability of those in power to protect and enhance their interests, not just misguided policy.

Numerous examples could be used to illustrate the severity of the effects of factor price distortions on the rural economy. A typical case is "industrialization first" development policies that provide preferential access to scarce capital inputs, resulting in overcapitalization in the modern enclave. In order to offset the negative impact of these policies on the agricultural sector, policy makers have often compounded the problem by providing differential access to scarce capital resources among farmers, thereby creating a dualism within the agricultural sector as well as between industry and agriculture (Bourne and Graham, 1981). Despres (1973, p. 142) described such a situation in Pakistan in 1956 and argued that "a serious case of underpricing of an acutely scarce resource is that of capital." He further noted that "the businessman who obtains an authorization to build a plant, an import permit, or bank credit gains command over a scarce and highly profitable resource at extremely favorable terms. At these favorable terms, there exists today a sizable unsatisfied demand for [capital in the form of] import permits, credit facilities, and other official authorizations" (Despres, 1973, p. 141).

The situation that Despres described is representative of many LDCs. Preferential allocation of capital at favorable terms to the commercial and industrial urban sector and the modern enclave of the agricultural sector results in a "sizable unsatisfied demand for credit" in the traditional agricultural sector. Berry and Cline (1979, p. 10) found that the "gap between the price of capital to large and small farmers frequently encourages the substitution of capital equipment for labor on the large farm." Consequently, the traditional sector is left with residual capital inputs and is forced to use labor-intensive technology.

The impact of factor price distortions on the allocation of resources and the distribution of income are relatively well known. The effects of factor price distortions on fertility behavior have not, however, received much attention, although such policy-induced changes in fertility behavior have potential long term economic consequences for rural areas. The purpose of this chapter is to analyze the effect of factor price distortions on fertility in the traditional sector. A household decision making model is used to analyze the effects of factor price distortions on the quantity and quality of children that farm families desire. If the income elasticity of fertility is negligible and fertility is not responsive to changes in children's wages, the analysis suggests that factor price distortions increase fertility in rural areas. A policy implication which follows from the static analysis is that a reduction or elimination of concessionary interest rates for the privileged borrowers and minimum wage rates for privileged workers in the modern sector, may decrease fertility in the traditional sector.   Finally, the development of an integrated financial market in rural areas would likely decrease fertility, if financial assets became a more attractive alternative to children as a means of transferring resources through time for old age security.

GOVERNMENT POLICY AND DUALISM WITHIN AGRICULTURE

As indicated earlier, governments often bias the terms of trade against agriculture and in favor of industry in an effort to accelerate the development of the country.   To counteract the adverse effects of these policies, governments frequently make credit available at concessionary rates to agriculture.   Subsidized credit and the resulting excess demand for capital in the traditional sector creates a bimodal distribution of capital in agriculture.   The modern sector has high capital-labor and capital-output ratios, while the traditional sector has low capital-labor and capital-output ratios.   Symptomatic of these distortions is the situation observed in LDCs where a farmer on one side of the road farms with a tractor, while a farmer on the other side uses only a hoe.

The government affects the relative prices of agricultural inputs including capital and labor through monetary policy, fiscal policy, foreign trade policy, and budget policy.   Monetary policy can influence both the nominal and the real rates of interest.   If the real rate of interest is negative, or very low, private sources of credit may not lend or may restrict lending to only the very best risks, who tend to be in the modern sector.   Farmers in the traditional sector may be unable to get private credit at concessionary rates.   As a result, excess demand for credit will exist in the traditional sector at the concessionary rates.

Foreign trade policy can influence the cost of capital through tariffs, quotas, import-licensing systems, and undervalued or multiple exchange rates.   Scarce foreign exchange, in turn, is allocated through import licenses for preferred items such as tractors.   The allocation of undervalued foreign exchange constitutes an import subsidy.   Fiscal policy can influence the price of capital through tax concessions, tax credits, and deductions.   Budget policy subsidies include subsidies for agricultural inputs, investment in agricultural infrastructure, and influence the level and direction of agricultural research and extension.   de Janvry (1978) argued that vested interests may influence the direction of agricultural research in LDCs away from output-increasing labor-saving techniques and toward labor-saving capital-intensive techniques.   When capital-using techniques become available those with access to credit and other capital subsidies quickly adopt the new technology.

The likely consequences of government policies in LDCs similar to those discussed above are summarized in Figure 1 under the "Low Interest Rate Policy" heading.   Low rates of interest provide little incentive to defer consumption and thus discourage saving within agriculture.   Deposit rates at savings institutions below the opportunity cost of capital induce savers to seek alternative investments to the

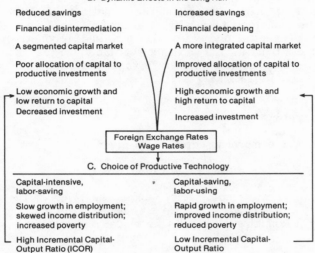

Low Interest Rates   **High Interest Rates**

A. Static Effects in the Short Run

Increased investment by privileged borrowers with access to official credit markets; decreased investment by small farmers.

More equal competition for capital in official credit markets.

B. Dynamic Effects in the Long Run

Low Interest Rates	High Interest Rates
Reduced savings	Increased savings
Financial disintermediation	Financial deepening
A segmented capital market	A more integrated capital market
Poor allocation of capital to productive investments	Improved allocation of capital to productive investments
Low economic growth and low return to capital Decreased investment	High economic growth and high return to capital Increased investment

Foreign Exchange Rates
Wage Rates

C. Choice of Productive Technology

Low Interest Rates	High Interest Rates
Capital-intensive, labor-saving	Capital-saving, labor-using
Slow growth in employment; skewed income distribution; increased poverty	Rapid growth in employment; improved income distribution; reduced poverty
High Incremental Capital-Output Ratio (ICOR)	Low Incremental Capital-Output Ratio

Figure 1.   The effects of alternative financial policies.   Source: adapted from Timmer (1982).

debt of established depository institutions.   "Disintermediation" develops in a fragmented capital market where a wide dispersion exists in the rates of return to various investments, resulting in an inefficient allocation of both existing capital and new investment.   The decreased savings and inefficient allocation of capital gives a high incremental capital–output ratio, a high capital–labor ratio, low rates of economic growth, and an unequal distribution of income.

"Subsidized" credit increases the inequality in the distribution of income.   Those who get loans at subsidized rates tend to be the prosperous farmers in the modern sector.   These farmers benefit from subsidized credit by (a) defaulting on loans, (b) obtaining credit at negative real interest rates, and (c) leveraging their equity in the project.   The effects of inequality in the distribution of income on fertility are discussed in Chapter 11.

In the sections below a two–sector model is used to demonstrate the impact of factor price distortions on the relative use of capital and labor in the modern and traditional sectors.   Then, a demand model of fertility behavior is posited and used to demonstrate the impact of changes in factor prices on fertility behavior.   The discussion of fertility behavior, in turn, provides the basis for an elaboration of the potential effects of financial reform on fertility.

THE TWO SECTOR MODEL

We assume that the modern sector receives preferential allocation of capital at concessionary rates and employs privileged workers at a wage above the free market wage.   The traditional sector receives residual capital and labor.   Let $y_1 = g(L_1,K_1)$ and $y_2 = f(L_2,K_2)$, respectively, denote the output in the traditional sector and the modern sector, where L_i and K_i are the amount of labor and capital employed in sector i.   The production functions of f(.) and g(.) are assumed to be monotone increasing, and strictly concave.   Assume that an increase in capital increases the marginal productivity of labor. Assume further that in the absence of factor price distortions the modern sector uses capital intensively and the traditional sector uses labor intensively, i.e., $K_2/L_2 > K_1/L_1$.

The Modern Sector

The profit of the modern sector π_2 is given by

$$\pi_2 = p_2 f(L_2,K_2) - r_2 K_2 - w_2 L_2, \qquad [1]$$

where p_2, r_2, and w_2, respectively, denote the price of the output, the interest rate, and the wage rate in the modern sector.   The first order condition for maximizing profits in the modern sector is

$$P_2 f_L(L_2,K_2) - w_2 = 0$$
$$P_2 f_K(L_2,K_2) - r_2 = 0, \qquad [2]$$

where f_L and f_K, respectively, denote the marginal product of labor and capital in the modern sector.   Differentiating Eq. [2] with respect to w_2 and r_2 gives

$$\partial L_2/\partial w_2 = p_2 f_{KK}/H \qquad [3]$$
$$\partial K_2/\partial r_2 = p_2 f_{LL}/H$$
$$\partial K_2/\partial w_2 = \partial L_2/\partial r_2 = p_2 f_{LK}/H$$

where $H = P_2^2(f_{LL}f_{KK} - f_{LK}^2)$ is the Hessian and is positive.   These equations indicate that an increase in the wage and/or a decrease in the interest rate lowers employment L_2, but increases the use of capital K_2 in the modern sector.

The Traditional Sector

Let L and K, respectively, denote the given labor and capital endowment of a LDC.   The traditional sector is assumed to employ the residual factors.   The residual labor L_1 and capital K_1 employed in the traditional sector are given by

$$L_1 = L - L_2(w_2,r_2), \qquad K_1 = K - K_2(w_2,r_2).$$

Thus the profit of the traditional sector π_1 can be written as

$$\pi_1 = p_1 g[L - L_2(w_2,r_2), K - K_2(w_2,r_2)], \qquad [4]$$

where p_1 is the price of the output in the traditional sector. The wage w_1 and the interest rate r_1 in the traditional sector are determined by the following equilibrium condition:

$$p_1 g_L[L - L_2(w_2,r_2), K - K_2(w_2,r_2)] = w_1 \qquad [5]$$
$$p_1 g_K[L - L_2(w_2,r_2), K - K_2(w_2,r_2)] = r_1.$$

Differentiate Eq. [5] with respect to r_2 to get

$$\partial w_1/\partial r_2 = -p_1 g_{LL}(\partial L_2/\partial r_2) - p_1 g_{LK}(\partial K_2/\partial r_2) > 0 \qquad [6a]$$
$$\partial r_1/\partial r_2 = -p_1 g_{KL}(\partial L_2/\partial r_2) - p_1 g_{KK}(\partial K_2/\partial r_2) < 0.$$

Thus the preferential allocation of capital at the concessionary rate to the modern sector depresses the wage and increases the cost of capital to the traditional sector. Differentiating Eq. [5] with respect to w_2 to get

$$\partial w_1/\partial w_2 = p_1 g_{LL}(\partial L_2/\partial w_2) - p_1 g_{LK}(\partial K_2/\partial w_2) < 0 \qquad [6b]$$
$$\partial r_1/\partial w_2 = -p_1 g_{KL}(\partial L_2/\partial w_2) - p_1 g_{KK}(\partial K_2/\partial w_2) > 0$$

It follows that the payment of wages above free market rates in the modern sector will depress the wage and increase the cost of capital in the traditional sector.

Lewis (1954) analyzed the effects of distorted factor prices on the growth of employment in the modern and traditional sectors. He demonstrated how an increase in the capital–output ratio (and/or an increase in the wage rate) in the modern sector decreases the rate of employment growth in that sector and increases the rate of growth in the labor force in the traditional sector. For example, in an economy where the labor force (population) is growing at 2.5 percent per annum and half of the labor force is in the traditional sector, employment in the modern sector must grow at 5 percent per annum to hold the labor force in the traditional sector at a constant level. Dovring's (1959) work also indicates that in a country where 63 percent of the labor force is in agriculture, if the total labor force is growing at a rate of 2.5 percent per year, and the rate of growth of urban employment is nearly 4 percent per year, it will take about 50 years before the labor force in agriculture will stabilize and stop growing (1). Therefore, high wages and low interest rates in the modern sector delay the time when the size of the agricultural labor force will begin to decline (2).

The effects of factor price distortions on the capital–labor ratios in the two sectors can be illustrated by the Edgeworth box diagram in Figure 2. A point in the Edgeworth box shows how the total endowments of L and K are allocated between the two sectors. The isoquants for the modern sector are convex to the southwest corner M and those for the traditional sector are convex to the northeast corner T of the box. In the absence of factor price distortions, an allocation

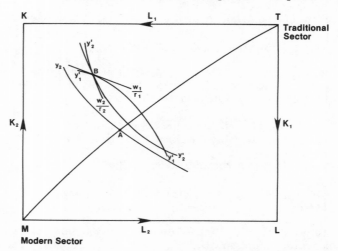

Figure 2.   The effects of factor price distortions on the sectoral allocation of labor and capital.

of the two factors on the contract curve can be achieved.   Since the
modern sector is capital intensive, the contract curve lies above the
diagonal connecting M and T and is concave to the southeast corner.
Assume that an initial allocation of the two factors occurs at point A
on the contract curve.   Preferential allocation of capital at the concessionary rate to the modern sector increases K_2 and decreases L_2,
causing movement from A to B, which lies on a higher isoquant for the
modern sector.   The slopes of the isoquants y_1' and y_2' at point B
represent the factor price ratios w_1/r_1 and w_2/r_2, respectively.   The
movement from A to B makes the modern sector more capital intensive
and the traditional sector more labor intensive.

A DEMAND MODEL OF FERTILITY BEHAVIOR

As Becker (1965) noted, family utility is a function of a vector of
nonmarketable, home-produced commodities.   To construct a fertility
model that is both empirically tractable and generally applicable, we
write the family utility function as

$$u[C,S]$$ [7]

where u[.] is a single-period family utility function, and C and S,
respectively, denote the "child services" and the composite commodity
representing the "standard of living" as in Willis (1973), De Tray (1973),
Gronau (1973), Becker and Lewis (1973), Rosenzweig (1977), Rosenzweig
and Evenson (1977), and Rosenzweig and Wolpin (1980).   The family
utility function indicates that all household decisions are made jointly
by parents and that the future is faced with perfect foresight.   Following De Tray, we assume that the production of child services requires

two home-produced factors.   Specifically, the production of child services is given by

$$C = C(N,Q) \qquad [8a]$$

where N and Q, respectively, denote the quantity and quality of children.   Implicit in De Tray's production function of child services is the assumption that parents choose an equal level of child quality without discrimination.   Additionally, we assume as in Willis (1973) and Michael (1973) that (a) there is not joint production of child quality, and (b) the child quality depends only on the schooling and parent's time devoted to each child.   The child quality production function is given by

$$Q = F(X,T) = F(x_1/N, t_1/N) = Q(x_1, t_1, N) \qquad [8b]$$

where X and T denote the schooling and parent's time per child, and x_1 = NX and t_1 = TX denote the total schooling and parental time all children receive.   The production of the composite commodity is given by

$$S = S(x_2, t_2) \qquad [8c]$$

where x_2 and t_2, respectively, denote the market good and the parental time input used in the production of S.

The household's capacity to produce child services and the composite commodity is not only constrained by the production technologies, but is also limited by the household time and budget constraints.   As in the Chicago approach we assume that the husband's time $t_h = 1$ is totally devoted to earning wage M in the labor market.   However, the wife's time is divided into three activities.   Let t_0, t_1, and t_2, respectively, denote the fraction of time the wife uses for market work, raising children, and producing the composite commodity.   The wife's time constraint is then given by

$$t_0 + t_1 + t_2 = 1. \qquad [8d]$$

Thus the wife's income depends on her wage W and the fraction of her time t_0 sold in the labor market, and is equal to Wt_0.

Parents in a LDC setting are strongly motivated to have children in order to derive satisfaction from them directly as consumer goods and indirectly as producer goods.   The motivation to have children depends on the satisfaction they provide in the form of child services as well as their contribution to the family income over time.   Thus Schultz (1973, p. S5) noted that "in poor countries children also contribute substantially to the future real income of their parents."   Rosenzweig and Evenson (1977, p. 128) also argued that "the desired quantity of children exceeds the amount that would be demanded if children were only production or consumption commodities."   Parents recognize this dual role of children, and weigh the cost of having children against the satisfaction they provide in the form of child services and their contribution to the family income.   Let w denote a child's contribution to the household income in the parents' life time. Then the household's total income is $M + Wt_0 + wN$. Let p_N denote the child rearing cost the parents must incur for each child prior to the schooling period, and let p_1 and p_2 denote the price of market goods for x_1 and x_2, respectively. Then the household's budget constraint can be written as

$$M + Wt_0 + (w-p_N)N - p_1x_1 - p_2x_2 = 0. \qquad [8e]$$

The household's problem is to maximize Eq. [7] subject to [8a] - [8e]. In order to make the model more tractable, we substitute the nonlinear production constraints [8a] - [8c] into the utility function to get

$$u[C(N,Q\{x_1,t_1,N\}),S(x_2,t_2)] = v[x_1,x_2,t_1,t_2,N]. \qquad [9]$$

In contrast to the utility function $u[C,S]$ which is expressed in terms of two final goods C and S, the utility function $v[x_1,x_2,t_1,t_2,N]$ has the analytical advantage that it expresses the household utility as a direct function of the family's input decisions. It should be noted that $u[C,S]$ is monotone increasing in C and S; C is monotone increasing in x_1 and t_1; and S is monotone increasing in x_2 and t_2. Thus $v[.]$ is monotone increasing in x_1, x_2, t_1, and t_2. However, v is not monotone increasing in N. This suggests that children can become a satiable good and that the income elasticity of fertility is low. The household's time and budget constraints in Eqs. [8d] and [8e] are combined to form a single constraint:

$$M + W - p_1x_1 - p_2x_2 - Wt_1 - Wt_2 - (w-p_N)N = 0. \qquad [10]$$

The household's problem is to choose x_1, x_2, t_1, t_2, and N to maximize Eq. [9] subject to Eq. [10]. The Lagrangian function associated with this problem can be written as

$$L = v[x_1,x_2,x_3,x_4,N] + \lambda[M+W-p_1x_1-p_2x_2-Wx_3-Wx_4-(p_N-w)N], \qquad [11]$$

where λ is the Lagrange multiplier, and $x_3 = t_1$ and $x_4 = t_2$ for convenience. The first order condition is

$$
\begin{aligned}
&v_1 - \lambda p_1 = 0 \\
&v_2 - \lambda p_2 = 0 \\
&v_3 - \lambda W = 0 \\
&v_4 - \lambda W = 0 \\
&v_N - \lambda(p_N-w) = 0 \\
&M + W - p_1x_1 - p_2x_2 - Wx_3 - Wx_4 = 0.
\end{aligned}
\qquad [12]
$$

This first order condition gives the input demand functions in terms of factor prices and wages:

$$
\begin{aligned}
&x_i^* + x^*(M,W,p_1,p_2,p_N-w), \ i = 1,2,3,4 \\
&N^* = N^*(M,W,p_1,p_2,p_N-w)
\end{aligned}
\qquad [13a]
$$

Substituting Eq. [13a] into the production constraints Eqs. [8a] to [8c] gives

$$Q^* = Q[x_1^*, t_1^*, N^*] = F(X^*, T^*) = Q^*(M, W, p_1, p_2, p_N-w) \qquad [13b]$$
$$C^* = C[N^*, Q^*] = C(M, W, p_1, p_2, p_N-w)$$
$$S^* = S[x_2^*, t_2^*] = S(M, W, p_1, p_2, p_N-w).$$

These indirect production functions indicate that the production of quality, child services, and the composite commodity depends on the factor prices, p_1, p_2, and p_N, and the wages M, W, and w. We now consider the effects of changes in wages on fertility related variables.

The Effects of the Husband's Wage

Differentiating Eq. [12] with respect to M gives

$$\partial x_i/\partial M = -H_{\lambda_i}/H \qquad [14a]$$
$$\partial N/\partial M = -H_{\lambda N}/H,$$

where H is now the bordered Hessian and H_{ij} is the cofactor of the ij-th element of H. If x_i is a normal factor, then $\partial x_i/\partial M$ is positive. There is considerable empirical evidence that children are normal goods. However, since v[.] is not monotone increasing in N, the income elasticity of N is likely to be small and less than unity. That is, children are a normal good but not a superior good. In light of the satiability of N, we assume that the income elasticity of x_i, $\varepsilon_{iM} \equiv (\partial x_i/\partial M)(M/x_i)$, is greater than the income elasticity of N, $\varepsilon_{NM} \equiv (\partial N/\partial M)(M/N)$, for all i = 1,2,3,4. This implies that the income elasticity of X and T, $\varepsilon_{XM} = \varepsilon_{1M} - \varepsilon_{NM}$ and $\varepsilon_{TM} = \varepsilon_{3M} - \varepsilon_{NM}$, are both positive. Differentiating Eq. [13b] with respect to M gives

$$\partial Q/\partial M = F_X(\partial X/\partial M) + F_T(\partial T/\partial M) > 0, \qquad [14b]$$

since ε_{XM} and ε_{TM} are both positive. It follows that if the income elasticity of fertility is negligible, an increase in income will increase the quality of children.

The Effects of the Wife's Wage

Differentiating Eq. [12] with respect to W gives

$$\partial x_i/\partial W = \lambda(H_{i3} + H_{i4})/H + t_0(\partial x_i/\partial M) \qquad [15a]$$
$$\partial N/\partial W = \lambda(H_{N3} + H_{N4})/H + t_0(\partial N/\partial M).$$

The effect of a rise in the wife's wage on fertility is generally indeterminate. Note that the substitution effects, $\lambda H_{N3}/H$ and $\lambda H_{N4}/H$, measure the changes in the wife's time for raising children and for producing the composite commodity induced by a change in W when the family is subject to a given level of utility. As the opportunity cost of the wife's time increases, she is likely to spend fewer hours in the household production activities. Therefore, if the income effect on fertility is negligible, an increase in the wife's wage is likely to decrease fertility, i.e., $\partial N/\partial W < 0$. Differentiating Eq. [13b] with respect to W gives

$$\partial Q/\partial W = F_X(\partial X/\partial W) + F_T(\partial T/\partial W). \qquad [15b]$$

The effect of a change in the wife's wage on the quality of children is also generally indeterminate. However, given that the income effect on fertility is negligible, an increase in W must decrease t_1 and t_2 and increase t_0, and hence the family income. Given that child services are a normal good, a rise in family income must increase the production of child services, which in turn requires an increase in quality to more than offset the decline in quantity.

The Effects of Children's Wage

Differentiating Eq. [12] with respect to w gives

$$\partial x_i/\partial w = -\lambda H_{iN}/H -N\ H_{i\lambda}/H = -\lambda H_{iN}/H + N(\partial x_i/\partial M) \qquad [16a]$$
$$\partial N/\partial w = -\lambda H_{NN}/H -N\ H_{N\lambda}/H = -\lambda H_{NN}/H + N(\partial N/\partial M).$$

Since children are a normal good and the substitution effect of a rise in children's wage on fertility is positive, fertility should increase with w. It should be noted that w represents a child's total contribution to the family income during the parents' lifetime. The higher the interest rate (discount rate) is, the smaller is a child's contribution to the family income. Hence, in the presence of high interest rates the effect of a rise in children's wage on fertility is likely to be small, i.e., the elasticity of fertility with respect to children's wage ε_{Nw} is small and less than unity. Differentiating Eq. [13b] with respect to w gives

$$\partial Q/\partial w = F_X(\partial X/\partial w) + F_T(\partial T/\partial w), \qquad [16b]$$

which is indeterminate.

Diagnosis of the Effects of Factor Price Distortions on Fertility

The analysis of the two sector model shows that privileged access to credit and wage rates above the free market level in the modern sector acts to decrease the wage rates and increase the cost of capital in the traditional sector. The static effects of this factor price distortion on fertility in the traditional sector operate through the income and price (substitution) effects of reduced wage rates for men, women, and children. The effects of a reduced male wage rate on fertility is generally analyzed in terms of the income effect. Since men are assumed to spend an insignificant amount of time raising children and producing child services, the substitution effect for male wages on the labor force time is ignored. Although children are assumed to be a normal good, empirical studies have reported a low income elasticity of fertility. Simon (1974, p. 98) stated that "the short run effect [of income on fertility] is not likely to be important of itself from a policy point of view in LDCs." In his study of U.S. fertility behavior Lindert (1978, p. 162) found that "the level of current income is of inconsistent sign and seldom significant." Therefore, the reduction in wage rates (productivity) for males resulting from distorted factor allocation would have little effect on fertility in the traditional sector.

The reduction in female productivity resulting from distorted factor prices has both income and substitution effects. The argument with regard to the income effect of a reduction in female wage is similar to that for male wage rates, but the former is weaker since women generally contribute less income to the family than men. Since the reduction in female wages decreases the opportunity cost of time spent raising children vis-a-vis other activities, fertility would increase. The reduction in children's wage would decrease fertility, but its effect is likely to be small.

THE EFFECTS OF FINANCIAL REFORM ON FERTILITY

The consequences of changes in government monetary, fiscal, foreign trade, and budget policy that increase the cost of capital to its "free market" prices are shown in Figure 1 under the "High Interest Rates Policy" column. The higher interest rates provide an incentive to delay consumption and therefore to increase savings. Increased competition among financial institutions for deposits and loans leads to financial deepening as institutions seek to provide financial assets that are more attractive to savers in terms of return, risk, liquidity, etc., and to make loans that are better tailored to the needs of borrowers.

Small farmers are more likely to make deposits in institutions when meaningful interest rate reform results in higher real rates of interest. In this way, private financial institutions can increase their loanable funds by attracting new deposits. In short, subsidized credit discourages financial institutions from attracting savings because they cannot afford to offer attractive rates of interest to depositors when borrowers can obtain funds at subsidized interest rates. Financial institutions will acquire a reputation for stability if their life exceeds that of institutions which make concessionary loans and go out of business when inflows of loanable funds are cut off by the domestic governments or by foreign governments that reduce foreign aid.

The capital market becomes more integrated as farmers shift from methods of self-finance to direct and indirect finance (McKinnon, 1973; Shaw, 1973). Rather than depending on family and relatives, farmers can borrow from and lend to financial institutions if they charge and pay competitive rates of interest. A survey in India in 1951 indicated that 14.2 percent of total loans to farmers came from relatives (Belshaw, 1959, p.58). The weakening of the economic functions of the family associated with the institutionalization of borrowing and lending will tend to reduce the number of children born in farm families. The competition among financial institutions will reduce the spread between the return to savings and the cost of capital to borrowers and as a result increase savings and investment.

The increased competition in financial markets and the integration of the capital market will reduce the dispersion in rates of return to investment in various projects and improve the efficiency with which existing capital and new investment are allocated. The "high interest rates" will encourage capital-saving, labor-using, output-increasing technology in agriculture and result in a low incremental capital-output ratio and a more rapid expansion of employment. Projects that were feasible only at subsidized rates of interest will be rationed out of the market and the returns to capital will increase. The rate of economic growth will increase and the distribution of income will become more equal. The abolition of subsidized credit and the ability of farmers with technological and managerial abilities to secure capital will reduce income inequality.

The creation and existence of financial assets as a means of transferring financial surpluses over time to deficit periods, particularly the transfer of surpluses accumulated during the most productive periods of life to old age, provide an alternative to children as a source of old-age security. Increases in returns on financial assets and on skilled labor will encourage farm families to adjust their asset portfolios by substituting financial assets and human capital for increased numbers of children.

An equalization of factor prices results in an increased demand for yield-increasing agricultural inputs in both the traditional and the modern agricultural sectors. Yield-increasing inputs such as biological, chemical, and agronomic inputs require managerial and skilled labor for their efficient application. The increase in demand for these inputs is at the expense of demand for machinery within the modern agricultural sector.

An increase in the demand for skilled labor associated with the expanded use of biological, chemical, and agronomic inputs tends to motivate the parents to have fewer but higher quality children. The study by Rosenzweig (1982) based on a survey of farm households in India between 1968 and 1971 provides empirical support for this hypothesis. Exposure and access to new technologies induced farmers to increase investment in children in the form of schooling and decrease the number of children. Rosenzweig found that access on a continuing basis to technical assistance, assured supplies of fertilizer and new higher yielding seed varieties, and access to primary school were important determinants of schooling and fertility. He reported that proximity to a school alone weakly increased both fertility and school attendance, but concluded that "farm households exposed to new technologies reduced their fertility and increased the allocation of resources to schooling despite the concomitant rise in the demand for unskilled labor" (Rosenzweig, 1982, p. 87).

Children's wage w was assumed to be exogenous in our model. An increased demand for skilled labor associated with yield increasing technologies makes the children's wage an increasing function of schooling, i.e., $w = w(X)$, $w'(X) > 0$. Consequently, schooling can enhance the family income and expand production (and consumption) possibilities. The effects of an increased demand for skilled labor is illustrated in Figure 3. The production possibilities curve BC shows various combinations of N and Q that can be produced for a given value of S by the household resources. Assume that initially the household chooses an equilibrium combination of N and Q at point A, where the indifference

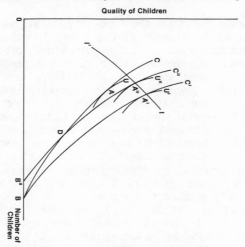

Figure 3. The effects of an increased demand for skilled labor on the number and quality of children demanded.

curve U is tangent to the production possibilities curve BC. If a rise in demand for skilled labor increases the wage of the children with schooling, then the production possibility curve shifts outward. If the consumption of the composite commodity is held constant the production possibilities curve rotates clockwise about B. The household moves from A to A' on the higher production possibilities curve BC', thereby producing and consuming higher quality children. Since some portion of the increased income is spent on the composite commodity, the production possibilities curve must shift inward from BC' to B"C". The net effect of a rise in children's wage is that the production possibilities curve rotates clockwise about D, where the initial and the final production possibilities curves intersect. Since a clockwise rotation of the production possibilities curves increases the opportunity cost of N and decreases that of Q, parents are likely to choose fewer but higher quality children. The final equilibrium occurs at A" which lies on the income consumption curve II'.

CONCLUSION

In rural areas of LDCs there is great diversity in the skills and talents of the population. Each individual has his own unique production opportunity. If his endowment of capital is not appropriate to his production opportunities, and a fragmented capital market in rural areas prevents him from borrowing or lending, the farmer may be constrained in his efforts to improve his situation. The development of a well-functioning capital market and the rationalization of factor prices make it possible for farmers to match access to resources with their ability to use resources productively to improve their economic position. As Timmer (1982, p. 16) states, the "surest bet [that the poor have for lifting themselves from their poverty] is an economic structure which allows them to make most of the effort themselves." Financial reform and the rationalization of factor prices help provide an environment where the poor can improve their economic position.   Moreover, if farmers find that present high levels of fertility are interfering with their ability to take advantage of new opportunities resulting from financial reforms, this may motivate them to have fewer children.

In an effort to interpret the decline of fertility during the demographic transition in northwest Europe and Japan, Davis (1963, p. 352) observed that "people found that their accustomed demographic behavior was handicapping them in their effort to take advantage of the opportunities being provided by the emerging economy.   They accordingly began changing their [fertility] behavior."   In other words, Davis suggested that fertility decline may occur as a result of changes which provide new opportunities for farmers to get ahead.   If the traditional fertility pattern is an obstacle to taking advantage of new opportunities, farmers would respond by reducing fertility.

In the case of financial reform, more equal access to capital markets may increase the demand for biological, chemical, and agronomic inputs. However, the adoption of the new technology is contingent upon the existence of skilled workers in agriculture.   If farmers want to take advantage of new opportunities with which they are presented, they need to provide their children with a higher level of education, i.e., demand higher quality children.   An obstacle to providing more education for each child would be the burden of educating all children in a large family.   Alternative adjustments to a decrease in fertility include, for example, providing higher levels of education for some children than others (perhaps more education for males than females, but discrimination is less likely among children of the same sex); encouraging some children to migrate to urban areas (the more educated children are likely to migrate); and infanticide.   All of these alternatives appear to have higher costs to the parents than a reduction in fertility, although the costs of a reduction in fertility may still be significant.

In this chapter we have shown how financial reform and the rationalization of factor prices would increase income and wage rates in the traditional agricultural sector and accelerate the expansion of employment in the modern sector.   Available evidence indicates that factors associated with overall economic growth (increased wage rates in the traditional sector and increases in the demand for higher quality children) decreases fertility.   But the strongest argument for these policies is not that they decrease fertility, but that they stimulate broad based economic growth and increase human welfare.   Government policy resulting in a bimodal distribution of capital within agriculture tends to increase fertility and retards economic growth.   A policy which provides equal access to resources at their "free market" prices and makes it possible for farmers to make the most of their unique talents will likely stimulate rapid economic growth and a decline in fertility.

NOTES

1. If the urban sector in the country includes an underemployed poor population working at low productivity with very little equipment

and a low level of skill, then the number of years before the labor force in low-productivity employment (agriculture and urban jobs where labor is underemployed) would stop growing would increase.

2. Since birth rates in rural areas are higher than those in urban areas, the factor price distortions which result in a larger share of the population in agriculture make for higher birth rates for the country.

REFERENCES

Becker, G.S. 1965. A theory of the allocation of time. Economic Journal 75:493–517.

_____ and H.G. Lewis. 1973. Interaction between quantity and quality of children. Journal of Political Economy 81:S279–S288.

Berry, R.A. and W.R. Cline. 1979. Agrarian Structure and Productivity in Developing Countries. Baltimore: Johns Hopkins University Press.

Belshaw, H. 1959. Agricultural Credit in Economically Underdeveloped Countries. Rome: Food and Agricultural Organization of the United States.

Bourne, C. and D.H. Graham. 1981. Problems with Supply-Leading Finance in Agricultural Development. Discussion Paper No. 8, Colloquium on Rural Finance, Economic Development Institute. Washington, D.C.: World Bank.

de Janvry, A. 1978. Social structure and biased technological change in Argentine agriculture. In: H. Binswanger and V. Ruttan (eds.) Induced Innovation: Technology, Institutions and Development, pp. 297–323. Baltimore: Johns Hopkins University Press.

De Tray, D.N. 1973. Child quality and the demand for children. Journal of Political Economy 81:S70–S95.

Davis, K. 1963. The theory of change and response in modern demographic history. Population Index 29:345–366.

Despres, E. 1973. Price distortions and development planning: Pakistan. In: G.M. Meier (ed.) International Economic Reform: Collected Papers of Emile Despres, pp. 133–145. New York: Oxford University Press.

Dovring, F. 1959. The share of agriculture in a growing population. Monthly Bulletin of Agricultural Economics and Statistics (FAO) 8:1–11.

Gronau, R. 1973. The effect of children on the housewife's value of time. Journal of Political Economy 81:S168–S199.

Lewis, W.A. 1954. Economic development with unlimited supplies of labour. The Manchester School of Economic and Social Studies 22:139–191.

Lindert, P.H. 1978. Fertility and Scarcity in America. Princeton: Princeton University Press.

McKinnon, R.I. 1973. Money and Capital in Economic Development. Washington, D.C.: The Brookings Institute.

Merrill, W.C. 1975. The Impact of Agricultural Mechanization on Employment and Food Production. Occasional Paper No. 1, Economics and Sector Planning Division, Office of Agriculture, Technical Assistance Bureau. Washington, D.C.: U.S. Agency for International Development.

Michael, R.T. 1973.   Education and the derived demand for children.
Journal of Political Economy 81:S128-S164.
Rosenzweig, M.R. 1977.   The demand for children in farm households.
Journal of Political Economy 85:123-146.
_____ 1982.   Educational subsidy, agricultural development, and fertility change. Quarterly Journal of Economics 97:68-88.
_____ and R. Evenson. 1977.   Fertility, schooling and the economic
contribution of children in rural India. Econometrica 45:1065-1079.
_____ and K.I. Wolpin. 1980.   Testing the quantity-quality fertility
model: The use of twins as a natural experiment. Econometrica 48:
227-240.
Schultz, T.W. 1973.   The value of children: An economic perspective.
Journal of Political Economy 81:S2-S13.
Shaw, E.S. 1973.   Financial Deepening in Economic Development.   New
York: Oxford University Press.
Simon, J.L. 1974.   The Effects of Income on Fertility.   Chapel Hill:
Carolina Population Center.
Timmer, C.P. 1982.   The financial aspects of macro food policy.   Paper
presented at World Financial Conditions and Agricultural Trade Con-
ference (Sept.) Minneapolis, Minnesota.
Todaro, M.P. 1981.   Economic Development in the Third World (2nd
ed.).   New York: Longman.
Willis, R.J. 1973.   A new approach to the economic theory of fertility
behavior. Journal of Political Economy 81:S14-S64.

CHAPTER 14

Fertility Control at the Community Level: A Review of Research and Community Programs

Rodolfo A. Bulatao

As a pivot between the nation and the household, the small community is sometimes considered the appropriate focus for population policy. Designing community policy translates into more direct contact with the realities affecting people's lives, thus appearing less formidable and more substantive a task than the often abstract, assumption–laden exercises involved in designing national policy. At the same time, a community focus still involves a broad social concern that extends beyond the individual household. This chapter is a review of the community focus in fertility research and programs. Given the relative novelty of this focus, the chapter does not attempt to go much beyond cataloging approaches.

The idea of community is one of the core concepts of sociology (Nisbet, 1966). Basically referring to some territorial unit within which individuals can live out their entire lives, it also carries notions of shared values, experiences, and goals as well as the sense of togetherness that motivates people to be intimately concerned with the welfare of others. However, in practice the concept of community often reduces to some specific settled administrative unit within the nation–state, within which there may be less sharing than rivalry and antagonism, less of common and more of opposing interests. This latter usage is perforce the one used here, but the more general understanding of community will be returned to below.

This investigation divides naturally into two parts: first, an account of research that attempts to identify community effects on fertility;

and, second, a selected account of attempts to influence fertility through interventions at the community level. Though there is considerable disjunction between research on this topic and practice, that in itself seems to be an important reason for considering both.

COMMUNITY EFFECTS ON FERTILITY

Social research on community effects on fertility is not easily segregated from research on group and institutional effects generally, and no sharp distinction will be made.   Classification seems essential here, though categorizing the work of other researchers is a chancy endeavor likely to generate as much heat as light. Approaches taken in investigating the impact of community factors on fertility might be classified as: (a) functionalist, (b) crude empiricist, and (c) applied diffusionist. The label functionalist will cover the work of Caldwell (1982, 1983) and McNicoll (1978, 1982), though neither of them use this label.   Related work by Cain (1982) and Potter (1983) might also be cited. Under crude empiricists, work by Hermalin and Mason (1980) and others who have used World Fertility Survey (WFS) data with the intention of identifying community effects should be considered.   Under applied diffusionists, work developing from or related to that of Rogers (e.g., Rogers and Kincaid, 1981) will be reviewed.

FUNCTIONALIST DISCUSSIONS OF COMMUNITY EFFECTS

The first research approach seeks to explain fertility by reference to functions that certain fertility levels serve for particular groups within the society. In this sense, the work falls in the functionalist tradition (Merton, 1968), though elements of other approaches are incorporated and the researchers may owe their inspiration to other sources.   The search for functions of fertility for social groups leads naturally to discussions of social structural and institutional factors related to the provision of these functions.

Of the work classified under this approach, Caldwell's (1982) is the most specific.   Following a suggestion by Ryder (see Berelson, 1971, p. 179), Caldwell has focused on the obligations children owe their parents as the key to explaining high fertility in developing countries. This focus is unexceptionable, as the importance for fertility of the economic gain or loss linked to each child has been a constant theme in fertility transition theory (e.g., Notestein, 1945).   Caldwell (1982, p. 338) takes it to the extreme, however, contending that "there are really only two kinds of societies from a demographic viewpoint: one where unlimited fertility is an economic advantage and the other where fertility is of no economic advantage."   This economic advantage accrues, Caldwell argues, because of the familial mode of production, and especially the control elders can exert under this system over the labor and consumption and fertility of others in the household.   In analyzing the breakdown of this system in the fertility transition, Caldwell stresses ideological changes, such as those stemming from

"Western" education, that produce alterations in family structure: the breakup of the extended family, depriving elders of the benefits they previously counted on from children; a decline in the willingness of children to turn over their earnings to their parents; and the increasingly felt compulsion for parents to provide more for their children. (Following a similar line in explaining high fertility in pretransition societies, Ryder, 1983, diverges in his account of the transition, choosing to stress instead mortality decline and consequent increases in family size as the chief factor.)

To this highly abbreviated account, only a few words need to be added to draw out the role of the small community. The community provides the setting in which household production takes place, but Caldwell notes that familial production can continue, for some time at least, in urban areas under industrial conditions. More important perhaps is the role of the community in enforcing children's obligations to their parents, above all by gossip: "scandal-mongering, ridicule, and stronger expressions of derision and even anger and disgust" when the younger generation refuses to yield (Caldwell, 1982, p. 172). The community may be especially motivated in this direction because numbers mean community strength and security. The image is, therefore, that of a tightly-knit, small community promoting fertility by keeping the young in their place and gradually coming under siege by "foreign" ideologies especially attractive to the young, propagated by Westernized, citified elite.

In contrast to Caldwell's full-blown theoretical enterprise, McNicoll's investigation of institutions and fertility has proceeded more haltingly, with a sharper focus on community factors (from the perspective of this chapter). From an initial belief that "a major reduction in fertility can be achieved through a unified community development program, provided that appropriate inducement is given to the social control of fertility" (McNicoll, 1975), McNicoll has progressed to teasing out specific institutional explanations from detailed accounts of fertility and social structure in selected countries or regions. For Bangladesh, for instance, continued high fertility is interpreted with reference to the increased span of control children provide for dominant families, coupled with the added labor peasants seek. In addition, he argues, the dominance of clans and lineages that cross village boundaries and the consequent weakness of village solidarities allow the leading families to avoid directly dealing with the burdens of high fertility. He suggests that, in general, community pressures will only be effective given village solidarity and an ability to contain negative community spillovers. For the Chinese province of Guangdong, a contrasting case with significant fertility decline, McNicoll (1982, p. 153) draws on Parish and Whyte's (1978) detailed account of social changes, concluding that the decline was "primarily a response by parents and communities to the changed rural social structure and consequent shift in economic incentives," though it was also facilitated by improved health care and government antinatal campaigns.

In moving gradually toward systematization of such insights, McNicoll (1979) has distinguished (in what he considers an arbitrary manner) three routes of institutional impact on fertility: (a) through economic benefits and costs connected with childbearing; (b) through social and administrative pressures; and (c) through internalized values. This distinction of routes of influence—which Potter (1983) takes up and illustrates with somewhat different examples—is not matched by a distinction among institutional forces, which remain inchoate, subject to the observer's choice and interpretation.

Both Caldwell and McNicoll, therefore, focus ultimately on functions— economic in a broad sense—that children provide for key social groups, and move on to discuss the institutional basis for ensuring these functions or altering them, as well as the cultural values underpinning institutional and individual behavior. Neither Caldwell nor McNicoll have so far attempted to test their insights into community effects in any systematic manner, relying on post hoc interpretations. Although specific propositions can be found throughout these works, evaluating their validity does not appear to have been given priority.

EMPIRICIST SEARCHES FOR COMMUNITY EFFECTS

In stark contrast, the empiricists appear to have plunged into data with more primitive conceptions of the specific community effects to investigate but much more sophisticated appreciation of the verification problems for these effects as against alternative interpretations.

Casterline (n.d.) reviews the work of this type that has used WFS data, including prescriptions for such analysis by Freedman (1974) and Hobcraft (1982), and various attempts at such analysis by Mason and Palan (1978), Nizamuddin (1979), Hermalin and Mason (1980), and others. Findings are classified by the locus of impact of the community factors: on contraceptive use, on fertility preferences, or on fertility itself. On contraceptive use, the impact of accessibility of family planning outlets has been verified (e.g., Knodel et al., 1980); however, perceived accessibility appears to have a stronger effect than actual accessibility (e.g., Rodriguez, 1978). Some differences in contraceptive use by household structure are also reported, though not consistently, as well as some differences by region within countries. Other attempts to relate use to such community characteristics as type of economic activity, the presence of modern means of communication, and the existence of educational institutions have generally found weak, nonsignificant relationships. With regard to fertility preferences, there is no obvious community factor like contraceptive access to consider, and the findings are rather varied. Some effect is noted for household structure and educational opportunities, but the studies are not all in agreement. On fertility itself, the main approach is that of Hermalin and Mason (1980; also Entwisle et al., 1982), in which coefficients from regressions within countries for fertility or its components are entered as dependent variables into regressions across countries. In principle, the approach could be applied to identify community rather than national factors, though the WFS samples are relatively thin for that purpose.

These findings appear mostly preliminary and provide little of the sense of interlocking social institutions that comes from Caldwell's or McNicoll's descriptions. In an attempt to point toward the broader possibilities for survey analysis, Casterline (n.d., p. 10) identifies four possible mechanisms for community effects: (a) direct effects of social norms; (b) direct effects of structural factors on individual incentives; (c) indirect effects through the determination of individual attributes and resources; and (d) effects through the provision of resources for acting on the intermediate variables. Analysis organized along such lines would improve the linkages with functionalist work, but Casterline does not find it easy to fit the little work available into this frame-work.

Is the considerable divergence between the theorizing of the func-tionalists and the investigations of the empiricists due to inherent limitations of census and survey data? That appears to be the view of the functionalists (Caldwell, 1982; McNicoll, 1982; Potter, 1983), but not necessarily of the empiricists, who seem to be of the opinion that much additional work is still possible (Casterline, n.d.; Entwisle et al., 1982).

DIFFUSIONIST ANALYSIS OF COMMUNITY EFFECTS

Still a different approach to community effects is represented in work growing out of the innovation–diffusion tradition. In the earlier phases of this work, the focus was on the process of adopting contraception and on characteristics of individuals that facilitated adoption (Rogers, 1962). Soon it became evident that social factors in the process of adoption were also of great importance. The theory of a two-step flow in communication was applied to contraceptive adoption, and attention turned to locating opinion leaders who might be responsible for spread-ing contraception more widely. More recently, the focus has shifted to the social groups themselves and their characteristics that facilitate the spread of information or provide support for the adoption of innova-tions.

As to communication networks, social groups are characterized with regard to the cliques into which they are divided, the strength of ties between members, homophily or heterophily of network links (similarity or dissimilarity between the linked members on key characteristics), and other similar features (Rogers and Kincaid, 1981). With data from several Korean villages, it is shown that network features have signifi-cant marginal explanatory power for contraceptive knowledge, attitudes, and adoption. Adoption is higher among those whose personal networks include more adopters (Rogers and Kincaid, 1981, p. 233); among those with greater connectedness to the community network (Lee, 1977); in villages where the mother's club leader has greater connectedness with the family planning communication network; and in villages where this family planning network overlaps most with the general communication network (Rogers and Kincaid, 1981, p. 279). In addition to these network variables, Rogers and Kincaid (1981, p. 279) find that a village's exposure to family planning mass media and the frequency of fieldworker visits also relate to village levels of adoption (also see Kim and Palmore, 1978).

One way to characterize the diffusionist approach is to see it as focused narrowly on the interpersonal mechanisms for providing access to contraceptive knowledge and supplies, the main community factor so far reliably identified in the empiricist approach. In addition, however, the network measures might also represent group pressures brought upon the individual.

CRITIQUE AND REFORMULATION

It seems apparent from this review that researchers have not so far produced a satisfactory paradigm within which to generate and test hypotheses about community effects on fertility. The disjunction between functionalist theorizing and empiricist analysis is notable, as is the failure of either group to integrate the diffusionist approach into their work.

One may ask how research into community effects has diverged, for reasons ranging from benign neglect to serious antipathy, from the microanalytic approach that attempts to explain fertility differentials from individual characteristics in the context of household decisions? For the diffusionists, it seems to be a case of a separate, coexisting research tradition that has never been fully integrated into mainstream fertility research (but see Retherford and Palmore, 1983). For the empiricists, the basic model generally still appears to be a household model, with not very satisfactory accretions to permit the investigation of additional group effects. The functionalists, in contrast, have explicitly abandoned the household decisions approach, at least in a rhetorical sense. Caldwell (1982, p. 132, 1983) regularly savages most mainstream research, accusing it of insensitivity to cultural settings, neglect of extended-family decision making, and crude and misleading measurement, or the total failure to measure variables of interest. McNicoll (1982, p. 150) argues that the fertility phenomenon "bursts the bounds" of the consumer demand model and, for empirical reasons, is unwilling to be satisfied with amendments to it. He does begin to sketch an alternative household model using bounded rationality as the chief principle (Simon, 1957; Leibenstein, 1976). Ryder (1983, p. 9) points out an important limitation of microanalytic work: a successful model would still leave aggregate fertility unexplained since it would not account for the distribution of households by the predictor characteristics.

Despite the validity of some of these objections, some clarity is certainly lost when these researchers attempt to leapfrog household models of fertility behavior, rather than building up from some variant of a household model toward group, community, and societal effects. That they have missed something is sometimes recognized: McNicoll (1982, p. 151), for instance, wants to have the "pure biology . . . disposed of" before he begins his exegesis, although such "biological" factors as breastfeeding and secondary sterility are not exogenous but actually part of the problem. While laying much stress on incentives for childbearing, the functionalists pays scant attention to the economic (Lindert, 1983) and psychosocial (Fawcett, 1983) measures essential to link institutional forms to the incentives individuals actually confront. The direction that could have been taken instead is illustrated in Table 1, in which Easterlin (1983) speculates about the impact of institutions

Table 1. Direction of Effect of Various Aspects of Modernization on Indicated Determinants of Deliberate Control

ASPECTS OF MODERNIZATION	FACTORS THROUGH WHICH FERTILITY CONTROL IS INFLUENCED[a]						
	Demand (Cd)			Supply (Cn)		Regulation Costs (RC)	
	Tastes	Income	Prices	Natural fertility	Survival prospects	Subjective costs	Market costs
Better public health and medical care				+	+		
Growth in formal education	−		−	+	+	−	−
Urbanization		−	−			−	−
New consumer goods	−						
New fertility control methods						−	−

[a]Note: Income is related in a complex fashion to all these factors and is discussed by Easterlin in more detail than can be conveniently summarized here.

Source: Easterlin (1983).

on fertility, with various household decision factors as intervening. The conception of institutions in this table, as well as in the discussion that accompanies it, is rather primitive; one searches vainly for some treatment combining the sophisticated appreciation of institutional workings and linkages the functionalists aspire toward with a differentiated and comprehensive view of household-level determinants.

From this perspective, Casterline's (n.d.) attempt to bring order to the empiricist approach appears to be eminently sensible. He recognizes the misleading implications in categorizing variables as either individual or community, pointing to the importance of indirect community effects for which household or individual variables are intervening. Thus the community level is not set up in opposition to an individual or household level, but rather acts through them in its impact on fertility. The essential nature of this conception is demonstrated by the findings of greater predictive power for perceived over actual contraceptive availability: in principle other individual decision factors, if properly measured as perceptual phenomena, should also be more predictive of fertility decisions than parallel objective or community measures. However, this does not invalidate a concern with the community characteristics that give rise to the particular perceptions, particularly when these characteristics are more amenable to direct manipulations.

It would be ideal, following this argument, to provide a list of relevant community institutions, a discussion of alternative patterns of their interrelationships, and a chart for the household decision factors each affects. Given the limitations of the research that has been reviewed, such a comprehensive approach would be at best highly speculative and possibly quite arid at this time. Instead, a simple representation of community factors is given in Figure 1, emphasizing those that are most prominent in the literature but leaving out all noncommunity factors—apart from those bearing directly on community organization—that affect fertility.

Three major community factors are distinguished: the access communities provide to fertility regulation information and methods; the social pressures they exert toward high or low fertility; and the features of community institutions that affect incentives for childbearing. Contraceptive access is the major community factor that empiricist work confirms as important (following much practical concern among family planners with access); it may also partly account for diffusionist findings. To allow for the inclusion of abortion, the term used here is access to regulation. Social pressures appear to be a major explanation for diffusionist findings and also appear in functionalist discussions, as in Caldwell's treatment. The structure of incentives, especially economic ones relating to children's contributions and costs and to employment opportunities for women, is a central factor in the functionalist approach.

To have impact as community factors, each of these depends on effective community organization, which in turn requires community solidarity as well as the approval or at least tolerance of higher authorities. These seem to be minimal organizational requisites for community factors to have some fertility impact. Cultural requisites,

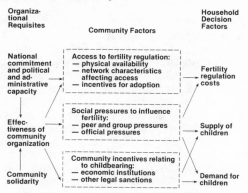

Figure 1. Selected community factors affecting fertility.

as belonging essentially to a different level of social organization, are not considered here. Community organization per se is neither pro nor antinatal. Only when organization is brought to bear to provide access, to impose pressures, or to control incentives should it have some impact. Thus it is listed not as a community factor itself but rather as a condition for the impact of other factors; the degree to which it is a necessary or sufficient condition is an empirical issue.

Several questions about the three community factors may be taken up: Do these operate at the community level, or are they rather features of higher-level entities like societies or lower-level entities like households? Are these factors satisfactorily distinct? Do these factors include all the major community forces relating to fertility control? These questions will be considered in order.

In rural areas of traditional or transitional societies, access to fertility regulation is likely to be a community matter, given the barriers posed by inadequate communication and transportation networks. For rural elites, local community access may be less significant, although lack of local access would still mean additional costs. Although access also could be seen as a property of households, the fact that a single family planning clinic within the community can affect access for many in the community makes it appropriate to treat access, for some purposes, as a community rather than household factor. Similarly, social pressures are most appropriately treated at the community level. Pressures can be exerted by a central government or by national organizations; however, short of direct coercion, these must be translated into pressures within the small, face-to-face groups existing within a community in order to have much effect. Pressures may also be exerted by individuals and families; however, concerted group pressures are likely to have the greatest effect. For the third group of factors, i.e., community institutions that structure childbearing incentives, the argument is perhaps least clear. Such institutions as the mode of production or land tenure systems may be essentially societal or national, though they may also show some community variation and be subject to some degree of local control. It is theoretically possible to design incentive systems specifically to impact on communities (McNicoll, 1975), which provides at least a minimal reason for considering this as a community factor.

The distinctions among these three factors can be clarified with reference to the household decision factors on which they impact, using Easterlin's (1978) classification of the latter.   The distinction between the first factor and the third factor is fairly obvious: access to fertility regulation affects the regulation costs the couple faces, both market or economic costs and psychic or subjective costs, whereas institutional incentives affect different household factors: the demand for children and the supply of children.   The second factor, social pressures, affects regulation costs, demand for children, and supply of children, though generally the psychic rather than the economic side of these household factors.   Pressures are considered here to consist essentially of public admonitions and the force of public approval or disapproval.   Where pressures are brought through providing tangible rewards or imposing penalties, this aspect may be more properly classified under one of the other two factors, depending on whether the rewards are connected specifically to adopting regulation or to affecting demand or supply.   This appears to be the main area of possible overlap, since separating concrete incentives from general social pressures may be difficult; and among incentives segregating those related to regulation from those related to demand is also complex, though in principle not impossible.

What community factors have been left out?   In Easterlin's (1978) classification of household factors, child survival combines with natural fertility to define the supply of children.   Child survival may be affected by community factors not represented, such as nutritional practices, hygienic conditions, and medical facilities.   These might reasonably be added to Figure 1.   Figure 1 does not include the general values·or mentalites that McNicoll (1979) and Potter (1983) consider important, nor the social norms that Casterline (n.d.) lists as an important influence.   It is not clear from their discussions whether these factors are properly community or essentially societal and cultural variables.   More important, perhaps, the essential force of these factors seems to be captured in the concept of social pressures: community norms may be treated as the patterns for behavior that pressures seek to impose.

COMMUNITY INVOLVEMENT IN FERTILITY CONTROL

The simplified model of Figure 1 provides a convenient framework for discussing the involvement of local communities in modern population control programs, which might be seen as progressing down the list of community factors.   Following this scheme, the first topic for discussion will be what are labeled community-based contraceptive distribution systems.   Then the use of community pressures will be discussed, and, finally, community incentives will be taken up.

There are several possible perspectives on community effects in relation to fertility control programs: one might be concerned with community effects produced by the program itself, or with effects that operate regardless of the program, or with the simultaneous operation or even interaction of both of these. Research has been predominantly concerned with program effects, which necessarily restricts the focus of this discussion. Thus a somewhat narrower understanding of community impact on fertility is used in this section: only effects resulting from deliberate community action or involvement are considered. Neither is any attempt made at a comprehensive picture of programs and their social settings. The focus is narrowly on community aspects, and implications that can be drawn are therefore circumscribed.

COMMUNITY-BASED CONTRACEPTIVE DISTRIBUTION

Following the pattern in the developed countries, family planning programs in the developing world were organized initially around physicians and clinics. In this model, clients were expected to come in for advice and contraceptive supplies. With health facilities and personnel typically in short supply, such programs reached few people. Attempts were therefore made to extend the reach of clinics, as well as to provide family planning advice and services through alternative delivery systems. Many of the alternative systems required the involvement of specific individuals or groups within communities; the term "community-based distribution" has been applied to these schemes. The ideal is to have delivery systems "not only based in the community, but also to become part of the community" (Foreit et al., 1978, p. 3). Community-based programs, ranging from small experimental ones to national programs, have grown exponentially since the early 1970s, and can now be found in at least 40 countries (Isaacs, 1981, p. 122).

Local residents are usually chosen as distributors for contraceptives, frequently with the advice and participation of community leaders. Besides willingness to participate, characteristics like leadership within the community, interpersonal skills, and sometimes literacy may be emphasized. The distributors are provided with short but intense training, given a supply of contraceptives, and required to keep some simple records. Local involvement may go further: it may include systematic canvassing of all residences and periodic visits. This distribution system may coexist and require some coordination with a clinic-based family planning or health delivery system.

Community-based distribution clearly improves access to contraceptives for the majority of potential users. Foreit et al. (1978) list several advantages provided by such programs: increased information (which may result partly from associated promotional campaigns), reduced distance to outlets, and fewer administrative hurdles for clients. Much study of these delivery systems has been concerned with their effects on contraceptive adoption, continuation, and fertility (e.g., Gaddala et al., 1980; Huber and Khan, 1979). Given their recency and great diversity, generalizations are difficult, but they are generally considered effective (e.g., Isaacs, 1981, p. 123; Foreit et al., 1978, p. 26). From the perspective of community effects, much concern has focused on the question of what type of community involvement is most appropriate in different settings. Many experiments are reported using different types of distributors, training and supervision patterns, mixes of services and commodities, and charging and remuneration policies (e.g., Cuca and Pierce, 1977; Foreit et al., 1978). Much less attention has been paid to the question of the conditions of community organization and external support under which community-based distribution systems can be introduced and are viable.

Another aspect of family planning programs that can have a community dimension is the degree of their integration with other development activities.   Integration can have many interpretations (Files, 1982); some of these, like the coordination of national population policy by interministerial councils, have little direct relevance to community effects.   In contrast, integration of service delivery should make some difference at the community level.   Some degree of integration with the health care system is common, but integration has also been tried with other development projects like agricultural extension and nonformal education. Although there are many arguments for it, there are also practical problems with integration, including possible conflicts of priorities and disputes about allocation of resources (Watson et al., 1979). It has been suggested that the most promising strategy may be to pursue integration specifically at the community level, allowing different patterns depending on the local institutions (Schearer and Financioglu, 1981, p. 77).

COMMUNITY PRESSURES

To have officially sanctioned contraceptive distribution within the community may in itself constitute a form of social pressure favoring adoption.   This must be considered at best a mild form of pressure, however, in contrast to the pressures that can be exerted by the entire community, or major sections of it, acting in some concerted fashion, identifying specific individuals or families, and promoting specific actions by them.   Group action like this has the potential to change behavior even apart from any concrete rewards or punishments the group may choose to impose.

Two cases may be discussed to illustrate group pressures: banjars in Bali and production teams in China. Banjars—traditional units of local self-government, which serve as centers for mutual aid and cooperative work—consist of all the male household heads in a hamlet or subvillage. The form is centuries old.   The traditional head of a banjar is democratically elected but has no official standing. Instead, the banjar also has a second, official head, who may be appointed and may have charge of more than one banjar (Hull, 1978).   Banjar meetings may be held every month (or 35 days), usually with perfect attendance (there is a system of fines for absence or lateness) and typically discuss development of the community and religious affairs (Astawa, 1979). Since 1974, these meetings have also included discussion of the family planning status of each family.   Each member is asked what he and his wife are doing about family planning.   A register is kept and a color-coded map of the community indicating eligible couples and their contraceptive status is prominently displayed in the banjar hall (Meier, 1979).

The decline in marital fertility in Bali of about 30 percent in less than a decade has been dramatic enough to be labeled a "demographic miracle" (Hull et al., 1977). How much of the change has been due to the community pressures exerted through the 3700 banjars is a difficult and probably unanswerable question. Other elements of the Balinese situation are notable, such as acute pressures on land, the fact that much agricultural land is worked collectively for the common benefit, the penetration of modern influences (through such means as consumer goods, communication and transportation systems, Western-style schooling, and tourism), and cultural factors like the relative independence of young couples—which may facilitate contraceptive decisions—and the fact that birth attendants have traditionally been male (Hull, 1978). Other elements of the family planning program probably contribute, from an effective logistical system to creative uses of native art forms to communicate family planning messages. In addition, the banjars' involvement was engineered by the national program and would probably not have materialized without its stable political backing, organizational strength, and operational flexibility. Thus the specific contribution of the social pressures exerted through the banjars is indeterminate, although it may be considered an important link in the interrelated factors favoring fertility control.

Production teams in China, which are usually the effective unit in rural areas for production and income sharing, consist of 30 to 40 households in a small village, within which kinship ties may be strong. Established in 1962 as the much more massive communes were threatened with breakdown, the production teams actually represented a return to earlier forms of collective organization under Communist rule, which were in turn based upon preexisting village and kinship alignments (Parish and Whyte, 1978). Although in one sense relatively new, production teams nevertheless follow the lines of natural communities with much longer histories. However, there is at least one significant discontinuity: where mutual cooperation was formerly organized along kinship lines that could span villages, the greatest amount of cooperation is now within production teams. In addition, strict migration controls keep men within their villages, and intravillage marriages reinforce the sharing of status and interest (Parish, 1981).

Production teams assume important responsibility for the fertility of their members. As part of the national "wan xi shao" campaign (named for the reproductive norms of later marriage, longer birth spacing, and fewer births) the production teams were responsible for deciding which couples could have births, in line with the reproductive norms and with team quotas set from above (Chen and Kols, 1982). The team birth-planning leadership group (the leaders all being local residents) might call all eligible couples to a meeting, at which their individual birth plans could be scrutinized and allocations made. Under the one-child campaign, which replaced the wan xi shao campaign in 1979, community birth-planning still takes place, though allocation of birth quotas follows different norms. As couples become familiar with the system, the time-consuming meetings to adjust birth plans may be dispensed with, and the leadership may simply notify couples of its decisions. Adherence is in theory voluntary, resting on persuasion and education. Such elements as adult study groups and visits from birth-planning delegations maintain the peer pressure (Chen, 1981). There are reports of more coercive measures being taken against recalcitrants, though the central authorities have criticized such practices.

As with the Balinese banjars, it is not possible to determine the specific impact of the social pressures exerted through production teams, which are only one element in the Chinese population program and which operate in a socioeconomic context that may now be signifi- cantly unfavorable to high fertility.   A more complete picture would have to include discussion of the dense network of the community-based contraceptive distribution system, the active promotion of specific methods and continuing research into appropriate ones, the design of incentives for having one child, as well as the essential and stable political commitment to population control (see Chen and Kols, 1982). Furthermore, it may be argued that collectivized agriculture and the employment of women in the fields have increasingly undermined the economic basis for high fertility (Parish and Whyte, 1978).

These two cases involve community pressures under conditions that might be considered favorable to fertility control, despite relatively low levels of development: apparently few economic rewards for having large families; employment of women outside the home; a firm national commitment to fertility reduction and the organizational capacity to implement it; extensive community-based distribution systems for con- traceptives; and a community structure of stability and legitimacy whose members share at least some economic rewards and costs within which working out group problems in common is an accepted practice. Which particular conditions among these are essential for community pressures to succeed, or even to be successfully mobilized, or whether some combination of these might have brought about fertility decline by themselves without the mobilization of the community, are unresolved questions.

COMMUNITY INCENTIVES AND DISINCENTIVES

A distinction is made in Figure 1 between incentives tied specifically to contraceptive adoption and incentives meant more generally to affect the costs of having children.   In the first category, small incremental payments might be made to motivate individuals to adopt a specific method, and somewhat larger ones to adopt a permanent form of contraception like sterilization.   In the latter category fall various payment schemes meant to reward nonpregnancy or the avoidance of a birth, not only cash payments but also such rewards as time off from work and educational benefits for children in smaller families.   In contrast to incentives, disincentives are more likely to be tied to family size than to adoption of specific methods, and similarly could cover a variety of sanctions, such as poor housing and restrictions on medical care.   Incentives and disincentives like these may be con- sidered community variables either because they are awarded to or imposed on communities as a whole or because they are imposed on families but controlled at the community level.   Community incentives of the first type are designed to force communities to exert pressure on their members; incentives of the second type are utilized by communities to control their members.

Experience with incentives imposed on communities as a whole has been relatively limited so far. Though various substantive incentives of this type have been proposed (e.g., McNicoll, 1975), the most common are the intangible sanctions of official approval and prestige that come from meeting or overfulfilling community quotas and the mainly symbolic prizes that may be awarded to more successful communities. Some attempt has also been made to tie public works grants and loans for income-generating activities for Indonesian villages to family-planning practice (Jacobsen, 1983).

Incentives controlled at the community level deserve special attention. Though they have been tried in a variety of countries (see, e.g., David, 1982), careful investigation of their effects is generally lacking. As an ideal setting in which incentives have been tried, the Singapore program is worth considering. Though it is not in any sense typical of the prospects for rural areas in other developing countries, the Singapore case has undergone some evaluation, and important implications can be drawn from this work.

In 1969, after fertility decline had been in progress for at least a decade, Singapore began to implement a set of disincentives to discourage fourth- and higher-order (and later third-order) births. These disincentives grew incrementally; in 1979, they included rising delivery fees for later children, priorities in choice of primary school for children (especially the first and second) of sterilized parents, the allocation of public housing flats irrespective of family size, income tax deductions only for three children, and maternity leaves in both the public and private sectors only for first and second births (Fawcett, 1979). Although these disincentives were not imposed on a community or neighborhood basis, it may be argued that, as a small, compact, urban society ruled by a comprehensive national party, Singapore as a whole may be considered the operative community. These incentives appear to have had an impact on fertility: the timing and pattern of declines since 1969 follows what one would predict if this were the case (Anderson et al., 1977). A more complex question is how these incentives have had their effect. In attempting to summarize a number of collected studies of these disincentives, Fawcett and Chen (1979) distinguish three possible types of effects: to educate people about the government's population policies, to facilitate or encourage rational decision making about childbearing, and to serve as barriers to large families among those inclined toward them. The disincentives have had the expected educational effect, increasing public awareness and conveying the "government's serious intent in matters relating to population control." Similarly, they served to "facilitate consideration of the costs and benefits of family size, even if they are not a major influence on the final decision" (Fawcett and Chen, 1979, p. 249). However, they were ineffective as barriers: they did not prevent couples from achieving the family sizes they desired.

Though it requires substantiation by other research, this conclusion suggests a different role for incentives than the obvious one. Incentives appear to be essentially an alternative form or an intensification of community pressure, rather than significant economic pluses or minuses that shift the demand for children in the desired direction. Incentives with greater impact, affecting child costs and benefits in more basic fashion, might in principle be designed, but it is difficult to see how they could be legitimized and effectively implemented elsewhere if this has not been done in Singapore.

SUMMARY

These examples indicate that, in appropriate circumstance, involvement of communities can contribute to fertility control. Community-based contraceptive distribution fairly clearly contributes to fertility decline when it is properly organized, but the conditions that make such organization possible have not been investigated here. Community pressures may also contribute, though their specific influence is more difficult to pin down. Also, the examples considered suggest special circumstances under which communities have been mobilized to exert pressures; what other circumstances would also allow mobilization and effective pressures cannot be said. Community-controlled incentives, again under very special conditions, also can have some fertility impact. However, there is no evidence that they can in fact produce significant changes in the economic utility of children; perhaps their major influence is to reinforce community pressures and demonstrate the firm intentions behind a population control program. If this argument is correct—that the incentives a population program is able to marshall cannot shift the net cost of children to households significantly—the implication need not be that incentives should not be resorted to. One might argue the reverse, that therefore even apparently inconsequential incentives should be seriously considered for their symbolic impact.

Examples have not been taken from pretransition European societies. Community influence appears in some accounts (e.g., Lesthaeghe, 1980; Smith, 1981), though mainly on nuptiality rather than marital fertility. It is not evident what can be learned from the significantly different community and societal settings in these cases (but see Potter, 1983).

Some reference should be made to the ethical questions related to community mobilization. Recognizing that ethical issues must be resolved within the context of the particularly heirarchy of values within a society or a community, Berelson and Lieberson (1979) nevertheless offer some general prescriptions. They find contraceptive distribution not only unobjectionable but also preferable to other approaches in permitting more scope for voluntary action. They regard positive incentives as acceptable, provided they are necessary and sufficiently understood by those affected. But with disincentives they are more cautious, because of the possibility of "potential harm to innocents." They are even more cautious about peer pressure, requiring that other more voluntary measures be tried first, that members of the affected community be consulted, and that dissenters from the community consensus be protected. The central value in Berelson and Lieberson's analysis is freedom or liberty. They do not consider the value of equity or distributive justice (Dyck, 1971), to which people sometimes assign a higher priority than freedom of choice if they are convinced of the need for population control (Bulatao, 1974). From the standpoint of equity, community pressure has the special advantage of usually being tied to collective monitoring and greater—or at least more obvious—sharing of sacrifices and rewards.

CONCLUSION

It is evident from this review that no adequate paradigm for the study of community effects yet exists. Community effects are often difficult to distinguish from the effects of other social aggregates or of cultural patterns, and communities themselves are often in transition between various degrees of independence or dependence and of integration into the nation-state. The research approaches taken appear fragmentary and often avoid focusing on aspects of community relevant to population programs.

Although there are no adequate answers to them, it is useful to try to restate the central questions about communities and fertility control. The basic question is whether what happens at the community level can make a difference to fertility. A subsidiary question is whether changes at this level are possible to promote fertility control. Following the threefold distinction of community variables in Figure 1, it may be said that the evidence is clearest with regard to access to regulation: this does affect fertility, and a reasonable case can be made for treating it as a community variable. The evidence is murkier for the other community variables, categorized here as community pressures and incentives structured at the community level. There are bits and pieces of research evidence for the importance of pressures and incentives, as well as more or less persuasive interpretations of specific social situations that appear to implicate these community variables. What may be covered under incentives is so wide, however, and so poorly defined to date, that the degree to which these are specifically community variables is not clear. On the subsidiary question of whether fertility control is possible through these community variables, only descriptive data are available. Again, they favor a role for community access, and possibly community pressures, but are more equivocal about community incentives. The skepticism Demeny (1975, p. 158) has expressed about restructuring development policies to provide incentives for lower fertility still seems apt:

> Given the existing state of the art of development planning and given the inadequate conceptual framework for analyzing population problems, it is, in fact, doubtful whether arguments based on fertility effects of development policies are ever strong enough appreciably to modify the mix of development measures that planners would otherwise propose.

If one grants that community variables can play a role in fertility, one might then ask whether this is an essential role. There does not seem to be any evidence directly on this point. The hypothesis might be worth exploring that the community role is not essential and might be dispensed with if all other conditions are favorable to fertility control, but is essential when control is being introduced as a new and untested innovation in a setting predominantly favoring large families.

Another question is what characteristics of communities or their social settings make it possible for them to play a role in fertility control. Figure 1 suggests some organizational requisites and points to the permeability of communities to decisions taken at the national level. Another requisite would seem to be reasonably small size. Acting on behalf of the group and monitoring the behavior of members become considerably more difficult as the group increases in size (e.g., Olson, 1965). It might be argued that a community must also be closed, in the sense that any environmental degradation, unemployment, or similar effects of demographic decisions be contained within the community (McNicoll, 1975). This requirement would seem to conflict with the requirement of smaller size, however, and the former may be more important. There certainly are other, cultural requisites for an effective community role: for instance, some degree of legitimacy for fertility control and some consensus that it is desirable.

It is worth asking whether the focus on territorially based administrative units has been too limiting and whether other forms of communities should be considered. The argument might be that communities defined by different criteria might better distinguish groups that evidence a stronger interest in mutual welfare or that share a common culture or subculture. In the first case, the alternative communities (kin groups aside) might be voluntary organizations; in the second case, they might be ethnic, linguistic, or religious groups. Voluntary organizations (such as peer groups and friendship circles, like mothers' clubs in Korea) may have significant effects on fertility even in rural, peasant settings. Ethnic groups generally lack the small size and immediate personal contact that seems to be crucial for exerting influence in the small community; nevertheless, ethnic differences in fertility are often notable and difficult to explain away (Berelson, 1978). These social forms are of some interest, particularly in the degree to which they represent cleavages that reinforce community divisions, but probably cannot be analyzed within the same framework applied to territorial communities here.

One final point concerns the degree to which individuals recognize the influence of communities, and in fact the influence of other people generally, on their fertility decisions. The great majority of respondents in the cross-national Value of Children surveys indicated that social pressures were irrelevant to or only minimal factors in their childbearing preferences (Arnold et al., 1975; Bulatao, 1975). It may be argued that a different selection of countries would have turned up greater social influence (though Singapore was included in these surveys), or that the survey method is inappropriate for detecting social influence. However, it is perhaps more important to note that, whether or not social influence was in fact part of the story, most respondents chose not to give it importance and preferred to take responsibility for their own fertility decisions.   Attempts at the community level to influence fertility are therefore likely to be more successful if they also provide individuals with sufficient information and arguments to convince themselves of the need for fertility control.

REFERENCES

Anderson, J.E., M.C.C. Cheng, and W. Fook-Kee. 1977. A components analysis of recent fertility decline in Singapore. Studies in Family Planning 8:282–287.

Astawa, I.B. 1979. Using the local community: Bali, Indonesia. In: M. Potts and P. Bhiwandiwala (eds.) Birth Control: An International Assessment, pp. 55–70. Baltimare: University Park Press.

Arnold, F., R.A. Bulatao, C. Buripakdi, B.J. Chung, J.T. Fawcett, T. Iritani, S.J. Lee, and T.-S. Wu. 1975. The Value of Children: A Cross-National Study, Vol. 1, Introduction and Comparative Analysis. Honolulu: East-West Population Institute.

Berelson, B. 1971. Population policy: Personal notes. Population Studies 25:173–182.

_____ 1978. Ethnicity and fertility: What and so what? In: V. Baras and M. Himmelfarb (eds.) Zero Population Growth. Westport, Connecticut: Greenwood Press.

_____ and Lieberson, J. 1979. Government efforts to influence fertility: The ethical issues. Population and Development Review 5:581–614.

Bulatao, R.A. 1974. Attitudes Toward Legal Measures for Population Control: Social-Psychological Factors Affecting Ethical-Cultural Acceptability. Quezon City: University of the Philippines.

_____ 1975. The Value of Children: A Cross-National Study, Vol. 2, Philippines. Honolulu: East-West Population Institute.

Cain, M. 1982. Perspectives on family and fertility in developing countries. Population Studies 36:159–175.

Caldwell, J.C. 1982. Theory of Fertility Decline. London: Academic Press.

_____ 1983. Direct economic costs and benefits of children. In: R.A. Bulatao and R.D. Lee (eds.) Determinants of Fertility in Developing Countries. New York: Academic Press.

Casterline, J. n.d. Community Effects on Individual Demographic Behavior: Multilevel Analysis of WFS Data. London: World Fertility Survey.

Chen, P.-C. 1981. China's birth planning program. In: National Research Council Committee on Population and Demography, Research on the Population of China, Proceedings of a Workshop, pp. 78–90. Washington, D.C.: National Academy Press.

_____ and A. Kols. 1982. Population and birth planning in the People's Republic of China. Population Reports 10(1) Series J, No. 25.

Cuca, R. and C.S. Pierce. 1977. Experiments in Family Planning. Baltimore: Johns Hopkins University Press.

David, H.P. 1982. Incentives, reproductive behavior, and integrated community development in Asia. Studies in Family Planning 13:159–173.

Demeny, P. 1975. Population policy: The role of national governments.
Population and Development Review 1:147-161.
Dyck, A.J. 1971. Population policies and ethical acceptability. In:
National Academy of Sciences, Rapid Population Growth, Vol. 2, pp.
618-638. Baltimore: Johns Hopkins University Press.
Easterlin, R.A. 1978. The economics and sociology of fertility: A syn-
thesis. In: C. Tilly (ed.) Historical Studies of Changing Fertility, pp.
57-113. Princeton: Princeton University Press.
_____ 1983. Modernization and fertility: A critical essay. In: R.A.
Bulatao and R.D. Lee (eds.) Determinants of Fertility in Developing
Countries. New York: Academic Press.
Entwisle, B., A.I. Hermalin, and W.M. Mason. 1982. Socioeconomic
Determinants of Fertility Behavior in Developing Nations: Theory
and Initial Results. Committee on Population and Demography Report
No. 17. Washington, D.C.: National Academy Press.
Fawcett, J.T. 1979. Singapore's population policies in perspective. In:
P.S.J. Chen and J.T. Fawcett (eds.) Public Policy and Population
Change in Singapore, pp. 3-17. New York: Population Council.
_____ 1983. Perceptions of the value of children: Satisfactions and
costs. In: R.A. Bulatao and R.D. Lee (eds.) Determinants of Fertility
in Developing Countries. New York: Academic Press.
_____ and P.S.J. Chen. 1979. Public policy and population change:
An appraisal of the Singapore experience. In: P.S.J. Chen and J.T.
Fawcett (eds.) Public Policy and Population Change in Singapore, pp.
243-258. New York: Population Council.
Files, L.A. 1982. A reexamination of integrated population acitivities.
Studies in Family Planning 13:297-302.
Foreit, J.R., M.E. Gorosh, D.G. Gillespie, and C.G. Merritt. 1978.
Community-based and commercial contraceptive distribution: An
inventory and appraisal. Population Reports Series J, No. 19.
Freedman, R. 1974. Community-Level Data in Fertility Surveys. Occa-
sional Paper No. 8. London: World Fertility Survey.
Gadalla, S., N. Nosseir, and D.G. Gillespie. 1980. Household distribu-
tion of contraceptives in rural Egypt. Studies in Family Planning 11:
105-113.
Hermalin, A.I. and W.M. Mason. 1980. A strategy for the comparative
analysis of WFS data, with illustrative examples. In: The United
Nations Programme for Comparative Analysis of World Fertility Survey Data, pp. 90-168. New York: United Nations Fund for Population Activities.
Hobcraft, J. 1982. Strategies for comparative analysis of WFS data.
In: World Fertility Survey Conference 1980: A Record of the Proceedings, Vol. 3. The Hague: International Statistical Institute.
Huber, D.H. and A.R. Khan. 1979. Contraceptive distribution in
Bangladesh villages: The initial impact. Studies in Family Planning
10:246-253.
Hull, T.H. 1978. Where credit is due: Policy implications of the
recent rapid fertility decline in Bali. Paper presented for the annual
meeting of the Population Association of America, Atlanta.
_____, V.J. Hull, and M. Singarimbun. 1977. Indonesia's family plan-
ning story: Success and challenge. Population Bulletin 32(6).

Isaacs, S.L. 1981. Annex to the background document: Review of the current status of family planning. In: Family Planning in the 1980s: Challenges and Opportunities, pp. 105-151. New York: United Nations Fund for Population Activities, International Planned Parenthood Federation, and Population Council.

Jacobsen, J. 1983. Promoting Population Stabilization: Incentives for Small Families. Worldwatch Paper 54. Washington, D.C.: Worldwatch Institute.

Kim, J.-I. and J.A. Palmore. 1978. Personal networks and the adoption of family planning in rural Korea. Unpublished paper. Honolulu: East-West Population Institute.

Knodel, J., N. Debavalya, and P. Kamnuansilpa. 1980. Thailand's continuing reproductive revolution. International Family Planning Perspectives 6:84-97.

Lee, S.-B. 1977. System Effects on Family Planning Innovativeness in Korean Villages. Ph.D. Thesis. Ann Arbor: University of Michigan.

Leibenstein, H. 1976. Beyond Economic Man. Cambridge, Massachusetts: Harvard University Press.

Lesthaeghe, R. 1980. On the social control of human reproduction. Population and Development Review 6:527-548.

Lindert, P.H. 1983. The changing economic costs and benefits of having children. In: R.A. Bulatao and R.D. Lee (eds.) Determinants of Fertility in Developing Countries. New York: Academic Press.

Mason, W.M. and V.T. Palan. 1978. Community-level variables and their effects on reproductive behavior in Malaysia. Paper prepared for the Conference on Comparative Fertility Transition in Asia, Tokyo.

McNicoll, G. 1975. Community-level population policy: An exploration. Population and Development Review 1:1-21.

_____ 1978. Population and development: Outlines for a structuralist approach. In: G. Hawthorn (ed.) Population and Development, pp. 79-99. London: Frank Cass.

_____ 1979. The demography of post-peasant society. In: Conference on Economic and Demographic Change: Issues for the 1980s (Helsinki, 1978) pp. 135-145. Liege, Belgium: International Union for the Scientific Study of Population.

_____ 1982. Institutional determinants of fertility change. In: C. Hohn and R. Mackensen (eds.) Determinants of Fertility Change: Theories Re-examined, pp. 147-168. Liege, Belgium: Ordina Editions.

Meier, G. 1979. Family planning in the banjars of Bali. International Family Planning Perspectives 5:63-66.

Merton, R.K. 1968. Social Theory and Social Structure, rev. ed. New York: Free Press.

Nisbet, R.A. 1966. The Sociological Tradition. New York: Basic Books.

Nizamuddin, M. 1979. The Impact of Community and Program Factors on the Fertility-Related Behavior of Rural Pakistani Women. Ph.D. Dissertation, School of Public Health. Ann Arbor: University of Michigan.

Notestein, F.W. 1945. Population: The long view. In: T.W. Schultz (ed.) Food for the World, pp. 36-57. Chicago: University of Chicago Press.

Olson, M., Jr. 1965.   The Logic of Collective Action: Public Goods and the Theory of Groups.   Cambridge, Massachusetts: Harvard University Press.

Parish, W.L. 1981.   Marriage and changes in the family in the People's Republic of China.   In: National Research Council Committee on Population and Demography, Research on the Population of China, Proceedings of a Workshop, pp. 93-120.   Washington, D.C.: National Academy Press.

_____ and M.K. Whyte. 1978.   Village and Family in Contemporary China.   Chicago: University of Chicago Press.

Potter, J.E. 1983.   Effects of societal and community institutions on fertility.   In: R.A. Bulatao and R.D. Lee (eds.) Determinants of Fertility in Developing Countries.   New York: Academic Press.

Retherford, R.D. and J.A. Palmore. 1983.   Diffusion processes affecting fertility regulation.   In: R.A. Bulatao and R.D. Lee (eds.) Determinants of Fertility in Developing Countries.   New York: Academic Press.

Rodriguez, G. 1978.   Family planning availability and contraceptive practice.   International Family Planning Perspectives 4:100-115.

Rogers, E.M. 1962. Diffusion of Innovations.   New York: Free Press.

_____ and D.L. Kincaid. 1981.   Communication Networks.   New York: Free Press.

Ryder, N.B. 1983.   Fertility and family structure.   Paper prepared for the Expert Group on Fertility and Family, New Delhi.

Schearer, S.B. and N. Financioglu. 1981.   Background document.   In: Family Planning in the 1980s: Challenges and Opportunities, pp. 53-104.   New York: United Nations Fund for Population Activities, International Planned Parenthood Federation, and Population Council.

Simon, H.A. 1957.   Administrative Behavior.   New York: Macmillan.

Smith, R.M. 1981.   Fertility, economy, and household formation in England over three centuries.   Population and Development Review 7: 595-622.

Watson, W., A. Rosenfield, M. Viravaidya, and K. Chanawongse. 1979.   Health, population, and nutrition: Interrelations, problems, and possible solutions.   In: P.M. Hauser (ed.) World Population and Development, pp. 145-173.   Syracuse, New York: Syracuse University Press.

CHAPTER 15

Conclusions and Policy Implications

Ozzie Simmons

The purpose of this volume is to examine the theoretical and empirical bases for the design of rural development policy that is fertility-sensitive. If such policy is to be designed and implemented, researchers and planners will have to work together to ensure that fertility effects will be in the desired direction without imposing major constraints on the achievement of appropriate rural development policy objectives. As the chapters in this volume show, current knowledge yields only a very broad understanding of the links between rural development policies and fertility. There is as yet no generally accepted theoretical framework for explaining the conditions, correlates, causes, and consequences of population change in the developing countries (LDCs), and within which to view relations between rural development policy and population growth. Nevertheless, the knowledge base that has been generated points to recurrent significant links, at least at the aggregate level, between fertility and such development factors as income, health and nutrition, education, and labor force participation. These links do provide useful departure points for the theoretical and empirical work that still needs to be done to clarify these relationships at national and subnational levels to yield an understanding of them that can be operationally useful for rural development planning and policy making.

Most of the world's severe poverty exists in the rural areas of the low-income countries. About two-thirds of the developing world's population gains its livelihood from agriculture as farmers and farm workers and these groups include the vast majority of the world's poorest people (International Bank, 1982).   As noted in Chapter 1, their reproduction rates are among the highest in the world, and the rural poor will account for most of the population growth in LDCs throughout the remainder of the century.   In three of the most populous countries in Asia, Bangladesh, India, and Indonesia, the percentage of the population living in urban areas is projected to be still only 22, 34, and 32, respectively, in the year 2000 (Todaro, 1981). Landless workers are the poorest of rural residents, and one writer (Cool, 1979) estimates that in South and Southeast Asia there may be upwards of 200 million landless or near-landless rural workers.   Cool claims that, on present evidence, this number is likely to grow both absolutely and as a percentage of total rural households at an unprecedented rate well into the future.

In view of these considerations, it is clear that the major thrust of development strategies for poverty reduction will have to be in the rural areas.   Since the early 1970s, development strategies have begun to shift away from "urban bias" and to emphasize the role of agriculture and the importance of increasing the incomes of the poorest people in a society, but as Todaro (1981, p. 8) observes, "To date . . . the commitment to this strategy has not been strong enough to significantly change the urbanization-industrialization policies of past decades."

Schutjer and Stokes (Chapter 1) make a distinction between rural development policies directed toward income enhancement and those directed toward improving the quality of life through access to resources other than income and point out that these sets of policies can influence both the demand and the supply of children.   These conceptions reflect the prominent shift in development objectives that has come about through the perception that the exclusive pursuit of economic growth was too narrow an objective and that other objectives, related to poverty reduction—enhancing income, increasing employment, and satisfying "basic needs"—must be taken into account (Morawetz, 1977).   What has been discovered (or in fact rediscovered, since these issues have been around for some time) is that production objectives cannot be separated from those of distribution.   Consequently, current thinking in the rural development literature is oriented to broad-based approaches that will bring increased access for the poor majorities in rural areas to resources needed for enhancing their economic and social well-being.

The principal calls are for improved agricultural productivity and returns to productivity, and expanded opportunities for nonagricultural employment in rural areas if rural incomes are to move upward; provision of public services for better health and nutrition and greater life expectancy; and investment in human capital, especially education for women and children.   Also needed is administrative and political decentralization to encourage and help rural groups and communities to organize themselves to plan their own programs for access to and management of resources and to identify the specific kinds of help they need from government and other outside sources for implementing these plans and programs.   This orientation to broad-based development offers an enhanced potential for the design of rural development policies that can be fertility-sensitive. Rural development policies that seek to reduce poverty and population policies aimed at reducing fertility can go hand in hand. All of the dimensions of broad-based rural development listed here—income, off-farm employment, health and nutrition, education, and greater popular participation and community-level action—largely coincide with the factors generally considered to constitute the important determinants of rural fertility. All the available evidence seems to point toward the proposition that fertility will decline as broad-based development brings improved well-being to the rural poor majorities in the LDC, which decades of economic growth by itself have failed to do. To the extent that a large proportion of the population can share in the benefits of development, they will also experience fertility decline that will eventually produce a greater aggregate-level fertility decline.

LINKS BETWEEN RURAL DEVELOPMENT AND FERTILITY

The chapters in this volume focus on these several links between rural development factors and fertility. For illustrative purposes, three of these links will be considered here: between fertility and income, health and nutrition, and female labor force participation.

Mueller (Chapter 7) observes that documentation of a pure income effect, i.e., demonstrating that a change in the demand for children is attributable solely to a change in income, is hard to come by. This is because income change may affect the demand for children indirectly through other variables that operate through changes in the value of time invested in children, costs of children, aspirations, perceived benefits from children, female and child labor force participation, and a family's sense of optimism and security regarding its financial future. These indirect effects are difficult to measure empirically.

Acknowledging these constraints, Mueller examines the process whereby rural development creates a need for a more literate and skilled labor force, leading to investment in educational facilities, and also increased availability of consumer goods, either through local production or importation. She hypothesizes that to the extent that as these new opportunities emerge in rural areas, they enhance consumption and educational aspirations which may then reduce the demand for children. Income change alters tastes in favor of educated children and new consumer goods at the expense of child quantity, and thus income increases could lead to a decline in the demand for children.

Mueller's review of the empirical evidence indicates that the relationship between income and fertility is negative in rural areas where development is relatively advanced, but positive where the benefits of development are yet to be received. Where rural development has appreciably progressed, negative indirect effects, including rising educational and consumption aspirations, may outweigh positive direct effects.

In looking at the relationship between income distribution and fertility, Kocher (Chapter 11) concludes, like Mueller, that the effect of income on fertility is not linear; it is positive at low levels of income (and in fact fertility may increase at these levels as income increases, but only up to a point) and negative at higher levels. In any case, from the few studies available of the relationship, Kocher derives the conclusion that lower fertility and more rapid fertility decline are generally associated with more egalitarian distributions of income and relatively greater access to education, employment, and health and social welfare services.

Given the paucity of both theory and empirical research for analysis of the interactions between fertility and income inequality, however, convincing generalizations in this area are still not within reach. The effects of demographic factors on income distribution, and vice versa, are mixed and inadequately understood. Although it does appear that higher fertility is associated with greater economic inequality, it is not clear whether the direction of causation is from fertility to inequality or the reverse, which may be just as likely.

The effect of food policy on fertility may be significant, but, as Pinstrup-Andersen and Kumar note (Chapter 12), demonstrating the pure effect is as difficult as in the case of income and fertility because the effect is usually indirect, operating through a number of other variables, including the proximate fertility determinants designated by Bongaarts (1978). Food policy influences nutrition through a series of factors, and nutritional status in turn may influence fertility through a number of biological mechanisms, as identified by the authors. They go on to say:

> The nutritional status may influence fertility through biological as well as behavioral relationships. The biological relationships influence potential fertility. The extent to which potential fertility is translated into actual fertility is determined by a number of behavioral factors. Thus, potential fertility may be viewed as the "supply" of fertility—what is biologically possible—while behavioral factors reflecting the desire to have children may be viewed as the "demand" for fertility. Interaction between supply and demand results in actual fertility.

A third set of relationships brings us back to economic factors. In particular, two such factors directly influenced by food policy are identified as of great importance for fertility: (a) the level and stability of real incomes of low-income households, and (b) the demand for and shadow cost of women's time.

Typically, declines in fertility have been preceded by declining infant mortality. Mortality decline appears to be leveling off in many LDCs at what are unacceptable levels, and this phenomenon makes the current groundswell for primary health care for the poor all the more important. It seems reasonable to believe that improved health care will eventually encourage some decline in rural fertility. There remain unanswered questions, however. Little is known about the determinants of the length of the lag between mortality and fertility decline and the resulting effect on population growth rates (Preston, 1978; Schultz, 1976). Although there is more evidence for than against the proposition that decreases in infant and child mortality will be followed by a fertility decline, such factors as family income, education, and economic growth affect both fertility and infant mortality and probably distort the results of attempts to measure the direct relationship between the two (Simmons, 1983).

The best answer that can be given to the question of whether the fertility of working women is lower than that of nonworking women is maybe (Kupinsky, 1977). A review of studies on female work status and fertility in Latin America showed no consistent inverse relationship between female labor force participation and fertility (Davidson, 1977). The inverse relationship was fairly predominant in large cities but virtually absent in small towns. The important factors related to female labor force participation were education, the number and ages of children, husband's income, the type of family (nuclear versus extended), urban-rural status of the community, and the stage of economic development of the country.

Weller's review (Chapter 8) of female employment and fertility reflects the ambiguous nature of the evidence. He strikes a hopeful note in pointing to research that relates female labor force participation to several of the intermediate variables that can lead to lower fertility, namely, a higher age at marriage and an increased use of contraception. But he concludes that current available evidence does not always show a negative association between female employment and fertility, especially in the rural areas of the LDCs. Moreover, even when present such a negative relationship is seldom strong and may have an ambiguous causal nature, so that any effects of female employment on fertility are likely to be long-term rather than short-term.

THE TASKS FOR THEORY

The foregoing brief consideration of what is known about the links between several key rural development factors and fertility reveals the deficiencies of the existing knowledge base in attempts to predict the fertility effects of these development factors. It yields only a very broad understanding of why fertility behaves as it does. The "mainstream" theories of fertility decline, such as demographic transition theory and microeconomic theory as applied to household decision making, have made useful contributions to this field, especially the subsequent revisionist versions, but the prevailing deficiencies can be attributed at least in part to the failure of these theories to take into account the ways in which changes in structural and cultural contexts may affect fertility. A number of writers (e.g. Burch, 1975; McNicoll, 1980) have argued for the importance of these contextual variables in explaining the relationships between developmental change and fertility decline.

High rates of population growth are a global problem, but, as Hawthorn (1978) has pointed out, it does not follow that this problem can have any general solution. Given the complexity and indirect nature of the interactions among rural development and demographic variables, the different levels and kinds of rural development associated with fertility reductions, and the fact that the relationships between fertility and its determinants vary considerably not only among countries but also among different groups within countries, a general solution, even if it were attainable, could only be of limited practical use.   Neverthe-less, even though it is not likely that definitive answers are within reach in the near future, theoretical work that seeks to identify possible chains of links between cause and effect through which a particular developmental change or intervention is or is not conducive to reducing fertility is a worthy objective to strive for in the interest of gaining greater precision in this field.

The key question is: Within the array of the most prominent candi-dates considered to be the determinants of fertility, what are the particular combinations of the fundamental variables at specific levels that constitute the necessary and sufficient conditions to precipitate a fertility decline?   There are no wholly adequate answers from the prevailing theoretical models.   When advocates of these models are accused of abstracting too much from the real world, they respond by adding such black boxes as the "influence of social institutions" and "cultural norms and values."   This volume has confronted these theo-retical deficits, particularly in the efforts of Turchi (Chapter 6) and Mueller (Chapter 7) to broaden the theoretical base,   Goldscheider's (Chapter 3) specification of the importance of the structural variables, and Vinovskis' (Chapter 5) contention that broad attitudinal and cultural shifts played a key role in the decline of American fertility.

Although basically economic, the model outlined by Turchi does take into account community-level factors affecting the demand for com-pleted family size and specifies a series of variables for research that constitute the "social/normative environment."   Mueller, in her diagram of the model of the relationship between income and fertility, accords a prominent place to "culture and social structure" as conditioning this relationship.   Moreover, in her analysis of the role of educational and consumption aspirations as intervening variables between income and fertility, she breathes life into the concept of "tastes," which has been treated largely as a residual category by economists.

To date, however, conceptualization about the relationships between rural development and fertility consists essentially of accounting schemes, frameworks for specifying what a theory must contain, rather than a theory as such.   To be able to verify or falsify the putative relationships, values have to be attached to the variables in a frame-work.   Only then could a testable and potentially explanatory theory be formulated.   Causal chains cannot be identified by citing attitudes, norms, values, and perceptions as determinants.   There is need to delve into how these variables are derived and formed by sociocultural and institutional contexts.

In his discussion of migration and rural fertility, Goldscheider identifies changes in social organization as one of the major types of effects of outmigration (of the permanent rather than the seasonal or temporary kind) on fertility.   In his view, two key processes are involved: structural differentiation, which entails a break with kinship dominance over economic resources and with family control over status, and expansion of opportunity structures, both at place of origin and of

destination, particularly for women. To the extent that these processes occur, outmigration will indirectly foster a more rapid decline in
fertility. Noting that these hypothesized effects require systematic and
detailed empirical testing, he maintains that the changes permanent
migration would induce in the family, in the status of women, and in
opportunity structures, would constitute the necessary and sufficient
conditions for reducing fertility as long as changes in all three were to
occur. Consistent with Goldscheider's position, Mason and Palan (1981),
in their study of female employment and fertility in Peninsular Malaysia,
emphasize the potential utility of the concept of opportunity structure
for explaining the full range of variation in the employment-fertility
relationship. In so doing, they also illustrate the complexity of the
relationships between fertility and structural changes in women's
employment, family labor patterns, childcare arrangements, and children's schooling.

Goldscheider expresses reservations regarding cultural factors as
forces in fertility change, contrary to the position advanced by Vinovskis. Goldscheider believes that opportunity structures are critical for
explaining changes in attitudes and values. Cultural traditions may
play a role, but, in his view, the key consideration is structural
changes of the kind opened up by migration.

The more fruitful approach, however, would seem to be to view both
structural (institutional) and cultural factors as major components of
the contexts that affect fertility behavior. In the view of McNicoll
(1978), e.g., three levels of analysis are to be distinguished: institutional analysis, which focuses on the fertility-relevant components of
social organization that mediate between individuals and families as
decision makers and national governments; evaluation of the local
objective realities that actually face individual decision makers or
potential clients of development programs; and exploration of the
meanings that attach to these realities in a given sociocultural
context. The second of these levels is seen as filling the gray area
between institutional and cultural analysis.

Institutional and cultural factors are hardly to be accorded exclusive
priority over economic factors. The economists have made a valuable
contribution in their work on the economic values and costs of children
by showing that under certain conditions high fertility is sustained
because parents perceive the added economic value of additional children as greater than the cost of having them, whereas under other
conditions fertility declines because the economic value of children is
perceived as decreasing or disappearing and preferences for other
benefits of the good life compete effectively with the preferences for
children. But this focus on the economic calculus leaves out of
systematic consideration what may be important structural or cultural
factors that mediate and are mediated by economic pressures and thus
influence the ways in which economic pressures affect parental and
societal decision making. To acknowledge that "tastes" have an important bearing on the economic calculus is not much help if in fact
tastes constitute a residual category. A principal theoretical issue is
not whether economic, structural, or cultural variables are the most
appropriate focus, but what are the conceptual requirements for speci-

fying the priorities with regard to the kinds of data needed to get at explanations, by identifying, for particular situations, the combinations of variables that are conducive to sustaining high fertility and to precipitating fertility decline.

THE TASKS FOR RESEARCH

A recurrent theme in this volume is that of the need for methodological approaches that can exploit aggregative, household, and individual data.   To meet theoretical requirements for generating explanatory power, all three levels need to be employed as units of analysis, with collection of data oriented to a more or less common conceptual frame to insure cumulative results for an adequate knowledge base.   This means that any debate about the virtues of cross-sectional, aggregate-level surveys versus community-specific and village-level studies is sterile.   A critical task is to combine these approaches to maximize the possibilities for causal analysis and increase thereby the explanatory power of research on the relationships between rural development and fertility.

Much dissatisfaction has been expressed with using only aggregate (or attribute) data to explain fertility behavior because the associations established on the basis of cross-sectional survey or census data usually do not answer the question of causality.   Further, such data cannot cope with the severe limitation imposed in having to cope with essentially indirect effects and the consequent problem of indeterminate time lags.   More specifically, Mueller observes that the research interest in the income/aspirations/fertility sequence reflects concern with a dynamic process that is believed to reduce the demand for children over time.   But cross-sectional data are not readily amenable to the study of dynamic change because the relevant time series are not available.   Johnson (Chapter 9) also states that cross-sectional data cannot confirm time-series relationships.   Kocher notes that an analysis of the relationships between the distribution of income and fertility requires more than simply knowing aggregate-level characteristics, and indeed requires more than an understanding of the determinants of fertility at the micro-level, although both are necessary.   As he says, there will frequently be long lag periods between "socioeconomic/cultural changes" which ultimately have important effects on fertility and the resultant fertility change.   During this process, there may be some segments of the population experiencing rising fertility, others experiencing declining fertility, and others essentially unchanged fertility. Aggregate-level data may mask these significant subaggregate differences, so that it may be difficult or impossible to identify important variations from such data.   And Bulatao (Chapter 14), in reporting that the great majority of respondents in the cross-national Value of Children surveys indicated that social pressures were irrelevant to or only minimal factors in their childbearing preferences, notes that it may be argued that the survey method is inappropriate for detecting social influence.

There have been increasing calls in the literature (Jones, 1978; Urzua, 1978; Population Council, 1981) for village-level studies as a way to document more concretely the economic, institutional, and sociocultural contexts of fertility behavior.   Cross-sectional surveys, designed only to identify statistical associations between fertility and its correlates, cannot, by virtue of their limitations, serve as adequate research instruments for the study of these contexts of fertility decision making.   To the extent that they are country- and region-specific, however, they can help provide a knowledge base for village-level studies to document the role of the contextual variables at the community and family levels.   Such an approach may not serve the cause of generality but it would yield closer approximations to reality.   And generality may also be served if the design of such studies were oriented to a more or less common conceptual framework.   Moreover, Chapman (1981, p. 87) maintains that "results from micro-studies reveal far more common ground and consequently a much greater ability to generalize than is commonly assumed."

This is not to say that comparative or cross-national research is of no value.   On the contrary, comparative treatment may very well strengthen particular explanations by placing them in a larger framework of what works and what does not, but only if the research documents the empirical reality of the setting in which reproduction occurs. Such work could be sufficiently specific to serve as the basis for policy decisions in that particular setting and at the same time permit more general conclusions.

What is needed is an articulation of the cross-sectional survey and village-level approaches with an orientation to a common conceptual framework.   Village-level studies, by themselves, are too likely to be anecdotal and idiosyncratic, but if research were designed to collect national- and community-level data on relevant variables on the one hand, and individual- and household-level data on the other, the findings could have substantial application potential that would be of importance for policy recommendations.   The relationships between fertility and its determinants vary not only among countries but among different socioeconomic, occupational, and cultural groups within countries.   A combined approach of the kind proposed here could focus on how changes in incomes and welfare affect reproductive behavior among different groups in the population, groups based on social class, rural or urban residence, kinship, occupation, and ethnicity or religion. With these problems in mind, research could be designed to test ongoing or projected innovative and experimental program interventions in rural development to determine their demographic impact.   More finely-honed survey approaches together with focused village-level studies could contribute to the identification and explanation of group differentials in fertility behavior.

If more can be learned about how fertility change occurs or does not occur in a range of particular settings in developing countries in relation to the range of rural development variables considered in this volume, such as income enhancement, health and nutrition, female education and employment, technical change and agricultural mechanization, migration effects, and access to land, perhaps ways can be found to induce fertility decline without waiting for comprehensive economic development to bring this about. The research findings reported in these chapters merit further research to strengthen the basis of evidence.

Greater light on how people can be induced to change their fertility behavior, the all-important policy question, will require systematic research on the relationships of these development variables to fertility in the context of economic, structural, and cultural factors. It is not at all clear which of these factors are more or less manipulable by policy interventions, but there is no better way of finding out than by subjecting them to research of the kind proposed here. Questions of manipulability are not easy to answer in this, any more than in other problem areas of the social sciences, but they are clearly important for making policy choices.

POLICY IMPLICATIONS

The foregoing discussion addresses the question of what could be done to improve the theoretical and empirical basis for the design of fertility-sensitive rural development policy. As stated in Chapter 1, the task of the present volume is not the exposition of a "set of policies," but rather a determination of the extent to which a consistent set of ideas and research findings are available that can serve as the basis for the design of rural policy. To that end, the ensuing discussion considers policy issues and implications as they relate to five major areas: technical change and mechanization; household-level considerations; population distribution; food policy and nutrition; and access to land.

Technical Change and Mechanization

As Boserup (Chapter 2) poses the issue of technical change, the choice between intensification of agriculture with labor-intensive methods or with mechanized inputs is of crucial importance for the use of child labor and may provide motivation for, or against, the reduction of fertility. She concludes that, to avoid further urban deterioration, rural employment opportunities and income must increase to stem out-migration, and that this is more important than rapid fertility decline. So she urges that an unqualified policy of rapid mechanization of agriculture should not be pursued, even though this might reduce fertility. Instead, rural development policy should be designed as a compromise between labor-intensive and modern-input methods, which seem the only way to improve both urban and rural levels of living.

Choi and Hicks (Chapter 13) are concerned only with agricultural mechanization policy, and conclude that financial reform aimed at ensuring more equal access for farmers to capital markets could increase the demand for new technology focused on mechanization. The new technology would promote economic growth and the factors associated with such growth, namely, increased wages and employment and increased demand for "higher quality" children (because of the need for more skilled workers), which would decrease fertility.

Household-Level Considerations

Mueller suggests that once advances in rural technology raise the marginal productivity of farm investments, the rising demand for investment funds would be conducive to lower fertility by raising the opportunity cost of children. A policy of creating conditions favorable to high investment aspirations for a broad range of rural households is not only desirable in its own right but also could lead to reduction of fertility. The question remains, however, whether children's labor facilitates investments or whether the costs of having more children to feed is perceived by parents as an obstacle to investment.

Noting that options for government policies aimed at redistributing income are limited, Kocher identifies three categories of policies that can, over a period of two or more decades, enhance income levels of the poor majority and thus lead to fertility decline. These measures tie in, for the most part, with those considered in the discussion thus far. They are: (a) major commitment of public resources to basic education, especially for girls, and provision of health and family planning services; (b) development strategies that emphasize investments to stimulate labor-intensive sectors; and (c) strategies aimed at development, promotion, and adoption of technology that complements rather than displaces labor, in both the rural and urban sectors.

The issues involved in a policy of income redistribution remain unclear and complex. Reference has already been made to the ambiguity of the direction of causation in the relationship between fertility and income inequality. Even if there is a causal relationship, the question is whether it could operate with sufficient strength and speed to justify a policy of income redistribution, since Kocher is talking about two decades or more. Mueller has made the point that income cannot be redistributed by putting it in a pool (1). The way redistribution is undertaken may be more important for fertility than redistribution itself. Perhaps the way to go is through family allowance, tax exemptions, and increased opportunities.

As stated earlier, Weller's review indicates that there is some evidence that female labor force participation is associated with increased age at marriage and contraceptive use, and that these in turn may be associated with decreases in family size or with delayed childbearing. But the available evidence about the female labor-fertility relationship is too ambiguous to support policies aimed at reducing fertility by increasing female labor-force participation. Nevertheless, enhancing the status of women by improving their opportunities for labor-force participation and for ownership of assets on equal terms with men, as well as by striving for gender equality in education, as proposed by Johnson, has its own justification. And gender equality in production and reproduction is certainly more likely to enhance the potential for fertility reduction in the long run if not in the short run.

Johnson argues that the value of children may differ markedly between husband and wife, between patriarch and son, and between daughter-in-law and others in the extended family. Moreover, children at low parity and high parity may be valued more or less by different members of the household at different stages of the life cycle. Consequently, actual fertility may represent a compromise between conflicting desires on the part of both husband and wife, as well as other family members.

Population Distribution

Internal migration, its determinants and consequences, and their links to rural development strategy constitute a problem area perhaps equal in importance to that of fertility. It is a reasonable proposition that the goals of development strategy in a country ultimately determine the spatial distribution of the population and changes in that distribution. If the principal goals include making the best use of natural and human resources where they are to be found and reducing the disparities in access to the benefits of development both between social classes and the rural and urban sectors, then it will be necessary to implement policy measures aimed at eliminating the urban bias and rural neglect that characterize so many developing countries. This should not be construed as downgrading the need for industrialization in countries that have the capacity for it. On the contrary, employment-oriented rural development is required to facilitate industrial development (Simmons, 1983).

Sun's study (Chapter 4) of urban-industrial development in Taiwan shows that, unlike the majority of LDCs where urban-industrial development has left most of the rural areas relatively untouched, in the case of Taiwan there has been rapid growth of an industrial population in rural areas, and urban-industrial development has had a significant impact on fertility change. He reasons that industrial development in rural Taiwan must have provided an increased number of opportunities for off-farm employment, which is considered to have negative effects on fertility. Unfortunately, limitations of the study did not permit examination of these propositions.

Although Goldscheider observes that outmigration may have positive, negative, or no effects on rural fertility depending on the particular case, his focus is on the ways in which selective migration may alter the social organization of rural communities, particularly by its effect in attenuating the control by the family of its individual members, changing the status of women, and expanding opportunity structures, all of which will foster, if only indirectly, more rapid fertility decline. In his view, policies should be adopted that foster outmigration because of its uprooting effects on social organization, and, indeed, he argues that the costs to both rural and urban populations of nonmigration "may slow down the differentiation process critical for modernization, in general, and for fertility reduction, in particular."

Bulatao states that too little is known about how community organizations and structure affect rural fertility to draw policy implications.

Nevertheless, his paper does make a start in indicating the increasing importance of the community as a unit for the focus of agricultural policy. Community-level action constitutes a complex area for development efforts, but it is the locus of where things happen and the level at which the differential effects of rural development on fertility behavior must be understood. McNicoll (1975), e.g., has argued for community-level policy as an intermediate level between national policy-making and fertility decisions made at the individual level, and the concomitant need to gain a purchase on community-level determinants of economic and demographic behavior.

Food Policy and Nutrition

As indicated earlier, food policy affects fertility largely through intermediate factors, so the principal task is to identify the factors through which food policy is most likely to have fertility-reducing, rather than fertility-enhancing effects. Pinstrup-Andersen and Kumar attach greatest importance to the level and stability of real incomes of low-income households and to the demand for and shadow cost of women's time. Their general recommendation, consistent with the goals and directions proposed by other authors in this volume, is that the goal of fertility reduction will be most effectively realized through the design of policies that will result in the largest self-sustained economic benefits for low-income households and for the most disadvantaged in such households, namely, women and children. This holds for the goals of improved nutrition as well. Perhaps the principal underlying cause of hunger and malnutrition is that those who need food do not have the money to buy it or produce it, not because food supplies are inadequate in some absolute sense.

Access to Land

Virtually all of the chapters in this volume subscribe to the proposition that agricultural and rural development policies oriented to enhancement of income and improvement of the quality of life among rural populations can provide delimited sets of policies to influence both the demand and supply of children. In some instances, the short-run effect of these policies is likely to be fertility-enhancing, but in all cases, the long-run effects would be fertility-reducing. Access to land is central to the well-being of rural populations, so that rural policies designed to effect changes in the basic institutional arrangements governing access to land could have a particularly substantial impact on fertility.

In their review of the research on the relationships between access to land and fertility, Stokes and Schutjer (Chapter 10) report that the size of landholdings has positive effects on fertility, while land ownership has negative effects. Access to more land leads to greater economic returns for child labor and the higher incomes associated with larger holdings could be expected to increase natural fertility and the survival prospects of children. Land ownership, however, has negative effects by substituting land for children as a source of old-age security. Moreover, the higher incomes associated with ownership may be expected to lead to greater investments in child quality, particularly additional schooling. Here too the short-run and long-run effects are expected to differ. The short-run effect is likely to be fertility-enhancing, but the long-run effect fertility-reducing.

Much more empirical research is needed to specify what the effects of size of holding and of land ownership on fertility might be in different institutional and cultural settings, so as to ascertain under what conditions the effects are complementary or work at cross-purposes. Nevertheless, the research done to date does have implications for the design of policies concerned with access to land. The perspective provided by this work indicates that the expectation that a policy of land redistribution will invariably lower fertility in its wake is simplistic, and constitutes a departure point for identifying the particular conditions under which land redistribution is likely to have either pronatalist or antinatalist effects. If agricultural policy and land reform programs that increase land ownership, in contrast to other tenurial arrangements, are likely to have the desired negative effect, then, in the long run at least, as Stokes and Schutjer say, "they may provide the necessary base for a sustained fertility decline and genuine improvement in the lot of the rural poor."

CONCLUSION

This summation of policy issues and implications that can be identified on the basis of available knowledge about relationships between rural development factors and fertility shows a substantial degree of consistency and consensus among the contributors to this volume. There is still a long way to go before a level of specificity is reached in analysis and research that can be operationally useful for comprehensive rural development planning and policy making. However, enough has been accomplished to provide the basis for limited consideration of fertility impacts of rural policy, and to affirm that the coordination of population and rural development policies is feasible and desirable.

Such coordination will not come about by itself but will require systematic organizational arrangements for its facilitation. For the most part, decisions about what research on population problems is undertaken rest largely with individual social scientists pursuing their own disciplinary interests, and relatively little attention is given to the needs of development planners and policy makers. In undertaking research at national, community, household, and individual levels and to insure that it has policy relevance, there is a need to bring to planners and policy makers an understanding of what is already known that is of policy relevance, to engage them with researchers in a common effort to identify the key questions that are researchable and need to be answered, and to provide policy makers with continuing consultation, based on the best available knowledge, of what options may be open to them, together with the anticipated effects, as they engage in the decision-making process (Simmons and Saunders, 1975).

A number of types of organizational arrangements for coordinating planning and policy making in development and population have been proposed, of which the most prominent, as called for by the World Population Plan of Action, is the establishment of a population policy and development planning unit "at a high level of the national administrative structure" (World Population Conference, 1975). Several Asian countries, including South Korea, Sri Lanka, and Thailand, have already established population units in their national development planning agencies, and a number of other countries in Asia, Latin America, and the Middle East and Africa have expressed the intention of creating such units (Population Council, 1980; United Nations Fund for Population Activities, 1979; United Nations Fund for Population Activities, 1979 to 1981).

Whether such arrangements can be effective in facilitating coordination remains to be seen, since the experience of such units, where they exist at all, is obviously still too recent and limited to provide any basis for assessment of performance. For present purposes, it is instructive to point to several serious constraints with which population policy analysts and researchers will have to cope in working with development planners and policy makers.

Advocates of the coordination of development and demographic policies often tend to view the problems posed by population growth and distribution as of central importance to development planning efforts and to the implementation of development goals, but it would be unrealistic as well as unreasonable to assume that this view is shared widely by planners and policy makers. Population policy objectives are not ends in themselves but intermediate to the ultimate objectives of development. From the point of view of planners and policy makers, these latter objectives are of much greater importance as they try to cope, on a relatively short-term basis, with the design and implementation of development projects, depending on their particular priorities, in such sectors as rural development and agricultural productivity, employment and income generation, health and education, industrialization, an array of needs in infrastructure, and so on. The fact that population factors are not at the top of the hierarchy of objectives requires that population policy analysts view demographic policies as instrumental, along with other kinds of policy measures, in achieving the goals of development plans and to sort out, in working with planners, what may be in a particular case the effect of alternative development policies on fertility as well as the anticipated effect of incorporating measures to induce fertility reduction into development policies and programs.

Differences in time frames is a second major constraint. Most development plans encompass at most five-year periods, but virtually all of the policy measures considered in this volume are not likely to have, in the view of the authors, desired fertility effects for three to four times that time span. Kocher, e.g., sees fertility-reducing policies as not having their effect for two or more decades. In the near term, even if populations increase by 10 to 15 percent over a five-year period, the effects of this growth are swamped by the pressures on planners and policy makers engendered by the short-run targets they set for their development efforts. Given this asymmetry in time frames, population analysts will have to complement the five-year orientations of planners with a vision of what the situation is likely to be a decade or two in the future with respect to the needs of a substantially larger population even if this cannot be done with any great degree of precision.

However persuasive population policy analysts can be in gaining the attention and collaboration of development planners, it is safe to say that lack of access to budget allocation authority is a limitation that will have to be lived with for the foreseeable future. As has been noted (Population Council, 1980, p. 14), population policy analysts can have data analysis, research, and advisory functions, but in advocating their particular perspectives on national development planning "they cannot exercise the traditionally most effective bureaucratic lever: access to or control over budgetary resources."

As if these limitations were not enough, it must be noted that there are serious constraints imposed on the situation within which development planning is itself carried out that will have to be taken into account. Development planners may or may not, depending on the country, be powerful arbiters of major development issues, but whoever the arbiters may be, their power is constrained by a variety of political and bureaucratic considerations.

The coordination of rural development and population policies is clearly a complex and formidable task. It can be made easier by organizational arrangements that can foster a mutual learning process, to help planners see the relevance of demographic factors to their problems and researchers understand better the constraints under which they and planners must operate.

As the conclusion to Chapter 1 indicates, what is still lacking is the broad base of empirical research and theoretical refinement needed for detailed policy analysis under the wide range of agronomic and institutional settings that prevail in the developing world. If policy analysts are to identify the fertility consequences of rural development policies at levels specific enough to be of use to planners, research of the kind advocated earlier in this discussion will have to be pursued, taking into systematic account the wide range of variation in economic, structural, cultural, and political factors that prevail among and within the countries of the developing world. Only when the knowledge base is available that can be generated by such research will analysts concerned with population policy be able to demonstrate to the makers of rural development policy that demographic variables are not only critical to the development process but that their course can be altered without adversely affecting the other goals of rural development.

NOTE

1. Remarks made at the Conference on Rural Development and Human Fertility, Pennsylvania State University, April 11–13, 1983.

REFERENCES

Bongaarts, J. 1978. A framework for analyzing the proximate determinants of fertility. Population and Development Review 4:105-132.

Burch, T.K. 1975. Theories of fertility as guides to population policy. Social Forces 54:126-138.

Chapman, M. 1981. Policy implications of circulation: Some answers from the grass roots. In: G.W. Jones and H.V. Richter (eds.) Population Mobility and Development: Southeast Asia and the Pacific, pp. 71-87. Canberra: Development Studies Centre Monograph No. 27.

Cool, J.C. 1979. Landlessness and rural poverty in Asia: The circular trap. Unpublished paper, The Ford Foundation.

Davidson, M. 1977. Female work status and fertility in Latin America. In: S. Kupinsky (ed.) The Fertility of Working Women: A Synthesis of International Research, pp. 342-354. New York: Praeger.

Hawthorn, G. 1978. Introduction. The Journal of Development Studies 14:1-21 (special issue on population and development).

International Bank for Reconstruction and Development. 1982. World Development Report 1982. Washington, D.C.: The World Bank.

Jones, G.W. 1978. Social science research on population and development in South-East and East Asia. Appendix 3 to C.A. Miro and J.E. Potter, Population Policy: Research Priorities in the Developing World. London: Frances Pinter Publishers, 1980. (Reproduced at El Colegio de Mexico, Mexico City, December, 1978.)

Kupinsky, S. 1977. Overview and policy implications. In: S. Kupinsky (ed.) The Fertility of Working Women: A Synthesis of International Research, pp. 369-380. New York: Praeger.

Mason, K.O. and V.T. Palan. 1981. Female employment and fertility in peninsular Malaysia: The maternal role incompatibility hypothesis reconsidered. Demography 18:549-575.

McNicoll, G. 1975. Community-level population policy: An exploration. Population and Development Review 1:1-21.

_____ 1978. Population and development: Outlines for a structural approach. The Journal of Development Studies 14:79-99.

_____ 1980. Institutional determinants of fertility change. Population and Development Review 6:441-462.

Morawetz, D. 1977. Twenty-five Years of Economic Development: 1950 to 1975. Washington, D.C.: The World Bank.

Population Council. 1980. Population Policy and Development Planning Units in Asia. Bangkok, Thailand: The Population Council.

_____ 1981. Research on the determinants of fertility: A note on priorities. Population and Development Review 7:311-324.

Preston, S.H. (ed.). 1978. The Effect of Infant and Child Mortality on Fertility. New York: Academic Press.

Schultz, T.P. 1976. Interrelations between mortality and fertility. In: R.G. Ridker (ed.) Population and Development: The Search for Selective Interventions, pp. 239-289. Baltimore: Johns Hopkins University Press.

Simmons, O.G. 1983. Development Perspectives and Population Change. Papers of the East-West Population Institute, No. 85. Honolulu: East-West Center.

_____ and L. Saunders. 1975. The Present and Prospective State of Policy Approaches to Fertility. Papers of the East-West Population Institute, No. 33. Honolulu: East-West Center.

Todaro, M.P. and J. Stilkind. 1981. City Bias and Rural Neglect: The Dilemma of Urban Development. New York: The Population Council.

United Nations Fund for Population Activities. 1979. The role of UNFPA in promoting integration of population and development planning. In: United Nations Fund for Population Activities, Report on Latin American Conference on Population and Development Planning, UNFPA/79/CDPP/LA/4, Annex 2, Document 3, pp. 1-17. Cartagena, Colombia: United Nations.

_____ 1979-1981. Report of Mission on Needs Assessment for Population Assistance. UNFPA, a series of 40 country reports. New York: United Nations.

Urzua, R. 1978. Social science research on population and development in Latin America. Appendix 11 to C.A. Miro and J.E. Potter, Population Policy: Research Priorities in the Developing World. London: Frances Pinter Publishers, 1980. (Reproduced at El Colegio de Mexico, Mexico City, December 1978.)

World Population Conference. 1975. World population plan of action. Population and Development Review 1:163-181.

Index

Abduraham, I., 163
Access to land
  and human fertility, 19, 195–
    210, 303–304
  and U.S. fertility decline, 79–
    86, 91–92, 180. See also
    Landholdings; Land reform
Africa
  demand for children in, 220,
    227–228
  patterns of migration in, 29
  predictions about rural-urban
    proportions in, 36–37
  women's roles as mothers and
    workers in, 157, 159. See
    also names of specific
    African countries
Age at first marriage. See
  Marriage patterns
Agricultural mechanization, and
  fertility, 252–266
Agricultural production
  and human fertility, 3–4
  impact of technology on, 4
  policies to increase, 15

and population density, 23–24
surplus in, 4–12
in Taiwan, 52
technolgoical vs. institutional
  changes in, 3
and urbanization, 9–12. See
  also Agricultural mechanization; Agricultural technology; Child labor; Intensification; Women's employment,
  in agriculture
Agricultural surplus, 4–12
Agricultural techology, and
  fertility, 12–13, 19, 23–32, 73.
  See also Instensification
  (agricultural)
Algeria, fertility study in, 153
Anderson, J., 115
Anker, R., 127, 134, 140, 152
Arnold, F., 141
Arowolo, O.O., 153
Aspirations (and fertility)
  consumption, 18, 121–123, 142–
    145
  educational, 121, 135–142, 208

309